MARKETS AND GROWTH IN EARLY MODERN EUROPE

Perspectives in Economic and Social History

Series Editors: *Robert E. Wright*
Andrew August

Titles in this Series

1 Migrants and Urban Change: Newcomers to Antwerp, 1760–1860
Anne Winter

2 Female Entrepreneurs in Nineteenth-Century Russia
Galina Ulianova

3 Barriers to Competition: The Evolution of the Debate
Ana Rosado Cubero

4 Rural Unwed Mothers: An American Experience, 1870–1950
Mazie Hough

5 English Catholics and the Education of the Poor, 1847–1902
Eric G. Tenbus

6 The World of Carolus Clusius: Natural History in the Making, 1550–1610
Florike Egmond

7 The Determinants of Entrepreneurship: Leadership, Culture, Institutions
José L. García-Ruiz and Pier Angelo Toninelli (eds)

8 London Clerical Workers, 1880–1914: Development of the Labour Market
Michael Heller

9 The Decline of Jute: Managing Industrial Change
Jim Tomlinson, Carlo Morelli and Valerie Wright

10 Mining and the State in Brazilian Development
Gail D. Triner

11 Global Trade and Commercial Networks: Eighteenth-Century Diamond Merchants
Tijl Vanneste

12 The Clothing Trade in Provincial England, 1800–1850
Alison Toplis

13 Sex in Japan's Globalization, 1870–1930: Prostitutes, Emigration and Nation Building
Bill Mihalopoulos

14 Financing India's Imperial Railways, 1875–1914
Stuart Sweeney

15 Energy, Trade and Finance in Asia: A Political and Economic Analysis
Justin Dargin and Tai Wei Lim

16 Violence and Racism in Football: Politics and Cultural Conflict in British Society, 1968–1998
Brett Bebber

17 The Economies of Latin America: New Cliometric Data
César Yáñez and Albert Carreras (eds)

18 Meat, Commerce and the City: The London Food Market, 1800–1855
Robyn S. Metcalfe

19 Merchant Colonies in the Early Modern Period
Victor N. Zakharov, Gelina Harlaftis and Olga Katsiardi-Hering (eds)

Forthcoming Titles

Welfare and Old Age in Europe and North America: The Development of Social Insurance
Bernard Harris (ed.)

Female Economic Strategies in the Modern World
Beatrice Moring (ed.)

Policing Prostitution, 1856–1886: Deviance, Surveillance and Morality
Catherine Lee

Respectability and the London Poor, 1780–1870: The Value of Virtue
Lynn MacKay

Narratives of Drunkenness: Belgium, 1830–1914
An Vleugels

Mercantilism and Economic Underdevelopment in Scotland, 1600–1783
Philipp Robinson Rössner

Crime and Community in Reformation Scotland: Negotiating Power in a Burgh Society
Robert Falconer

Residential Institutions in Britain, 1725–1950: Inmates and Environments
Jane Hamlett, Lesley Hoskins and Rebecca Preston (eds)

Consuls and the Institutions of Global Capitalism, 1783–1914
Ferry de Goey

MARKETS AND GROWTH IN EARLY MODERN EUROPE

BY

Victoria N. Bateman

Routledge
Taylor & Francis Group
LONDON AND NEW YORK

First published 2012 by Pickering & Chatto (Publishers) Limited

Published 2016 by Routledge
2 Park Square, Milton Park, Abingdon, Oxfordshire OX14 4RN
711 Third Avenue, New York, NY 10017, USA

First issued in paperback 2015

Routledge is an imprint of the Taylor & Francis Group, an informa business

BRITISH LIBRARY CATALOGUING IN PUBLICATION DATA

Bateman, Victoria N. (Victoria Naomi), 1979–
Markets and growth in early modern Europe. – (Perspectives in economic and social history)
1. Capitalism – Europe – History – 16th century. 2. Capitalism – Europe – History – 17th century. 3. Capitalism – Europe – History – 18th century. 4. Europe – Economic conditions – 16th century. 5. Europe – Economic conditions – 17th century. 6. Europe – Economic conditions – 18th century.
I. Title II. Series
330.1'22'094'0903-dc23

ISBN-13: 978-1-138-66176-9 (pbk)
ISBN-13: 978-1-8489-3258-6 (hbk)

Typeset by Pickering & Chatto (Publishers) Limited

CONTENTS

LIST OF FIGURES AND TABLES

ACKNOWLEDGEMENTS

Academic research is a collective endeavour and as such this work stands on the shoulders of many giants. I owe a great debt of gratitude to all of the economic historians around the world who have worked tirelessly and in numerous languages uncovering price data in archives, making a work of this kind possible today. I must also acknowledge the contribution of those who have worked carefully on a specialist period or aspect of economic history, without which my 'long-span' approach would not be possible.

On an individual level, I am greatly appreciative of all the economic historians I was fortunate enough to meet in the course of my graduate studies at the University of Oxford between 2001 and 2006. There could have been no more conducive and stimulating an atmosphere as the one created by Avner Offer as Chichele Professor of Economic History, alongside Bob Allen, Jane Humphries, Knick Harley, Nicholas Dimsdale and others. More than anyone else, I owe a great debt to Bob Allen, from whom I learnt so much and whose support proved invaluable in the process of writing my DPhil, in which the seeds of this book were sown.

Before my time at Oxford, Michelle Baddeley and Iain Macpherson nurtured my interest in economics and in particular economic history at the University of Cambridge. It was with great sadness to everyone who knew him that Iain passed away during the summer of 2011, and it is with great humility that I now walk in his footsteps as a Fellow of Gonville and Caius College.

One person has been at my side since my first step into the scholarly domain: my husband, James Bateman, who has patiently and lovingly supported my meanderings through economic history and has also spent a good few hours reading a number of the chapters in this book. I cannot ever thank him enough. This book is dedicated to him.

PREFACE

Markets and Growth in Early Modern Europe has been designed to be accessible to a broad readership, encompassing not only economists and economic historians but also any reader with an interest in the topic. For the general reader, I would recommend the Introduction, Chapter 1 and Chapter 7 as the main areas likely to be of interest, which also convey the central messages of the work. Whilst the remaining chapters are inevitably more technical, the empirical and econometric work has been moved to endnotes and appendices wherever possible. The specialist reader will be familiar with much of the ground covered in the Introduction and Chapter 1, so I would suggest briefly glancing through these areas before moving on to the rest of the book.

INTRODUCTION

For much of history, the standard of living was poor and subject to little improvement. For many, life was 'poor, nasty, brutish, and short', and people could not look forward to a better life for their children and grandchildren.[1] Today, we expect our incomes to rise year on year, and hope that our children will experience a life of which their great-grandparents could only have dreamed. The economic growth that has enabled this to occur began with the onset of the British Industrial Revolution in the late eighteenth century. It completely transformed the economy and the way in which we lived our lives, ushering in the near-continuous economic growth that we now take for granted.

One of the most important questions that economic historians seek to answer, is how to explain this take-off to modern economic growth: How did we go from a situation in which for centuries the average level of economic growth was close to zero, to a new era from the early nineteenth century onwards in which incomes rose year on year? And, related to this, why was Europe the first region to see this process of 'modern economic growth'? As one notable economist famously said, 'once one starts to think about [this question] ... it is hard to think of anything else'.[2] That sustained long-run economic growth can lift large parts of a population out of poverty means that the benefits to understanding its causes are very great indeed. It is therefore unsurprising that economists and economic historians in particular have researched and debated the issue at great length.

One particularly popular answer to the question of what created long-run economic growth is the development of markets. This book aims to assess the validity of this assertion. Markets involve the ability to freely produce, buy and sell goods, and they lie at the very centre of economics. The advantages of markets were put forward centuries ago by Adam Smith in his *Wealth of Nations*, now so famous that, at the time of writing, he appears on the reverse side of the British twenty-pound note.[3] Writing in 1776, Smith asked us to consider a simple hunter-gatherer society, in which each person produces everything they need for themselves. In the morning, you may go out hunting, returning to cook and eat at lunch. In the afternoon, you may make clothes from the animal skins that are left over from hunting, and undertake any urgent repairs to your shelter. The problem with this arrangement is that it is not very efficient. We are not all, for example, good hunters, and it wastes time moving between the different tasks of the day. People tend to have different natural abilities. If you are not good at hunting, you may instead be good at making clothes, but you may find that you have little time left to do the sewing as you are spending all of your day hopelessly chasing deer. It therefore makes sense for the talented seamstress to find someone who is good at hunting and strike up an exchange – agree that he will hunt for you both, and you will make the clothes for both of you. It is in this way that Adam Smith argues that exchange and trade start to arise. As individuals specialize in the task at which they are most productive, each person ends up getting a greater amount of, in this example, meat and clothing, than they would if they tried to do everything for themselves. Total output is increased, and, as a result of markets, everyone is happier.

The benefits of markets do not end there, as Smith went on to show: as population expands, specialization grows ever deeper. Now there may be ten people rather than a single individual in your village performing each task, in which case some of them might start to work together and sub-divide the tasks between themselves. Some might start to form 'firms' which then draw in people from their lives of subsistence farming, stimulating the development of a labour market. To illustrate, Smith uses the example of pin-making. Rather than each pin-maker making pins from start to finish, one may draw out the wire, another cut it into pieces, another put the point on the end, and another put the head on the opposite end. Smith argues that this specialization and 'division of labour' between different tasks both raises efficiency and importantly increases the likelihood of technological advance: if you specialize in one particular task, rather than spreading your energies across a number of tasks, your abilities and understanding of this task improve. This means that you are more likely to work out ways of improving the manner in which you produce. This generates technological progress, which further raises output and incomes in the economy.

Over time, people start to conduct their trades using a medium of exchange ('money'). Early on, it may make sense to swap an item of clothing for a leg of deer – you can find a direct exchange that is mutually beneficial. As population rises, people increasingly strike exchanges in terms of a commonly accepted medium (such as silver). You may have clothes to sell, but someone who wants to buy them may not have the leg of deer that you want in return. Hence, she instead agrees to pay you in silver, which in turn you can then give to the hunter for his leg of deer – so long, of course, as he is happy to accept it, in the knowledge that he can also use it to buy what he wants in return. In this way, a money-using economy starts to arise.

With the development of money, capital markets emerge. Some people may wish to save – in other words, they may not wish to spend everything they earn at a particular point in time. They want to save the excess to spend in the future instead. At the same time, other people may wish to spend more than they currently earn, in which case they would like to borrow. If the two can come together, they can agree a mutually beneficial exchange of funds. The saver can 'invest' with the person who wants to borrow, and the borrower can then repay in the future in a way that makes the exchange worthwhile for each party (effectively agreeing a rate of interest with which they are both happy). The borrower gains by getting access to the funds he desires, and the saver gains by getting a return on her savings. Initially, it may be necessary to strike the exchange with someone you know and trust (who will not run off with your money!). Alternatively, there may be a friend in common who can act as an intermediary in the exchange. Over time, banking institutions – more formalized intermediaries between savers and investors – start to develop to facilitate these types of exchange. Hence, once goods and labour markets have developed, so by logical progression do capital markets.[4]

As specialization grows deeper and banks start to emerge, the economy becomes increasingly complex. R&D and machinery can be funded, improving the efficiency of production and thereby expanding output, goods become increasingly sophisticated – through both the process of specialization and technological advance – and new goods start to appear.[5] Whilst the economy and its productive ability becomes more complex, life for each person becomes, in many ways, simpler. Each person produces just one type of product, and yet is able to obtain access (through exchange via the market) to a whole host of varied and sophisticated products and services. The supposed beauty of the market is that whilst each person does what is best for themselves – 'maximizes their own utility or profit' in economists' language – this does not lead to chaos. People's different consumption and production requirements are made consistent through the market force that is the price mechanism.[6] If there is an excess supply of a particular good, the price of the good will fall – discouraging its production and encouraging its consumption until demand and supply of the good become equal. If there is an excess demand for a good, the price will rise – sending a signal for producers to produce more, and putting off those who might not value the good as highly as others. If the market is allowed to function, prices will therefore naturally reach the point at which supply is equal to demand. It is on this basis that economists suggest that the market is 'informationally efficient' – the only thing that people need to know in order for their desires to be made consistent with each other is the price of the good they produce and the price of the goods they may wish to consume.[7] The market looks after the rest. According to pro-market economists, individual desires do not, therefore, lead to chaos, but to order. Without a market, the state would have to develop a plan, predicting what people want to consume, and then direct the associated production. Pro-market economists note that this would require the state to collect a great deal of information on what everyone wants and what everyone is capable (or willing) to produce. On top of that, the state would then have to create the necessary incentives for production, rather than leaving it to prices to signal and incentivize producers to produce exactly what people want. As many communist governments have found, this can be very difficult to successfully achieve.

Given such advantages of a market economy, it is unsurprising that a number of authors have suggested that the reason why economies were poor for so much of the past was that markets were virtually non-existent or were prevented from functioning.[8] Markets, it has been hypothesized, were held back by poor institutions, which raised the costs of exchange and trade (i.e. increased 'transaction costs'). These included inadequate property rights, government regulations and a lack of competition (e.g. guilds and monopoly trading privileges). Property rights are necessary to underpin the market – one cannot buy and sell goods in which one has no rights or certainty of ownership. As Adam Smith conjectures, 'commerce and manufactures can seldom flourish long in any state which does not enjoy a regular administration of justice, in which the people do not feel themselves secure in the possession of their property'.[9] In history, these property rights were supposedly undermined by absolutist leaders and monarchs who expropriated private property, used taxation and the courts to unfairly extract wealth, and defaulted on their debt. The standard historical explanation is that improvements in institutions only took place in Europe from the seventeenth and eighteenth centuries onwards, enabling greater use of and reliance on the market. The Glorious Revolution in England in 1688 led to reduced power of the monarch and, in its place, greater power of the elected parliament: with this shift came greater enforcement of property rights. Policy also increasingly moved away from a 'mercantilist' interventionist approach to a Smithian laissez-faire approach, with greater freedom for the market. Regulations concerning capital markets (e.g. 'Usury laws')[10], labour markets (e.g. Statute of Artificers)[11] and goods markets were increasingly relaxed. The monopoly power of producers, merchants and guilds was being further undermined as a result of the rise of production of manufactured goods outside of established cities, which introduced greater competition into the market. The power of merchants to control international trade in goods was also diminished by a movement towards free trade. Altogether, Polanyi posits a *Great Transformation* to a market economy in the eighteenth and nineteenth centuries, seemingly correlating well with the start of economic growth.[12]

Clearly, this market-based explanation of western economic growth has been very popular amongst economists as it fitted well with their capitalist political leanings. The fall of communism in the Soviet Union in the 1980s and the success of more market oriented policies in China and India added greater credence to this view. It has also greatly influenced the development advice given by western powers to the poor economies of today. As summed up in the 'Washington Consensus', developing economies are told that by putting in place market-based policies, and integrating into the world market, they can follow the west on the route to riches.[13] The fortunes of large parts of this planet, and the ability of populations to rise out of extreme poverty, therefore hinge on the argument that markets explain economic growth. If this is not the case, billions of people are condemned to the life of poverty, and billions of aid are being wasted.

Economists do, of course, accept that markets are not always perfect. Even if they function well, raising the overall level of output in the economy, they do little to guarantee that the output is distributed equitably amongst the population. This is something that is particularly visible, for example, in the contrast between the slums of India and the growing number of Indian billionaires. Recognizing this fact, many governments have created systems of redistribution, which work through the taxation and benefit system, to transfer income from those with more to those who have little, guaranteeing at least a minimum standard of living for all. Through state-provided education in many countries, emphasis is also placed on creating opportunities for all, allowing each person to exploit their natural ability and talents and so raise their future income.[14] Clearly, however, there is a trade-off; the more the government tries to redistribute, the more it risks reducing total output in the economy, by lowering incentives to produce for those who are facing taxation. According to free-market economists, if we significantly harm wealth-creation in the economy through 'excessive' redistribution, there will be substantially less to redistribute to those without. In other words, everyone will be poor. It is argued that only if we were not disincentivized to produce upon having the fruits of our labour redistributed to others would it be possible to ensure that everyone is equally well off. Given that as human beings we are at least partly self-interested, most economists argue that such a redistribution of wealth is a rather romantic and idealized (and ultimately futile) goal; there are limits to the extent to which inequality can be reduced.

Aside from the question of how the pie of output is distributed, economists also recognize that markets do not always maximize the size of the pie in the first place: 'market failures' may naturally occur. For markets to function in the best possible way, we need to live in a world in which, for example, individuals face the full consequences of their decisions on what to produce and consume (there are no 'externalities'), where they are also not able to strategically hide information from another party to an exchange, and where there are enough market producers and consumers for people to be able to 'shop around'.[15] Each of these and other assumptions which need to be made for markets to be shown to be 'efficient' is violated in the real world, meaning that markets can create inefficiencies, or 'fail'. Pollution and congestion are obvious examples of situations in which individuals' self-interested decisions create spillover effects on others. A further case is the reduced incentive to innovate when an inventor cannot reap the full benefits of his invention due to the possibility of imitation by others.[16] However, free-market economists have pointed out that this first example of market failure actually arises from missing markets, and that these can be created by establishing, for example, property rights for knowledge (through patents), thereby limiting the need for government intervention.[17] In that sense, it is not really a market failure at all – rather it is the failure of a market to be established. Asymmetries of information between individuals in the market is the second situation in which markets can fail, leading to 'moral hazard' and 'adverse selection'. An example of this problem can be seen in insurance. By insulating a person from risk, insurance protects individuals from experiencing the full consequences of their behaviour, which is hidden from the insurer, and so may lead them to be less careful (creating 'moral hazard'). Banks who behave in too risky a manner in the belief that governments will bail them out if things go wrong is a similar example. An example of the third source of market failure is monopoly power, such as cases in which one firm has command over the market for a particular good. In this type of situation, one side of an exchange has the ability to 'take advantage' of the other side. Finally, markets are not well equipped to produce exactly the types of 'public goods' that they need to be able to function, including transport infrastructure, a legal system to support property rights, and defence to minimize the risks of invasion.[18]

Pro-market economists have, however, worked hard to demonstrate how the market might naturally find solutions to many of these problems and, where it cannot, how the costs of failure are relatively minimal compared with the longer-run advantages of the market.[19] They suggest that even if in theory a case can be made for state intervention, such interference risks replacing market inefficiency with inefficient government officials and, according to Hayek, may even put us on a slippery slope in which the market is disposed of altogether.[20] On this basis, their recommendation is to leave markets to their own devices and for the state to intervene only where absolutely necessary, such as in the provision of some public goods.

Perhaps the greatest critique of leaving the market to its own devices came with John Maynard Keynes's *General Theory*, written during the Great Depression, which argued that free markets may, at times, generate mass unemployment and economic instability (in the form of boom and bust).[21] If correct, this is a potentially much more serious problem than many of the 'micro' level inefficiencies considered above. To understand Keynes's argument we need to begin by noting that the value of everything that an economy produces will always be paid out to workers and capitalists (through wages, rents and profits), meaning that in theory there should be enough spending (or demand) in the economy to 'mop up' all of the goods that are being produced. This spending will consist of both consumption and investment. Whilst some consumers might save some of their income (which detracts from spending), 'Classical' free-market economists tell us that there is no need to worry as these savings make their way through the banking system (as discussed earlier) into the hands of people wanting to borrow to invest. This supposedly works through the natural adjustment of the interest rate, which will move to ensure that savings equal investment. If, for example, there is an excess of savings (and so too little spending and demand in the economy), this will put downward pressure on interest rates, which encourages more investment and puts people off saving, creating demand. Hence, total spending (consumption plus investment) will never fall below the value of what is being produced – the economy will never have goods that it has produced going unsold. Furthermore, Classical economists tell us that the amount that the economy will be producing will always be exactly equal to that which ensures that everyone who wants a job has a job. This works through the adjustment of wages in the economy. If a significant number of people are unemployed, this will place downward pressure on wages, meaning that firms are willing to employ more people.

However, Keynes was unconvinced on both counts. Observing the desperately poor unemployed workers waiting in dole queues in Britain in the 1920s and 30s, he reasoned that something must be wrong with Classical free-market economic theory. He argued, firstly, that workers may not be able to 'price' themselves back into work by accepting lower wages. If a worker accepts a lower wage (in money terms) in the midst of a recession, firms may pass on the lower wages to consumers in the form of lower prices, the result of which is that the real cost of employing the worker (the money wage relative to the prices at which goods are sold) is no different to before. The second point he made was that not all saving makes its way into investment. If the economic future looks gloomy, even very low interest rates may not be enough to induce firms to invest an amount equivalent to the savings in the economy. As a result, spending remains too low and so ouptut and incomes fall. He therefore proposed that governments need to be on hand ready to make up the difference, in the form of government spending, to get the economy out of recession.

According to Keynes, therefore, the 'visible hand' of state intervention may be required alongside the 'invisible hand' of the market to ensure that recessions are avoided. Recognizing Keynes's arguments, governments after World War Two followed demand management policies, aiming to ensure that demand was strong enough to 'mop up' the supply of goods at which the economy would be fully employed. However, despite seemingly following Keynes's advice, the scourge of mass unemployment returned in the 1970s and 1980s. By that time, Keynesian expansionary policies seemed only to raise prices, rather than lower unemployment – a situation called 'stagflation' (stagnation and inflation combined). Those with a pro-market view came back to the fore and argued that Keynesian policies were misplaced, building a new theory of the economy that accepted that mass unemployment and indeed the 'business cycle' could occur, but which argued that they were the result of voluntary decisions on behalf of workers – i.e. of workers choosing not to work – and so were not a failure of the market in the sense that Keynes had suggested. This 'Real Business Cycle Theory' showed that if the economy suffers a productivity shock (such as the type of oil shocks occurring in the 1970s), and so firms cannot afford to pay the same wage as before, workers will choose to take time out of their jobs because work is no longer worth the loss of leisure time. Furthermore, even if workers are not directly choosing to be made unemployed, they may indirectly be choosing to be so by preventing firms from cutting wages in response to the shock (as a result of trade unions or through voting for minimum wages and benefits). In other words, unemployment was a result of choice and/or interferences in the free workings of the labour market. Were firms free to cut wages, unemployment would not occur except where workers voluntarily opted for it. Based on such theory, Keynesianism was declared dead and stories of the Great Depression were retold in which trade unions and benefits were to blame rather than any failure of the market to create sufficient demand. In the words of one paper, 'The army of unemployed standing watch in Britain at the publication of the *General Theory* was largely a volunteer army'.[22] Influenced by this theory, the policies in the 1980s of Thatcher (in the UK) and Reagan (in the US) deregulated, privatized and liberalized markets. Those who believed in the new theory – including a President of the American Economic Association – predicted that we would never have another deep and concerning recession, that economic growth would rise and that unemployment would stay low.[23] Against these optimistic predictions, the global recession of the late 2000s to the present day has come as a great shock. It is much to the surprise of many eminent economists that the economy now faces, at best, the gravest situation since the Great Depression of the 1930s. Few of them predicted it: in fact, they expected the opposite.

For the first time since Keynes in the 1930s, economists' faith in the market is once again being tested. Since the market is at the root of economics, this current debate has the potential to create a revolution in our understanding of the economy and the policies we design. Now more than ever we need to ask how much markets really contribute to economic growth. If markets really are strong enough to guarantee long-run economic growth, then a case can be made that their long-run advantages offset any shorter term disadvantages: without them, we could all still be living as hunters and gatherers. If so, we should be wary of 'throwing the baby out with the bath water' when considering responding to the current recession with what free-marketeers would argue is a knee-jerk reaction of clamping down on free markets and imposing regulation.

So, what is the evidence that markets were key to the arrival of long-run economic growth from the nineteenth century onwards? Rather surprisingly, the link has scarcely been tested using the long spanning historical data that would be required to do so.[24] The view that markets sowed the seeds of economic growth has simply been assumed to be correct by most economists, perhaps driven more by ideology rather than empirical evidence. This represents a major gap in the discipline that this book aims to fill.

In order to examine the link between markets and economic growth, it is necessary to first of all establish the path of market development in history. According to the market based view, markets were poorly developed throughout much of history, only becoming developed in the seventeenth and eighteenth centuries in the run up to the Industrial Revolution, coinciding very neatly with the start of economic growth. Seemingly confirming this story, most studies conducted by economic historians tend to show that markets moved from a state of under-development to one of high development between the seventeenth century and the early-nineteenth century.[25] However, whilst attractive to economists, this vision is not consistent with other available evidence. Firstly, the work of medieval (and even ancient) historians suggests that markets were already relatively well developed in earlier times and that economies were much more 'commercial' early on than has typically been thought.[26] If correct, the fact that modern economic growth did not begin in these earlier times – despite their well-developed markets – implies that markets are simply not enough for sustained economic growth. Secondly, the work of authors such as Ha-Joon Chang (*Kicking Away the Ladder*) and David Ormrod (*The Rise of Commercial Empires*) suggests that *non* free-market policies may have played a crucial role in the sustained economic growth of the west. They have argued that the now rich economies (Britain, US, Germany, East Asia) became rich by going against the market – by using tariffs and other anti-market policies to carve out for themselves a place in the world economy. Thirdly, comparative work on China and Europe suggests that markets were as well developed in parts of the east on the eve of the Industrial Revolution as those in Europe and yet, despite this, the east did not begin to industrialize until the twentieth century.[27]

Given these inconsistencies, together with the significance of the issue for economics and policy-making, this book aims to build a more complete and consistent story of markets in the long span of European economic history. This then forms the basis for examining whether markets were responsible for the emergence of modern economic growth in the nineteenth century. Chapter 1 pieces together recent research by economic historians on markets from Roman times to the present day, presenting a long-run history of markets. The vision of markets suggested is one at odds with that of many economists, but is in need of more formal and empirical testing. In an effort to provide this, Chapters 2–4 formally measure markets from the perspective of both the individual countries of Europe and the two major regions of Europe (the Mediterranean and the north-west), before aggregating the results to calculate the Europe-wide trend. The common method for measuring market development (or, 'market integration') is to gather information on prices from various locations and look for evidence as to whether these prices have been converging over time. In theory, this should be the case if markets are becoming increasingly developed, as price differences between locations will be arbitraged out through the process of trade: if the price of a good is high in location A and low in location B, then traders will buy the good in the cheaper location and ship it to the more expensive location, guided by the incentive of making a profit. This process increases the supply of the good in the more expensive location (pushing the price there down) and does the opposite in the cheap location, therefore acting to converge the prices. Furthermore, if markets are becoming better developed, we would expect that they can better deal with shocks, meaning that prices become less volatile and the speeds at which prices adjust increase. This gives us three good ways of measuring markets: price convergence, price volatility and the speed of price adjustment.

Once market development has been measured, Chapter 5 is in a position to explain the trend it has taken over time. The results enable us to understand how certain parts of Europe entered a virtuous circle resulting in the development of markets far earlier on in history than the eighteenth century, whilst others either failed to do so (having to wait for the transport revolution of the nineteenth century) or even experienced the opposite: disintegration. Geography, institutions and population density are shown to be the key factors at work. Chapter 6 builds on the previous chapters, using the market estimates of the earlier chapters to empirically test the connection between markets and economic growth from 1400–1900. This represents, to date, the longest historical test conducted of the link between markets and growth in history. It considers various measures of economic performance – urbanization, agricultural productivity, population density and real wages – alongside each of the three measures of market development. It argues that whilst markets might be a necessary precondition for growth, they are in no way sufficient. The state and the Enlightenment – rather than markets – were what triggered the beginning of continuous economic growth in the nineteenth century, and these involved important non-market elements. Chapter 7 summarizes the findings and considers how they can help us to understand why so many economies are still poor today, and what policies can be used to encourage their escape from poverty. In light of the current economic turmoil, it aims to contribute towards a new agenda for economics and policy not only in the poorer, but also the richer, economies.

1 MARKETS IN HISTORY: A SURVEY

As we have seen, markets are central to the explanations that have been put forward for the sustained economic growth that began with the British Industrial Revolution and continues to the present day. Having great influence over the formation of this market-led view is a particular vision of life in Europe before the Industrial Revolution. The economy is seen as backward commercially and, as a consequence, technologically, leaving little room for growth. Whilst in the modern world people come into contact with the market every day of their lives – through the goods they buy, the daily work they undertake for businesses and the banks that look after their money – people of the past are often seen as having had minimal contact with goods, labour and financial markets. We might not quite all have been living as hermits in wooden huts, subsisting on our own patch of land, but something not far from this is probably a fair depiction of what many people have in mind. This all supposedly changed in the seventeenth and eighteenth centuries, preparing the way for the Industrial Revolution. It is on this understanding of the past that the poor economies of today are told that liberalizing markets will result in them catching up with the rich west. By taking a chronological journey through history from Roman times towards the present day, this chapter questions the historical understanding on which this advice is given. It knits together the economic history of the different periods, helping to identify where and when markets developed. Rather than finding poorly developed markets in history, we will see that waves of integration and disintegration have existed across time. Markets are certainly not a modern invention – they have been present for thousands of years. Taken together with the fact that sustained economic growth is a recent phenomenon, this suggests that whilst markets may be necessary for economic growth, they are certainly not sufficient.

The chronology begins in a period in which much of Europe was dominated by Roman power. Augustus had not long gained his status as Emperor after defeating Antony and Cleopatra at the Battle of Actium in 31 BC, and Britain was ripe for its invasion in AD 42. By the second century AD, the Roman Empire had expanded so successfully that it 'stretched from Hadrian's Wall in drizzle-soaked northern England to the sunbaked banks of the Euphrates in Syria'.[1] In many ways, the achievements of Roman times are truly impressive, particularly when it comes to the construction and architecture of such still-famous buildings as the Colosseum, and more generally the temples, villas and engineering feats such as the aqueducts and road system. However, despite its great size and visible achievements, the general belief of older scholars, such as Finley, was that the economies of the ancient world were 'primitive' and 'backward', marking them out as different to those of the modern day.[2] Whilst some present day authors still subscribe to this view,[3] others present a revisionist account, identifying 'good' institutions which they argue supported the market and enabled it to develop, thereby raising standards of living in the economy.[4] The well-developed and unified Roman state – covering an extensive area – had a number of significant advantages for the development of markets.[5] Merchants trading in far-flung parts of the Empire did not face uncertainty with regard to the legal regime, taxation or a multitude of weights and measures and were relatively free from the threat of physical harm or discrimination. The centralized tax system was able to fund the well-known transport infrastructure of the age, enabling merchants to travel at reasonably low cost. The stable and trusted coinage meant that the economy could develop beyond barter, supporting transactions between anonymous buyers and sellers and a higher level of specialization in the marketplace. The legal system and capital markets were also well enough developed to support markets. In a recent survey of research, Silver notes how 'Roman law recognized bargaining and freedom of contract', that Romans 'knew deposit banking and fractional reserves' and that there is 'evidence that Roman banks and other visibly active credit intermediaries made loans to businesses'.[6] Given such institutions, it seems plausible that markets were able to function reasonably well in the Roman economy. Archaeological evidence supports this notion, finding ceramics that were 'distributed very widely' and that 'the percentage of imported pottery, as opposed to local wares, is impressively high',[7] indicating a reasonable degree of long-distance trade. The abundance of Roman coins which are always found in archaeological digs throughout Europe similarly suggests the existence of a highly commercialized economy. At a more technical level, Temin argues that prices from Roman times display the statistical properties that one would expect from relatively well-developed markets.[8]

Given the extensive potential market in the Roman world, one would expect to find a high degree of specialization leading to technological developments which helped to support a high standard of living. Perhaps unsurprisingly to the visitors of museums and archaeological sites, historians and archaeologists are revising upwards their views of the wealth and levels of development achieved in the Roman economy.[9] Whilst estimates of income are clearly open to error, we do find evidence of rising consumption of luxury goods (such as meat and wine) an accepted indicator of rising incomes.[10] Population growth and urbanization in the period could also be interpreted similarly.[11] We also know that the Romans were relatively literate and had an understanding of key mathematical concepts (such as geometry), built water wheels, which provided mechanical energy, and made manufactured goods such as cloth and glass.[12] Taken together, the co-existence of markets and economic advance early on in history is certainly consistent with the idea that markets are a necessary feature of a successful economy. However, why the Roman economy did not go on to industrialize becomes a more difficult question to answer; markets may not have been enough.

By the fourth century AD, the western part of the Roman Empire was starting to disintegrate. In response, Emperor Constantine shifted his capital to the more stable eastern part of the Empire, to the city he named Constantinople (modern day Istanbul).[13] By the death of Emperor Theodosius in the fifth century, the Empire was completely divided between two sons: Honorius in the west and Arcadius in the east. Perhaps it was the former who drew the short straw as it was in the east – not west – that the economy was flourishing. Whilst the western part of the Empire was crumbling, the east survived and carried forward the mantle of knowledge left over from the ancient world. Trade links were developed with the Orient, which was the technological leader of the world of the time.[14] Along the Silk Road from China flowed not only exotic goods but also skills and new knowledge.[15] Becoming known as the Byzantine (later Ottoman) Empire, the region housed the largest cities in Europe and remained the wealthiest part of the old Roman Empire for centuries to come.[16] Islamic expansion and conquest in the seventh to ninth centuries united the region further: Muslims were keen learners and further advanced the knowledge left over from the Ancient world and through their contacts with the Orient.[17] At least until the thirteenth century, Muslim Europe was far more advanced technologically and educationally than Christian Europe and housed all the great European centers of industry.[18]

In contrast to the vibrancy found in the Byzantine world, western Europe fell into what has become known as the Dark Ages.[19] Lacking the unity of the east, rule became increasingly fragmented. Following Barbarian attacks in the fifth century, a number of early dark-age kingdoms emerged, including the Visgoths in Spain (484–711), Lombards in Italy (568–774) and Merovingians in Gaul (511–751).[20] Moreover, upon the death of a king, inheritance was divided between sons, leading to increased fragmentation and conflict.[21] Control was increasingly localized, and peace was continually interrupted by local conflict and invaders (including the infamous Vikings), who could take advantage of the poor state of defence. The reduction in law and order lowered population and led to a retreat from markets. Selling produce outside of the local area was more expensive as there was no central law to uphold the rights of buyers and sellers, together with deteriorating transport infrastructure and the lack of a uniform and stable coinage.[22] Using the market also became riskier – not only was there a threat to physical security from robbers, invaders and strangers but with the fall in population one could no longer guarantee being able to sell one's specialist goods in the marketplace and in return purchase the vital requisites for subsistence. Hence, individuals had an incentive to move away from specializing and instead produce everything they needed for themselves. As Wickham comments, this 'was not a period in which the structures of exchange were reliable enough to overcome much subsistence risk in the West'.[23] As individuals turned away from markets, the goods on offer and reliability of the market further deteriorated, progressively lowering the benefits of using them and so encouraging others to turn away. A process of de-specialization and falling trade followed; Rome halved in size and many cities were completely deserted.[24] From AD 400–700, population fell from 36 million to 22 million.[25] With a lesser degree of specialization, techniques became more rudimentary and the technologies and learning of Roman times faded into the past:[26] the economy was caught in a vicious circle.[27] Whilst revisionist accounts have recently tried to argue that there was more light in the dark ages than we have traditionally thought,[28] seeing it as a period of restructuring as opposed to simple decline, it is still difficult to imagine how the period can be seen in a distinctly positive light.[29]

Many have argued that the real death-blow to the western Roman world came with the Arab conquests of the seventh to ninth centuries.[30] Not only did these conquests swallow up the land of the Byzantine Empire and the entirety of the coastal regions of North Africa, they also absorbed Iberia and the tip of the Italian peninsula (including Sicily). According to Pirenne, the Christian and Arab world became cut off from one another and the west was forced to re-centre itself north of the Alps, away from its traditional focus around the Mediterranean. However, evidence is that significant contact between the two regions still took place: using accounts of 669 travellers (including pilgrims and diplomats), together with evidence of the movement of coins and slaves, McCormick argues that contact between the two regions actually increased in the period from the eighth to the tenth century compared with the earlier post-Roman years. He contends that this was to the benefit of the west, providing 'the wealth and markets which would fire the first rise of western Europe' in the late eighth century,[31] a large part of which is attributable to the sales of European slaves to the Arab world. According to McCormick, the result was actually a new-found strength for the Frankish King, Charlemagne, who in AD 800 was crowned Holy Roman Emperor over the lands covering modern day France, the Low Countries, Germany and northern Italy. Whilst the states he unified were disparate and often remained at war, he is commonly seen as providing a degree of harmony and so is sometimes referred to as the founding father of Europe. The greater political order and stability meant that market exchange was now both less costly and less risky compared to the time of 'Barbarian' invasion, helping to bring about a recovery in markets. Local, regional and even some interregional trade increased and cities started to redevelop.[32]

In 843, the Treaty of Verdun divided the Carolingian Empire into three regions – one which provided the basis for the development of a French state, another which resembles modern day Germany, although reaching further south, with the third a strip in between, which ran from modern day Netherlands south to the upper half of Italy. Whilst this return to the 'bad old days' of fragmentation was not ideal for markets, many historians have in fact argued that it proved helpful for technological diffusion and development. Being behind the Muslim and Orient lands, and having forgotten a lot of the knowledge built up in the classical world, Europe had a lot to learn. This included techniques for the manufacture of glass, paper, chemicals and cloth, together with the mathematical methods that supported the development of finance. The fact that Europe was composed of disparate states, all of whom were in competition with each other, meant, according to some historians, that they could not afford to 'rest on their laurels'. As knowledge and technology started to move westwards, often first appearing in Venice, the hub for contact with the east, there was a great incentive to learn about and adopt it in order to avoid falling behind competitors in Europe. Furthermore, division meant that there was no single state who could 'turn off the lights'. If any one province did so, knowledge and skills could simply move to another part of Europe, thereby sustaining technological advancement. Mokyr argues that it was because the onus of technological change was on private individuals (as opposed to a strong state) and because it was undertaken in a 'decentralized, politically competitive setting' that it could thrive, develop and be sustained.[33] Whilst this may be an advantage of division, if such division simultaneously proves unfavourable for markets, limiting specialization and eroding the incentives to adopt better technologies, it is difficult to imagine how these benefits would be realized. Fortuitously, out of the fragmentation emerged a set of institutions which acted as a substitute for an overarching and strong state, supporting markets and enabling a continued commercial – and technological – expansion well into the second millennium.

The most well-known institution on the rise at the time was that of serfdom (or feudalism). With the lack of a strong state and more geographically fragmented political power than in Roman times, knights and lords had strong power at the local level. The knights maintained themselves and their castle by extracting dues from local peasants (or serfs). The peasants generally possessed their own means of production but had limited geographical mobility and freedom. Their forfeit of freedom can be interpreted as a voluntary payment for the security and protection provided by the knight and his castle in a time of diminished law and order. More sceptically, of course, it can be seen as a consequence of the enhanced power of landowners. Following the population decline that came with the Roman break-up, land was plentiful and labour scarce. Landowners therefore commanded low market rents whilst labourers could demand high real wages. By restricting the mobility of peasants, serfdom prevented labourers from exploiting their bargaining power and gave landlords a means of extracting dues, sustaining a luxurious lifestyle for the elite.[34] According to Duby, this rather dark cloud had a silver lining; it encouraged the recovery of trade as lords improved order and set up and licensed markets (encouraged by the tax income they brought to the manor). It also created a demand for luxury goods, stimulating longer-distance trade (including that between the Arab and Christian worlds).[35] However, whilst serfdom may have been beneficial in these senses, it also created a ceiling above which markets could not rise. Clearly, if peasants surrender a large proportion of the goods they produce, there is likely to be little incentive to maximize production, and if they do not have freedom to move, it is unlikely that they will find the most productive employment. Similarly, the potential and almost continuous risks of conflict that came from the competition between lords can be seen as lowering the incentives to participate in market exchange, and to invest and innovate. Hence, Marxist authors have long argued that it was only with the decline of the feudal system that the economy could make a transition to a more market-oriented and capitalist base.

Evidence suggests that from the twelfth century onwards there was a tendency to replace both feudal payment in kind with payment in money and the old system of seigneurial demesne with one in which land was leased out to tenants in return for rent, creating incentives for direct producers to raise productivity and participate in the market. The reasons behind the decline of serfdom have been the subject of much debate: some authors have highlighted the transformative power of factors external to the feudal system, whilst others point to the self-destructive nature of the system itself. Dobb places emphasis on the combination of, firstly, the inability of the feudal system to expand production, and, secondly, the increasing number of lords over time, which brought increased conflict and placed increased pressure on a system unable to cope with these extra demands. The simple fact that the population was naturally expanding over time may have been enough to dissolve the feudal means of production. With a rising population, the balance of power shifted away from labourers and towards landowners, as land became the relatively scarce factor. As a result, landowners no longer needed to limit the mobility of peasants; they could now instead source labour cheaply using the labour market[36] – the peasantry were therefore granted freedom, with which came a greater incentive to produce and to sell goods in the marketplace.

Growing commercialization may also have acted to undermine the system of serfdom, including through the recovery of international trade[37] and the building of towns, some of which had Roman origins but many of which were new,[38] providing an alternative way of raising income for both peasants and knights. At the root of this commercial recovery and expansion was a combination of newly emerging top-down and bottom-up institutions. At the top-down level, Christendom had grown to fill the power vacuum left by fragmented and weak states and had been further encouraged under the Carolingians.[39] According to Mann, the church 're-discovered' Roman law, moved in the direction of 'written-down law' and pushed for equality for all before the law. Hence, from the eleventh century onwards, law and order increased and property right abuses of monarchs were restricted (as seen, for example, in the Magna Carta).[40] At the same time, the increasing authority of the church stimulated the use of a common language (Latin), literacy and printing (as necessary for the reproduction and use of biblical texts).[41] Attempts to construct cathedrals that could reach high to the heavens stimulated skills and techniques, many of which are visible in the famous Chartres Cathedral.[42] Religion is often seen as having a potentially adverse effect on the development of science, but many historians of science are keen to point out that Christianity aided learning in medieval Europe.[43] At first, education was undertaken in monasteries, but by 1200, three universities had emerged: Bologna, Paris and Oxford. In terms of their independence and the freedom they provided scholars to debate and criticize ideas, an essential element to move knowledge forward, these institutions were unique to Europe.[44] Educational institutions promoted theology and law together with providing a channel through which techniques lost in post-Roman Europe – but which had lived on in the east and were now spreading back to the west (including mathematics) – could be relearnt and diffused.[45] From the bottom-up level, institutions also emerged to resolve the collective action problems that markets faced as a result of political fragmentation. As studied, amongst others, by Grief, Milgrom and Weingast, Grief, and de Moor,[46] these consisted of privately-created institutions, such as merchant guilds, city 'communes' and craft guilds, which all substituted for the functions otherwise performed by the public institutions of a well-developed state. Communes were associations of inhabitants (often of a city) who governed themselves through councils and parliaments, enhancing the property rights and freedoms of the population. Well-known communes emerged from around the eleventh century and included Venice, Padua, Verona, Milan, Genoa, Augsburg and Cologne.[47] Whilst communes were successful in supporting the market within a particular city, merchant guilds also helped to support merchants when operating outside of their home city. At a time when the state (and so public law and order enforcement) were lacking, merchants involved in long-distance trade in Europe risked being discriminated against, having contracts torn up, being cheated on by agents operating on their behalf in distant cities, or even having their goods forcibly removed. It was difficult for a merchant acting alone to present a sufficient threat to ensure fair treatment when dealing with strangers, particularly when they were not present in person or when the contract involved delayed payment or receipt of goods. However, when acting together as a group, merchants had the power to effect a painful trade embargo against the home cities of merchants who did not respect their rights, therefore ensuring that trading and contractual rights were respected.[48] Craft guilds, meanwhile, were associations of producers in particular sectors who, it is argued, acted to ensure that quality controls were met, hence ensuring that customers had confidence in the purchase of goods, and that skills and techniques were diffused across generations (through apprenticeships).[49] Altogether, these institutions acted as a substitute for the state, lowering the risks and transaction costs associated with participating in the market, and so stimulated market expansion.

With the newly developing top-down and bottom-up institutions, together with declining serfdom, trade and markets recovered, leading to the commercial boom of the High Middle Ages, lasting from as early as Carolingian times to the end of the thirteenth century.[50] Commercialization is noted across Europe, as is clear in the work of Britnell and Campbell, Masschaele and Clark on the English economy, van Bavel et al. and Unger on the Low Countries, and Epstein on Italy.[51] Across western Europe, markets existed for both agricultural and manufactured products, as is evident in the expanding fairs and urbanization taking place in the period.[52] Writing on the cloth trade in the thirteenth century, Chorley concludes that there was 'a highly developed and extensive market … Altogether the European market for northern cloth was much more differentiated and reached further down the social scale than the accepted view allows'.[53] As towns and trade expanded, so did technological knowledge. New technologies included simple mechanical devices (such as gearing) which allowed the development of water and wind mills, providing a source of power that could replace both human and animal exertion; agricultural improvements, such as crop rotations, animal breeding, irrigation systems and the plough; and chemical and metallurgical processes that enabled dying and new types of weaponry.[54] Knowledge of these technologies travelled to the west both through the peaceful medium of east–west trade (with transfer aided by Genghis Khan's Mongolian Empire which spanned from China into the Middle East)[55] and through the less peaceful contact between the Arab and Christian worlds that came as they battled for supremacy in the Crusades of the eleventh to thirteenth centuries. The twelfth century in particular witnessed a dramatic increase in the number of texts that were translated from Arabic or original Greek into Latin, including those found in the newly Christianized parts of Europe when the Arabs were pushed back (such as Toledo in Spain).[56] The economy was in a virtuous circle of improving markets, rising specialization, improving techniques and increasing population. This is evident in the fact that European population trebled in the period between 800 and 1300, from roughly 25 million to 79 million.[57] The ground was now prepared for the Renaissance.

As it had in Roman times, Italy led Europe in the medieval era of commercialization. Lacking a unified state, the Italian success stories came in the form of the city-states of maritime Venice, Pisa and Genoa. With little in the way of their own agricultural land to feed their population, but with advantageous coastal positions, including notably that close to the east, such cities had a natural inclination to search for trading opportunities overseas. This stimulated developments in shipping, with which came naval strength, which could be used to great commercial benefit at a time of both political fragmentation within Europe and Muslim–Christian battles in the south and east. After helping the Byzantine Empire resist invasion, Venice was granted trading privileges with the 'rich' east through Constantinople and amassed great wealth as a result.[58] Merchants of the city imported many great luxuries – silks and spices – selling them at monopoly prices to European consumers; the result is visible in the famous paintings of Canaletto. Geographically well positioned on the western side of Italy, Pisa became the chief maritime nation in the western Mediterranean. The city used seaborne military might to help re-conquer Muslim territories in the area (such as the Balaeric Islands and parts of southern Spain) and after supporting Frederick I in the battle between the Pope and the Holy Roman Emperor, Pisan merchants were granted the freedom to trade unhindered in his southern Italian territory. Pisa's chief rival, Genoa, defeated the Pisan fleet in the late thirteenth century, thereafter becoming the dominant of the two powers.[59] Like the other two great Italian cities, trading opportunities were in part formed on the back of military victories. Trading privileges with the east were granted after providing assistance to the Byzantine Emperor, access to Sicilian grain was granted after helping Sicily fend off the Angevin Kings, defeating the Pisans brought access to (amongst other things) the iron mines of the Elba and help with reconquering Iberia from Muslim hands brought trading opportunities in the Peninsula.[60] The focus of Genoese merchants on bulky cargoes of grain and alum (which commanded relatively low prices compared with the lightweight small packages of spices) encouraged developments in shipping and navigation which cut the costs of transportation. Genoese merchants were, for example, some of the first to successfully tackle winter seas.[61] Better shipping practices spilled over to other cities, further expanding the range of goods for which trade was profitable and also the locations between which trade could take place. Sea connections through Gibraltar to London and Bruges were first established by the Genoese, and vessels were regularly using the route by the late thirteenth and fourteenth centuries, connecting the north and south of Europe by sea.[62] With the increasing trade of the great Italian cities came a demand for credit, so Italy became the first financial centre of Europe, as evidenced by the fact that many financial and banking terms have Italian origins, including the symbols for the British currency (L., s. and d.).[63] A major development of the European capital market followed, as is clear in the significant decline in interest rates at this time.[64]

Within Europe, Italy's growing principal rival in terms of wealth was Flanders. In the words of one author:

> No observer at the turn of the [first] millennium ... would have been likely to predict that the county of Flanders would become the commercial and industrial center of northwestern Europe ... Flanders was anything but an economic leader; rather, contemporaries considered it backward ... Yet, rather suddenly, in the late eleventh century, Flanders became the hub of a northwestern economic region.[65]

The manorial system was breaking down, commercial settlements in the region were expanding, a number of new towns ('coastal emporia') developed focused on trade, and a rising number of fairs suggest vitality in the region.[66] Three explanations have been put forward for the rise of the region: firstly, her production of woolen cloth, an outgrowth of sheep farming from Roman times; secondly, her geographic position as a gateway to markets in the Eastern Low Countries and Germany (through the Meuse and the Scheldt); and thirdly her concentrated population, which gave her a potential role as a consumer. These forces combined to create economic success: international merchants had a dual incentive to travel to Flanders, as her population and geographical ease of access to consumers in mainland Europe provided a ready demand for their goods, whilst Flemish cloth provided a valuable return cargo to accompany them home (which could in turn be used to settle payment deficits for spices in the east). Trading through Flanders was therefore doubly profitable, giving an economic outcome that was more than the sum of its parts.[67]

Between Italy and Flanders, the main focal point for north–south trade was overland, through the Champagne Fairs. Here, Flemish wool and cloth were exchanged for Italian spices, luxuries and financial services – its attraction underpinned by the concentration of buyers and sellers in one place, guaranteeing a market for all. The fairs developed from the middle of the twelfth century, rotating between four towns in the Champagne region and operated for a period of six weeks in each. Significant debate exists as to whether the success of the fairs was a result of publicly – or privately – provided institutions, the latter relating to the bottom-up institutional developments in the medieval period. Milgrom, North and Weingast have argued strongly in favour of the latter, contending that a private code of law and private judges emerged to report on the reputation of a potential party to a trade (lowering risks associated with market exchange) with the implications that market success is not completely dependent on the state.[68] Ogilvie has recently presented a strong case in the other direction: she argues that the fairs rested on strong public institutions, evidenced by the fact that the Fairs went into decline following the region's absorption into French control in 1284, which undermined these institutions.[69] This together with the emerging maritime trade between Italy and the north-west of Europe diverted more trade directly to Flanders itself, leading to the expansion of Bruges. As we have seen, Flanders specialized in providing cloth and Italian merchants, attracted by the quality and value of the cloth, provided shipping and financial services that took it to the far corners of Europe.[70]

Through their trade along this north–south axis of Europe, the Italians came into contact with merchants involved in the east–west European trade which was conducted between the Hansa towns of northern, central and eastern Europe. Whilst their financial and commercial practices were not as advanced as the Italians, the Hansa had a well-organized network of trade and soon absorbed best practices from the southern merchants.[71] This 'League of Hansa Cities' was founded in Lübeck on the Baltic coast in the middle of the twelfth century and was initially a group of just north German cities. At a time of political fragmentation the merchants from these cities were seeking greater certainty – a means of reducing the riskiness of long-distance trade. This gave each city a common interest: for one's own merchants to be granted trading privileges in the other cities, it was necessary to allow merchants from those other cities to trade freely in the home city. This common interest resulted in reciprocal trading agreements on the basis of which trade expanded to the benefit of all involved. Merchants from the Hansa cities spread out to found new towns[72] in areas conveniently located for trade and to strengthen already established commercial links between places such as Cologne and London.[73] In towns outside of the League, the Hansa sought privileges for their merchants, including exclusivity of trade and/or freedom from customs dues: towns who failed to grant or uphold such privileges could find themselves being forced into submission through a blockade. The more the Hansa came to dominate trade, the more painful such a blockade would become, and so the fewer cities that would protest, meaning that Hansa merchants soon came to monopolize east–west trade.[74] The League soon included around 200 cities reaching as far as the Zuider Zee and the Gulf of Finland, and spanning the area from the Baltic in the north down to Thuringia in the south.[75] The main trading route followed Novgorod–Reval–Lübeck–Hamburg–Bruges–London. From this axis inland connections were formed to south Germany, France and Italy (via the Rhine) as well as maritime connections to France and, by the end of the fifteenth century, Spain and Portugal as well.[76] Through this network of cities, goods could be traded with relative ease – both from east to west and from north to south. As Dollinger writes:

> To the people of that period the Baltic was not a cul-de-sac shut in by ice-bound shores: it was a trade route, giving easy access to the Russian rivers and leading to the great markets of Novgorod and Smolensk, to which came by long weary roads rare and precious goods from distant countries, from the shores of the White Sea as well as from Byzantium and Moslem lands.[77]

Whilst the Italian city-states and the Hansa were focusing their energies on developing long-distance European trade, between the north and the south and the east and the west of Europe, England and the Netherlands were achieving a high level of market development in a very different sphere: within their own economies. Whilst the development of local markets in Italy and Germany were encumbered by political fragmentation and, in parts, by unfavourable geography (distant from the coast and of a mountainous nature), England and the Netherlands had a number of advantages which pushed forward the internal development of markets. The first is natural geography, both in terms of a long coastline and relatively flat land, meaning low costs of transportation. The second concerns the level of cooperation between local areas, which proves helpful both for the provision of market-supporting infrastructure and mutually beneficial exchange. In England, this was facilitated by a strong state with little in the way of strong urban centres to act as potential vested interests against development.[78] In the Netherlands, there was no overarching state, but a number of evenly sized cities, with no dominant interest, all of whom were mutually dependent and so acted cooperatively to the benefit of markets and trade.[79] Whilst the development of internal markets in north-western Europe was less noticeable and seemingly less impressive to both contemporaries and modern day historians than the more obvious long-distance trade of Italian and Hansa merchants, it provided a more solid foundation for later development and meant that when more international trade came to their shores, the benefits would be multiplied as they reverberated through the whole economy.

The downside of the medieval European recovery and development of markets and international trade was that disease could now travel with the distance and speed at which goods were being traded. In 1346, whilst Tartars from the east were laying siege to one of Genoa's colonies, Caffa, the corpses of plague victims were catapulted into the city's interior walls. Infected Genoese sailors returned to Italy – via Constantinople – from where the illness travelled onboard Italian ships out to all corners of Europe.[80] The Black Death of 1348–51 was the result and stands as testament to the extensive trade of the times;[81] it was also one of the most important shocks in history. In fact, the fourteenth century played host to a number of extreme demographic shocks, with the Great Famine of northern Europe in 1315–22, the Black Death of 1348–51 and repeated plagues in the latter half of the fourteenth century. During the Great Famine, 10–15 per cent of the population of southern England lost their lives,[82] and with the Black Death the population of Europe as a whole declined by between one third and one quarter (from around 80 million to around 55 million).[83] It took until the end of the sixteenth century for population in Europe to recover.[84] To some, the Black Death is viewed as shaking up what would otherwise have been a relatively stable system – an economy that would have, without this shock, continued expanding. Others (including Postan and Titow) adopt a Malthusian view, seeing demographic crisis as an inevitable consequence of the medieval economic expansion which, as we have seen, had been taking place for some centuries.[85]

According to this view, there is a maximum number of people that the land can feed and support. As population rose in response to favourable economic times, which lowered mortality and caused an increasing number of births, the pressure on food and raw materials pushed up prices, causing the standard of living to fall. The result was rising mortality and fewer births, leading population to fall until it was once again in line with the availability of land.[86] Population estimates suggest that England had reached around 5 million inhabitants by the beginning of the fourteenth century, a level she did not reach again until the seventeenth century.[87] In 1377, following the demographic shock, population amounted to little more than it had at the time of the Domesday Book.[88]

However, whilst the collapse in population adversely affected markets in the immediate term (completely decimating some towns and villages), it has also been argued to have structurally changed the economy in a way that enhanced markets in the longer term. This worked through three different channels. The first of these operated through wages: as labour was now scarce, the market value of peasants (i.e. what they could earn by selling their labour) rose, whilst the now relatively abundant land meant that rental rates for landowners were pushed downwards. The resultant change in the economic power of labourers relative to landowners posed a great threat to the power system in Europe. The Peasants' Revolt in England is just one example of the tensions that ensued. According to Brenner,[89] the resolution of the situation was a reflection of varying constraints on class-conflict in the different parts of Europe. In eastern Europe and the Arab World,[90] where political power rested strongly with the landlord classes, landowners were able – in a repeat of the post-Roman decline – to limit labour mobility, resurrecting the feudal system. In contrast, in much of the rest of Europe (e.g. France) some political power had already spread to peasants, and so it was difficult for landowners to reassert feudalism. Instead, peasants could now take advantage of their increased power to increase their land holdings, at the cost of the lord, and eliminate the need to pay dues to the lord (thereby gaining full possession of the means of production). The lords had to find alternative ways to support themselves, including through the state and taxation system. In equity terms, this change may have been beneficial and the result is evident today in the large number of small family-owned farms in the French countryside. However, Brenner argues that compared to Britain the new found ability of peasants to live self-sufficiently created a slower rate of market development. In England, as in western Europe, lords failed to intensify the feudal system, but they were at least able to prevent peasants from gaining full property rights over their plots (assigning leasehold status which required payment of ground rent to the lord). According to Brenner, this separation of English peasants from the full means of production left them with no choice but to produce for the market (in order to earn the funds to pay their rent), leading to the rise of a class of tenant farmers who employed wage labour from the labour market. Once they were producing for the market it became clear that they could further gain from increasing production, specializing, investing and innovating, leading to rising productivity, declining food costs and the possibility of supporting urban and industrial development. Goods and labour markets became increasingly developed as a result: around 50 per cent of England's population was involved in the labour market in the period 1300–1520.[91]

The second effect of the Black Death was an acceleration of the development of states.[92] Europe was, in large parts, highly politically fragmented after the breakdown of the earlier empires, which created limits to trade through, for example, the numerous borders (at which tariffs and tolls were charged) and a lack of public goods (such as centrally provided transport infrastructure and common laws).[93] Epstein has argued that the warfare that naturally resulted from this fragmentation was starting to push in the direction of the development of states. Funding warfare requires taxation, and taxation requires building a political consensus, state sovereignty and an administrative system.[94] As famously argued by authors such as Tilly and Hintze, warfare thereby created the momentum for state formation.[95] According to Epstein, the Black Death accelerated this process by creating 'a wave of Schumpeterian creative destruction', on the basis of which markets could break through bottlenecks and further advance.[96] This was to the greatest benefit in areas in which urban jurisdictions were not strong (such as England compared to Italy). Where cities had a dominant position and a monopoly on the local area, such as was the case with the Italian cities, they had a vested interest in preventing freer and easier trade in their vicinity and so were reluctant to abdicate power to a body representing a wider area and a broader interest, leading to more delayed state formation.

The third effect of the Black Death was felt particularly strongly in the economies of north-western Europe, where domestic markets had already advanced. According to de Moor and van Zanden, the combination of reduced population and already well-developed internal markets led to a unique north-western 'European Marriage Pattern' – 'Girlpower' – which was to further propel the region forwards in the years ahead.[97] The fall in population raised the value of labour, and developed markets allowed labour to exploit this value. This in turn created opportunities for younger people to survive on their own means, independent of their parents, including most notably young women. With economic freedom came freedom for individuals to select whether, when and whom to marry (free from parental interference) and the creation of small nuclear families. The result was a higher average age of marriage (which created fewer births, meaning less pressure on food and raw materials),[98] higher levels of human capital formation and lower family ties. The latter increased saving (stimulating capital markets) as people could no longer 'fall back' on kin in the event of an adverse shock. In other words, the Black Death paved the way for the rise of the north-west region of Europe in the years to come.

Through whatever channels it operated, the Black Death meant higher incomes for those who were lucky enough to survive. In turn, these higher incomes led to an increasing demand for luxury goods, further spurring trade between distant places. Once again, trade and technology expanded together. According to Fara, 'fuelled by international exploration. Commercial trade stimulated the global exchange of skills [and] knowledge ....'[99] Europe entered the period known as the Renaissance, an 'intellectual fizz' which began in Florence in the fourteenth century.[100] As we have seen, maritime connections across Europe had already been expanding, with the Italians reaching north to England and the Low Countries in the latter thirteenth century. By the late fifteenth century the Hansa had stretched south[101] and the Dutch had started to regularly ship bulky goods between the different parts of Europe. In both the luxury and the bulk trades, the Baltic and Mediterranean were linked by sea in the late fifteenth century.[102] However, the reach of Europe was not enough: it was the east with whom everyone really wanted to make contact. Developments in shipping, navigation and cartography – in part stimulated by this desire – now made this possible. The Orient was of particular interest not only on an intellectual level for the unexplored and mystical element (which only increased following the explorations of Marco Polo) but, more importantly, on a financial level. Venice was the envy of the rest of Europe, and in an effort to attain the wealth of Venice, merchants elsewhere in Europe were desperate to find their own route eastwards in the hope of destroying the Venetian trading monopoly and amassing great fortunes. With support from Spain, Christopher Columbus sailed around the world westwards to find a backdoor to the east. He was convinced that he had found it, but had actually landed in the Americas:[103] the Atlantic economy was born. Vasco Da Gama took an alternative route which went south and east, travelling around the Cape of Africa and up into the Indian Ocean. The result was the establishment of trade between Portugal and the eastern world. The resultant Portuguese cargoes first landed in Antwerp in 1501 and the city became the key distributing hub in the Portuguese spice trade.[104] Here, Portuguese merchants offloaded their finds and bought cloth and metals to take back to the east as payment for spices. Once silver began to flow out of the South American mines, there was an even readier source of payment on hand: trade with the Americas and with the east were fundamentally linked.[105] The extra competition in the spice trade is visible in the reduction in the real prices charged for eastern goods in Europe, bringing clear benefits for consumers.[106] Not only did the prices of such imported goods fall relative to home-grown products, but the volumes imported expanded significantly in response. The growth of world trade in the first half of the sixteenth century (at 2.4 per cent p.a.) was not far from that in the twentieth century (3.44

per cent p.a.).[107] To some, this age of international exploration and expansion marks the start of western domination of the entire globe. It gives rise to colonization, the slave economy, and the destruction of the indigenous population of the Americas. It can also be argued to mark the start of the west overtaking the east, a process only beginning to perhaps reverse itself today.

Within Europe, the consequence of the oceanic adventures was that economic success shifted towards Iberia, which began to carve out the first European colonies across the globe.[108] However, Iberian success was not sustained for long. Much of the colonial trade was monopolized and regulated, with the state being heavily involved, rather than being in the hands of a class of private individuals.[109] Poor internal markets hampered by unfavourable geography and poor institutions also limited the extent to which the benefits of colonial trade could spread deep into the economy. Poor institutions not only hampered markets, but are also likely to have held back technological and scientific development: without an internal dynamic, the Iberian economy soon stagnated, and any nascent industry that did exist was made uncompetitive by the inflows of silver which pushed up prices.[110] The lack of internal sources of growth meant that as other economies also began to enter the race for colonies, Spain and Portugal were not in a sufficiently strong enough position to maintain their hold. The economy was ultimately doomed.

Perhaps the key institution that most historians have argued was holding back the Spanish economy was absolutism: the excessive power of the monarch.[111] Indeed, rising absolutism is argued to have beset much of Europe in the sixteenth and seventeenth centuries, which could be argued to have ushered in a more general economic decline across the continent, known as the seventeenth-century crisis. Everywhere, states were becoming stronger. According to some, these larger entities could aid the development of the market at the local (or national) level if the state used its powers to overcome the problems associated with the fragmentation experienced in Europe since Roman times, such as by eliminating internal tariffs, putting in place a common legal system and ensuring a standard currency.[112] However, the result, others argue, was often the opposite. Many developed in an absolutist direction, and used their power to undermine institutions which had grown to serve markets, foregoing the potential benefits they could bring.[113] These included the pro-market medieval 'bottom-up' institutions discussed earlier, such as urban autonomy and parliaments (the French Estates General, for example, did not meet at all between 1614 and 1789).[114] Fiscal pressures from heavy state expenditure, uncertainty over property rights,[115] a perversion of the course of justice (e.g. in France and Spain[116]), and religious intolerance often followed. In the first of these, the fiscal domain, increasing conspicuous consumption at the court level, together with rising military expenses as the absolutists embarked upon military campaigns, placed great pressure on the nation's finances. Much of this pressure was borne in the form of heavy taxation by those with the least political privilege and power – the less well-off small-scale producers and workers. In turn, this restricted investment by small-scale producers in new technologies. According to North and Weingast, bond markets were not keen to lend to those with absolutist monarchs who regularly defaulted on debt.[117] The fiscal pressures also raised uncertainty regarding property rights and eroded the system of justice. By expropriating private property and using the courts to unfairly extract wealth, absolutists found a simple short-term solution to their fiscal problems. The longer-term consequence, however, was clearly an environment in which economic incentives were damaged. In England, the result was a stand-off between the monarch and Parliament, which resulted in the Civil Wars in the middle of the seventeenth century. The final side effect of rising absolutism, religious intolerance, became particularly clear with the onset of the Reformation. Intolerance against growing non-Catholic adherents is particularly evident in France during the Wars of Religion and in Spain with the expulsion of the Moriscos and the Spanish inquisition. Craftsmen of non-Catholic faith fled from Spain, France and the Spanish part of the Netherlands (including Flanders). It was perhaps only as a result of Henry VIII's desire for a divorce that the English monarch put his weight behind the Protestant as opposed to Catholic cause, albeit still with the consequence of a bitter struggle between Catholics and Protestants in England that lasted until the late seventeenth century. Not only did the rise of absolutist states supposedly hinder market development at the national level through abusing property rights, disrespecting the law and persecuting individuals on the basis of their religion, it also created inter-state conflict that resulted in a series of wars that disrupted not just local but long-distance trade. Germany, for example, suffered badly in the seventeenth century as a result of The Thirty Years War, which arguably had its origins in both religious and inter-state conflict. Poland suffered as surrounding states sought to extend into the region, with the ensuing warfare having serious effects on trade.

Whilst many economic historians see the economic decline that came in the seventeenth century as a consequence of rising absolutism, others see it in a more straightforward Malthusian sense. Neo-Malthusians argue that during the 200 years since the Black Death, the economy and population had recovered and so was once again starting to exceed resources in the economy, pushing up the price of food and raw materials, causing the standard of living to decline. In western Europe, estimates suggest that the population rose from around 57 million in 1500 to around 74 million by the end of the century. Evidence of rising food prices, falling real wages and deteriorating agricultural productivity at the same time as rising population could be interpreted as supportive of this view. However, those who focus on deteriorating institutions argue that had institutions been superior, the rising population would not have caused falling real wages and rising agricultural prices. The increasing supply of labour would have been met with a rising demand for labour, as better institutions would have enabled stronger markets which would have created incentives for productivity improvement, stimulating economic growth. Similarly, food production would have expanded at a greater rate, preventing the fall in agricultural productivity and consequent rising food prices. Authors who take this view point to two economies in particular who both escaped economic crisis and where institutions were favourable: the Netherlands and England.

The performance of these economies looks remarkable when placed in a comparative context and brought about a full-scale reorientation of the axis of economic power away from the Mediterranean for the first time in history. The figures below place the performance of the two economies in the context of the rest of Europe. Figure 1.1 demonstrates the urbanization that was taking place.

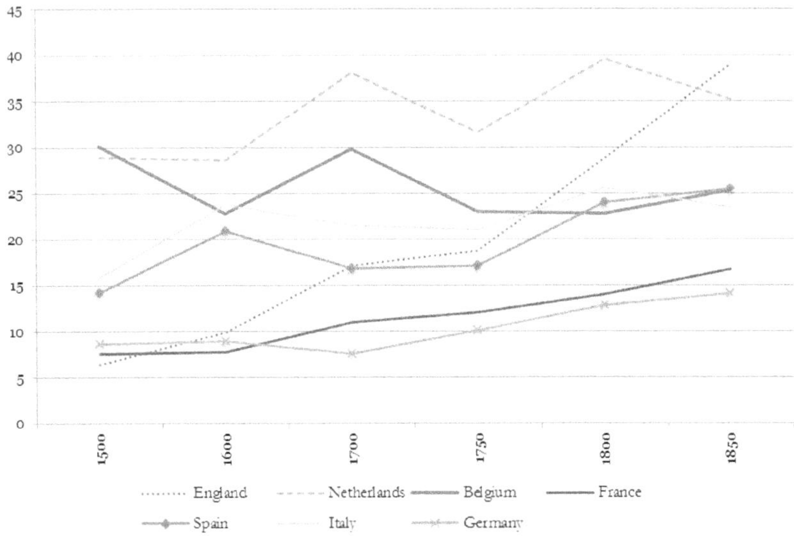

Figure 1.1: Urbanization rates in Europe, 1500–1850.
Source: D. Acemoglu, S. Johnson and J. A. Robinson, 'The Rise of Europe: Atlantic Trade, Institutional Change, and Economic Growth', *NBER Working Paper 9378* (2002).

In most parts of Europe, agricultural employment represented around 75 per cent of the population in 1500.[118] The initial economic leadership of southern Europe and the Low Countries is apparent, as these areas have the largest urban share of population at 15–30 per cent with only 60 per cent in agriculture in 1500. However, Figure 1.1 also suggests that by the end of the early modern period, England had undergone remarkable urbanization: by 1750, England had only 45 per cent of its population in agriculture and The Netherlands had reduced hers to 42 per cent. In contrast with England, in southern Europe, the Spanish and Italian shares saw little change from their medieval levels.[119] It was not until the nineteenth or even twentieth century that the other European economies had transformed themselves. Austria, France, Germany and Poland only experienced a small change in their economic structures during the pre-modern period. Indeed, even after World War 2, Germany still had 25 per cent of her workforce in agriculture compared with only 5 per cent for Britain.

Figure 1.2 presents estimates of agricultural productivity during the same time period.[120] Clearly, in theory, high agricultural productivity tends to be representative of an economy with a lower agricultural share, as it leaves more resources free for the urban non-agricultural sector. Also, rising agricultural productivity tends to occur concurrently with structural change out of agriculture and into the urban sector of the economy.

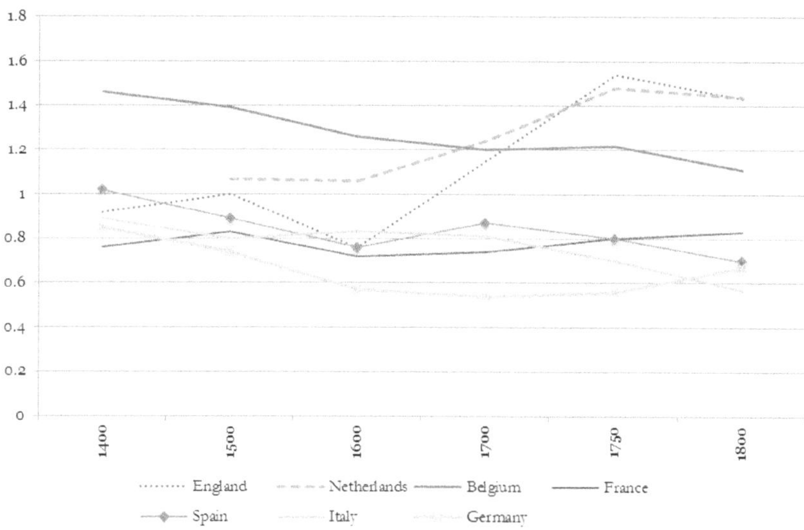

Figure 1.2: Agricultural productivity in Europe, 1400–1800.
Source: Allen, R. C., 'Economic Structure and Agricultural Productivity in Europe, 1300–1800', ***European Review of Economic History*****, 4 (2000), pp. 1–25.**

Hence, given her relatively large urban share at the start of the early modern period, it is unsurprising to see that Belgium also had a high agricultural productivity. Subsequently, the Netherlands and England underwent agricultural revolutions, catching up with the agricultural productivity of Belgium. In the rest of Europe, agricultural productivity generally stagnated at relatively low levels (and even declined).[121]

Figure 1.3 provides an indication of what was happening to the real wage or standard of living of unskilled workers in Europe, using Allen's 'Welfare Ratios', for which a value above one indicates that 'families had extra income over and above their basic needs' when working 250 days a year.[122] A value of less than one indicates that families would have had to cut back on their basic consumption of goods such as food or work for more than 250 days per year. During the medieval years of the fourteenth and fifteenth centuries, real wages had risen across Europe in response to the labour scarcity which followed the Black Death. By the early sixteenth century, however, real wages were marching downwards in Europe. Population had recovered to its pre-Black Death levels and so was arguably once again stretching the fixed resources of the economy, pushing up the prices of land-based goods (food and energy) and so lowering the real wage. Exceptionally, in the early seventeenth century real wages in the Netherlands were recovering, as they then did in England by the second half of the century. It therefore appears that economic events in the north-west were sufficiently favourable to counteract the decline in the real wage which was resulting from excessive population pressure. This suggests that the demand for labour was rising sufficiently to 'mop up' the growing population, indicative of economic advance unlike anywhere else in Europe. This leaves a divergence in real wages across the continent.

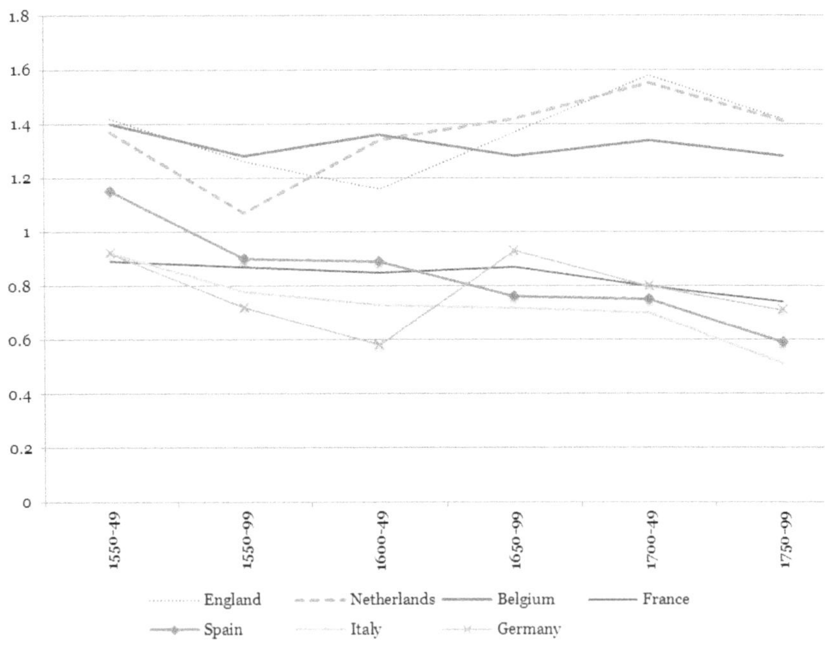

Figure 1.3: Welfare ratios of building labourers in Europe, 1500–1799. Source: R. C. Allen, 'The Great Divergence in European Wages and Prices', *Explorations in Economic History*, 38 (2001), p. 428.

As is perhaps clear from the figures, the Netherlands was the first economy to whom economic leadership passed in the early modern period, with her economy experiencing a 'Golden Age' during the seventeenth century at the very same time that many others were experiencing crisis. The Low Countries were under Spanish control in the sixteenth century, but there was a growing desire for independence when the absolutist claws began to dig deeper: the result was a lengthy and costly war for independence. The war seemed distinctly in Spain's favour, but three factors worked to the advantage of the Dutch: Spanish military distractions in France and England, which diverted its military resources away from the Low Countries, the immense Dutch fiscal raising powers that enabled it to fund its own military expenditure, and rivers that made battles more easily won in the north than those in the southern Netherlands (modern day Belgium). The result was that whilst the modern day territory of Belgium failed to gain independence, the Netherlands successfully managed to do so, 'kicking out' the Spanish absolutists for good. The cooperation of the Dutch provinces in the process – formalized in the Union of Utrecht – marks the beginning of the modern day country of the Netherlands, of which the province known as Holland was the richest and most powerful.[123] From this point on, the Dutch rise was magisterial. 'It seems a wonder to the world,' wrote Thomas Munn, a seventeenth-century English economist and mercantilist writer, that despite being small in terms of population, natural resources and land, the Netherlands became the greatest trading nation the world had ever seen.[124] As summarized by Israel, it was 'the hub of world commerce' and much more exceptional than Venice or Antwerp before it. It was not simply a regional entrepot or a place that linked many different markets, but instead dominated 'the markets of all continents' – the first truly global entrepot.[125] By 1670, the Dutch had three times the tonnage of England, and more than all of the other major economies combined.[126] To other countries, the Netherlands was the most hated but at the same time most envied and admired country of seventeenth-century Europe. Whilst they were experiencing the pains of the seventeenth century, the Dutch were witnessing all manner of success. In fact, irrespective of whether one blames Malthusian strains or rising absolutism for the seventeenth-century European crisis, the Dutch were in a position to benefit.

During the fifteenth century, the Netherlands had carved out a role as the carrier of bulk low-value goods for the rest of Europe, including grain, wood, salt, wine and fish, on the back of the large Dutch shipping fleet and low Dutch freight charges. The oldest register of tolls on the Danish Sound (from 1497) records that more than half of the ships passing through – and so involved in Baltic trade – were Dutch.[127] The strength of the Netherlands in the bulk trade is also evident in the fact that its cargo capacity was twice that of Venice.[128] By the early seventeenth century, Braudel argues that these goods became increasingly important relative to the 'rich trades' of cities like Venice, Genoa, Lisbon, Seville, Lyons, Bruges, Nuremberg, Lübeck and Antwerp. Population growth was rising and in the face of limited land this meant that there was an increasing demand for food, including from the richer Mediterranean part of Europe. As a result, the balance of power tipped in favour of the Dutch. Israel argues that the 'bulk trades' are not enough to explain Dutch success, and that the 'rich-trades' – including the new opportunities provided by colonization and the opening up of the world – became increasingly important to its trade in the seventeenth century.[129] In actual fact, these two trades were mutually supportive: the rich-trades provided a valuable cargo to ship to the Baltic in return for grain.[130] Hence, both aspects of trade grew together.

Why did one single economy come to be global entrepot for all this trade? T.P. van der Kooy argues that the world economy was developing within the constraint of relatively high transport costs and with greater uncertainty in demand and supply relative to the later age of rail and steam in the nineteenth century. This created an advantage in having a staple market that could act as a focal point for trade, enabled the stockpiling of goods in a single location, and provided storage, marketing, insurance and transport services to all.[131] This central point could help to match demand and supply and it was thanks to Dutch geography (accessible for the Atlantic, Rhine and Baltic) that it took on the role. Kooy gives an example of French wine, for which the harvest came too late in the year to enable shipping the goods directly into the Baltic and around northern Scandinavia. Many would agree that there is an important element of truth in this idea, but more than just geography (and, through that, trade) aided the development of the Dutch trading position. The policies of the state working through the formation of big international trading companies, the most famous of which was the Dutch East India Company, and a well-developed broader economy – agriculturally, industrially and financially – also helped. Indeed, one could argue that it was on the back of this well-developed internal economy that the Dutch economy's trading position could flourish and could give rise to great stimulus across the entire economy.

Indeed, Dutch economic success was much broader based than many of the previous economies so far discussed, which gave it 'staying power'.[132] In addition to trade, the economy was already home to a developing textile sector around the cities of Leiden and Haarlem and there were important developments in the herring fishing industry, including the ability to cure fish whilst at sea together with specialized boats.[133] Shipbuilding also flourished in response to trade, and an early dominance in bulky low value goods stimulated the design of cheaper ships, lowering transport costs, and culminated in the famous 'flute' ship, first launched in 1595.[134] Dutch agriculture benefited from being able to shift away from grain (thanks to the ready supply being brought from the Baltic), but was on shaky ground due to a rising sea level and excessive peat-digging.[135] However, the engineering skills of the Dutch, supporting the reclamation of land, together with developing a specialization in crops and animal-rearing more suited to wet conditions, turned the agricultural situation into a success. Finance was also an area of strength in the Dutch economy, including the development of a stock exchange, the Amsterdam Exchange Bank (1611)[136] and an extensive market for government debt, which enabled the economy to finance the costly wars against the Spanish. Before long, Dutch capital 'could be found draining French marshes, developing the Swedish copper and iron industry, and exploiting the monopoly of Austrian quicksilver'. Each sector's success created favourable spillover effects on the other sectors, further fuelling expansion and placing the economy in a virtuous circle benefiting from positive feedback effects:[137] finance allowed merchants involved in sourcing foreign goods to buy in bulk ahead of harvest or production, putting them at an advantage relative to the merchants of other countries, and also provided funds for investment in manufacturing;[138] manufacturing in turn required foreign raw materials which further boosted trade; the inflow of grain allowed the agricultural sector to specialize (e.g. in the production of cheese and butter), which raised agricultural productivity, released labour for manufacturing and provided a valuable export good which pushed forward the involvement of the Dutch in the European carrying-trade.

Behind this broad-based development of the economy lay a set of markets and institutions which acted as strong foundations. As we saw earlier, internal markets had already developed relatively early on. The Netherlands was also unique in Europe in terms of being a republic and so avoiding the tightening grip of rising absolutism (including by fighting off the Spanish). It was also relatively unusual in the sense of being religiously tolerant of all sects at a time of serious religious disputes surrounding the Reformation and Counter-Reformation which were causing disturbances elsewhere and which attracted talent to the Netherlands in flight from persecution (including from Flanders).[139] The Dutch economy was therefore like a modern day industrial cluster, providing a growth pole which pulled talent towards it. However, its advanced commercial nature failed to generate sustained economic growth: the Dutch economy stagnated. It seems that well-developed markets and institutions may not have been enough to ensure continued success.

By the eighteenth century, England was overtaking Holland; urbanization was increasing, an agricultural revolution was taking place and real wages made up for ground lost in the previous century. According to the market-based view, the rise of England was the result of improving markets in the eighteenth century, supported by institutional improvements in the late seventeenth century. Whilst markets elsewhere were undermined by rising absolutism, and monopoly trading companies started to weaken the Netherlands' success, England saw the Glorious Revolution of the late seventeenth century. According to North and Weingast, this led to improved property rights, underpinning improvements in markets, together with more representative economic policies that did not succumb to vested interests.[140] In stark contrast, however, others argue that England had already experienced internal market development, originating in Anglo-Saxon times, and that the absolutism of Tudor and Stuart monarchs was only a temporary interruption. If this is the case, it is difficult to argue that markets reached significantly new heights and led to the Industrial Revolution.[141] Indeed, some of the most recent contributions to the literature have identified factors other than markets: state intervention in the trading arena, high wages, the Enlightenment and coal.

Much of Britain's involvement in the global trading sphere from the seventeenth century onwards was led by the state as opposed to the free market. In an effort to capture European and colonial trade from the hands of the Dutch and the longer established Italians, the strong English state successfully implemented mercantilist policy and carved out colonies.[142] Amsterdam merchants blamed their falling behind on the difficulties caused by English protectionism.[143] Whilst the amount of colonial trade and the associated profits have been shown to have been too small to have made a substantial direct contribution to economic growth,[144] trade could have affected the economy indirectly. According to the recent work of Allen, England's trading fortunes raised the demand for labour, preventing her real wage from falling. When combined with fortuitously cheap coal, this high wage incentivized labour-saving inventions and technological adoption, ultimately leading to the Industrial Revolution.[145] High wages also facilitated education by providing families with the income necessary to send their children to school. Furthermore, they acted to stimulate change in the countryside, as agriculturalists battled to raise the productivity of the land in an effort to keep up with growth of the cities.[146] In the Malthusian vein, Pomeranz argues that Atlantic trade freed England from the Malthusian trap, enabling sustained growth,[147] and so preventing a return of the supposed Malthusian-driven economic collapse of the fourteenth and seventeenth centuries. On the demand side Davis writes, 'The process of industrialization in England from the second quarter of the eighteenth century was to an important extent a response to colonial demand for nails, axes, firearms, buckets, coaches, clocks, saddles, handkerchiefs, buttons, cordage and a thousand other things'.[148] Davis also notes how trade reduced prices of imported goods, thereby enabling mass markets.[149] More recently, the work of Maxine Berg has emphasized the way in which imports of eastern manufactured goods stimulated import substitution and consumerism, thereby contributing to the industrialization. The goods produced in the colonies (which produced trade surpluses) enabled England to import increasing amounts of goods from the east – goods for which Europeans had a great appetite.

Whilst some economic historians argue that trade was sufficient to ignite the British Industrial Revolution, others argue that the roots are to be found elsewhere, and that trade was perhaps a consequence as opposed to the cause. Technological change – the development of the steam engine, metal manufacture and new cotton machines – is central to the Industrial Revolution and Mokyr argues that these were not so much the result of trade but of the Enlightenment which was sweeping across Europe at the time.[150] This movement led scientists to work together with engineers and businessmen to push forward the frontiers of technology, raising the productivity of the economy. It also ushered in changes to policy making, including the Smithian laissez-faire policy approach, which Mokyr argues aided the development of the economy by making the state more reluctant to support vested interests who might be upset by technological change, such as workers who might see the values of their skills eroded or the owners of now obsolete technologies. This meant that nothing stood in the way of continued progress. Since the Enlightenment was happening across Europe, Mokyr argues that Britain was not essential for the Industrial Revolution (it would have soon happened elsewhere). Of course, by downplaying Britain, Mokyr downplays the importance of Britain-specific factors in the start of modern economic growth.

No one can mention the Industrial Revolution without thinking of coal, and if coal was important, then perhaps Britain really did have an edge over many other parts of Europe. According to Wrigley, the abundance of coal in Britain explains why once the economy started to grow, whether as a result of trade or the enlightenment, it could keep on growing.[151] Neo-Malthusians argue that economic expansion had always ended in stagnation earlier in history, including for the Dutch. As an economy grows, it increases the demand for food and raw materials, including energy resources, which makes these goods more expensive, raising costs to producers and so limiting expansion. Indeed, before Britain used coal, wood was used as a source of energy. The result was that as the economy expanded, it began to run out of trees; very few old oak trees still exist in England today – a mass deforestation occurred between Tudor times and the eighteenth century. As the price of wood increased in response to growing scarcity, people began to look for other options. Fortuitously, readily accessible coal reserves situated not far from the coast could be brought into use. Whilst coal is, like any resource, limited, it is much more abundant as a source of energy than wood. This also made it very cheap: cheap coal could literally fuel the expansion of the economy, allowing it to keep on growing. Of course, those who focus on technological change as being at the root of growth are to some extent reluctant to accept that resources are also important for growth. Any resource limit can in theory be overcome by technological advances which lessen dependence on natural resources. However, with the current global economy seeing dramatic increases in food and raw material prices, which is acting to raise the costs of production for firms and lower the standard of living of consumers, we may soon find out whether or not this is always the case.

The Industrial Revolution marks the first time in history that economic growth was sustained and, based on the recent work of authors such as Allen, Mokyr and Wrigley, was a result of much more than markets. However, even if markets were not enough to cause the Industrial Revolution, the consequences for global markets were tremendous. New steam and iron technologies led to the building of railways across the globe and the birth of steam shipping, drastically lowering transport costs.[152] New information and communication technologies such as the telegraph in the 1850s further added to the mix.[153] Institutional developments such as the Gold Standard and Imperial connections also helped to boost trade.[154] The result was a dramatic transformation in European and cross-national markets leading to a major globalization of the world economy in the latter half of the nineteenth century.[155] The world was metaphorically smaller and flatter as a consequence of growth. Now that Britain had become successful, she shed her mercantilist practices, replacing tariffs with free trade policies. In fact, not only were goods markets experiencing rapid integration, but so were labour and capital markets, as evidenced by flows of labour and capital together with a convergence in wages and interest rates.[156] Around 30 million people emigrated from Europe to the USA in the century after 1820.[157] British capital-exports funded the building of infrastructure and opened up large tracts of land to produce for international markets. Writing in 1982, one author noted that never before or since had one economy invested so much across the world.[158] Here we see the creation of all types of global markets as very much a consequence as opposed to cause of growth. However, despite this globalization, the newly industrializing economies of the US and Germany that were trying to catch up with Britain were not afraid to use tariffs to their advantage.[159] Tariffs in the US were equivalent to a uniform rate of 40 per cent between 1870 and 1913,[160] and Germany put tariffs in place from 1879. It was whilst protecting infant industries that these economies managed to catch up with Britain.[161]

Having achieved new heights of development in the latter half of the nineteenth century, international markets disintegrated in the interwar period between World War I and World War 2: tariffs rose in response to the Great Depression of the 1930s, and revolutions and fascism increased the number of countries pursuing autarky. Economic growth was contracting and with it so was world trade, creating a vicious downward circle. Global trade unraveled and restrictions on labour markets (including immigration policies) increased: the world economy de-globalized.[162] The share of exports relative to output that existed in 1913 in some of the world's major economies was not seen again until 1973.[163] Following this interwar experience, policymakers arrived at two conclusions that greatly influenced policy after World War 2. Firstly, they decided that a complete reliance on markets internally could not always guarantee full employment: Keynesian demand-management policies and the welfare state were born. Internally, therefore, a 'mixed' as opposed to fully free market economy was pursued. Secondly, when it came to international markets, tariff policies were shown to have been self-defeating as they resulted in a contraction of international demand which hurt not just the rest of the world but also the domestic economy. International markets were to be freed. A more supportive fixed exchange rate system – Bretton Woods – was introduced after the war and tariff negotiations started to take place. The new system relied on the freedom of international goods markets but restrictions on flows of capital between countries, which were seen as potentially destabilizing. Against this backdrop, the world economy entered the Golden Age of the 1950s and 1960s. Nowhere experienced this more than Europe: unemployment was low, as was inflation, and trade and investment were booming. By the late 1960s, however, the fixed exchange rate system was coming under pressure and so a wholesale shift to flexible exchange rates occurred in the 1970s. At the same time, capital markets were deregulated. Whilst domestic markets were being 'managed', international markets recovered to the levels of integration seen in the late nineteenth century.

Despite this re-globalization, by the 1970s and 1980s the scourge of unemployment returned and economic growth slowed. This time the response was very different to that of the interwar period, as we saw in the Introduction. Too little reliance on the invisible hand of the market as opposed to too much reliance was argued to be the culprit – trade unions were 'stamped on', the welfare state was 'rolled back' and capital markets were further de-regulated (the 'Big Bang' of the 1980s). The result was that by the latter decades of the twentieth century, both internal and international markets were 'freed', and globalization reached new heights.[164]

Summary

Economic history is very simple for pro-market economists. Nothing much of interest happened until the late seventeenth and eighteenth centuries when markets began to emerge, spurring the growth take-off that began with the Industrial Revolution. The long-span history presented in this chapter, which knits together the work of much old and new research in economic history, paints a very different picture. We have seen that markets existed as far back as Roman times but as the Roman Empire disintegrated in the west, markets unraveled and Europe entered the Dark Ages. Out of the darkness emerged substitutes for the state in the form of market-supporting institutions, on the basis of which markets rebuilt themselves. Whilst leading to trauma in the short term, the Black Death structurally changed politics and society in a way that introduced further opportunities for market expansion. Markets reached new heights as a result. By the seventeenth century, however, markets may have taken a backward move or, at the very least, stagnated. The Dutch and the English economies were the outliers to the 'crisis' occurring elsewhere in Europe. By the late eighteenth century, the Industrial Revolution was underway, which was followed by the next major phase of market integration – the nineteenth-century globalization. By the interwar period, growth was slowing and markets disintegrated, only overtaking their late nineteenth-century levels from the 1970s onwards. If the Great Depression is any guide, markets are now set for a further disintegration. One lesson we should learn from history is that markets cannot be taken for granted: they have unraveled in the past and they may do so in the future. The recent banking crisis put capital markets on a knife-edge, which only narrowly escaped a complete breakdown through the substantial intervention of the state. Whilst a complete failure of capital markets has been avoided, we still stand in the midst of recession with both governments and consumers who are more indebted than ever before. The global economy is far from safe.

This alternative narrative suggests that there is a much more complicated relationship between markets and growth than is typically thought. We seem to find the co-existence of markets and periods of economic prosperity throughout history, in Roman, medieval and modern times. Internal markets seem particularly correlated with success – in light of mercantilist policy, external markets arguably less so. However, if markets were reasonably well developed in Medieval times (and in the seventeenth-century Dutch economy), and yet did not produce sustained economic growth, can markets really be sufficient? Similarly, if England (and other early industrializers) did not pursue free trade, this may question the extent to which free international markets are at the root of growth. Furthermore, if markets are enough by themselves, why has the increasing reliance on them culminated in the worst global recession since the Great Depression? Perhaps when we see the simultaneous existence of markets and growth, we would be wise to remember that the former can be a function of the latter, as the nineteenth century shows.

In light of the significant implications that this new economic history narrative is pointing us towards, the path of markets in history and their relationship with economic growth deserves to be more formally explored. This is the task of the remainder of the book. The first task is to measure market development in the long span of history in a quantitative way, which is carried out in the next three chapters. Many studies exist which have econometrically measured markets in a particular country or at a particular time, but the different methods and data that they have used make comparisons on the basis of such work impossible. What we therefore need to do is measure markets in Europe for as long a period as the data allows.[165] We can then use the quantitative results to answer a number of questions which are crucial to confirming the alternative narrative presented in this chapter: To what extent did markets develop between ancient and medieval times? Were markets already reasonably well developed by medieval times? Did markets disintegrate in the Mediterranean and plough ahead in the northwest in the course of the early modern era? Did markets achieve new heights on the eve of the Industrial Revolution (or had they been similarly developed early on)? With the details pinned down, Chapters 5 and 6 are then in a position to place the market estimates alongside measures of economic performance to directly test for a link between the two. In other words, to formally test the basic tenet of the bible of economics, Smith's *Wealth of Nations*.

2 THE COURSE OF EARLY MODERN MARKET INTEGRATION: COUNTRY-LEVEL RESULTS

Few of us are good at everything. When it comes to meeting the basic needs of life, it is difficult to imagine how we could do it alone. Countries are no different.[1] However, when markets are poorly developed and the cost of exchanging goods is high, individual countries and regions produce everything they require for their own subsistence – exporting and importing goods is simply too costly. Only high value goods tend to be traded over long distances, and these represent only a small proportion of consumers' baskets. As transport costs (or more generally, the costs of making transactions) fall, it becomes feasible and profitable for different countries to trade with each other. A country producing a particular good relatively cheaply will find that it receives orders from far-flung places. Indeed, merchants will have an incentive to buy the good in the cheaper location and ship it to the more expensive location, induced by making a profit on the difference in price between the two. As a result, each country starts to export the good for which it is most suited – which it can produce locally relatively cheaply – and in return imports products that are relatively more cheaply produced elsewhere. Resources are pulled out of the sectors for which goods can now be more cheaply imported and towards the export sectors of the economy. The economy's structure of production changes and it becomes increasingly specialized; the volume of trade rises as a consequence. With trade comes technology transfer and economies of scale, further acting to raise income in the economy. Through this process of market development, economies therefore become richer.[2]

In this chapter we will examine the extent to which the individual countries of Europe were undergoing this process of market development from the medieval period through to the nineteenth century. This provides a useful means through which we can start to gauge whether trends in markets can help to explain the economic development of the different parts of Europe during this formative period of history. Unlike existing studies that tend to focus on measuring markets in just one or two countries or for a restricted period of time, the approach adopted here allows us to directly compare the relative level of market development in each country over a long-run period, identifying not only the trend markets took within and between each country, but also which countries had better developed markets relative to others. This will provide a strong basis from which to more formally test the relationship between markets and economic growth later on in the book.

In what follows, the first section discusses the techniques and data used to measure markets, formulating a set of 'market estimates' that form the basis for establishing the trends in markets at the country level, and also the regional and overall European level, which we will go on to consider in the next couple of chapters. On the basis of the country-level results, the second section presents market histories for the various European countries, examining trends in economic performance alongside the evolution of markets.

Measuring Markets

Our image of the process of market development suggests a number of different ways in which markets could be measured. This could include looking for evidence of falling costs of transactions, such as shipping costs, an increasing degree of specialization and a rising volume of trade. However, a more common approach, and one for which data is much more readily available, involves gathering and examining the behaviour of prices of a commonly used good from different locations.[3] As we will see, this approach strikes more fundamentally at the heart of what is happening as markets become increasingly connected, providing the ultimate means through which to track the evolution of markets. In order to provide a sufficiently broad perspective, three price-based measures are adopted in what follows: price convergence, price volatility and speeds of price adjustment.

The first price-based measure relies on the notion that if markets are becoming better developed, the prices of a particular good in different locations should be converging. The logic is as follows. Suppose that we have two countries, which we will refer to as country 1 and country 2. Country 1 has an abundance of high quality land but has a scarcity of skilled labour, and country 2 has an abundance of skilled labour but relatively little land. We will assume that the production of grain is intensive in the use of land whilst the production of manufactured goods is intensive in the use of skilled labour. In country 1, where there is lots of land but little skilled labour, the price of grain is likely to be very cheap, but the price of manufactured goods very expensive, with the opposite in country 2. Once markets open up between the two countries, it then makes sense for country 2 to import grain from country 1, where it is cheap, and in return for country 1 to import manufactured goods. The increase in demand for grain in country 1 pushes the price up, whilst the increase in imports of grain in country 2 pulls the price there downwards, as a result of which the prices of grain converge between the two countries. This is similarly the case for the prices of manufactured goods.

It is these resultant price changes that help to send signals to reshuffle resources in the economy towards producing the goods and services for which it is most suited: grain in the case of country 1 and manufactured goods in the case of country 2, leading to specialization and greater consumption opportunities for each economy, increasing the standard of living.[4] Without the changes in prices, the economy's production structure would not be fundamentally changed and so trade would have a minimal effect. Hence, if markets are truly becoming better connected, then we should observe a convergence in prices.

The second price-based measure relies on the assumption that if markets are becoming better developed, the volatility of prices should be falling. Markets are inevitably subject to local shocks which cause prices to fluctuate in the short run. However, as markets develop, one would expect to find a reduction in the volatility of prices as the effect of a local shock on local prices is mitigated by new sources of supply which are opened up by trade.[5] Given that harvest shocks tend to be local in nature, if one region falls short, another is likely in excess, and arbitrage will even out the difference between the two. In addition, trade allows consumers access to a greater range of goods, including substitute goods for those they regularly consume. Consumption possibilities are more diverse. Hence, the effect of a local shock on local prices will also be mitigated as consumers can respond to changing prices by switching to other products. If markets are improving, the volatility of prices should therefore fall, and the standard of living of consumers improves as their ability to buy goods is now more stable.

The third price-based measure is grounded in the belief that if markets are becoming better developed, we would expect to observe an increase in the speed at which prices adjust back to their 'normal' level following a shock. This is because if markets are integrated, exports in abundant times and imports in times of scarcity will help to quickly adjust prices back to their usual levels.

In total, an examination of prices therefore gives three ways in which market integration can be measured. Each of the associated measures has its own particular advantages and disadvantages, and so it is important to draw conclusions from the full range of results. Altogether, if we are able to find price convergence, falling volatility and rising speeds of adjustment then it would provide consistent evidence of improving market integration. In contrast, if we find little evidence of price convergence, and little change in volatility and speeds of adjustment, it would suggest that market integration did not improve.[6]

It is to the great benefit of modern day economic historians who are trying to measure markets that our ancestors were such good accountants. Bursars at historic institutions such as the colleges of Oxford and Cambridge Universities, government departments and religious institutions have long kept accounts of the prices of goods they have bought to feed their inhabitants or the value of the goods sold from the great swathes of farmland they leased out to tenants. Much of this grain price data has been painstakingly unearthed by economic historians from the primary sources, with a flurry of activity inspired by the International Scientific Committee on Price History (ISCPH) from 1929.[7] The time series which provide the longest period of coverage and which are available for a vast array of cities are grain price data, and particularly wheat prices. As a result, grain prices form the bedrock of data used in existing studies of market development. Whilst one may hesitate at the thought of using grain price data as a means to measure market integration more generally, there are in fact three strong justifications, aside from its ease of availability.

First and foremost, agriculture comprised the vast majority of national output in this period of history, and grain in particular was both supplied and demanded in all regions of Europe, making it a good product with which to study market integration. Wheat was the predominant grain consumed in Europe and average consumption was around 170–360 kg per year per person.[8] This means that grain supplied around 80 per cent of average calorie intake.[9] Whilst much grain was traded relatively locally,[10] it was also exported over longer distances and in significant quantities to urbanized regions such as the Low Countries and northern Italy. For example, grain from northern France and eastern Germany supplied Belgium, being taken along the Scheldt and other Flemish rivers to the cities of Douai, Bruges, Ghent and Ypres.[11] In medieval times, grain also made its way to Flanders from England,[12] whilst the lower Rhineland and northern France supplied the Netherlands. As is well reported in the records from the Danish Sound, exports of grain from the Baltic to the Low Countries – initially in the hands of the Hanse but increasingly the Dutch themselves – grew significantly at the start of the early modern era, fell in the seventeenth century and then stabilized.[13] In the Mediterranean the principal grain growing areas included Calabria, Apulia and Sicily, which supplied the deficit regions in northern Italy.[14] It was also not unknown for Mediterranean grain to reach northern Europe, as in the Great Famine of 1317.[15] By the end of the sixteenth century, northern ships laden with Baltic grain were regularly penetrating the Mediterranean. Grain was not only traded between agricultural and urban regions, but also between specialized agricultural regions. For example, English grain was exported to Gascony, which specialized in viticulture.[16] This evidence of an extensive trade in grain suggests that using grain prices to measure the integration between different parts of Europe seems sensible.

The second reason for using grain prices is provided by the fact that grain was the basic necessity of life and so it was only when the grain market became integrated and so regular access to imported grain could be guaranteed that areas could specialize according to their comparative advantage – whether that be industrial or agricultural – generating the associated welfare gains.[17] Hence, grain market integration was essential for the broader processes of structural change and market development and so represents a useful proxy for market development more generally in the economy.

The final justification for using prices of grain to measure markets more generally is that the potential causes of grain market integration (including transport and institutional improvements) are likely to be similar to those for other products. As a result, the trend in grain market integration will likely be in some way representative of integration of other markets.

Altogether, this provides a compelling set of reasons for studying the development of markets through the price of a grain product such as wheat. Two types of wheat price data are in fact used in the present study: annual and monthly. Perhaps the most commonly used data is monthly, such as in the well-known study of European markets undertaken by Persson.[18] The high frequency nature of this data supports the careful measurement of not only price gaps but also volatility and speeds of adjustment. The data has been gathered by the current author from a broad set of sources detailed in the previous work of the author.[19] As each city's prices are quoted in a different monetary and physical unit, it was necessary to convert the original series into a single unit, grams of silver per litre. This process produced comparable monthly grain prices for a number of cities in early modern Europe: Antwerp (from 1608), Brussels (from 1568), Cologne (from 1550), London (from 1683), Munich (from 1690), Paris (from 1550), Pisa (from 1550), Ruremonde (from 1650), Siena (from 1550), Toulouse (from 1563), Utrecht (from 1550) and Vienna (from 1692). The existing studies which have made use of these prices have concluded that markets in early modern Europe witnessed improvement.[20] However, given the relatively late date at which these price series begin, such a conclusion is formed on the basis of comparing the late sixteenth and seventeenth centuries with the eighteenth century, which is not ideal given what historians have identified as a 'General Crisis' in most parts of Europe at some point between c.1550–1700.[21] This crisis is certainly evident in the trade data available to economic historians: O'Rourke and Williamson find a strong contraction in the growth of European international trade in the late sixteenth and seventeenth century, from 2.42 per cent p.a. in 1500–49 to 0.12 per cent p.a. in 1550–99, 0.75 per cent p.a. in 1600–49 and 0.55 per cent p.a. in 1650–99.[22] Within Europe, evidence from the Sound Tolls suggests that grain shipments and the number of ships operating to and from Europe's bread-basket – the Baltic – were also witnessing significant decline in the seventeenth century, following growth in the century beforehand.[23] Both of these aspects of European trade then show recovery in the eighteenth century. Hence, the suggestion that markets integrated between the seventeenth and eighteenth centuries is hardly surprising given an understanding of the historical context, and should not necessarily be taken as indicating that markets achieved new previously unseen heights; instead, they may have simply recovered. If we truly want to judge whether markets on the eve of the Industrial Revolution were better integrated than ever before, we need to push further back in time, and this is where annual price data proves to be particularly valuable.

Most of the annual data has already been expertly compiled from the secondary sources (which grew out of the ISCPH) by Allen and Unger in their grain price data set and is now in common usage.[24] A number of additional price series are available through the International Institute of Social History[25] and from other sources documented in Appendix 1. This data enables us to measure market integration as far back as the fourteenth century and for a larger number of cities than the monthly data allows. The cities and the time periods for which data is available (together with sources) are indicated in Appendix 1. Figure 2.1 shows the prices for a selection of cities for which we have the longest coverage (in grams of silver per litre using a 20 year moving average).

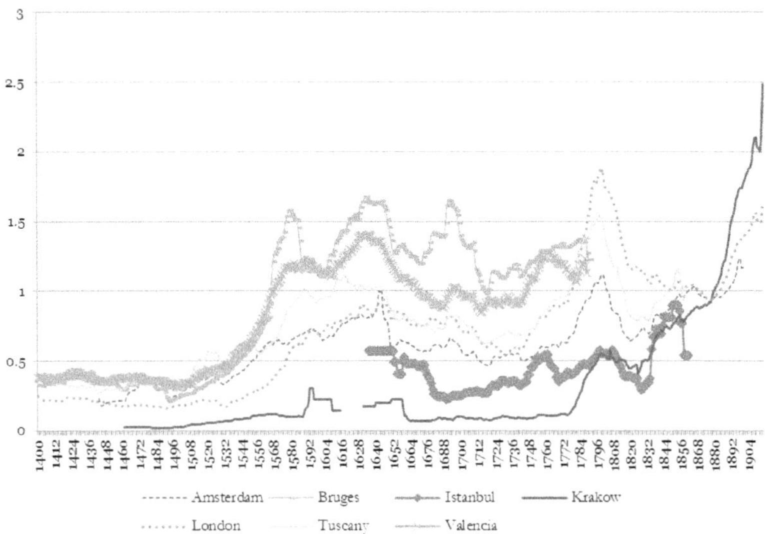

Figure 2.1: Annual grain prices (grams of silver per litre).

One of the most visible features of this data is the price revolution of the sixteenth century. On average the price of wheat goes from just under 0.5 grams of silver per litre in the fifteenth century to around double that level by the seventeenth century. There exists a debate as to the causes of this price increase, with both increasing population pressure and increasing supplies of silver from the New World being the two possible factors at work.[26] The figure also reveals areas in which prices are either relatively high or relatively low. Poland, for example, initially stands out for its relatively low prices, which could be explained in terms of having an abundance of land relative to people. Over time, these prices increase and converge with prices elsewhere in Europe. One could easily infer that falling transaction costs made exports from the area more viable, leading to a convergence of prices. In western and central Europe, prices begin quite close together, becoming more dispersed from the late sixteenth century. This is indicative of a dislocation of markets in the long seventeenth century. In the nineteenth century, prices appear to re-converge. This initial look at the data confirms the importance of measuring markets across a longer span of history than can typically be found in the existing literature. Even before we begin our formal measurements, this cursory glance suggests that markets may have been similarly integrated at the start and end of the early modern period (1500–1800), with an intermediate dislocation. Focusing only on the late sixteenth century onwards merely picks up one half of this apparent U-shaped trend, and so leads to a seriously incorrect vision of market development in history.

For our first measure of market development, price convergence, the long and abundant annual wheat price data are employed. On the basis of this data, percentage price gaps are calculated between a large number of cities for as long as the data permits.[27] More than forty-three cities are used to enable broad coverage both geographically and across time, giving almost 1,000 city-pairs between which price gaps are estimated for consecutive fifty yearly periods between 1400 and 1900.[28] Using the resulting panel of price gaps together with panel data techniques, the average price gap within each country and between each economy and the rest of Europe can be calculated.[29] Given that some countries are much smaller than others and so have cities located closer together, the within-country price gaps are made comparable by a process of 'distance-adjusting'. The results together with more discussion can be found in Appendix 2.

The second measure of market development, price volatility, can also be measured on the basis of the annual price data. When measuring volatility we are essentially looking at how often and to what extent prices are subject to change in a particular period – in other words, whether prices are smooth or whether they are moving up and down significantly. To do this, the coefficient of variation for each city was calculated for rolling ten yearly periods and then averaged to give a figure for each fifty yearly period. As is usual, a falling coefficient of variation indicates a reduction in volatility and so rising market integration. The results expressed as an average for each country can be found in Appendix 2.[30] The monthly wheat prices provide a useful complement to the annual data when measuring volatility. Whilst they cover a shorter period, the high frequency nature of this data allows us to more precisely capture monthly and seasonal price fluctuations which allows us to track changes in market integration which might not be picked up by the annual price observations. The results of calculating the coefficient of variation for each of the cities for which monthly data is available appear in Appendix 2. The coefficient of variation is a relatively simple means through which to measure volatility. An alternative and more sophisticated approach which is regularly used in modern day finance to measure the volatility of stock markets is the GARCH model, which separates explainable from unexplainable volatility. Reassuringly, the results of applying this approach to the price data prove to be highly consistent with those arrived at using the coefficient of variation. Further details and discussion can be found in Appendix 2.

For our third measure of market integration, speeds of market adjustment, the high frequency monthly data is by far the most useful. Annual data is inadequate if markets adjust in less than the space of a year. Hence, speeds of adjustment are calculated between each pair of cities for which monthly data is available for consecutive fifty yearly periods. The Johansen vector-error-correction-model (VECM) is used for this purpose.[31] The average speed between each city and the other cities in the data set is then calculated allowing us to see which cities had the fastest speeds of adjustment, and how these speeds changed over time. Appendix 2 records and discusses the results, including adjustments made for the different distances between cities.

The vast majority of existing studies of market development have relied upon grain price data alone, though for shorter intervals of times or for smaller sets of cities than used herein. However, as a result of work conducted by Robert C. Allen, data on a number of other products are now easily available, albeit for fewer cities and of a more patchy nature than the wheat data.[32] With a couple of notable exceptions (including Özmucur and Pamuk, and O'Rourke and Williamson) few existing studies of market integration have exploited such data.[33] In what follows, non-wheat price data is therefore used alongside the wheat prices to help provide a broader picture of market development. We calculate price gaps for soap, candles and linen at the level of the individual countries of Europe in order to see whether prices for manufactured goods were converging. Appendix 2 contains the results.[34]

In the next section, we will look at the estimates of price gaps, volatility and speeds of market adjustment through the lens of the individual countries of Europe.

Market Histories by Country

From Carolingian times to the end of the nineteenth century, the present day map of Europe was in the process of formation: today's countries were being born, albeit some much earlier than others. Despite what is often seen as minimal growth, significant changes in economic leadership were taking place alongside the formation of these nation states. At the start of the era, parts of modern day Italy and Spain led the way, with present day Belgium representing the connection to the north-west. Over time, these countries experienced relative decline, whilst the Dutch underwent a Golden Age and England rose to become the first industrial nation. Furthermore, unlike the other countries, economic advance in England was sustained, continuously up to the present day. To what extent does this hierarchy of economic wealth and the associated change in leadership correlate with developments in markets? And, to what extent could differences in markets between England and the other countries help to explain how, unlike the other countries, economic advance pushed as far as an Industrial Revolution, ushering in the sustained economic growth we experience in the modern world? By building market histories for each economy we can begin to shed light on these questions. In what follows, market histories are presented for Italy, Spain, Belgium, The Netherlands, England, France, Germany, Poland and the Ottoman lands.

Whilst some may object to the notion of calculating market development on the basis of modern day country boundaries (with one exception herein of the Ottoman Empire), there are two good reasons for doing so in this book. Firstly, there is an enduring interest in country-level history, which makes this unit of analysis a very worthwhile pursuit. If people are interested in how the economy of the country they inhabit today has developed, then it will be very useful to have a knowledge of how markets have evolved over time within the same boundaries. Secondly, and very importantly for our purposes, much of the evidence on economic performance is available at the level of modern day countries, and so when it comes to testing the relationship between markets and growth, it is necessary to have estimates of markets at the same level.

Italy

Our market histories begin with the richest economy at the start of the early modern era, Italy. In medieval times, Italy was one of the most economically advanced and wealthiest parts of Europe. Whilst mountainous terrain meant that agricultural development was somewhat limited, natural harbours and a long coastline in proximity to the rich Byzantine lands gave the country an offsetting natural advantage of a very different kind.[35] Early on, Venice successfully used its position to gain a monopoly on the spice trade through the eastern part of the Mediterranean. The commercial riches that resulted led to the magnificent buildings that still line the Venetian canals and surround St Mark's Square today. Italy's trade with the Byzantine world did not only benefit Italy – it also created an impetus for Italian merchants to expand trade links into western, northern and central Europe.[36] As well as being necessary to facilitate sales of the exotic goods much in demand by European elites, this was also a means through which to source products that would be in demand in eastern markets which could therefore be used to finance the purchases of spices. For these purposes, Italian merchants sourced woollen cloth in Flanders (initially at the Champagne Fairs and later through Bruges) and, following the revival of mining in the fifteenth century, precious metals in Central Europe.[37] In other words, Italian trade with the east stimulated Italy's integration with large parts of Europe.

Manufactures and financial services also played a role in Italy's early success. By the fourteenth century Italy had one of the largest urbanized sectors, hosting twelve out of the twenty European cities with a population above 40,000.[38] According to Britnell, 16 per cent of the population in northern Italy lived in cities with a population above 10,000, and these were hives of specialization, filled with metal workers, ship-builders, shoemakers, tanners, weavers and tailors, together with retailers, money changers, lawyers and clerks. Italian capital markets led the way in Europe, in part as a result of techniques learnt whilst in contact with the east, and the property market was reasonably well developed, featuring fixed rent leases and crop-sharing agreements.[39] Hence, in addition to trading other people's goods, Italy also increasingly traded her own manufactures and financial services across Europe.

Given the centrality of Italian merchants in the European trading network it is unsurprising to find that Italian markets for such products as linen and soap appear to have been relatively well integrated with the rest of Europe early on.[40] Italy has some of the lowest between country price gaps for manufactured goods in the early sixteenth century. Feeding the vast urban populations also required access to agricultural supplies. Indeed, it is only possible for an economy to become specialized in manufactures and commerce if it can reliably and consistently source the more basic necessities of existence in return for its exports. Hence, one would also expect to find that Italy was relatively well connected with agricultural markets across Europe. Looking at the wheat price gaps between Italy and the rest of Europe we do indeed find that the Italian gaps are the lowest in the period 1400–50 at 53 per cent, although not dramatically below those elsewhere in Europe (which range 55–60 per cent).

Compared with the rest of Europe, however, Italy's internal market integration was poor. This was not just a result of the high transport costs resulting from the mountainous geography of inland Italy, but also from the fragmented nature of political rule.[41] Before the nineteenth century, modern day Italy comprised multiple states (including city states), which meant that there was regular conflict, little in the way of a coordinated transport network, multiple currencies and internal tolls. Furthermore, in smaller political entities, the power of a particular big urban centre can be very strong, and for this reason many of Italy's cities held a dominant position over the countryside. This included exercising monopoly rights through, for example, putting in place regulations to limit the development of markets outside of the city.[42] Of course, having been based on long distance trade and urban manufactures, Italy's economic success had not depended on well-developed internal markets, which created little in the way of an incentive to improve domestic integration. All of this may help to explain why the average wheat price gap within Italy was 35 per cent in the early sixteenth century, compared with only 23 per cent for Europe as a whole. The annual coefficient of variation (CV) of wheat prices was 0.33 in the fourteenth and fifteenth century, compared with 0.17–33 in the north-west. Only the city of Catania on Sicily (a major agricultural supplier) exhibited low price volatility. However, by the late sixteenth century the price gap fell significantly to an average of 19 per cent, which is just under the average for western Europe, suggesting that domestic markets were improving.[43] Epstein also finds evidence of an improvement in Italian markets between the fifteenth and sixteenth centuries and argues that it was the result of a decline in political fragmentation.[44] By the mid-fifteenth century, six major states had formed out of what had been a much larger number of smaller principalities and city states (Venice, Florence, the Duchy of Milan, the Papal States of Central Italy and the Kingdoms of Naples and Sicily). By the early sixteenth century, Lombardy, Naples and Sicily were consolidated under the Spanish crown and many state authorities were becoming stronger relative to local jurisdictions (such as cities). With waning local power came lower tariffs, lower taxes on trade, less regulation of the countryside,[45] the rationalization of road networks and greater stability, all acting to improve market integration.[46]

In the seventeenth century, internal price gaps suffered a substantial setback, suggesting that a temporary disintegration was taking place. On the international front, whilst Italy's price gaps declined, implying increasing integration with Europe, those in the Netherlands and England had fallen by even more, to around 40 per cent (versus 49 per cent in Italy). In terms of the speed of wheat market adjustment, Italy was also behind north-western Europe in the period 1550–1750. Hence, by this middle part of the early modern period, parts of the north-west appear to have overtaken Italy in terms of the level of both within country and between country integration. The seventeenth century was also a period in which Italy was falling behind more generally. Developments in manufactures elsewhere in Europe came to rival the higher quality, but as a result higher-priced, Italian goods. In theory, the fact that Italy was no longer a monopoly producer and supplier of such goods provided the potential to further push the degree of economic specialization and act as a stimulus to innovation, raising output. However, local guilds and policy arguably acted to resist this market pressure. In some areas, regulations were put in place to limit the use of new (lower quality and cheaper) dyes, to impose strict quality controls and to limit the number of machines that could be used in a single workplace.[47] As a result, customers were tempted away from the high priced Italian goods to the cheaper alternatives, leading to an economic decline.

By the late seventeenth and eighteenth centuries, Italian wheat market integration with the rest of Europe had caught up with the north-west: speeds of adjustment rose, volatility fell and price gaps declined. Grain was regularly on offer in the Mediterranean from the Baltic. Whilst price gaps for the manufactured products for which we have data (linen and soap) soared in the eighteenth century, this was a common feature of many European economies at this time, reflecting the development of protectionist policies for manufacturing industries. Italy's resistance to foreign competition no doubt also contributed. Internally, wheat markets had by now recovered from their temporary setback. The average internal price gap returned to 19 per cent, where it stood in the late sixteenth century, and price volatility declined below earlier levels, suggesting that domestic wheat markets were witnessing improvement. However, the situation is not as encouraging when it comes to goods other than wheat. Considering olive oil, for which price data is available from Tuscany, Milan and Naples in the eighteenth century, there is no evidence that price convergence within Italy was taking place. For candles we also find no evidence of price convergence when using the data on Naples, Florence and Modena, available up to the mid-seventeenth century. We conclude similarly for the case of cloth when using the Milanese linen and Naples mattress cover data.[48]

Overall, the wheat price evidence for Italy suggests that both internal markets and integration with the rest of Europe improved between the fifteenth century and the eve of the Industrial Revolution (albeit with a temporary setback in domestic markets). However, as with many other countries, this was not the case for markets other than wheat. In comparative terms, and by the time that England was undergoing an Industrial Revolution in the late eighteenth century, we find that Italy's integration with the rest of the continent was on a par with the north-west, and above that of England, whilst internal markets are close to the average for Europe, although behind England. Altogether, this suggests that there is no straightforward link between markets and Italy's eclipse by other countries.

Spain

On the eve of the early modern period, and similar to Italy, Spain was a fragmented country in comparison with the present day. Multiple small political entities had gradually formed into two principal states: Castile and Aragon. Castile was the most southerly and had been a recurrent frontier of Christian–Muslim battles, having been conquered by the Moslem World in the eighth century.[49] Perhaps unsurprisingly, therefore, Castile is loosely translated as 'land of castles'. The smaller north-easterly state of Aragon had formed from a number of independent northern counties, partly as an alliance to stem Muslim and Frankish invasions. In terms of its maritime connections, Barcelona held an important place within Aragon. It expanded its frontiers across the Mediterranean to include land in the Balearic Islands, Sardinia, Sicily and Naples and formed an important connection with the north of Europe, through the Hansa network.[50] Hence, through Barcelona, Aragon had links with the rest of the Mediterranean and with northern Europe.

In the latter half of the fifteenth century, Castile and Aragon were united by the marriage of Queen Isabella of Castile and Ferdinand II of Aragon.[51] With a new Spain came a new age. The years 1481–92 saw the final Christian–Muslim War in which Spain conquered Granada, pushing the Muslim Moors out of the Iberian peninsula after almost 800 years. Spain then reached outwards in an effort to achieve the type of global connections from which Italy earned great benefit, giving support to the four voyages (between 1492–1504) of a Genoese navigator, known as Christopher Columbus, which were to become the most famous in history.[52]

The Spanish economy soon became recognizable for its riches. However, compared with Italy, these were to a much lesser extent attributable to a successful internal economy and were less commercial in nature. Instead they flowed from the exploitation and ruthless extraction of resources from the colonies carved out of the back of their oceanic adventures. Hence, whilst Spanish urbanization was high compared with the rest of Europe, and on a par with Italy, the largest cities – including Madrid and Seville – were built on a foundation of colonial imports and colonial administration. Domestic agriculture was far from advanced, as witnessed by the comparisons of agricultural productivity across Europe, and as such these urban areas were prone to food shortages. In addition, there was relatively little in the way of a developed manufacturing sector. One notable exception was the Catalan textile industry. This industry had developed during the commercial boom of the medieval ages, in part stimulated by techniques learnt from the neighbouring Muslim and French worlds.[53] Specialization was in low to medium quality cloths, and resulted in a dominant early position in the Mediterranean textile market.[54] The region had a number of geographic advantages favouring textiles: access to a high quality raw material in the form of prized Spanish wool, plenty of natural rivers, a high population in mountainous areas that were crying out for by-employment, and the easy access to Mediterranean markets that came with Barcelona's trading position. However, by the early fifteenth century, Catalan cloth was being out-competed by that from England and France.[55] Some revival did come in the sixteenth century, but was based almost purely on the increasing domestic demand that came with Castile's new-found riches, which stimulated exports of cloth from Barcelona to Castile via the port of Seville, and a flow of wheat in return.[56] The earlier prosperity was never reestablished as the industry never attained technological leadership and, as a result, failed to develop in the way of the Italian, Belgian, English and French industries.[57] Furthermore, any industry that did exist within Spain suffered as imports of colonial silver pushed up prices, making domestic goods relatively uncompetitive, reducing exports and increasing imports of foreign goods.[58] The net result was that the Spanish economy lacked strong foundations at home and, perhaps as a result, went into decline.

Fundamentally, the lack of strong foundations could ultimately be blamed on poor domestic markets. The heavy direct involvement of the state in Spain's colonial domain – which arguably proved to be less lucrative in the long term than the private merchant-led model used by later colonizers (such as England) – may have been partly a consequence of poor domestic markets. The lack of agricultural advancement and manufacturing success within the domestic economy could also be tied to poor domestic markets. As we saw in the previous chapter, many hold poor institutions – the rise of absolutism – responsible for poor markets. These institutions may in part be endogenous. The lack of development of a merchant class that was independent of the state and could lobby and push for institutional improvement, as seems to have happened in England, could help to explain a failure of Spanish institutions, and so why initially poor markets remained poor. However, the extent to which absolutism can be blamed has recently been questioned by Voth.[59] He and Grafe separately suggest that an alternative explanation could be found in the political fragmentation of Spain, which resulted in, for example, a decentralized taxation system, internal customs barriers,[60] poor transport[61] and multiple monetary systems.[62] Despite the unions that resulted in the formation of Castile and Aragon, and subsequently the joining of the two in the late fifteenth century, rule was far from centralized, meaning that many of these problems remained.[63] Geography was also unfavourable. Whilst coastal areas were well placed to participate in exchanges with each other and with Mediterranean markets more generally, the mountainous internal terrain made connections between the inland and coastal areas naturally more difficult to forge. Furthermore, as Ringrose points out, no other major city in early modern Europe was so poorly located to stimulate market-oriented exchange as Madrid.[64]

Our market estimates allow us to gauge exactly how poorly developed Spain's internal markets were relative to other countries. The within country price gaps begin at a high level compared with the rest of Europe, at 31 per cent in the fifteenth and early sixteenth centuries (when the western European average is 23 per cent). Whilst this subsequently fell to 15 per cent in the sixteenth century, the period in which Castilian growth was stimulating domestic trade, by the late seventeenth century gaps are once again at the higher level. It is notable that the lowest price gaps are between the coastal cities for which we have data, Valencia and Barcelona.[65] Volatility is also low in these coastal cities and looks good in comparison with the rest of Europe.[66] It therefore appears that markets on the Spanish coast were reasonably well integrated with each other. This supports Ringrose's suggestion of a dualism between the coast and interior of the Spanish economy. He finds that in the sixteenth century, year to year fluctuations in prices were more extreme in Castile than in Valencia,[67] and in 1804, when wheat prices temporarily increased by 100 per cent in Valencia, in Old Castile they rose by around 350 per cent.[68] Markets in the interior did not catch up with the level of integration on the coast, as wheat price gaps between the coast and interior show no decline. Some more mixed findings are arrived at when we turn to look at other products, but overall do not suggest a generalized improvement. For soap, we find a rise in the coefficient of variation (CV) across the set of prices from Valencia, Old Castile and Barcelona and a fall in the speed of adjustment for Valencia–Old Castile in the late sixteenth/early seventeenth centuries.[69] In the eighteenth century, there are signs of a recovery with a fall in the CV (and rise in the speed of adjustment) between Barcelona and Madrid. Using linen price data for Old Castile, Madrid and Valencia we see no improvement in the CV.[70] Using additional data on nails available for Spain (from New- and Old-Castile), we find a rise in the CV for the years in which the data is available.[71] The only case in which we find a clear improvement is olive oil, for which there was a significant reduction in the price gap and a rise in the speed of adjustment between Madrid and Barcelona in the years 1507–1800, but with a temporary setback in the latter half of the seventeenth century.[72]

Taken together, the evidence therefore suggests that interior Spanish markets were not particularly well integrated compared with other countries and improved little over time. In the early nineteenth century, the internal price gap was as high as in the fifteenth century and well above that for the average western European country. It appears that market integration in the Spanish interior had to wait a long time – for the liberal reforms and transport developments of the later nineteenth century – and even then Spanish integration still remained poor compared with the rest of Europe.[73]

When looking at markets between Spain and the rest of Europe from the point of view of price gaps, the situation looks more positive. For wheat, we find no improvement in the long period from 1400 to 1700, during which the gap stands at 55 per cent, and then a decline in the eighteenth century to 46 per cent. Compared with other western European countries, this situation does not look particularly concerning as the Spanish between country price gap is almost exactly equal to the European average until the latter half of the eighteenth century. In terms of price gaps for manufactured goods, the situation actually looks favourable, with low between country price gaps for Spain. Looking at some of the individual cities, the average wheat price gap between Valencia and the other European cities is relatively high, at 64 per cent throughout the early modern period, but the gaps for Barcelona are much lower (to 47–51 per cent by the eighteenth century). However, in the early nineteenth century, markets take a significant backward move and Spain fell behind.

Overall, Spain's connections with the rest of Europe do not look particularly poor until the end of the early modern period, but domestic markets show cause for concern from early on. Hence, if markets are in any way responsible for Spain's relative decline in the early modern era, domestic markets are most likely to hold the blame. With an initial stimulus of exploitative colonization that would inevitably run out of steam,[74] together with internal markets that were too undeveloped to respond to external stimuli or to generate an internal dynamic of their own, the Spanish economy was unlikely to succeed for long. In the middle of the seventeenth century, population in Castile fell by 25 per cent and by as much as 40 per cent in Madrid, and the state had already declared bankruptcy.[75] As Dupuy and Dupuy remark, 'within a century Spain reached, then passed, the apogee of world power'.[76]

Belgium

Outside of the Mediterranean, the modern day territory of Belgium began the early modern period as arguably the most advanced part of Europe, as is clear from the evidence of a high level of both urbanization and agricultural productivity. According to Pirenne, the high level of urbanization had its roots in the woollen cloth industry, which provided a strong basis for trade.[77] Belgian textiles provided a valuable good that was in great demand across Europe: Italian merchants required cloth as a return cargo that could be sold in the east in payment for spices, and were already regularly buying Belgian cloth in the twelfth century.[78] At the same time, merchants from Germany and the Hansa cities demanded cloth to exchange for the goods of north and eastern Europe, which included furs, metals and grain. Flemish cloth was therefore vital to sustaining the commercial contact between the north and south of Europe and the east and west of Europe, and so also brought these two axes of Europe into contact with each other. During the commercial boom of the medieval period, much of this trade was taking place through the Champagne Fairs, but increasingly merchants sourced their goods directly in Belgium. Hence, in Belgium's case, and unlike many parts of the Mediterranean, trade seems to have been the consequence – as opposed to the cause – of success. In addition to its domestic textile industry and associated urbanization, and again unlike the Mediterranean, Belgium had a high level of agricultural productivity (in fact the highest in Europe).[79] This helped to provide support for the cities in the form of food supplies. Compared with much of the Mediterranean, Belgium's development therefore appears to have been based on a strong internal – as opposed to external trade-based – stimuli.

Consistent with this story we find better developed internal markets in Belgium than the Mediterranean and a relatively high level of connectedness with the rest of Europe. The existing literature already suggests that internal markets in the Low Countries were well integrated in medieval times, but our estimates enable a more formal comparison with the rest of Europe.[80] In the fourteenth century, volatility is exceptionally low in comparative terms and the wheat price gap within Belgium in the early fifteenth century is only 15 per cent (which is half the level of Spain and Italy in the sixteenth century). As Pirenne suggests,

Belgium was also relatively well integrated with European markets, with a wheat price gap below the western European average and only slightly higher than Italy (at 56 per cent versus 53 per cent at the opening of the fifteenth century).

As time progressed, Belgium faced challenges to which it needed to adapt. In the thirteenth and fourteenth century the woollen cloth industry came under pressure. According to the evidence, the percentage of the citizens of Bruges involved in woollen textiles fell from 44.63 per cent in 1302 to 15.09 per cent in 1394–6 and the number of textiles given a lead seal in Ypres had fallen by 60 per cent in the period 1312–1360s.[81] Once woollen cloth manufacture in England and Italy started to emerge, the power of Flemish guilds began to price Flemish cloth out of the market. England's switch to producing woollen cloth – in part stimulated by protectionist policy – meant that she exported less raw wool, reducing the amount of this exported to Flanders, depriving her of an important source of inputs. Furthermore, the decline of the Champagne Fairs together with rising insecurity on traditional trading routes (such as those through France in the west and as a result of the Mongol and Ottoman conquests in the east) made overland trade profitable only for the most expensive cloth.[82] However, whilst some Belgian towns went into decline, others rose to the challenge and successfully adapted to the situation by shifting into both higher quality (more expensive) cloths and by pioneering new draperies, the latter of which required both less skilled labour and less wool.[83] Bruges, in particular, was successful in making the shift, and soon took over from the Champagne Fairs as the centre for the textile trade.[84] Genoese and Hansa merchants flooded in. The Italians also brought their financial skills with them, making the city the money market for the Low Countries.[85]

By the late fifteenth century, Bruges' trading position began to suffer as a result of the silting up of her access to the sea along the Zwin.[86] Price gaps within Belgium rose and volatility increased. Trade shifted out of Bruges to Antwerp, which is easily accessible to the open sea through the Scheldt. According to Braudel, the city became 'the centre of the entire international economy' – the most important trading hub of its age and not just for intra-European trade but for all the trade being newly created by the age of exploration.[87] Portuguese ships – laden with eastern goods from their oceanic adventures – were attracted to the city by the copper and silver metals on sale from Central Europe. Like woollen cloth, these metals provided a means of payment for spices in the east. Shortly after 1500 Antwerp became the official entrepot for the Portuguese spice trade.[88] Spanish traders were also attracted to the city, bringing in goods from the Americas, such as silver, sugar and cocoa (the last of which made Belgium famous for chocolate). By the middle of the sixteenth century, 75 per cent of all the Low Countries' trade was conducted through this single city.[89] This is reflected in Belgium's between country wheat price gap, which fell to 43 per cent in the early sixteenth century, and suggests that Belgium was by then the most integrated economy with the rest of Europe (now ahead of Italy). In the words of Israel, 'here were stockpiled the sugar and spices of the Portuguese colonial empire, the silks and luxury goods of Italy and the Levant, the copper and iron goods of Germany, and the woollen cloth of England'.[90]

However, Belgium's success did not continue. Under Spanish rule in the sixteenth century, the Low Countries were becoming increasingly restless. Religious policies together with taxation led to a fight for independence beginning in 1566;[91] the region 'boiled'.[92] During an epic siege lasting from 1584 to 1585 merchants had little choice but to turn away from Antwerp. Whilst the southern provinces that constitute modern day Belgium were not successful in their attempt to gain independence, the northern provinces (the modern day Netherlands) managed to fend off the Spanish, forming the Dutch Republic. In an effort to hurt the Spanish through their Belgian holdings, the Dutch navy closed the Scheldt to navigation, bringing the waterway into the hands of Dutch shipping and customs dues.[93] For Antwerp, this was disastrous, resulting in a permanent loss of trade to the Dutch cities. Merchants and financiers migrated northward, taking their skills and trade contacts with them to Holland. In search of freedom from the Spanish, many craftsmen also emigrated along with their techniques. According to Veraghtert (1983), Belgium became a 'sleeping beauty'.[94]

The impact of these dramatic late sixteenth-century events on trade and markets is very clearly reflected in our market estimates, which show that domestic price gaps soared and volatility increased in the latter half of the sixteenth century. For Bruges, integration never recovered to earlier levels, with the price gap remaining persistently higher. Markets between Belgium and the rest of Europe also disintegrated in the late sixteenth century relative to the first half of the century, with the wheat price gap rising from 43 per cent back to 56 per cent. Belgium had lost its position as the most integrated economy in Europe, and by the late seventeenth century had in fact moved towards the bottom of the country rankings. Looking at the non-wheat products, we find that the price gaps for linen and soap were also high in the late sixteenth century and were even higher by the late eighteenth century. Price gaps for candles were the only exception, disintegrating but then recovering and ending the period lower than they began. Despite the serious shock, markets did keep trying to reassert themselves. The speed of adjustment in Antwerp was high in the latter half of the seventeenth and eighteenth centuries and rose in Brussels in the late eighteenth century. In addition, low volatility kept returning, although was not consistently maintained. Taken together, the evidence suggests that markets were turbulent.

In conclusion, our market estimates suggest that Belgian markets were the most developed within themselves and with the rest of Europe in the first half of the sixteenth century. However, thereafter, they show no signs of improvement, and instead witnessed a degree of disintegration both within themselves and with the rest of Europe.[95] By the nineteenth century, the economic situation in Belgium was looking significantly improved. Industry witnessed a noteworthy revival in the eighteenth and nineteenth centuries.[96] Trade awoke when the Scheldt was re-opened in 1794, soon after which Belgium bought out the Netherlands' rights to custom dues in the area. Developments in internal transport, such as the road system, also helped to boost internal integration.[97] As is shown by Jacks (2005), Belgium was one of the most well integrated economies in Europe at this point in time.[98] The situation had come full circle.

The Netherlands

As Italy, Spain and Belgium went into decline, the Netherlands saw a spectacular rise, and the axis of economic power shifted decisively away from the Mediterranean. This rise is nothing but remarkable. In the early eleventh century, Holland consisted of great expanses of peat bogs which were largely inhospitable and so uninhabited. In an effort to increase income and military potential, the Counts of Holland organized large-scale land reclamation, offering favourable terms to immigrants who were willing to undertake the reclamation work. Unlike elsewhere in Europe, this meant that feudalism never really existed; instead, settlers were given absolute rights over the land in return for paying taxes.[99] This encouraged the early development of free labour, land and capital markets (the latter of which developed on the basis of offering mortgages on the privately owned land).[100] It also meant that there was a much higher degree of social mobility and income equality than in much of the rest of Europe.[101] Furthermore, the unsuitability of the soil for basic grains meant that inhabitants had to look outwards to import grain, which had the side effect of necessitating the development of export sectors (providing goods which could be exchanged for imports).[102] From its origins in the eleventh century, Holland was, therefore, a very commercial economy.[103]

In 1433, Holland came under Burgundian rule, and in 1506 it passed into Habsburg (and Spanish) hands, which culminated in growing discontent. Whilst fighting for independence, Holland and the surrounding provinces joined together to establish a confederation (known as the Union of Utrecht).[104] Despite being small in terms of land area, population and natural resources, within years of independence this new Dutch Republic became 'the hub of world commerce, the universal intermediary of trade, possessing at its height roughly half of the world's total stock of seagoing ships'.[105] According to Prak, the province of Holland grew as fast as 1.5 per cent p.a. between 1580 and 1650, a period known as the Golden Age.[106] The famous tulip mania of 1637, in which tulip bulbs sold for ever increasing prices before suddenly crashing, was likely a reflection of such growth.[107]

To some, this 'Golden Age' was the outcome of exogenous factors which propelled the Dutch economy forward whilst also holding other countries back.

These forces are argued to include the decline of Belgium (just considered), wars in neighbouring countries, and famines in Europe, the latter of which increased the trade of grain in which Holland was a big player.[108] However, Dutch economic historians are at pains to remind us that the region was already a well-developed market-based economy, as we have just seen. According to De Vries and Van der Woude, Holland was the pioneer of economic modernity – 'the first modern economy'.[109] Indeed, at the start of the sixteenth century, Holland had a small agricultural share of employment at around 25 per cent,[110] an urbanization rate that was second only to Belgium[111] and arguably the highest estimated GDP per capita in Europe.[112] This advanced nature has been argued to have had its roots in the way in which Holland was settled, as previously explained. On this basis, it seems more likely that it was only because of well-developed Dutch markets that the economy was able to gain so successfully from the external circumstances in the late sixteenth and seventeenth centuries. Without the domestic economic incentives provided by a favourable internal economy, skilled craftsmen fleeing from war and absolutism elsewhere (including Belgium) may not have chosen Holland, nor would they have been able to easily and successfully begin production there. In addition, without the large economic potential provided by the favourable domestic markets and institutions, the incentive and ability to expel Spanish control, maintaining herself as a non-absolutist state amongst the sea of absolutist Europe (avoiding the associated adverse consequences), would have been somewhat reduced. Also, whilst the Dutch certainly gained in trading terms when harvests failed across Europe in the seventeenth century, it took an earlier establishment of markets and success in the bulk trades (dating back to the late fifteenth century) to take advantage of the situation. The Dutch already had an 'unprecedented' stock of merchant ships, 'incomparably low freight rates' and an 'unrivalled capacity to transfer bulky goods cheaply and in large quantities quickly'.[113] Altogether, it therefore makes more sense to argue that an advanced internal market economy combined fortuitously with a number of external factors to propel the Netherlands (and Holland in particular) into a virtuous economic cycle.

A number of studies have formally measured markets in the Dutch Republic and confirmed that they were indeed well advanced from early on.[114] According to our estimates, which enable a fuller comparison with the rest of Europe, volatility was exceptionally low at the start of the fifteenth century (on a par with Belgium). There was then a setback in the period 1450–1550, after which low volatility reasserted itself until the mid-seventeenth century. Within country wheat price gaps were also reasonably low at 20 per cent, and by the seventeenth century had fallen to only 6 per cent. Wheat price gaps with the rest of Europe also declined, from 60 per cent in the fifteenth century to 51 per cent in the sixteenth century and then 40 per cent by the seventeenth century. On the basis of the price gap, volatility and speed of adjustment evidence, we can safely say that by the latter half of the sixteenth century, the Netherlands had overtaken Belgium to become the most integrated economy in Europe.

Like the other economies so far considered, Dutch leadership did not last, despite strong market foundations. By the eighteenth century, Dutch trade and the wider economy were being challenged by the English. By way of an explanation, some have pointed to the heavy Dutch fiscal demands as a result of both the hefty debt servicing on previous war expenditure and the need for continued defence against foreign incursions.[115] One author writes that the Anglo-Dutch Wars against England and the War of the Spanish succession 'broke the Dutch as a great naval and land power'.[116] In 1695, the Dutch tax rate was two and a half times the English rate.[117] These high taxes could be argued to have reduced the competitiveness of the Dutch economy and lowered incentives to work and produce. However, the tax burden might have been easier to spread and so bear had the economy kept growing. To look for a more complete explanation, we therefore need to ask why the growth rate started to slow down. One potential answer could be found in the rise of strong states elsewhere in Europe, with which came the practice of mercantilism, starting with the English navigation Act of 1651.[118] In the 1640s, the average annual value of Dutch trade was 300–400 million guilders. By the 1660s, this had fallen to 200–250 million.[119] Many Amsterdam merchants held English protectionism responsible,[120] and left Holland for England after 1689.[121] The structure of Dutch international trade may not have helped, as Dutch trade was based upon formal and informal monopoly, as opposed to the English model of private trade (particularly following the Glorious Revolution).[122] Monopoly precluded new entrants and foreigners, and was less responsive to changing consumption patterns. Perhaps linked to this point, some Dutch economic historians are starting to argue that growth brought previously unseen material and political inequality, and that this may have started to hold back the economy.[123] Of course, international trade was not the only significant element in the Dutch economy. As we saw in the previous chapter, the Dutch economy had a broad base which included significant manufacturing. Here, the neo-Malthusians blame the downturn on a mounting energy crisis, pointing out that England had one vital resource that the Dutch lacked: coal. Accordingly to Wrigley, this meant that, unlike the other economies we have considered so far, once the English economy started to grow, it could keep on growing.[124]

Given that Dutch markets seem to be closely related to Dutch success in the seventeenth century, it also makes sense to consider whether slower economic growth can be explained by a market deterioration. The between-country price gap actually remained the lowest in Europe, and in the eighteenth century at around 37 per cent was in fact below that during the Golden Age. This makes it difficult to argue that Dutch decline was a result of the economy becoming less connected with Europe. However, the within country price gap reverted to its pre-Golden Age value of 20 per cent, which was above that of England (where it stood at less than 10 per cent by the eighteenth century). Hence, if we are trying to understand how Britain overtook the Netherlands, it was not a result of the former becoming better integrated with Europe. If markets were important, then domestic as opposed to cross-country markets hold the key.

England

England underwent significant economic change in the early modern period – perhaps witnessing the greatest improvement of all the European economies under consideration. At the beginning of the era, many have argued that she was an underperforming economy, with a relatively low urbanization rate and low GDP per capita,[125] but by the end of the period she had overtaken the other economies of Europe, undergone an agricultural transformation and stood on the eve of the first Industrial Revolution. Her population rose by an average of 0.39 per cent p.a. in the early modern period compared with only 0.15 per cent pa in the rest of Europe, suggesting a remarkable capacity for expansion.[126]

North and Weingast explain England's rise in terms of a major change on the institutional front which took place in the seventeenth century – The Glorious Revolution of 1688 – which they argue transformed markets and so in turn set the stage for investment and technological change that culminated in the Industrial Revolution.[127] The Glorious Revolution marked the triumph of Parliament over the monarch at the end of a bitter century of Civil Wars and ultimately broke the economy free of the absolutism seen elsewhere in Europe (with the exception of the Netherlands), securing property rights and so raising the incentive to invest and invent. However, this explanation has been criticized on a number of grounds, three of which we will highlight here.

The first criticism, as we have already seen, is that well-developed markets and the avoidance of absolutism in the Dutch Republic did not give birth to an Industrial Revolution in seventeenth-century Holland. Secondly, some have argued that the opposite of the market – mercantilist policy – provided a strong stimulus to the English economy (whilst at the same time helping to explain Dutch decline).[128] Mercantilist policy began with the 1651 Navigation Act, and continued until the middle of the nineteenth century. The fact that this policy seems to have so successfully shifted trade out of the hands of the Dutch, and with it stimulated a British shipbuilding industry and British finance industry (to provide insurance and credit), along with an endless list of related industries (cloth for sailors' uniforms, metal for anchors, rope-making and so on) suggests that this should not be discounted. Britain's involvement in world trade is a key characteristic of her ascent, and given the Dutch position in world trade, it is difficult to imagine how the British would have 'got a look in' without using protectionist policy to nurture its infant trade.[129] However, for mercantilism to have its maximum effect on the economy, the domestic economy needs to be highly responsive. Institutions need to be able to adapt to meet the needs of a growing commercial sector, which seems to have been the case in Britain. In this sense, Acemoglu, Johnson and Robinson have implicitly argued that the Glorious Revolution was a consequence rather than cause of Britain's growing commercialization.[130] Furthermore, markets at home also needed to be reasonably well developed so that they were ready to act in response to the stimulus provided to trade and exports. Well-developed internal markets with backward and forward linkages between each other mean that a positive stimulus can have a larger multiplier effect throughout the economy. Better-developed markets also mean that inputs can be provided to support the development of the trade sector. Hence, if mercantilist policy did benefit the economy, it is likely to have done so in combination with internally responsive markets and institutions. Thirdly, even if we accept that domestic markets were important in this combined way, this is still not enough to give full support to the Glorious Revolution hypothesis, as existing work suggests that market development in England began well before the Glorious Revolution. Hence, if markets are important for explaining England's rise, we need to start our chronology much further back in time.

According to Jones, a market economy in England emerged as far back as the eleventh century, in Anglo-Saxon times.[131] He argues that an 'emergency conversion' to the market took place in response to the constant and actual threat of invasion from the Vikings in the north (and the Welsh in the west). Power was shifted from the local level to a central body (or 'state') in order to facilitate the formulation of a defence strategy, including the construction of fortified towns. With this came the need to tax in order to fund the defence systems. In order to pay taxes, individuals had to start producing and selling at least some goods on the market and the central body had to 'monetize' the economy (issuing and controlling coinage).[132] Furthermore, to help make sure that these taxes were accepted by the masses, this central body provided something additional in return: law and order. With the beginnings of a tax system also came the capacity to fund expenditure on public goods, such as roads and other infrastructure, which lowered the costs of trade and so further stimulated the market. Bell has recently shown that through such activity, the state played a vital role in the development of markets at this time.[133] All of this added together with favourable natural geography (including a long coastline and few of the mountain ranges seen in mainland Europe) to encourage market activity in the economy. Hence, in the eleventh century one contemporary wrote that 'he who has pennies or silver can get anything he pleases'.[134]

The period from the twelfth to the fourteenth century brought a further growth of market activity in Britain.[135] Masschaele's study of medieval transport costs highlights a number of improvements driving down these costs in the thirteenth century, 'including the transition from oxen to horses, the dramatic expansion in the number of bridges, the integration of roads and rivers with an increasingly sophisticated urban network, and the proliferation of markets and marketing'.[136] Using evidence on the costs of transport from sheriffs' accounts he shows that the costs were 'remarkably low' in fourteenth-century England and changed little between then and the middle of the eighteenth century. In other words, transport costs had achieved low levels very early on in England's history. He argues that this helped to underpin the commercialization and growth of the economy during the 'long' thirteenth century. Dyer provides evidence, such as the large distances travelled by merchants, to demonstrate that 'by the late thirteenth century all sectors of society participated in a complex commercial network'.[137]

As the market grew larger, it inevitably created challenges that needed to be addressed if it was to continue to flourish: standardization and enforcement of weights and measures, a stable coinage, a fair and reliable legal system, and prevention of monopoly activity. The early development of the state in England meant that there was a natural body who could rise to the challenges and, according to Britnell, the English state did this very successfully.[138] As we have already discussed, Epstein places great emphasis on the importance of the state for market development. He suggests that the lack of well-established internationally oriented urban centres in England (unlike Italy) may actually have aided internal market development, as there were no strong vested interests to object to the state's market-widening measures within the country.[139]

On the basis of our estimates we can gauge England's level of market development relative to that elsewhere in Europe. This confirms that in terms of domestic markets, England was relatively well developed from early on. In the fifteenth century, the average internal price gap was 16 per cent, very close to that of Belgium. Price gaps temporarily rose in the latter half of the sixteenth century to 25 per cent. There are a number of reasons why markets may have become disintegrated at this time, including wars with the Spanish (1585–1604) and between the Spanish and Dutch (from 1566), which disrupted sea-based trade routes, and increasing market regulation under the Tudors.[140] However, after this period, the percentage price gap quickly recovered. In the seventeenth century it fell to 13 per cent, then to 9 per cent in the early eighteenth century and to a little over 5 per cent by the end of the century. Whilst there is a lack of monthly data with which to most accurately calculate speeds of adjustment early on, using the annual data gives a high speed showing that between 70–100 per cent of price disequilibria were eliminated in the space of a year during the earlier centuries.[141]

The price data can also be used to see the extent to which the economy was well integrated with the rest of the continent on a comparative basis. As we saw in the previous chapter, England had trading connections with the rest of Europe from quite early on. In the fifteenth century, the Italians were trading through

Southampton, sending three or four galleys a year to the port.[142] One of the clearest pieces of evidence is the English customs accounts and Italian records which demonstrate the persistent attempt by the Italians to avoid paying the associated custom dues. Ruddock tells of one report from 1423 of a customs official boarding an Italian vessel at the port and insisting that customs were paid: the captain refused and asked the official to leave. A stalemate between the two ensued resulting in the ship setting sail with the customs official still onboard, before he finally gave in and disembarked on the Isle of Wight.[143] Clearly, the Italians were regular traders with the English, even if they were sometimes reluctant to pay their dues. Through these Italian merchants, England was connected to the Flanders cloth markets, supplying raw wool and purchasing cloth in return, and imported products from the Mediterranean and Far east, including oil, soap, silks, spices and sweet wines.[144] From the middle of the twelfth century, England was also connected with northern and eastern Europe through the Hansa network that ended in London.[145] However, the existence of connections does not prove that the economy was well integrated with the rest of the continent. Britain was marginal rather than central to the European and global economies of the time.[146] She was an exporter of primary (agricultural) products such as wool, hides, lead and tin, and manufactures were imported rather than domestically produced.[147] Compared with most other countries in Europe, our evidence suggests that the average price gap was reasonably high at 59 per cent in the fifteenth century. In fact, this is very similar to the level for the Netherlands at the time.[148] The Dutch price gap fell in the early sixteenth century and again in the seventeenth century, achieving a level of 40 per cent, which is well below that of most of the rest of Europe. In England, the price gap fell to a similarly low level of 41 per cent in the early seventeenth century (notably before the Glorious Revolution). From this point on, England's between country price gaps remained below the western European average, but were on the increase (rather than decrease), until, in the first half of the nineteenth century, they were back at their old level of 59 per cent. This trend is consistent with the rise in tariffs during the eighteenth century, which reached around 30 per cent on average by 1779.[149] In the century after 1750, only Spain and Belgium had a higher price gap out of the group of western and central European countries. Hence, England was becoming less and not more integrated with the rest of Europe during the Industrial Revolution. Price gaps between England and the rest of Europe for soap and candles mirror those of wheat, showing improvement in the seventeenth century followed by a rise in the eighteenth century. With the exception of linen, the non-wheat price gaps are the highest in Europe in the eighteenth century. In terms of volatility, which can be seen as a combined indicator of both domestic and foreign integration, England remained behind Belgium and the Netherlands with a CV (based on annual data) that ranges 0.21–0.32 in the period 1300–1750, never achieving the lows of 0.17

witnessed during the height of Dutch dominance. Whilst the speed of adjustment was very high, indicating that 22 per cent of any deviation of prices from the normal price gap was eliminated in the space of a single month, the 'normal' price gap to which prices would have been adjusting in the event of shocks was, as we have seen, an increasing one, from the low in 1600 to a high in 1849. Hence, unlike on the eve of the Dutch Golden Age, England's integration with the rest of Europe was not improving in the course of her ascendancy.

Very clearly, therefore, England's economy industrialized whilst experiencing a deterioration in integration with the rest of Europe. Only after industrialization did both tariffs fall and a shift to free trade policy take place (including the Repeal of the Corn Laws protecting grain). It was this post-Industrial Revolution policy shift together with the dramatic falls in transport costs (enabled by the new technologies of the Industrial Revolution) that brought about an integration of the English economy with the rest of Europe, and helped generate the globalization of the world economy. International market integration was a consequence as opposed to cause of Britain's Industrial Revolution.

In sum, and based on the experience of England alone, it would seem that domestic market development may indeed help to lay the foundations for economic growth – although that may not be sufficient. Free-market connections with the rest of the world, however, appear to be more questionably related to growth. Whilst England was not badly integrated with Europe in the seventeenth and eighteenth centuries, this level of integration was declining, and by the early nineteenth century (when the Industrial Revolution was in full steam) was well behind the western European average. Rapid international integration seems to have been an outcome as opposed to cause of growth in England's case.

France

In the fifteenth century, France was marred by civil war and was, in some regions at least, overrun by the English. Over the course of the century, the English were pushed out, in part under the inspirational leadership of Joan of Arc, and feudal anarchy was replaced by state building.[150] In the early modern period that followed, the performance of the French economy sits between the extremes of economic decline witnessed in Italy, Spain and Belgium and the economic rise seen in the Netherlands and later England. Cursory estimates of French GDP per capita suggest little improvement from 1500 to 1800.[151] Whilst the urban percentage of population approximately doubled between 1500 and 1800, it still remained low relative to the rest of Europe by the end of the early modern period.[152]

A lack of strong domestic market foundations in comparison with the Dutch and English economies could potentially help to explain the failure of the French economy to advance significantly.[153] Hoffman points to the adverse effects of taxation, war and the small size of the urban sector on French market development.[154] The Wars of Religion in 1560–98, for example, seriously disrupted trade in some parts of the country, as did the Fronde (1648–53). The last of these also greatly enhanced the power of Louis XIV, leading to the rise of absolutism in the country, which some would see as a further obstacle to market development. However, the underdevelopment of French domestic markets can be understood at an even more fundamental level as some form of 'trap'. French geography was relatively less favourable than in the north-west of Europe, with a more rugged terrain and an average location more distant from the coast. It would therefore have required more investment in transport infrastructure to attain the same level of domestic market development as in the Dutch and English economies. However, following Meuvret we could argue that the economy was in a vicious circle from which it was difficult to break free.[155] Poor and costly transportation limited the potential reach and so demand for goods, as a result of which areas were reluctant to specialize and could not exploit economies of scale to improve the production process. But, with a lack of specialization and production for the market, there was no demand for improving the transport infrastructure as there were few goods requiring transportation outside of the immediate locality. Further pushing in this direction, according to Brenner, was the structure of French farming that resulted from the Black Death, in which peasants were able to subsist on the basis of their own small plot of land without paying rents (unlike England), which therefore did not compel participation in the market.[156] Hence, investments in infrastructure were not profitable. What this implies is that poor markets led to poor transport, which then fed back to give poor markets – a self-confirming outcome. Also reinforcing this poor market 'trap' was the fact that poor markets were more likely to be regulated in an effort to help avoid the starvation and social unrest that could result from food shortages, but which ultimately worsened rather than helped the situation by disincentivizing production for, and so use of, the market (as the Physiocrats later went on to argue). In other words, the economy was trapped in a high transport cost, high regulation and poor market equilibrium, in which all three proved mutually reinforcing, making it difficult to break free.[157]

The evidence suggests that French markets started to break out of this trap in the course of the early modern period. Ladurie and Meuvret point to a number of positive developments in French markets, such as in the cultivation of vines, maize and beans, with Hoffman finding evidence of increasing agricultural efficiency in the Paris basin from the sixteenth to the late eighteenth century (although with stagnant agricultural efficiency elsewhere in France).[158] O'Gráda and Chevet find evidence that prices were moving closer together, showing that the disparity of wheat prices for thirty-five French towns and cities was declining between 1690 and 1790.[159] Our market estimates also suggest that an improvement was taking place, with evidence of both falling volatility and declining wheat price gaps. If we begin in the first half of the fifteenth century, when the CV was 0.51, we find evidence of market improvement almost straight away: the CV fell to 0.28 in the latter half of the century. However, the value for the early fifteenth century is likely inflated by the significant amount of warfare in France at this time. If we therefore instead compare the value in the late fifteenth century (0.28) with what came afterwards, we find that a market improvement began in the seventeenth century, when the CV fell to 0.22. This is followed by a further improvement in the latter half of the eighteenth century, when the CV fell to 0.15 (albeit with a temporary setback between 1700–49). Turning to the wheat price gaps, we also find evidence of improvement towards the end of the early modern period. The average French wheat price gap fell from 24 per cent during 1500–1749, to 18 per cent in the latter half of the eighteenth century.

This improvement in domestic markets could be explained in terms of the emergence of the French nation state which, by the middle of the seventeenth century, began to improve the transport infrastructure of the country, helping to break markets out of the 'trap' alluded to earlier. Perhaps the key aspect of these improvements was the development of a canal system, which aided the cheaper water transport of goods.[160] The network included the opening of the Midi canal connecting Toulouse to the Mediterranean in 1681, and the Briare canal connecting the Loire with the Seine River in 1642.[161] Further help to break free of the trap came in the eighteenth century, when the French Physiocratic school of thought began campaigning for a deregulation of the grain trade. There were a number of moves in this direction, starting with the Edicts of 1763 and 1764, and later in 1774 under Turgot.[162] Such reforms, which included the repeal of tolls levied on grain and the abolition of laws requiring merchants to register their transactions, were in part a response to growing contemporary concern for French agricultural production, a desire for fiscal reform and growing cities.[163] Unfortunately, these moves suffered serious setbacks as a result of poor harvests – which brought the usual popular unrest and saw a return to regulative policies – and the outbreak of the French Revolution.[164] Hence, by the end of the eighteenth century, whilst domestic markets in France had advanced, they still remained underdeveloped compared with those of England, where the price gap had fallen to a mere 5 per cent.

Alongside an improvement in domestic markets, the evidence also points towards a period of significant market integration between France and the rest of Europe. The between-country price gap fell from 73 per cent in the late fifteenth century to 50 per cent in the first half of the sixteenth century, and then to 41 per cent in the eighteenth century (below the western European average). In the first half of the nineteenth century, France had the lowest between country price gap, which stood at 30 per cent. The speeds of adjustment are 0.16 for Toulouse and 0.12 Paris, in line with those outside of the north-west. Taken together, this meant that by as early as the sixteenth century, France was positioned in the better half of countries with regard to cross-country integration. However, despite this, France did not achieve the level of economic success experienced in England at this time.

Altogether, we find evidence of market improvement in France both internally and externally in the course of the early modern period. In comparison with other countries, French domestic markets look rather average: the average wheat price gap between French cities was 24 per cent for much of the early modern era, which compared unfavourably with England and Holland but much more favourably with the price gaps in Spain and Italy (seen previously). However, connections with the rest of Europe look relatively stronger: except for the very start of the period for which we have data (1450–99), the between-country wheat price gap was consistently below the western European average (with the narrow exception of the period of warfare in 1550–99). In comparison with England, perhaps the most striking difference was in terms of domestic markets, which could suggest that domestic markets as opposed to international market connections are more useful as foundations for economic growth.

Germany

Germany is traditionally argued to have experienced little in the way of economic advance during the early modern period.[165] However, in medieval times, as was seen in the previous chapter, German cities were heavily involved in European trade through the Hanseatic League. In the sixteenth century, the 'rich trades' of eastern and central Europe were dominated by the German city of Lübeck whilst the cheap bulk trades in the area were left to the Dutch. As late as 1580, this meant that much of the international trade of the Baltic was in Hansa hands.[166] The dramatic siege of Antwerp in 1584–5 created new opportunities for surrounding regions, and it initially seemed that Germany would be the one to benefit. German merchants were starting to adopt some of the superior Dutch trading practices associated with the bulk trades and were benefiting from inflows of migrants from the Low Countries relocating to Germany to escape turmoil at home, taking their valuable skills with them. At the same time, Dutch trade was being hurt by both the Spanish and Portuguese embargos (1585–9) and Spain's attempt to close the waterways linking the Netherlands to Germany, together with the more generally uncertain military and political situation.[167] It looked like Germany was therefore set to inherit Belgium's lead, consolidating its position as the leading trading economy of the north. However, once it became clear that the Dutch were able to fend off the Spanish, and as Spain began to lift its punitive measures against Dutch trade, it was evident that the Dutch were the ones to whom leadership was passing.

As early as 1590, within just five years of the Antwerp siege, the Hanseatic League was in 'full decline', and not just Belgian but German trade was increasingly falling into Dutch hands.[168] For a number of reasons, the Dutch were in too fundamentally a strong position relative to Germany. Firstly, Holland's greater experience in handling large scale traffic, due to its dominance of the bulk trades, had given it the necessary skills to deal with the 'growing scale and complexity' of trade.[169] This same dominance also gave rise to relatively more technological advances in shipping.[170] For cheap and bulky goods, the effect on profits of lowering transport costs was much greater than for light expensive ('rich trade') goods. Hence, there was a greater drive to improve shipping techniques for countries involved in the former rather than the latter. The result was that a country like Holland was able to out-compete others, thereby acquiring dominance in both types of trade. Secondly, the geographic position of the Dutch was better suited to the increasing trade between the Baltic, France, the Mediterranean and the Atlantic. As Israel writes, '[t]he Dutch could send a ship to south west Europe for salt, then on to the Baltic to exchange the salt for grain, returning home before the cold winter set in. This was near impossible for the Baltic ports'.[171] Hence, with maritime trade expanding between the north and south of Europe from the fifteenth century, together with the growing Atlantic trade, it was inevitably going to be difficult for the German economy to stay ahead. The tables had already turned too much in favour of the Dutch.[172]

The change in Germany's trading position from one of dominance in medieval times to being overtaken by the Dutch in the late sixteenth century is borne out by our market estimates. We find reasonably low wheat price volatility in the sixteenth century, with an annual CV of 0.22–0.24. Whilst this is not at the Dutch low of 0.17, it is still low compared with much of Europe and is below that of England at the time. Using the monthly data available for Cologne reveals particularly low volatility in this city, which was well connected with the Low Countries. In terms of price gaps with other European cities, the majority of the non-wheat gaps look relatively low to begin with, at, for example, 19 per cent for candles and 15 per cent for linen in Augsburg. For wheat, the average gap was 55 per cent in the sixteenth century. This was close to average for Europe at the time, and below the 59 per cent in England. However, thereafter, markets showed little further improvement – if anything, the opposite. Volatility rose significantly in the seventeenth century in the cities of Munich, Leipzig and Wurzburg. The between-country price gap also rose in the seventeenth century, reaching 60 per cent. Similarly, many of the non-wheat price gaps increased to higher levels. Part of the deterioration was likely associated with the devastating Thirty Year War, which raged during the period 1618–48. One author talks of Germany being returned to the Dark Ages,[173] whilst another refers to the loss of life and physical devastation as 'the most severe in Europe since the Mongol invasion'.[174] As a direct consequence of the war, income and population growth declined and a rise in tolls on important trading arteries, such as the Rhine, took place, all of which are likely to have adversely affected market integration and the economy more generally. Following the War, an intensification of feudalism occurred in regions such as Saxony,[175] which disrupted economic advance further.

By the early eighteenth century, German wheat markets were recovering and showing signs of improvement in a number of different ways. The between country price gap fell from 60 per cent to 41 per cent, which was equal to that of France and Italy and not far from that of England (39 per cent) or the Netherlands (37 per cent). The within country price gap also fell, from 23 per cent to 14 per cent, and volatility declined. However, the situation deteriorates in the latter half of the century, meaning that by 1800, the level of German market development looked broadly similar to that in 1500.

Altogether, German markets exhibited virtually no improvement in the years 1500–1800. Compared with those elsewhere in Europe, domestic markets were (at best) average, and connections with the rest of Europe fell below the western European average after 1600, when the Hansa went into decline and the Thirty Years War took place. This meant that by the end of the eighteenth century, other economies had overtaken Germany in terms of the level of market development. The German market experience could help to explain the economy's failure to push ahead in the manner of either the Dutch or English.

Poland

Like much of Europe, Poland experienced significant commercial development between the ninth and thirteenth centuries, during the medieval commercial boom.[176] The thirteenth and fourteenth centuries continued to be a time of prosperity: constitutions were reformed and the urban network developed.[177] By the fifteenth century, Poland housed cities involved in both the wider European north–south trade, through which spices flowed from the Far East via the Balkans, and the European east–west trade, through which grain, skins, furs, metals and textiles were exchanged.[178] The historic trading records of Cracow reveal that exchange in the fifteenth century regularly involved products from locations as far as the Black Sea in the east, eastern England in the west, northern Italy in the south, and the Baltic in the north.[179] Domestically produced and abundant bulky goods such as grain, which were much cheaper than elsewhere in Europe (as we saw earlier), were being shipped by the Dutch to western Europe where prices were higher. Hence, Poland was very much a part of the European trading network. Nevertheless, the between-country wheat price gap was very high, suggesting that despite the trade in grain, grain markets between east and west had not yet converged. However, price volatility was low (with an average CV of 0.18 in the sixteenth century), perhaps indicating that internal markets were not too poorly developed.

Despite the favourable start, the late sixteenth to eighteenth centuries brought serious disruptions for Polish trade and the economy faltered.[180] Ottoman expansion in the Mediterranean disrupted the overland trade in spices coming through the Balkans into Poland, from where it was then traditionally distributed to other parts of central and eastern Europe.[181] Furthermore, and despite its seeming distance away, Poland was not untouched by the oceanic adventures which reoriented trade out of the Mediterranean and towards the Atlantic, pulling spices and other prized international goods away from the eastern Mediterranean and along global maritime routes to the Low Countries. In response, cities like Cracow lost their role as international trading emporia, and instead reoriented themselves to involvement in the trade in cheaper central and eastern European raw materials.

Poland's role in the rich-trades was not the only aspect of trade under pressure. Trade based on domestically produced goods also began to suffer as a result of events closer to home. Continuing through to the eighteenth century, European wars and the determination of surrounding economies (such as Prussia, Russia and Austria) to extend their territory into Polish areas regularly wreaked havoc on trade. The Swedish–Polish war (1655–60) saw the port of Danzig blockaded, and 'ravaged' much of the northern and central parts of Poland.[182] The result was that exports of domestic products goods such as grain were heavily disrupted.[183] In fact, such incursions were so successful that by 1792, Poland had completely vanished from the map of Europe, only to show its presence once again after World War One.[184]

War was not the only problem affecting domestic markets. Unlike in the west, feudalism was on the rise in eastern Europe.[185] Every family was expected to give service to the landowner in return for being given their own plot of land, together with paying other dues. On a per annum basis, the number of days of service rose from 'just a handful' for a whole family before the sixteenth century to six days for every family member by around 1600.[186] The explanation for deepening feudalism at this time has two parts.[187] Firstly, there was an increasing demand for cereals across Europe as population expanded, particularly in the west. Secondly, the fact that in eastern Europe, land was in plentiful supply relative to population made the area a natural exporter of cereals, as they could be supplied at a low price. It also meant that if landowners wanted to make high profits from these sales of grain, it was necessary to restrict the freedom of peasants. Paying peasants their true market value by formally employing them on a labour market would have been simply too expensive given that labour was in relatively short supply. Kriedte calculates that profits were 50 per cent higher as a result of using serf (as opposed to free) labour.[188] The rise in feudalism might help to explain the declining yield ratios, as it likely blunted incentives to produce, which in turn meant that grain was both less abundant and less cheap.[189] In 1664, a mere 29,000 lasts of grain were shipped out of Poland by the Dutch.[190]

In total, and as records from the Sound tolls reveal, 18 per cent less grain was shipped by the Dutch from the Baltic in the latter half of the seventeenth century compared with the first half of the century, after which grain shipments fell further in the first half of the eighteenth century.[191]

Our market estimates strongly suggest that the events of the seventeenth and eighteenth centuries caused a backward move for markets. The average CV in the eighteenth century was 0.28, compared with 0.18 two centuries earlier, rising further to 0.32 in the first half of the nineteenth century. The cities of Lwow and Gdansk also saw increasing price gaps with the rest of Europe.[192]

In the nineteenth century, the situation in Poland appears to have improved and the economy began to integrate. The coefficient of variation returned to its earlier lows, the within-country price gap fell from 90 per cent to 31 per cent, and the price gaps between Polish cities and the rest of Europe fell dramatically to 19 per cent, altogether indicating that markets achieved new heights. Whilst low prices of grain in eastern Europe had always stimulated the export of grain to western Europe, it took until the nineteenth century for full-scale market integration to occur between eastern and western Europe. It was at this time that eastern grain came to increasingly penetrate European markets, a period known as the 'Grain Invasion'. Despite the integration, however, Poland did not go on to experience the type of economic growth witnessed in western Europe.

Ottoman Empire

Whilst today we are accustomed to thinking about western Europe as being the wealthiest part of the continent, southern Europe was for many centuries its economic powerhouse. Part of this lead came as a result of connections with the east, through Constantinople (modern day Istanbul), which was the largest city in early modern Europe. In the fifteenth century, Constantinople came under the control of the Ottoman Empire, which was expanding across large parts of south-eastern Europe, including the Balkans, the Levantine coast and the Middle East.

As with the days of Muslim expansion in the eastern Mediterranean, Ottoman enlargement did not result in a cutting of ties with the rest of Europe. Connections between the two regions were still firmly in place, but international trade was very much left in the hands of foreign merchants.[193] Cairo, Bursa and Aleppo along with the giant that was Constantinople were leading distribution centres open to traders from across Europe.[194] 'Privileges' granted to European countries in an effort to facilitate the flow of luxury goods from the east to Europe (and the associated profits and favours) seem to have indulged foreign at the cost of home-grown merchant activity.[195] In exchange for spices, imports from Europe were welcomed, but there was little in the way of home-grown exports. The Balkans was a vast grain-growing region within the Empire, and prices of grain were well below those in western Europe, in theory providing a source of exports. However, transport costs meant that exports of grain into the Mediterranean region were not in general profitable[196] and there was relatively little help from the state (in terms of developing transport infrastructure) to help overcome this. The only times at which noticeable grain exports took place was during the price revolution and at the end of the eighteenth century, when prices in western Europe increased but those of the Ottoman world lagged behind, meaning that exports became profitable (until price gaps then narrowed once more).[197] Looking at manufactured goods, prices in the sixteenth century appear to be higher at home than they were abroad (including for metals and cloth) or, at best, on a par (in cases such as soap and candles).[198] Taken together, this situation created little stimulus to export either agricultural or manufactured goods, and a rather major incentive to import the latter. English foreign merchants, for example, regularly supplied English cloth to many Ottoman cities such as Constantinople, Aleppo, Alexandria and Smyrna through the Levant Company (created in 1581).[199]

Compared with the rest of Europe, the situation in the Ottoman Empire looks a little unusual. Elsewhere, states (such as seventeenth-century England) were increasingly taking action to encourage the development of home-grown export sectors whilst putting in place tariffs to discourage imports, particularly of manufactured goods.[200] What explains this striking difference? The spice trade may provide part of the answer. Spices flowed out of the Ottoman Empire into the rest of Europe, leaving the latter in deficit to the former, and so a need to export something in return.[201] The Ottoman appetite for imports could therefore be explained in terms of the fact that they represented a return payment for spices, helping to balance trade between western Europe and the Ottoman lands. Furthermore, the Ottoman ability to use revenues from sales of spices to pay for foreign imports meant that there was less need to export domestically produced goods. As a result, there was little incentive to, for example, build transport infrastructure to facilitate flows of such goods or to protect and stimulate manufacturing sectors.[202] This could help to explain why Ottoman policy was seemingly the opposite of the mercantilist policy used elsewhere in Europe, where there was more of a need to generate export revenues in order to help pay for the imported goods from the east. A lack of infant industry protection together with 'Dutch Disease' could then help explain the failed development of the Ottoman economy relative to north-western Europe.

Of course, we must be careful not to paint too overly rosy a picture of the international trading arena facing foreigners in Ottoman lands. There were repeated wars with the Spanish, Austrians and Venetians, and during such periods foreign ships were often prohibited from entering the Black Sea. Foreigners complained of feeling insecure at Constantinople in the seventeenth century, and some ships began to bypass the port.[203] Furthermore, according to the work of historians of Poland, evidence suggests that trade from the east into Poland suffered as the Ottomans gained ground.[204] Based on existing literature, it is therefore not clear whether increasing or decreasing integration between the Ottomans and Europeans was taking place in the early modern period. Using our price data will help to provide a clearer answer.

Examining the level of integration between Istanbul and the rest of Europe using wheat prices, we find price gaps that were on average around 65 per cent. This was higher than the European average but not dramatically so. However, the gap showed little improvement before the nineteenth century, which is in line with Berov's view that transport costs were too high.[205] In the latter half of the nineteenth century, however, the price gap fell, indicating that by this time the Ottoman part of Europe was becoming connected with the wider European agricultural market. This was of course the time at which transport costs fell dramatically due to the building of railroads (such as that from Istanbul to Belova and Nova Zagora) and the introduction of steamships.[206] Markets for higher value and non-perishable goods, including cloth, soap and candles, also showed signs of increasing integration between the Ottoman region and other parts of Europe, albeit towards the end of the period.[207] This was apparent in the cloth data between Istanbul and Milan in the nineteenth century, and in the soap data between Istanbul and Naples in the eighteenth century and Istanbul and Amsterdam from the latter half of the eighteenth century. On this basis at least, it is not fair to say that the region was becoming disconnected from the European market place as Ottoman rule expanded, as we do not find an increase in price gaps, although improvements in integration did not come until the nineteenth century. As with Poland, when they did arrive, it is questionable whether they had a positive stimulus on economic growth.[208] The spice trade followed by exports of land-based goods from the nineteenth century may have de-industrialized the economy. Turkey still remains behind western Europe today.[209]

There is perhaps reason to be even less optimistic about the Ottoman Empire's domestic markets than there is in its foreign trading arena. Whilst increasing regional trade between the newly conquered and unified Ottoman lands might in theory have presented opportunities for markets to integrate, as was the case in the Roman world, this does not necessarily mean that this potential was realized. When it comes to the Ottoman Empire, the mammoth central bureaucracy and 'interventionism' of the state springs to mind. Ottoman rulers are generally described as being disinterested in trade.[210] Pamuk writes that 'the Ottoman government did not hesitate to intervene in local and long-distance trade to regulate markets and ensure the availability of goods for the military, the palace, and, more generally, the urban economy'.[211] Whilst extensive supplies of goods were regularly being made to the capital city, which was the largest city in Europe with a population of half a million in the sixteenth century,[212] these were far from free-market flows and were often regulated and conducted at state enforced fixed prices.[213] Furthermore, the situation regarding the ownership of land did little to encourage commercialization. As much as three quarters of land was owned by the state (and farmed by peasants) and was not transferred into private hands until the latter half of the nineteenth century.[214] Hence, within the economy it is questionable whether markets were well integrated. The Ottoman international trading situation also likely had negative effects on domestic markets. The lack of encouragement of the export of domestically produced goods in the early modern period provided little incentive to build hubs, transport infrastructure, networks and distribution channels from production areas within the domestic economy to the coast. The lack of support for the activities of Ottoman merchants overseas also meant that there was less opportunity for the transfer of trading skills to the domestic economy. To some extent, it was a vicious circle. With few merchants at home, reliance was placed on those from overseas, the result of which was that there was little in the way of a domestic merchant class to push for institutions and policy that would aid markets at home or be favourable to exports, meaning that markets at home would not develop.[215] Undeveloped markets then made the state more likely to regulate and fix prices in an effort to try to obtain provisions to feed the vast capital city, also meaning that markets would stay poor. The situation in Spain appears to be in many ways similar. Little wonder that middle eastern traders are often depicted somewhat derogatively as 'peddlar' in nature, suggesting that there may have been little in the form of internal market integration.[216]

More recent literature has tended to be more sympathetic to the existence of markets within Ottoman lands. Based on new archival evidence on the issuance of fixed prices, Pamuk argues that state interventionism has been overplayed, that it became more 'selective' and was anyway much less used when it came to cities other than Constaninople.[217] It has been suggested that peasants were regularly involved with the market, and 'that trade constituted an element essential to the cohesion of Ottoman state and society'.[218] So, does the evidence from our price data suggest that Ottoman markets were improving? We can use grain price data from the grain producing region of the Balkans and the urban centre of Bursa to see whether integration appears to have been increasing or decreasing with the capital city, Istanbul. For the Balkans, we use the two most regular price series which are available from Berov.[219] Other data comes from Pamuk.[220] In terms of the analysis of the data, it must be remembered that Ottoman authorities were not afraid of interfering with the market, setting and adjusting prices where they wished.[221] Hence, any examination of price data must be treated with some caution. Furthermore, the data is very patchy, and certainly precludes estimation of volatility and speeds of adjustment, meaning that the evidence is purely based on what little it is possible to say about price convergence. Nevertheless, Berov's detailed work tells us that there was a price gap of around 50 per cent between

Istanbul and the Balkans and that this tended to fall in the nineteenth century.[222] Looking at the Istanbul wheat flour data of Pamuk and Berov's Balkan wheat price data suggests that these areas were certainly commercially well connected in the long period 1489–1777 in the sense of prices being 'cointegrated'.[223] Between Istanbul and one of the Balkan series we find no reduction in the price gap, whilst for the other there is a clear and very significant visual reduction in the price gap in the latter half of the eighteenth century. Whilst we have fewer observations for the city of Bursa, we find a significant decrease in the price gap between Bursa and Istanbul in the nineteenth century. Hence, evidence suggests that domestic markets existed and that they improved from the latter half of the eighteenth century in the case of the Balkans and a century or so later elsewhere. Pamuk talks of there being only limited commercialization in Ottoman agriculture until the nineteenth century, with the possible exception of the Balkans, which seems to accord well with these results.[224] In terms of the non-wheat products, price data for which is available from Pamuk, the evidence is more mixed.[225] Considering olive oil prices from Istanbul, Edirne and Bursa we find evidence of markets being connected.[226] However, Istanbul and Damascus reveal a lack of cointegration.[227] Using prices of butter in Istanbul, Damascus and Bursa for the extended period of 1490–1856, we find evidence that markets were also connected, but with no change in the price gap and so no evidence of actual improvements.[228]

Summary

This chapter has examined the trends in market development in a number of European countries and compared the levels of market development within and between them. Set alongside trends in economic development, this can help us to uncover the relationship between markets and growth.

The findings suggest that there was some variety in market experience at the country level. Some economies experienced improvements, including Italy and France, some witnessed relatively little change until the nineteenth century, including Germany and the Ottoman Empire, whilst others suffered some form of disintegration, including Belgium and Poland. The question is whether this variety of experience can help to explain the changing economic leadership between the various economies.

A number of economies appear to display a strong link in terms of markets and growth. The Spanish and Belgian economies went into decline at the same time that markets experienced decline. In Germany, markets did not show improvement, and neither did the economy. In the Netherlands, markets improved as the economy rose to its peak success. However, improving markets were not enough to sustain the Dutch expansion or to stimulate the French or Italian economies, whilst England's connections with the rest of Europe faltered at exactly the time the economy was on the rise.

Whilst well-developed markets within an economy seem to be associated with economic advance (and, similarly, domestic market deteriorations are consistently connected with economic decline), we are still to formally test whether domestic markets are sufficient for economic growth. Furthermore, we are still left wondering about the relationship between economic growth and an economy's connectedness with European markets. Whilst integration between the Netherlands and Europe improved during its Golden Age, England became less and not more integrated with Europe as the Industrial Revolution set in, whilst other economies that were well integrated with Europe failed to advance. The relationship between markets and growth is far from proven by our country-level evidence.

Appendix 1: Annual Wheat Price Data

The two main sources for wheat price data are as follows:

Allen and Unger grain price data set:
www.history.ubc.ca/faculty/Unger/ECPdb/Submit.html (referred to as Allen-Unger below)

International Institute of Social History (historic prices and wages data files):
www.iisg.nl/hpw/data.php (referred to as IISH below)

Other data sources are referenced below.

The cities, time periods and sources are as follows:

Netherlands
Amsterdam (1462–1900), Arnhem (1568–1901), Leiden (1392–1792), Utrecht (1462–1792) (Source: Allen-Unger data set)

Belgium
Antwerp (1608–1870), Brussels (1401–1500), Bruges (1365–1791), Lier (1427–1600), Louvain (1404–1499) (Source: Allen-Unger data set); Dixmude (1525–1615, monthly), Ghent (1800–1914, monthly), Brussels (1800–1890, monthly) (Source: Verlinden[229])

England
Exeter (1316–1816), London (1260–1914), Eton (1594–1816), Windsor (1700–1801), Winchester (1630–1816) (Source: Allen-Unger data set)

Scotland
Edinburgh (1556–1780) (Source: Allen-Unger data set)

Germany
Augsburg (1668–1820), Cologne (1531–1796), Leipzig (1564–1810), Munich (1507–1790), Wurzburg (1500–1799) (Source: Allen-Unger data set)

Austria
Vienna (1439–1810), Wels (1472–1769) (Source: Allen-Unger data set)

Poland

Gdansk (1703–1815), Krakow (1480–1914), Lwow (1520–1914), Warsaw (1526–1914) (Source: Allen-Unger grain price data set)

France

Aix (1570–1789), Angers (1580–1789), Arles (1570–1789), Bezier (1587–1758), Grenoble (1501–1780), Paris (1431–1913), Toulouse (1486–1792) (Source: Allen-Unger grain price data set); Angouleme (1820–79) (Source: Frédéric Michaud, IISH)

Italy

Ancona (1700–1825), Catania (1512–1630), Milan (1701–1860), Naples (1474–1803), Pesaro (1700–1825), Sansepolcro (1500–1631), Udine 1 (1600–1799), Udine 2 (1700–1825) (Source: Allen-Unger grain price data set); Tuscany (1263–1859) (Source: Paolo Malanima, IISH)

Spain

Andalucia (1554–1650), Aragon (1397–1497), Bilbao (1700–1826), Madrid (1501–1799),[230] Valencia (1413–1789) (Source: Allen-Unger grain price data set); Barcelona (1494–1808) (Source: IISH[231]); Gerona (1815–1883), Granada (1815–1883) (Source: Rafael Barquín Gil , IISH)

Ottoman/Eastern Mediterranean

Istanbul (wheat flour 1467–1808; wheat 1654–1861), Bursa (1689–1864). Additional data is available for: Edirne (1617–1794), Konya (1682–1751) (Source: Pamuk,[232] Istanbul data is also available at IISH); two Balkan series (1423–1866 and 1455–1802) (Source: Berov, *Dvizhenieto*)[233]

Appendix 2: Country-level Market Estimates

A note on the method for calculating country-level wheat price gaps and country-level annual volatility

The vast number of cities for which annual data is available means that we have a large number of price gap and volatility estimates for each country. In an effort to find an average value for each country, one could simply take the simple average for each country for every fifty or 100 years from 1400–1900. However, for some cities prices (and so price gap and volatility estimates) are not available across the whole period. This means that cities would drop in and out of the calculation of the country averages, potentially biasing conclusions. Hence, in order to extract a more accurate average trend for each country (and similarly for each region in the chapter which follows), panel data techniques are employed. A fixed effects panel regression incorporating a series of time dummies is applied to the set of individual estimates available for each country. Insignificant time dummies are eliminated one by one in order to arrive at a specification which captures any significant moves in price gaps or volatility across the country as a whole. In order to extract the 'average' price gap and volatility together with its trend over time, the constant term and the coefficients on the time dummy are added together (for each respective period). This method helps to avoid the problems which arise from missing data.

Wheat Price Gaps: Between-Country

Wheat price gaps are calculated between each of the following cities (excluding those in the same 'country'): Naples, Tuscany, Milan, Sansepolcro, Udine, Pesaro, Cantania, Ancona, Toulouse, Paris, Angers, Aix, Arles, Beziers, Grenoble, Angouleme, Istanbul (wheat), Istanbul (wheat flour),[234] Bursa, Madrid, Valencia, Barcelona, Gerona, Granada, Amsterdam, Leiden, Arnhem, Utrecht, London, Exeter, Edinburgh, Antwerp, Louvain, Lier, Bruges, Brussels, Wels, Vienna, Munich, Cologne, Augsburg, Leipzig, Wurzburg, Warsaw, Lwow, Gdansk and Krakow.

The standard formula is applied to each city-pair: $Gap_{i,j,t} = \ln(P_{i,t}/P_{j,t})$.

The data has been chosen to include all of the cities or areas for which a long and regular series of prices is available, with cities for which only shorter series are available being used where necessary to ensure sufficient coverage of all countries and time periods.

Table 2.1 records the average percentage price gap between each country and the rest of Europe.

Table 2.1: Between-country wheat price-gaps

	Netherlands	Belgium	England	Italy	Spain	France	Ottoman	Austria	Germany	Poland
1400–49	0.60	0.56	0.59	0.53	0.55					
1450–99	0.60	0.56	0.59	0.67	0.55	0.75		0.44		0.99
1500–49	0.51	0.43	0.59	0.58	0.55	0.51		0.59	0.55	0.99
1550–99	0.51	0.56	0.59	0.53	0.55	0.56	0.65	0.59	0.55	1.22
1600–49	0.40	0.56	0.41	0.49	0.55	0.46	0.65	0.58	0.55	0.99
1650–99	0.45	0.76	0.49	0.53	0.55	0.50	0.65	0.44	0.60	0.99
1700–49	0.37	0.67	0.39	0.40	0.46	0.41	0.65	0.44	0.41	0.91
1750–99	0.38	0.56	0.44	0.40	0.51	0.41	0.65	0.44	0.52	0.99
1800–49	0.38	0.56	0.59	0.32	0.88	0.31		0.44	0.41	0.80
1850–99	0.08	0.27	0.07	0.15	0.55	0.06				0.19

In the early fifteenth century, price gaps are in the region of 50–60 per cent for all of the countries for which data is available. By the early sixteenth century, price gaps between Belgium and non-Belgian cities have fallen to the relatively low level of 43 per cent, consistent with the growing importance of Belgium as a trading centre in medieval Europe. By 1600, price gaps in Belgium have risen whilst those of the Netherlands and England have fallen to around 40 per cent, indicative of a move in trade away from Belgium and towards the Dutch and English. Indeed, the levels of integration achieved in the north-west by 1600 are not significantly improved upon again until after the mid-nineteenth century. French and Italian price gaps have also fallen by 1600, but are at a slightly higher level of 46–49 per cent. By 1700 their price gaps have fallen further, indicating that their level of integration with the rest of Europe had caught up with that in the north-west. German price gaps also started to decline at this time, although to a much lesser degree, standing at 52 per cent in 1750 compared with 55 per cent in 1500. By the early nineteenth century, price gaps between each of France, Italy and Poland and the rest of Europe were significantly below earlier levels. However, those of Belgium, England, the Netherlands, Spain and Austria were at similar levels to those existing at least 200 years before. Only in the second half of the nineteenth century do price gaps across the whole of Europe witness a further significant decline, with values dropping to under 10 per cent in a number of cases.

To facilitate comparisons between countries, it is worth noting that the average of the country-level results in western Europe (i.e. excluding Poland and the Ottoman region), are as follows: 1500–49 (54 per cent); 1550–99 (55 per cent); 1600–49 (50 per cent); 1650–99 (54 per cent); 1700–49 (44 per cent); 1750–99 (46 per cent); 1800–49 (49 per cent); 1850–99 (20 per cent). These are referred to as 'the western European average' in the text.

Wheat Price Gaps: Within-Country

Wheat price gaps are calculated between the following cities within each of the following countries (where data allows):

Italy (Naples, Tuscany, Milan, Sansepolcro, Udine, Pesaro, Cantania, Ancona)

France (Toulouse, Paris, Angers, Aix, Arles, Beziers, Grenoble, Angouleme)

Spain (Madrid, Valencia, Barcelona, Gerona, Granada, Andalusia, Aragon, Bilbao)

Netherlands (Amsterdam, Leiden, Arnhem, Utrecht)

England (London, Exeter, Winchester, Windsor, Eton)

Belgium (Antwerp, Louvain, Lier, Bruges, Brussels, Dixmude, Ghent)

Austria (Wels, Vienna)

Germany (Munich, Cologne, Augsburg, Leipzig, Wurzburg)

Poland (Warsaw, Lwow, Gdansk, Krakow)

When it comes to comparing the resultant price gaps, one stumbling block which had to be overcome was the difference in distance between each pair of cities resulting from the very different sizes of each country. For example, the Belgian cities are generally located less than 100 km apart, the English cities are within 250 km of each other but the Italian and French cities are located up to around 700 km apart. Hence, the difference in raw price gaps within each country will in part reflect geography. In order to control for this, the raw price gaps can be 'distance adjusted'. This process involves regressing the raw price gaps on the distance between each city and then using the coefficient on the distance term to arrive at distance adjusted price gaps.[235]

After distance adjusting the price gap between each city-pair, the average within-country price gap is arrived at by applying a fixed effects regression with time dummies to the data for each separate country.[236] Table 2.2 reports the results.

Table 2.2: Within-country wheat price-gaps.

	Netherlands	Belgium	England	Italy	Spain	France	Austria	Germany	Poland
1400–49		0.15	0.16		0.31				
1450–99	0.20	0.22	0.16		0.31				
1500–49	0.20	0.15	0.16	0.35	0.31	0.24	0.21	0.23	
1550–99	0.20	0.40	0.25	0.19	0.15	0.24	0.21	0.23	
1600–49	0.06	0.39	0.16	0.30	0.13	0.24	0.34	0.23	
1650–99	0.20	0.42	0.13	0.39	0.31	0.24	0.18	0.23	
1700–49	0.20	0.15	0.09	0.26	0.31	0.24	0.17	0.14	0.98
1750–99	0.20	0.49	0.05	0.19	0.24	0.18	0.11	0.23	0.90
1800–49	0.20		0.07	0.19	0.31			0.08	0.31
1850–99	0.20								0.31

Belgium and England stand out for their particularly low initial price gaps of around 15–16 per cent in the fifteenth century. Most other parts of Europe have a similar level of price gap at around 20–24 per cent. Italy and Spain exhibit relatively high internal price gaps of over 30 per cent, but given the more rugged terrain, this is still quite respectable compared with flat lowland north-western countries. In the early seventeenth century, price gaps in the Netherlands fall substantially, to under 10 per cent, at the same time as we see a reduction in the gaps between the Netherlands and the rest of Europe. By contrast, Belgian price gaps increase significantly (as do the price gaps between Belgium and the rest of Europe). Hence, in terms of both within and between price gaps, we see the Netherlands becoming better integrated as Belgium does the opposite, consistent with the differing directions of the two economies at this time. Italian and Spanish price gaps fall significantly to 15–19 per cent in the late sixteenth century, but then subsequently increase again. Hence, by the seventeenth century not only has

Belgium seemingly witnessed a dislocation in markets, but so has Spain, Italy and (as can be seen in the table) Austria. Whilst in Italy gaps return to a lower level in the eighteenth century, in Spain they do not return to the same level. If we compare the price gaps in the late eighteenth century with those early on, we see no change in the Netherlands and Germany, an improvement in Italy (which takes place by 1600), an improvement in England, France and Austria, most of which takes place in the eighteenth century, and a deterioration in Belgium and Spain. Altogether, this suggests a great variety in the market experience.

To facilitate comparisons between countries, it is worth noting that the average of the country-level results in the table (excluding Poland and the Ottoman region) are as follows: 1500–49 (23 per cent); 1550–99 (23 per cent); 1600–49 (23 per cent); 1650–99 (26 per cent); 1700–49 (20 per cent); 1750–99 (21 per cent); 1800–49 (17 per cent). These are referred to as 'the western European average' in the text.

Wheat Price Volatility: Annual Data

Volatility has been calculated for each of the following cities:

Italy (Naples, Tuscany, Milan, Sansepolcro, Udine, Pesaro, Cantania, Ancona)

France (Toulouse, Paris, Angers, Aix, Arles, Beziers, Grenoble, Angouleme)

Spain (Madrid, Valencia, Barcelona, Gerona, Granada, Andalusia, Aragon, Bilbao)

Netherlands (Amsterdam, Leiden, Arnhem, Utrecht)

England (London, Exeter, Winchester, Windsor, Eton, Chester)

Belgium (Antwerp, Louvain, Lier, Bruges, Brussels, Dixmude, Ghent)

Austria (Wels, Vienna)

Germany (Munich, Cologne, Augsburg, Leipzig, Wurzburg)

Poland (Warsaw, Lwow, Gdansk, Krakow)

Ottoman (Istanbul wheat flour)

The coefficient of variation (CV) was calculated for each of these cities for rolling ten yearly periods and then averaged to give a figure for each fifty yearly period.[237] As is standard, a higher CV indicates a higher level of volatility and so less developed markets.

Table 2.3 shows the average results by country, which are arrived at by applying a fixed effects regression with time dummies to the set of city-level CV results within each country.

Table 2.3: Country-level annual wheat price volatility.

	Netherlands	Belgium	England	Scotland	Italy	Spain	France	Istanbul	Austria	Germany	Poland
1300–49			0.32		0.33						
1350–99		0.18	0.26		0.33						
1400–49	0.17	0.27	0.26		0.33		0.51				
1450–99	0.33	0.33	0.24		0.33		0.28				
1500–49	0.23	0.24	0.32		0.33	0.19	0.31		0.27	0.24	0.18
1550–99	0.17	0.29	0.32	0.27	0.25	0.19	0.29	0.33	0.27	0.22	0.18
1600–49	0.17	0.18	0.21	0.20	0.23	0.19	0.22	0.25	0.27	0.31	
1650–99	0.24	0.23	0.25	0.25	0.17	0.19	0.22	0.43	0.27	0.31	0.18
1700–49	0.25	0.28	0.24	0.17	0.16	0.19	0.27		0.27	0.19	0.28
1750–99	0.17	0.11	0.20	0.13	0.17	0.19	0.15		0.27	0.23	0.28
1800–49	0.28	0.26	0.21		0.25		0.15		0.27	0.31	0.32
1850–99	0.17	0.18	0.14				0.12				0.18

The initial level of volatility in Belgium and the Netherlands is relatively low, indicative of well-developed markets early on. In Belgium, the CV begins at 0.18, but this subsequently increases (as do the price gaps), recovering back to its original level in the latter half of the early modern period. In the Netherlands, the CV begins at a similar initial level of 0.17, with a temporary setback in the late fifteenth century, late seventeenth century and early nineteenth century. Hence, low levels of volatility were achieved relatively early on in these economies, after which setbacks occurred. In England, France and Italy, volatility begins at a relatively high level (ranging from 0.33 for England to 0.51 for France), but then undergoes a significant decline early on, followed by a further decline later on. In England, the first major decline occurs between the fourteenth and fifteenth centuries, when the CV falls from 0.32 to 0.24. Higher levels of volatility then return in the sixteenth century. The second major decline occurs in the nineteenth century, when the CV falls from 0.21 to 0.14. In Scotland, volatility declines in the eighteenth century, the time at which Scotland and England were unified. In Italy, the CV undergoes a significant decline from 0.33 to 0.25 by the late sixteenth century. By the end of the seventeenth century this has fallen further to 0.17. In France, volatility also witnesses a significant decline early on, from 0.51 to 0.28 in the late fifteenth century, with a further decline to 0.22 in the seventeenth century, and a still further decline to 0.15 in the latter half of the eighteenth century. The final set of economies, Spain, Austria and Germany, witness no improvement in terms of this volatility measure of market development. In Germany, volatility displays no significant decline, and increases in the seventeenth century. In Spain and Austria, volatility remains at a stable level of 0.19 and 0.27 respectively. Interestingly, this level is rather low in the case of Spain, and results from low volatility in the coastal cities of Barcelona and Valencia. However, this is the only indicator on which Spain performs well.

Wheat Price Volatility: Monthly Data

The table below shows the results of calculating the CV using the monthly wheat price data on a five-year rolling basis and then averaging the results for consecutive ten yearly periods.

Table 2.4: City-level monthly wheat price volatility.

	Toulouse	Paris	Cologne	Munich	Siena	Pisa	Vienna	Antwerp	Brussels	London	Utrecht	Ruremonde
1550–9		0.24	0.18		0.39	0.35					0.28	
1560–9	0.34	0.37	0.20		0.28	0.32			0.19		0.24	
1570–9	0.27	0.31	0.12		0.18	0.21			0.16		0.15	
1580–9	0.19	0.49	0.22		0.19	0.18			0.42		0.14	
1590–9	0.34	0.26	0.11		0.23	0.23			0.15		0.13	
1600–9	0.27	0.14	0.09		0.16	0.17		0.14	0.18		0.14	
1610–9	0.25	0.16	0.19		0.17	0.14		0.18	0.23		0.16	
1620–9	0.34	0.23	0.20		0.17	0.13		0.14	0.19		0.16	
1630–9	0.29	0.15	0.15		0.37	0.28		0.13	0.07		0.11	
1640–9	0.31	0.31	0.19		0.24	0.19			0.17			
1650–9	0.29	0.27	0.19		0.16	0.16		0.21	0.17			0.17
1660–9	0.17	0.19	0.15		0.18	0.14			0.15			0.15
1670–9	0.17	0.17	0.16		0.32	0.23			0.15			0.16
1680-9	0.23	0.27	0.19		0.21	0.20			0.20	0.20		0.20
1690–9	0.23	0.49	0.23	0.25	0.13	0.10	0.18		0.21	0.24		0.22
1700–9	0.31		0.20	0.20	0.21	0.16	0.18	0.38		0.32		0.26
1710–9	0.28		0.14	0.17	0.22	0.14	0.20	0.22		0.15		0.13
1720–9	0.27		0.12	0.18	0.21	0.16	0.21		0.21	0.17		0.12
1730–9	0.12		0.16	0.19	0.18	0.11	0.15		0.21	0.19		0.18
1740–9	0.20		0.12	0.20	0.15	0.10	0.16		0.15	0.17		0.17
1750–9	0.20		0.16	0.15	0.20	0.11	0.19			0.23	0.23	0.16
1760–9	0.13		0.17	0.18	0.29	0.17	0.18			0.16	0.17	0.15
1770–9	0.17		0.15	0.30		0.17	0.19	0.09	0.09	0.13	0.18	0.12
1780–9	0.13					0.12	0.22	0.13	0.12	0.13	0.13	0.16
1790–9						0.17	0.21			0.28		

Once again, these results confirm that the cities with low volatility towards the start of the period can be found in the north-west. Volatility in Pisa and Siena subsequently falls, particularly rapidly in the latter part of the sixteenth and early part of the seventeenth century. In Paris and Toulouse, volatility also declines, although with setbacks along the way. Data for Munich and Vienna is only available for the latter part of the early modern period and suggests that no sustainable improvement was taking place, consistent with the results of the other measures.

Whilst as a measure of volatility the coefficient of variation used so far has the advantage of being easy to understand, it is not always ideal as a measure of market development. The results may in part capture the effect of trending prices (although we have at least attempted to mitigate this using small intervals of time) and factors such as the nature of demand and agricultural structure (which are more difficult to counter). For example, if there are many substitutes available for a particular good in a particular area, prices will tend to be less volatile as consumers can substitute away if prices start to rise and are attracted to the good if prices fall, which has the effect of dampening any change in price. In order to remove the effect of such factors from the variance of prices (and so our measure of volatility) it is necessary to explicitly model prices using, for example, lagged prices, time trends and seasonal dummies. The residuals from the price model capture unpredictable price changes (as opposed to predictable), and it is this unpredictability which we should be attempting to measure (i.e. the element of price fluctuations which is not caused by the seasons or time trends). The technique that can be used to implement this approach is borrowed from empirical finance, the GARCH model.[238] This involves modeling both prices and the variance of the associated residuals. By incorporating lagged residual variance in the latter model, we can control for a well-known empirical fact: the standard deviation (equivalently, variance) of price movements displays clustering behaviour. A large price movement in one month is likely to be followed by other such large movements, meaning that the variance is not constant.[239] Indeed, it is often found that a period of high volatility is followed by a period of low volatility, as seen in the stock market. For this reason, the GARCH model has been shown to have a good fit to real world data. Bateman (2013) estimates GARCH models for a number of wheat price series. The results suggest that volatility in Amsterdam remained unchanged in the period 1462–1900, suggesting that Amsterdam had already achieved a well-developed market early on. Similar results were found for London 1267–1799. For Bruges, the results suggest that volatility was rising in the period 1370–1499, consistent with our earlier findings. For Toulouse and Tuscany, the findings indicate that volatility was declining, again consistent with the earlier results.

Wheat Price Speed of Adjustment: Monthly Data

The speed of adjustment between each pair of cities for which we have monthly wheat price data has been calculated using the vector error correction method. The data was logged before applying the VECM model, which assumes that transaction costs are proportional.[240] A time trend (where significant) together with monthly dummies were included in the VECM specification. Where serial correlation was present, lagged difference terms were included up to the level necessary to eliminate the problem.[241] In the rare cases where there was no co-integration between a pair of cities or where no adjustment was identified in either direction, the speed was valued at zero.

Given that a large number of the cities for which monthly data is available are located in the north-west, the average speeds for each of the north-western cities is higher than for the other cities, in part reflecting the simple fact that they are geographically close to many of the cities against which their speed of adjustment is being measured. Hence, as with the within-country price gaps, 'distance adjusted' speeds were calculated for each pair of cities.[242] The 'average speed' for a particular city (for each fifty yearly time periods) is then calculated by applying a fixed effects regression with time dummies to all of the city-pairs which contain that particular city.[243] Table 2.5 provides the results.

Table 2.5: Distance adjusted speeds of adjustment.

	1550–99	1600–49	1650–99	1700–49	1750–99
Antwerp		0.21			0.21
Brussels	0.13	0.13	0.17	0.13	0.18
Ruremonde			0.16	0.16	0.16
Utrecht	0.16	0.16			
London			0.22	0.22	0.22
Pisa	0.14	0.14	0.14	0.14	0.18
Siena	0.14	0.14	0.14	0.14	0.25
Toulouse	0.16	0.13	0.16	0.16	0.16
Paris	0.12	0.12	0.12		
Cologne	0.12	0.12	0.15	0.12	0.12
Munich				0.12	0.12
Vienna				0.14	0.14

As with the wheat price gaps, and as already alluded to, the raw results suggest that the Low Countries appear to have the highest level of integration with the rest of Europe in the sixteenth and seventeenth centuries, with the highest speeds of adjustment being found in Utrecht, Brussels, Antwerp and Ruremonde. Brussels, Utrecht and Ruremonde have raw speeds of around 0.07–0.09, whilst Antwerp is even higher at 0.16. A speed of adjustment of about 0.1 implies that around 10 per cent of disequilibria are eliminated in a month (and gives a half-life of 6.34 months). This suggests that the Low Countries were not too far from the 3–4 month half-lives calculated by Persson for the mid-nineteenth century.[244] Whilst we only have monthly data for London from the late seventeenth century, it also indicates a high speed of adjustment at this time and one which is on a par with the speed (and so arguably level of integration) in the later eighteenth century (on the eve of the Industrial Revolution). Given the predominance of Low Country cities in our data set (a total of four out of twelve), it is perhaps unsurprising that we find higher raw speeds on average for the north-west cities as they are geographically close to many other cities in the data set. However, even controlling for distance between cities, we find that the north-west cities are in general well integrated with the other cities, with speeds of 0.16 for Utrecht in the late sixteenth century, 0.21 for Antwerp in the seventeenth and eighteenth centuries, and 0.22 for London. Hence, England, Belgium and the Netherlands appear well integrated with the rest of Europe from relatively early on. With the exception of Brussels, the speeds of adjustment in the late eighteenth century were on a par with those earlier in the period. Hence, as was found with the price gap and volatility measures, many markets in the north-west appear to be as well integrated in the sixteenth and seventeenth centuries as on the eve of the Industrial Revolution.

The Italian cities have the lowest raw speeds in the sixteenth and early seventeenth centuries (at around 0.05), but these subsequently rise in the later seventeenth and early eighteenth century, indicating that market development was taking place in this part of Europe in the early modern period, as also suggested by the price gap and volatility results. Of course, Siena and Pisa are distant to many of the cities found in our data set. Hence, their lower speeds are arguably still very respectable. It is certainly therefore possible that better located cities in Italy had speeds similar to the best integrated north-western cities in early modern times. Indeed, controlling for distance, the speeds of adjustment for Pisa and Siena at 0.14 are only slightly lower than those of Utrecht (at 0.16) in the late sixteenth century, although below Antwerp's level of 0.21 (measured in the early seventeenth century). By the late eighteenth century, Pisa's distance controlled speed has risen to 0.18 and Siena's to 0.25 – close to the 0.21 of Antwerp and 0.22 of London in the same time period. Hence, consistent with the price gap results, Italian integration had caught up with that of the north-west. German and French cities (Paris, Toulouse and Cologne) begin the period with intermediate speeds (around 0.06). Distance controlled speeds range from 0.12 for Paris and Cologne to 0.16 for Toulouse. As with Italy, these are not too far below the types of levels seen in north-western cities at the start of the early modern period. However, unlike in Italy, French and German speeds see no sustained improvement across the period. Hence, by the end of the eighteenth century, German distance controlled speeds in particular are some of the lowest at 0.12 compared with 0.18–25 in Italy, 0.22 in England and 0.16–0.21 in the Low Countries. On the basis of the speed of adjustment results it also becomes clear that Austria is one of the least integrated areas with the rest of Europe – the speed of adjustment for Vienna is only 0.043 in the eighteenth century (only Munich is at a similarly low level). Even adjusting for distance between cities, the speed is 0.14 in the eighteenth century, well below the eighteenth-century values in the north-west at this time. Overall, the hierarchy of integration suggested by the speeds of adjustment seems to be in broad agreement with that arrived at using the wheat price gaps. The cities (or countries) which are best integrated with the rest of Europe tend to be found in the north-west, followed by Italy, France, Germany and Austria.

Price Gaps for Non Wheat Products

Price data from a number of cities for goods other than wheat (soap, candles and linen) are used to calculate between country price gaps. The price data were collated by Allen, for his paper 'The Great Divergence' and have kindly been made available on the web. The following cities were used:

- Soap: London, Antwerp,[245] Amsterdam, Vienna, Naples, Strasbourg and Madrid
- Candles: London, Antwerp, Augsburg,[246] Vienna, Madrid, Strasbourg and Naples
- Linen: London, Antwerp, Augsburg, Munich, Leipzig, Strasbourg, Madrid and an amalgamation of Florence and Milan prices

An average European price was calculated for each product, on the basis of which price gaps between each country and the rest of Europe could be calculated.[247] Table 2.6 records the results.

Table 2.6: Non wheat price-gaps.

	Antwerp	Amsterdam	Naples/Florence/Milan	London	Vienna	Augsburg	Leipzig	Munich	Madrid	Strasbourg
Soap										
1550–99	0.43	0.31	0.18	0.35						0.33
1600–45	0.30	0.23	0.13	0.33	0.29					0.38
1734–78	0.46	0.42	0.46	0.72	0.19				0.13	0.21
Candles										
1503–49	0.17	0.13		0.32	0.27	0.19			0.26	0.14
1550–99	0.21	0.32		0.28	0.57	0.36			0.26	0.33
1600–49	0.14	0.29		0.21	0.47	0.21			0.2	0.29
1650–99	0.14	0.16		0.12	0.31	0.30			0.16	0.16
1700–49	0.08			0.26	0.18	0.27			0.10	0.18
1750–79	0.11			0.31	0.19	0.12			0.05	0.05
Linen										
1564–99	0.63		0.20	0.12		0.15	0.10	0.32		0.28
1600–20	0.74		0.17	0.19		0.16	0.13	0.24		0.12
1701–41	0.44		0.48	0.18		0.66	0.48	0.30	0.17	0.27
1750–90	0.84		0.69	0.09		0.64	0.88	0.10	0.5	0.43

Whilst the results are mixed, it is possible to extract some general findings. For Italy, we find a number of low price gaps, consistent with the importance of trade to Italy early on. In later years, the data reveals a significant rise in price gaps, indicating a growing disconnection of Italy from the rest of Europe in non-agricultural markets by the eighteenth century. In the case of Belgium, we previously saw that the wheat price gaps achieved low levels early on but were not sustained. Consistent with this we find high price gaps relative to most of the other countries for soap and linen. For the Netherlands, we find a decline in the soap price gap between the sixteenth and seventeenth centuries and in the case of candles we find low to average price gaps. In the case of England, we find relatively low price gaps in the case of linen, which end the early modern period below where they began. However, for soap and candles we find much higher price gaps relative to other countries. This suggests that not all markets in England were well integrated with the rest of Europe. For Austria and Germany we find a number of low price gaps, many of which increase around the time of the seventeenth century. Taken together with the wheat price data, it seems questionable whether these economies were becoming better integrated in the early modern period. For Spain, it is notable that the price gap for candles declines in the seventeenth and eighteenth century, indicating an improvement in the associated market by the end of the early modern era. However, it would be unwise to argue for a more general market improvement when the other evidence points consistently in the opposite direction.

In addition to calculating price gaps between each country and the rest of Europe, price gaps for such goods as soap, candles, olive oil and linen were calculated within each country where data permitted. To facilitate this, the non-wheat price data from Allen was supplemented with additional data from IISH (http://www.iisg.nl/hpw/data.php) and Pamuk (*500 years*). The cities involved and results are discussed in the main text.

3 THE COURSE OF EARLY MODERN MARKET INTEGRATION: THE MEDITERRANEAN AND THE NORTH-WEST REGION

'According to the best authenticated history', writes Adam Smith in his *Wealth of Nations*, the parts of the world that first developed 'were those that dwelt round the coast of the Mediterranean Sea'.[1] From ancient times to the middle of the second millennium, the Mediterranean was the wealthiest part of Europe and, from religions to the Renaissance, gave birth to major historical movements. During the early modern period, however, economic leadership shifted decisively away from the region and towards north-western Europe. Hobsbawm writes that the Mediterranean became an 'impoverished backwater' and that Venice became little more than a tourist centre on the European map.[2] Italy and Spain were in decline, and the Netherlands and England were on the rise. Whilst in the former the level of urbanization and agricultural productivity stagnated and real wages fell, in north-western Europe agricultural productivity was transformed, real wages held their ground and the level of English urbanization rose spectacularly from 7 per cent to 29 per cent of the population.[3] By the late eighteenth century, the British Industrial Revolution was well underway, and the rest, as they say, is history.

As we have seen, increasing trade and market integration are commonly held responsible for the rise of the north-west and, as such, markets in the region have been the subject of intense investigation.[4] What is disappointing, however, is that this literature makes little reference to the significant commercial exchange of the Mediterranean and makes no attempt to compare the level of market development in the two regions. The implicit belief seems to be that north-western markets were unique in terms of their level of development – that they had pushed ahead of those in the Mediterranean, or that the latter disintegrated. In order to see whether or not this was the case, the present chapter aims to provide a comparison of markets in the two regions. If we find that Mediterranean market development was overtaken by the north-west and/or that Mediterranean markets disintegrated, this would be entirely consistent with a market-based story of growth. By contrast, if we find that markets in the Mediterranean were as well developed as those in the north-west and did not disintegrate, this would lead us to question whether markets are sufficient for sustained economic growth.

In what follows, the first section considers the existing historical literature, which suggests some form of disintegration in the early modern Mediterranean. After questioning this literature, the second section proceeds to formally measure and compare the level of market development in the two regions.

The Early Modern Mediterranean: Evidence of Disintegration or Integration?

The 'Great Sea', as it is known to some, has always linked a diverse set of lands, rich in a great variety of products, at relatively low cost, creating an incentive for trade. At the medieval markets that framed its shores, one could regularly find on offer grain from Sicily, Egypt or the Balkans, oil from southern Italy and Spain, soap from Bari, sugar from Crete and Cyprus, raw wool from Spain, silk from Messina and spices all the way from the Malaccan Islands. In the western part of the region, trade was in the hands of Florence and Genoa, the last of whom carved out a trading position in heavy foodstuffs such as grain, salt and cheese. On the Spanish coast, Barcelona and Valencia were the significant maritime powers. Barcelona possessed land holdings across the Mediterranean, including Sicily and Sardinia, and had links to northern Europe through the Hansa. Valencia was the more popular of the two cities when it came to trade between the Mediterranean and Atlantic, owing to its more southerly position on the Spanish coast.[5]

In the Eastern half of the Great Sea, Venice dominated trade, including the trade in spices.[6] As one author writes of the city, 'she never was, she never will be wholly of the West'.[7] The valuable trade in spices meant that the Mediterranean was far from being a world of its own. The spice trade stimulated Mediterranean contact not only with the Orient but the rest of Europe. Spices from India, Ceylon, Indonesia and other parts of the East were gathered by the Chinese and shipped from Malacca into the hands of Arab traders in the Middle East. Continuing along the Silk Road they passed through the Levant and Ottoman Empire, into the hands of the Venetians.[8] From here they were taken to all parts of Europe, as Venetian merchants searched for markets in which to sell their exotic luxuries and valuable products that could be used as return cargo, completing the circle of east–west trade. From as early as the thirteenth century, following developments in Genoese shipping, Italian ships carrying Mediterranean and Eastern goods were regularly traversing north-western Europe. These trading connections were, for the time being at least, firmly in the hands of Italian merchants.

Altogether, it therefore seems accurate to depict the Mediterranean Sea at the onset of the early modern period as a rather lively place housing 'an integrated and expansive network of production and trade'.[9] However, we know that over the course of the early modern era, two major developments from outside the Mediterranean seriously reshaped the trading life of the region. The first involved the Portuguese and Dutch explorations in the East, along the Cape of Good Hope and up into the Indian Ocean. The second came in the form of increasing trade in the Atlantic and growing competition from Atlantic powers. This included the arrival of northern ships laden with Baltic grain and northern European manufactured goods, supposedly 'invading' Mediterranean markets, reaching as far as the traditionally Italian domain of the Levant.[10] From as early as 1511, the English successfully established regular trading relations with Leghorn, Sicily, Crete and Cyprus,[11] selling cloth and tin, and they were not the only ones. In 1593, out of a total of 219 ships which arrived at Leghorn, of which 73 brought grain from the north, 34 belonged to Hanseatic towns, 12 to the Dutch, 7 to England, 4 to Belgium, 2 to Norway and 1 to Riga.[12] However, the Hanseatic market share soon declined, leaving the French, English and Dutch. In 1581 the (English) Levant Company received its charter with the Turks.[13] By 1597 the Dutch had reached Syria, and under the French flag traded with Turkish ports, gaining independent trading rights with the Ottomans in 1612.[14]

As a result of these two developments, the Mediterranean moves from being at the heart of global trade to little more than a 'mill pond' in an expanding global economy.[15] According to much of the historical literature, the result was that the unity of the region was 'lacerated and torn', as a result of which it lost its 'integrative force'.[16] Tabak summarizes this literature by saying that, '[i]t is as if the Mediterranean was torn asunder by the tempestuous gales of the Atlantic and what was left behind was merely the debris of the Inner Sea ... brought to an end [only] by the arrival of the steamship in the Mediterranean in the mid-nineteenth century'.[17] One is left with a rather gloomy impression of a Mediterranean struggling to maintain its foothold in the marketplace, as a result of which the region goes into decline, whilst markets in the north-west plough ahead, leading to an eclipse.

There are, however, two major problems with this interpretation of the situation in the early modern Mediterranean. Firstly, it must be remembered that Mediterranean merchants had for centuries been operating in the north-west. Hence, it would be unfair to automatically assume that the arrival of Dutch and English merchants in the Mediterranean represented some form of overtaking or disintegration of the region. Instead, it could simply indicate that the north had 'caught up' in terms of exploiting cross-European trading opportunities. As the north began to develop and trade outside of its traditional realm, it would inevitably eat into the market shares of Mediterranean producers, trade and shipping, but that does not mean that the Mediterranean was in any way 'failing' or witnessing a backward move on the market front. Instead, it was just that the Mediterranean was no longer expanding into a vacuum, facing foreign competition in the European trading realm. The increasing presence of northern ships and the goods they carried is therefore not enough on the basis of which to argue that the Mediterranean was being overtaken by the north-west. Secondly, whilst the Mediterranean was certainly facing new competition, biting into some of its traditional activities, it also created new opportunities, allowing the Mediterranean to specialize in activities for which it was most suited. The result may therefore have been an increase, rather than decrease, in the region's integration with wider Europe and, indeed, the world. To see how the Mediterranean was responding and adapting to the new challenges of the early modern age, and whether these are indicative of decreasing or increasing integration, we will consider each of agriculture, manufacturing and commerce in turn, before moving on to more formally measure markets.[18]

(i) Agriculture

According to Braudel, by the sixteenth century, growing population was regularly placing strain on food supplies in the Mediterranean.[19] The growing demand for food caused by rising population was met by a reduced supply. This reduced supply was in part a result of the increased incidence of flooding and climatic variability that came with the 'Little Ice Age'.[20] Initially, the situation was eased by sourcing additional grain from the Ottoman areas of the Eastern Mediterranean, principally the Balkans. By the middle of the sixteenth century, between a half and a quarter of all grain 'thrown into circulation' each year on the Mediterranean market came from the Ottoman lands, most notably Romania.[21] Then, as soon as the Spanish embargo on Dutch trade in the Mediterranean was lifted, grain also began to arrive from the Baltic. With their unrivalled shipping capacity, the Dutch were in a position to profit from supplying Baltic grain to Mediterranean consumers.[22] The first Dutch ship sailed through the Mediterranean in 1590. Thereafter, between two and three hundred ships arrived each year.[23] In response to the changing climatic conditions and the newly available cheap grain, the cultivation of grain went into decline in the Mediterranean region. In addition to grain, the cultivation of sugar was also moving out of the Mediterranean, first into the Atlantic islands and then to the newly discovered West Indies and Brazil, where sugar could be produced at low cost with the use of slave labour.[24] However, the decline of sugar and grain was far from a loss for the Mediterranean; instead, it allowed the region to specialize in the production of agricultural goods to which it was most suited. Sales of grain and sugar were replaced by increasing production and sales of olive oil and wine. In response, cultivation and settlement moved away from the lowlands to the hillsides of the Mediterranean,[25] making the Mediterranean famous for the landscapes and hillside villages with which we are familiar today.

The image painted here is one of the regions of Europe, and in the wider world, responding to new European and global trading opportunities by increasingly specializing in the production of agricultural crops to which they were most suited and then exchanging the goods through long distance trade. To an economist, this suggests that Mediterranean markets were well connected with the wider world, which therefore deserves to be seen in a positive as opposed to negative light. The evidence from our wheat price gaps suggests that the difference in price between Mediterranean and north-western grain was indeed falling significantly over time, indicating increasing integration between the north-western and Mediterranean markets. The average price gap falls from 51 per cent in 1400–49 to 40 per cent in 1600–49, 34 per cent in 1750–99 and 19 per cent in 1850–9.[26] The Ottoman region integrates later than the rest of the Mediterranean, in the nineteenth century. Olive oil was the major input into soap production, and so we would expect soap prices to converge if the prices of olive oil were converging. The results of calculating the soap price-gap between the north-west and the Mediterranean indeed reveal evidence of a decline (i.e. increase in integration). With the exception of Barcelona, we find price convergence between all other city-pairs. For the western region (Naples and Madrid) this occurs in the seventeenth and early eighteenth centuries, whilst for the eastern region (Istanbul) it occurs later, in the nineteenth century. The fact that soap and wheat prices were converging is indicative of increasingly integrated agricultural markets between the two regions.

An acknowledgement of the response of the Mediterranean agricultural sector to the changing conditions of the time also suggests a revision to the now accepted view of 'backwardness' in Mediterranean agriculture. Economic historians are frequently critical of the progress of agriculture in the early modern Mediterranean. Given that agricultural revolutions were taking place in the north-west but seemingly not in the Mediterranean, agricultural productivity looks as if it had fallen behind. This 'failure' to advance has been attributed to 'the draconian rule and political eight of landowners, tax farming, and large flock owners as well as to the complexity of patterns of ownership and tenure'.[27] However, what comparisons of agricultural productivity miss is that much of the action in the Mediterranean was taking place not like the north-west, on low-lying land, but on the hills and mountainsides of the region. Comparisons of agricultural productivity based on the grain yield on low-lands are stacked against the Mediterranean, in the way that comparisons of yield of vineyards between the two regions would be stacked against the north-west. It is difficult to compare like with like when the two regions are beginning to specialize in very different areas of agriculture. The low yields of grain in the Mediterranean are unsurprising given that the Little Ice Age 'turned the cultivation of lowlands into a toilsome and worse, unpredictable, undertaking'[28] and that in many ways the region is better suited to the cultivation of olive trees and vines.

Our vision of Mediterranean agriculture deserves to be revised to one in which the economy is successfully adapting to new trading opportunities, which enabled it to specialize, and away from one of a withdrawal from markets and a failure of productivity.

(ii) Manufacturing

Alongside the production of agricultural goods, the Mediterranean had long been a producer of high quality manufactured goods, particularly northern Italy. Venice manufactured a number of luxury items, including woolen cloth, glass, soap and silk. Increasing competition in the spice trade, as a result of the oceanic adventures, encouraged Venetians to shift even more towards the production of manufactured goods, meaning that Venice became increasingly 'industrialized' in the latter half of the sixteenth century and early part of the seventeenth century.[29] However, northern ships soon carried north-western manufactures into the Mediterranean, presenting increasing competition for Venice and other manufacturing districts. The ability of the north-west to compete in Mediterranean markets was based on their development of a new lighter type of cloth, known as the new draperies, which cut costs of production by requiring less raw material input and less skilled labour. This new product, together with imitations of Italian cloths, could undercut the more expensive quality cloths produced by Mediterranean suppliers.[30] By the 1630s, English and Dutch cloth surpassed Italian cloth in the Levant marketplace.[31] By the mid-seventeenth century, the Mediterranean was the largest single market for London's exports, with woolen cloth featuring as the leading commodity.[32] Florentine production of cloth had fallen from 30,000 pieces in 1560–80 to 6,000 in 1641–45; by 1709 Milan had only one surviving firm out of more than sixty a century before and the output of Venetian cloth producers had fallen back to its level at the opening of the sixteenth century.[33] Employment in the woolworkers guilds of Venice fell from 3,321 in 1595 to 770 in 1690,[34] and over the same period total export-related employment fell from 45 per cent of the guild workforce to 33 per cent.[35] In soap manufacturing, the number of cauldrons fell from 40 to 7, with a decline in production from 13 million pounds in 1600 to 2.5 million by 1700.[36] In Venice in particular, construction, retailing and food services grew to replace the previous manufactured goods – in part aided by public building and tourism.[37] Manufacturing did not disappear from the Mediterranean, however. Instead, it shifted out of the cities and into the countryside (including north of the Alps), where the raw material (wool) was often more easily accessible and where labour costs were cheaper. The cities (including Venice and Genoa) shifted from specializing in producing the products themselves to organizing and financing their production in rural areas and getting the goods to markets, including in Leipzig and Cracow.[38] In fact, this process was not only particular to the Mediterranean, but was also taking place in the north of Europe.[39]

Whilst competition inevitably created problems for incumbent producers in the short run, it also created opportunities. It encouraged economies to further develop their techniques and products, and to specialize in areas to which they were most suited. However, such gains only went furthest where change was not resisted. Rapp argues that the industrial decline in Venice in the seventeenth century was not indicative of incompetence on behalf of producers, but the inevitable result of state authorities failing to respond to the new competition in an appropriate way by, for example, maintaining tight controls on the minimum quality of goods and regulating in a way that limited the use of new cloth dyes and new machinery.[40] As a result, the potential for market integration between Italy and the north-west was not fully exploited. Hence, whilst we find that the price gap for cloth declined between Istanbul and London, the price gap between London and Milan showed no decline. The price gap for other manufactured goods, such as candles, also failed to decline between the Italian cities and the north-west, even though it did so between Spain and the north-west.[41] Hence, whilst some parts of the Mediterranean took advantage of the supplies of cheap north-western goods, others acted to resist, and as a result did not rise to the challenge. The result is that whilst some parts of the Mediterranean integrated with the north-west in terms of the market for manufactures, this was not without exception.

(iii) Shipping

Perhaps one of the most obvious sources of competition facing the established powers in the Mediterranean was in the area of shipping, the means through which grain and manufactured goods were being carried through the Mediterranean Sea. Early in the sixteenth century, trade with the north was conducted almost exclusively on Venetian and Genoese ships. Genoa had long been a leader in shipbuilding and shipping – they were the first to navigate to the north-west from the Mediterranean and their ability to navigate during the winter months was a marvel to the French and Greeks.[42] Being a big player in the bulk trade, Genoese ships had also been built to carry high volumes of goods. The Venetian shipbuilding and shipping industry was also at the cutting edge, and specialized in the transport of luxury goods.[43] However, depletion of wood supplies and difficulties sourcing wood in the north (during the Thirty Years War)[44] raised the costs facing the Mediterranean ship-building industry, whilst simultaneously the Dutch and English were pushing ahead the design of their own ships (for example, to increase carrying capacity).[45] The Venetian merchant marine halved between 1550 and 1590.[46] The other side of the coin was an increasing presence of northern ships in the Mediterranean. According to many writers they 'swarmed into the Mediterranean with their superior sailing ships early in the seventeenth century, and seized control of the sea's commercial, financial and maritime life'.[47]

However, as Molly Greene argues, the image of the northern powers overtaking Mediterranean shipping needs to be revised.[48] Firstly, the increase in northern shipping through the Mediterranean was far from smooth. There existed an 'interregnum' in which the Venetians and Genoese were in decline, and yet the northern ships were not yet strong enough in presence.[49] The result was an unfavourable security situation. In the words of Leon:

> The last quarter of the sixteenth and first half of the seventeenth centuries was indeed a most difficult period for the policing of the seas: Turkey had now withdrawn to the eastern Mediterranean; the navies of the Italian states had declined; French naval power had been exhausted during the Wars of Religion and the Spanish navy had been exhausted by the Dutch and Elizabethan wars. International anarchy and the exhaustion of the Mediterranean naval powers proved a fertile soil for piracy.[50]

The presence of northern ships in the seventeenth century was therefore 'intermittent'.[51] The side effect was the creation of a new 'industry' for the Mediterranean, providing protection for northern ships.[52] Secondly, northerners were not the only people who stood to gain from the decline of Venice and Genoese shipping. Indeed, whilst the northern ships made an inroad on long distance trade to and from the Mediterranean, much of the 'carrying trade' between the various ports of the Sea remained in Mediterranean hands until at least the end of the seventeenth century.[53] Northern ships had particular difficulties establishing themselves in the eastern Mediterranean, where the Greeks had much more success and where in the Aegen the Ottomans had a firm hold.[54] In the western part of the sea, Italians and increasingly the French handled 'most of the traffic' between the North African coast and the rest of the Mediterranean.[55] Furthermore, whilst long distance trade through Venice and Genoa might have been in decline that through Leghorn and Marseille witnessed a substantial increase in the second half of the early modern era: Venice had issued a decree that limited the ability of Dutch and English ships to take on cargo from Venice,[56] which acted to divert trade elsewhere in the Mediterranean, particularly toward Leghorn, which as a consequence became 'probably the most important European port in the Mediterranean', followed by Marseille after 1715.[57] Hence, whilst the shipping of Venice and Genoa was in decline, other actors in the Mediterranean – the Greeks, Ottomans, Tuscans and French – were filling the gap. In the words of Greene, '[t]he northern Europeans, then, were just one group among many in the complex of commercial activity in the seventeenth century. They were not in a position to impose their will on the market-place; nor was anyone else'.[58]

Even if we accept that northern ships were replacing those of Mediterranean providers (in long distance trade in particular), from the point of view of an economist this provided an opportunity that the Mediterranean could exploit, and does not deserve to be interpreted as a failing of the region. The Genoese were in fact quick to recognize and respond to the opportunities open to them, shifting increasingly into organizing and financing shipping, rather than doing the shipping themselves.[59] Where northern ships proved less adept was in organizing and financing their trade in the Mediterranean, an area in which the Italians were expert. Given their experience in the Mediterranean shipping business, the Genoese (and Venetians) were therefore able to carve out a niche. Just because the ships that were carrying goods were increasingly from the north did not mean that the Mediterranean was not - in some discreet and more sophisticated way - very much involved. Furthermore, this advantage over bigger northern ships meant that the Venetian shipping industry managed to maintain a very respectable market share, even if it was in decline. In 1775, 4,000 of the 4,421 ships visiting Leghorn and Trieste were Venetian.[60] Whilst the Italian ships were smaller, this is still remarkable.

(iv) Finance

Italian cities were the pioneers of banking in Europe, providing financial services across the continent through networks such as the Medici.[61] The global discoveries presented additional opportunities. Through its connections to Habsburg Spain, Genoa was given the responsibility of administering the flows of silver between Seville and Spain's two outposts in Europe, Milan and Antwerp.[62] Between 1557, when the privilege was granted, and the middle of the seventeenth century, Genoa's position as a financial centre thereby received a distinct boost. Genoa shifted out of shipping and increasingly into finance, further evidence of specialization in the Mediterranean in response to the new global opportunities. Rather than being at odds, the Atlantic and the Mediterranean were in this way complements: the Italians provided the banking and financial services necessary to build the Atlantic economy, and the trade in the Atlantic created a demand for this Italian service. As one would expect, as the north-west advanced, it developed its own financial sector, which meant that Genoa faced growing competition from Amsterdam. However, despite the competition and despite a number of bankruptcies of the Spanish crown, to whom Genoa were the major lenders, Genoa maintained its position as a provider of financial services in the Mediterranean, including financing Marseille's increasing trade in the Levant.[63]

(v) Spice Trade

Until the oceanic discoveries of the late fifteenth and early sixteenth centuries, the spice trade was almost wholly in Venetian hands, allowing Venetian merchants to sell spices at monopoly prices to European elites.[64] Whilst the initial maritime voyages to the east (led by Vasco de Gamo) did relatively little harm to this trade, the later voyages of the Dutch had a much greater effect, diverting spices away from the overland spice route through the eastern Mediterranean and so out of the hands of the Venetians.[65] Evidence of increasing competition in the spice trade can be found in the reduction in the relative prices charged to European consumers for a number of spices, as recently examined by O'Rourke and Williamson.[66] The inevitable decline in spices passing through the Mediterranean was temporarily postponed as a result of Genoa's control over the flows of precious metals emanating from Spain's Atlantic discoveries. The great appetite for silver in Ming China and the Indian Ocean facilitated a revival of spice flows through the Mediterranean. Nevertheless, it was clear that with greater competition and lower profits in the spice market, Venice needed to adjust. New products suitable for western markets were therefore sourced, including silk, coffee, drugs and, later, cotton, helping to fill the void.[67] Where Venice lost market share in these new areas, it tended to be at the hands of another Mediterranean port that had growing relations with the Ottoman world in the seventeenth and eighteenth century, Marseille.[68]

In summary, the new forces acting on the Mediterranean in the early modern period, and their effects on the various sectors of the economy, should not necessarily be interpreted as causing a loss of unity on the part of the Mediterranean. Our evidence suggests that the Mediterranean was not being 'cut off' by the opening of the Atlantic and maritime connections to the east. Changes in agriculture, manufacturing and commerce, including the increased presence of Baltic grain, manufactured goods and northern ships should not be instantly interpreted as evidence that north-western markets had developed to a level beyond those of the Mediterranean. Mediterranean merchants had operated in the north for centuries, and it was only inevitable that they would start to do the reverse as they caught up. In fact, the Mediterranean adapted to the situation by specializing in what it was best at, successfully specializing in the cultivation of vines and olive trees, high end luxury manufactures, the provision of finance, and the transit trade in coffee, silk and cotton. Where the Mediterranean did not resist competition, they adapted in exactly the way that an economist would predict, to the benefit of themselves and the rest of Europe, including the new Atlantic trade.

Markets in the Mediterranean and the North-west: A Formal Comparison

Given that the traditional image of Mediterranean disintegration can be questioned, there is good reason to formally examine the relative level of market development in the Mediterranean compared with north-west region. In what follows, this will be carried out by making use of the panel of market estimates discussed in Chapter 2, but rather than looking through the lens of individual countries, we will instead look through the lens of the two regions. Looking at price gaps, volatility and speeds of adjustment in the wheat market, we will examine markets within each of the regions and between each of the regions and wider Europe.

Our investigation begins with the evidence provided by the wheat price gaps. Figure 3.1 shows the average price gap within each of the two regions, which includes twenty-one cities within the Mediterranean and twelve within the north-west.[69]

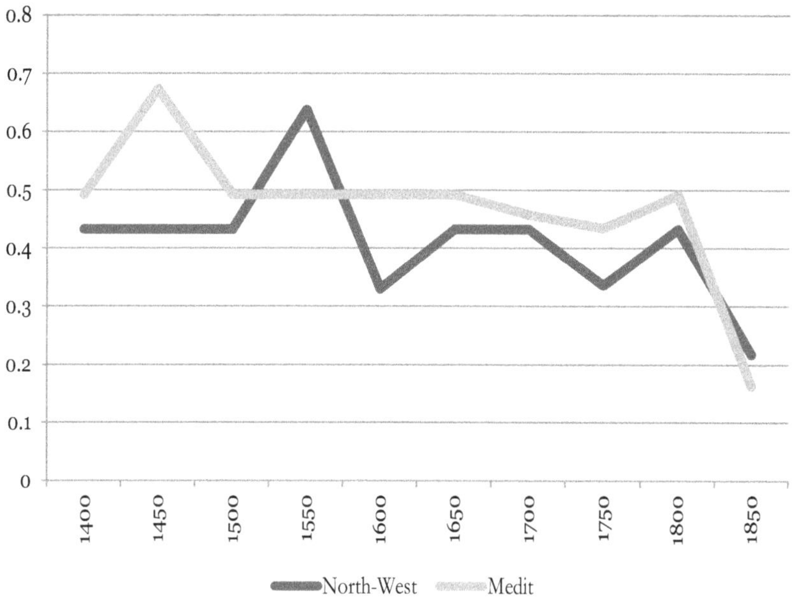

Figure 3.1: Price gaps – Mediterranean versus north-west.

In the Mediterranean, there was a clear adverse shock affecting markets in the late fifteenth century (the time of Ottoman expansion), after which markets recover and look reasonably stable until the rapid falls in price gaps in the nineteenth century. There is certainly no sign of an early modern market disruption or dislocation of the form envisioned by much of the historical literature.

In the north-west, markets also see a temporary setback, but this time in the late sixteenth century, which could be explained by the impact of the fight for independence in the Low Countries on markets in the area. It is worth noting that if we were to compare the late sixteenth century with the eighteenth century, as is usual in the literature, it would look as though north-western markets were witnessing significant improvement. However, comparing the fifteenth with the eighteenth and early nineteenth centuries suggests a very different story, one which is consistent with the notion of well-developed markets earlier on in history. As the chart reveals, the most significant improvement in integration actually arrives after the beginning of modern economic growth, in the nineteenth century, rather than beforehand.

Aside from illuminating the trends in each of the two regions, the figure also allows us to compare the level of market development in the two regions. Before the nineteenth century, the average price gap between cities in the Mediterranean was around 49 per cent and for cities in the north-west, it was 43 per cent.[70] Given that the north-western cities are generally closer together, this suggests that markets in each region were similarly well developed.

In order to see how well integrated each region was with the rest of Europe, we can look at the average price gap between each city and the other European cities. As we saw in the previous chapter, in 1400 all of the north-western and Mediterranean economies had a price gap on average with the rest of Europe of 50–60 per cent. Within this range, the Mediterranean economies of Italy and Spain had the lowest gaps. The gaps in 1450–1500 were high in Italy and France, reflecting the temporary period of disintegration previously identified. In the sixteenth century, the gaps for France, Italy and Spain were on a par with those of England, although were not as low as those for the Low Countries. However, by the start of the eighteenth century, this temporary gap had closed. Hence, on the eve of the Industrial Revolution, there was no noticeable difference in terms of the degree of integration with wider Europe of the group of Mediterranean and the group of north-western economies. Not only was integration within the two regions at a similar level, but integration between each of the regions and Europe more generally was also equally matched.

The second measure of market development, volatility, also suggests that the two regions were reasonably well matched. The average coefficient of variation for the Mediterranean cities (using annual data) is 0.27 in 1300–1550, falling to 0.16 by 1750–99. For the north-western economies, the values are in general slightly higher. Even if we restrict the north-western data to the cities in England and Holland, the CV is only slightly lower than the Mediterranean level, at 0.25 in 1300–1550, and actually higher than the Mediterranean value in 1650–1799. Only in the latter half of the nineteenth century does the CV in the north-west fall significantly below that in the Mediterranean. Table 3.1 reports the comparisons.

Table 3.1: Coefficients of Variation (annual data) – Mediterranean versus north-west.

	Med	NW
1300–49	0.27	0.30
1350–99	0.27	0.24
1400–49	0.27	0.26
1450–99	0.27	0.30
1500–49	0.27	0.26
1550–99	0.23	0.25
1600–49	0.20	0.20
1650–99	0.20	0.25
1700–49	0.19	0.24
1750–99	0.16	0.17
1800–49	0.27	0.23
1850–99	0.27	0.15

The speed of adjustment is our final measure of market integration. This is best calculated using the high frequency monthly price data, which captures seasonal price fluctuations. In order to compare markets within each of the two regions, we consider the speeds of adjustment between all of the north-western cities (Antwerp, Brussels, Ruremonde, London and Utrecht) and the speeds of adjustment between the Mediterranean cities (Pisa, Toulouse and Sienna). The average speed of adjustment for each of these groups (after distance adjusting) is presented in Figure 3.2.[71]

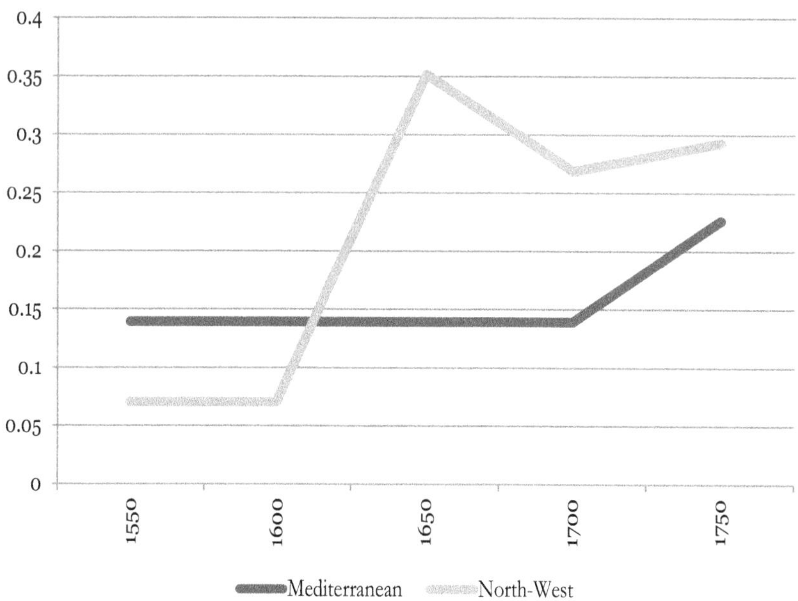

Figure 3.2: Speeds of adjustment – Mediterranean versus north-west.

Initially, the Mediterranean has the highest speed of adjustment, at 0.14 compared with 0.07 in the north-west. This value for the north-west is, however, likely to be a temporary low point (in light of the price gap findings, which suggest that the latter half of the sixteenth century was a temporarily bad time for markets in the region). Moving ahead in time, we find that the north-west is ahead of the Mediterranean in the latter half of the seventeenth century. In the eighteenth century, the Mediterranean starts to catch up, but still does not achieve the rapidity of price adjustment seen in the north-west. Hence, whilst in terms of price gaps and volatility markets within the Mediterranean are on a par with the north-west, in terms of short run price adjustment they were behind.

We can also use speeds of adjustment to compare the level of integration of each region with wider Europe. The Appendix to Chapter 2 provided the average speed of adjustment between each of the cities and the rest of Europe. Taking an average of the cities in the north-west, we arrive at a speed of 0.19 in 1750–99. For the Mediterranean cities, the value was almost exactly identical at 0.20 respectively. On this basis, and as with the wheat price gaps, it appears that the north-west region was no better integrated with the rest of Europe than was the Mediterranean on the eve of the Industrial Revolution.

Summary

After centuries of preeminence, the early modern period gave birth to the eclipse of the Mediterranean economy by the north-west; a shift in the axis of economic fortune which persists to the present day. In terms of explaining this shift, the existing literature has a rather major defect: whilst it investigates markets in the north-west, no effort has been made to compare markets in the two regions. As historians well know, cross-country and cross-region comparisons are necessary to sort through consistent and inconsistent explanations, and when searching for explanations of growth, a comparison of the north-west and Mediterranean regions is particularly relevant. Given the increasing presence of the north-west in Mediterranean markets together with the theme of disintegration that runs through the literature on the early modern Mediterranean, the existing literature could be forgiven. However, this chapter has argued that the theme of Mediterranean disintegration deserves to be revised. As our qualitative and quantitative evidence suggest, Mediterranean markets did not disintegrate. Furthermore, their level of integration was in many ways surprisingly similar to that of the north-west. The Mediterranean was as well integrated with wider Europe as was the north-west. In terms of the development of markets within each region, only one of our three measures places the north-west ahead, whilst the other two suggest they are reasonably equal. Hence, it seems highly questionable whether the development of markets is enough to explain why the Industrial Revolution occurred in the north-west and not in the Mediterranean. If markets are in any way important, then the focus should be placed not on international market connections but on markets at home.

4 EARLY MODERN MARKET INTEGRATION IN A LONGER RUN PERSPECTIVE

Were market foundations significantly stronger in Europe on the eve of the Industrial Revolution than ever before? Until recently, the answer was a definitive yes. However, evidence of the existence of markets from as far back as ancient times now forces us to think more carefully about this question. Clearly, the very existence of markets does not rule out the possibility that they achieved a higher level of development in the seventeenth and eighteenth centuries, but we can no longer afford to assume that the greatest strides were taken in this period on the run up to the Industrial Revolution, as opposed to earlier and later. In order to provide a picture of the evolution of markets across the long run of history, this chapter looks to the formal measurement of market development in Europe across the long span of history, thereby allowing us to see the early modern period in much greater perspective.

The chapter begins by considering the new and exciting literature which has attempted to measure the extent of market development between Ancient times and the end of the medieval age, in an effort to gauge the extent of improvement early on in history. Using the market estimates which formed the basis of the previous two chapters, this chapter then goes on to measure the overall extent of market improvement between the close of the medieval era and the nineteenth century. So far we have examined markets at the level of the individual countries and the major regions of Europe, which revealed a degree of variety in market experience. In some cases markets were already developed early on and so showed little further improvement over time. In other cases, markets showed a clearer improvement, including those of Italy and France. In still other cases, including Belgium and Poland, markets deteriorated. What we are therefore considering is whether the cases of market advance were numerous and strong enough to cancel out cases in which markets deteriorated, leaving Europe in a better state than at the onset of the early modern era. The final section of the chapter broadens the discussion from goods markets to factor markets, surveying the recent literature on the development of land, capital and labour markets.

By the end of the chapter, we should have a more fully informed quantitative impression of market developments over time that both neatly complements and allows us to 'test' the more qualitative picture constructed in the first chapter. As is consistent with this, we will see how on average both goods and factor markets witnessed their most pronounced developments in the medieval period and in the course of the nineteenth century, either side of the period which is traditionally emphasized (the seventeenth and eighteenth centuries). This significant change in the dating of when markets developed, moving it away from the run up to the industrial Revolution, suggests that the relationship between markets and growth is much less simple than economists have in mind.

European Markets from Ancient Times to the End of the Medieval Period

How well developed were markets in the fourteenth century compared with those of Ancient times? In Chapter 1 we saw how markets disintegrated in Europe after the fall of the Classical world but then recovered in the commercial boom of medieval times. This leaves us wondering whether the commercial boom resulted in markets advancing beyond the level that existed in the ancient world. In an effort to find an answer, the inevitable problem we face is the rather limited data available before the fourteenth century. As we have seen, measuring market development generally relies on price data, by calculating price gaps, price volatility and speeds of price adjustment. Each of these measures has its own advantages and disadvantages. However, out of all three measures, volatility gives us the greatest potential to compare markets in ancient times with more recent history.[1] The reason is simple – volatility can be calculated on the basis of a single price-series, unlike price gaps and speeds, which require at least two series. Volatility is also much easier to compare across time and place than the other measures as it does not require adjustments to be made for differences in quality or distance between locations.

Volatility comparisons between the Ancient world and medieval Europe have recently been conducted by Péter Földvári, Bas van Leeuwen, Jan Luiten van Zanden and also by the present author.[2] Naturally, when making comparisons across very distant time periods, the results need to be taken with a pinch of salt and should not in any way be seen as precise. Nevertheless, they do at least allow us to gauge whether markets were significantly different in the two periods. Bateman finds that the coefficients of variation for grain prices in Ancient Babylonia was around 0.48 which compares with values for the period between 1200 and 1500 of 0.24 in England, 0.27 in Antwerp and 0.31 in Vienna. This suggests that volatility in the ancient world was around double that of medieval Europe. Estimating volatility using the more sophisticated GARCH techniques borrowed from empirical finance suggests that volatility was about three times as high in ancient Babylonia. Hence, the implication seems to be that markets were significantly more advanced by the start of the early modern period, possibly up to two or three times as advanced as those of Ancient Babylonia. Péter Földvári, Bas van Leeuwen and Jan Luiten van Zanden consider volatility in a number of different parts of the eastern Mediterranean and Middle East and identify a significant structural break in medieval times for the Eastern Mediterranean and in the western parts of the Middle East (such as Turkey), with no such improvement in Mecca, as a result of which much of the Middle East started to trail behind.

Taken together these studies suggest that markets had already developed a long way in Europe by the end of the medieval period. Based upon our survey in Chapter 1, a likely period of advance was during the commercial boom that began in the eleventh century and lasted to the fourteenth and fifteenth centuries. As shown by Epstein, the price data available for Douai, Florence, Milan, Saragossa, Utrecht and Exeter reveal a dramatic fall in volatility of fifty per cent or more over the course of the fourteenth and fifteenth centuries. As we will see later, this was also a period which experienced similarly dramatic improvements in capital markets, as is shown by Epstein using interest rate evidence.[3]

European Markets from the Close of the Medieval Period to the Nineteenth Century

Did markets across Europe make a further significant stride between medieval times and the onset of the Industrial Revolution? Early modern markets have been the subject of intense investigation by a number of authors.[4] Some have suggested that markets did indeed advance at this time. Persson's *Grain Markets in Europe* was one of the first to apply advanced formal measurement to the price data for a selection of cities spanning Europe as a whole, measuring speeds of adjustment and volatility on the basis of monthly price data. The results suggested that markets advanced between the seventeenth and nineteenth centuries. One of the most recent works, conducted by Chilosi, Murphy and Studer, seems to agree. It argues that there was a decrease in the costs of trade from the late seventeenth century that resulted in improvements in market efficiency in the eighteenth century. Regional markets in particular were experiencing integration. On this basis they suggest that Smithian growth is 'plausible as an explanation of the industrial revolution'.[5]

However, as we discussed in Chapter 2, the problem with many of the existing studies is that they begin their measurement of markets relatively late on in the early modern period. Chilosi, Murphy and Studer begin in 1620, for example. In light of the evidence of a painful seventeenth century in many parts of Europe, evidence of which became clear in our country-level market histories, such a starting point is potentially flawed, biasing the results in the direction of suggesting that markets reached significantly new heights by the end of the eighteenth century. Studies which have considered a longer period of time are relatively scarce, but express doubts about whether markets advanced in early modern times. This includes Özmucur and Pamuk, which looks at the prices for a range of goods in cities around the Mediterranean, and Bateman, which looks at wheat prices for a larger span of cities across Europe.[6]

In what follows we will help to shed more light on the question of whether and when markets improved by assimilating the large number of market estimates that underpinned the results of the last couple of chapters. The number of cities included, the use of both monthly and annual data, the number of products for which we have used data and the length of time periods adopted allow us to take a significant step on from existing studies, including the previous work of the author. For wheat prices we have a vast quantity of evidence on price convergence, volatility and speeds of market adjustment giving us three large data sets which provide market estimates at the level of a large number of cities. We could estimate the average European trend by simply calculating the mean price gap, volatility and speed of adjustment across all of these cities for successive time intervals. However, the problem is that not all cities have data for each period, which makes comparisons across time potentially problematic. For example, if cities that had always been badly integrated disappear from our data set in the last couple of periods, then our calculated averages would suddenly suggest improvement, biasing our conclusions. The way to deal with this missing data problem is to find a means of decomposing the estimated level of integration for each city (or city-pair) into two components: a component which stays constant over time (which may be affected by, for example, access to the coast) and a component that picks up any changes over time. We can then isolate the latter component in order to calculate the average trend.[7]

Beginning with the volatility estimates, Figure 4.1 shows the path of the average coefficient of variation when measured on the basis of the monthly wheat price data. The results suggest that volatility in the latter half of the sixteenth century was just over 0.2, falling to 0.16 in the years 1770–89, before returning to the higher level in the last decade of the eighteenth century. This suggests that some improvement was taking place in the eighteenth century, but that it was not sustained. To see volatility in greater perspective, we need use the coefficients of variation based on the annual price data. This data suggests that the average CV had already fallen from around 0.33 in fourteenth-century England and Italy to 0.22 by the start of the seventeenth century, after which it declined to 0.19 on average in the last half of the eighteenth century.[8] Hence, it seems that the majority of the improvement in volatility took place before 1600, rather than between 1600 and 1800. In the first half of the nineteenth century, volatility witnessed a temporary setback, as a result of which volatility was not much lower than it was in the fifteenth century, but by the latter half of the century it had fallen to 0.15, which is around half the level of that in the fourteenth century.[9] Hence, we find reductions in volatility both well before and after the Industrial Revolution.

The volatility measure of market development captures the effects of market integration from the point of view of consumers. It reflects the tendency for better developed markets to reduce fluctuations in prices, meaning that a given wage can buy a more predictable amount of goods each week. As a result, the standard of living is more stable and life is less risky. However, from the point of view of production and so raising the level of output in the economy, price convergence is arguably the most important aspect of market integration. It is through relative price changes – brought about by convergence – that economies will naturally reallocate resources in a way that raises the level of income, as was discussed in Chapter 2. If price convergence was taking place in early modern Europe, we should be able to pick it up through the annual price data, which provides a larger set of estimates (for over forty cities and so over 800 pairs of cities) than when using the monthly data. Table 4.1 shows the results of calculating the average between-country price gap for Europe 1400–1900.[10] Given that wheat constituted an important good in the early modern economy, any wheat-price convergence would in theory have had a potentially powerful effect on the economy.

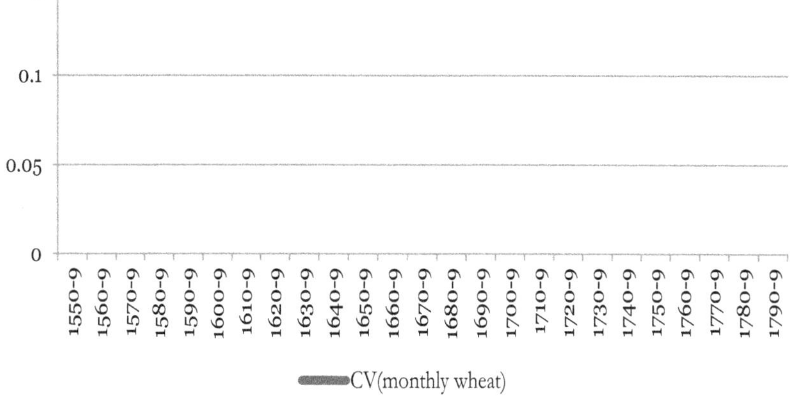

Figure 4.1: Coefficient of variation (monthly data) – long-run trend.

Table 4.1: Between-country price-gap long run trend.

	Average price-gap
1400	0.62
1450	0.62
1500	0.58
1550	0.62
1600	0.53
1650	0.57
1700	0.46
1750	0.50
1800	0.45
1850	0.04

The results reveal a reduction in the price gap in the centuries before the Industrial Revolution. However, most of this decline occured by 1600. The price gap fell from 62 per cent in the fifteenth century to 53 per cent by the early seventeenth century, a fall of almost 10 percentage points. There was then a deterioration in markets, as the price gap rose to 57 per cent in the latter half of the seventeenth century. By the end of the eighteenth century the price gap stood at 50 per cent, not much below where it was in the early seventeenth century. By far the most significant decline occured in the nineteenth century when the average gap falls to only 4 per cent.

Within countries, the results suggest only a minor improvement before the Industrial Revolution. The average within-country price gap fell from 23 per cent in the fifteenth century to 21 per cent by the late eighteenth century, with a temporary deterioration in the seventeenth century (to 26 per cent). This improvement between the start and end of the early modern period pales in comparison with the dramatic fall to only 5 per cent in the nineteenth century, most of which occured after 1850.

Taken together the within and between country price gap evidence suggests that little price convergence was in general taking place in Europe in the run up to the Industrial Revolution. Instead, and consistent with the volatility evidence, price gaps fell by much more between 1400 and 1600 and then very dramatically indeed in the nineteenth century period after the Industrial Revolution.

The final measure of market integration considers the speed at which markets adjust to shocks. If markets are becoming better developed, local prices should be responding more quickly to changes in prices occurring elsewhere in Europe. Since speeds of adjustment relate to short-run changes in prices, it is necessary to use the monthly data. Chapter 2 applied the vector error correction method to each pair of cities for which monthly data is available. On average we find that the raw speed remains stable at a value of 0.07 throughout the whole period 1550–1749, after which it rises to 0.1 in the latter half of the eighteenth century, equivalent to a half-life of just over six months.[11] However, of all the twelve cities considered, only three experienced an increase: Brussels, Pisa and Siena. For the vast majority of cities, there was no sustained improvement between the end of the sixteenth century and the late eighteenth century. This means that any increase in the average speed of adjustment was not experienced widely across Europe. Furthermore, some caution is necessary owing to the fact that the monthly data does not go as far back as the annual data, and so we cannot compare speeds in the fifteenth or early sixteenth centuries with those later in the period to see whether there was an improvement from start to end. Even if we assume that the speed did reach a new height, the improvement was dwarfed by the experience of the nineteenth century, when, as Persson calculates, adjustment speeds doubled or tripled, taking the half-life down to around three months on average.[12]

So far we have considered the market for wheat, which was the largest agricultural market in Europe, comprising around 80 per cent of calorie intake.[13] However, a limited amount of price data is available for a number of other agricultural goods, including olive oil, honey, butter and meat, allowing us to see whether the trend in the wheat market was representative of agricultural markets more generally. Examining these prices, Özmucur and Pamuk found little evidence of integration between 1500 and 1800, with the exception being olive oil.[14]

Whilst the agricultural sector was dominant in the pre-modern economy, manufactured goods were becoming increasingly important over time, and so it is also useful to investigate whether markets for these goods were becoming significantly more integrated in early modern times. Prices are available for a number of cities for soap, candles and linen. To investigate whether the markets for these goods showed signs of integration in the early modern period, we calculate the coefficient of variation across each of the sets of prices (a measure of price convergence), the results of which are displayed in Figures 4.2, 4.3 and 4.4 below.[15]

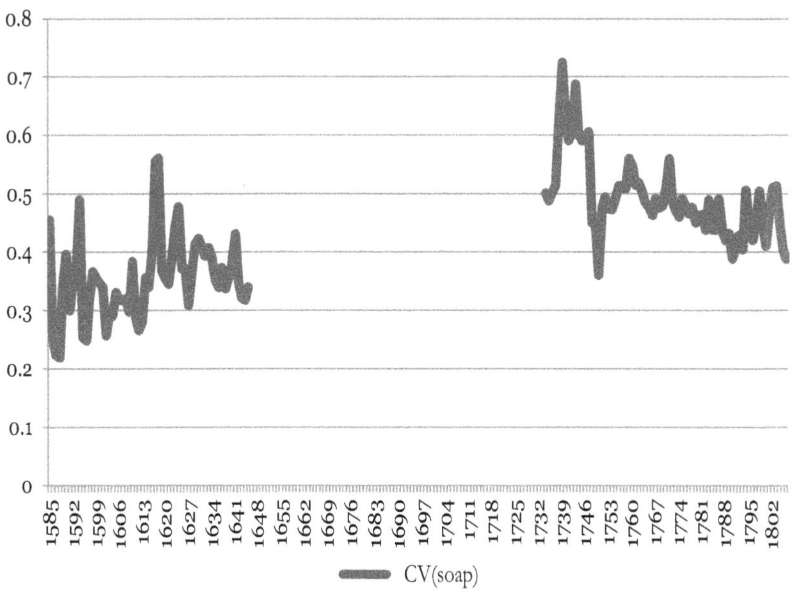

Figure 4.2: Examining price convergence for soap (London, Antwerp, Amsterdam, Vienna, Madrid and Naples).

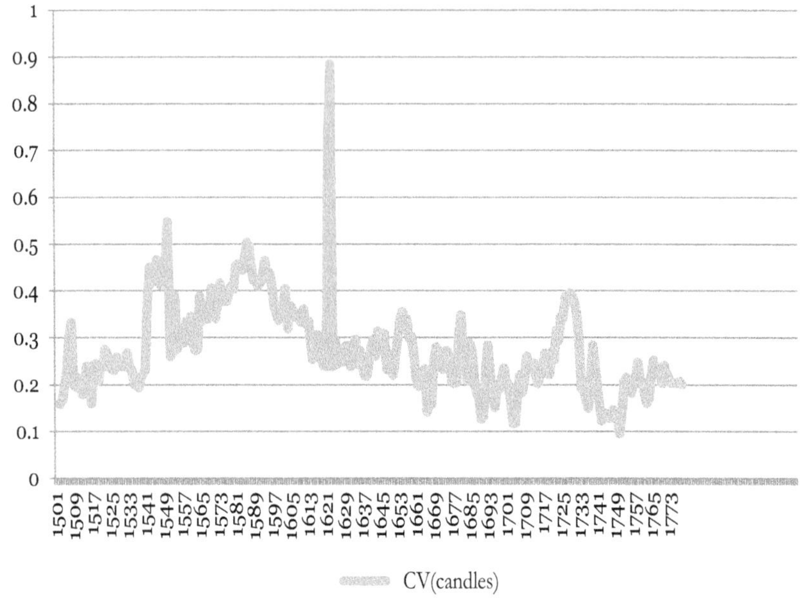

Figure 4.3: Examining price convergence for candles (London, Antwerp, Augsburg, Vienna, Madrid and Strasbourg).

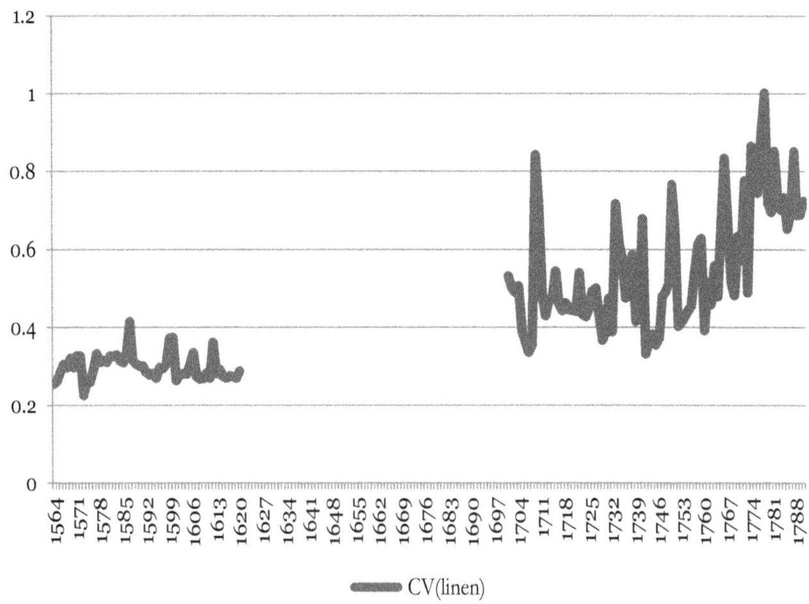

Figure 4.4: Examining price convergence for linen (London, Antwerp, Augsburg, Munich, Leipzig, Strasbourg and Florence/Milan).

For soap and candles, we find no reduction in the coefficient of variation across each respective set of prices between the start and end of the period, indicating that prices were not moving closer together over time. We also find evidence of a significant disintegration in these markets around the late sixteenth or seventeenth centuries. For linen, we find an increase in the coefficient of variation across the set of linen prices, indicating the opposite of price convergence.

In addition to the domestically produced agricultural and manufactured goods considered so far, the other types of goods on offer in Europe were those imported from the east or (following the oceanic adventures) the Atlantic. O'Rourke and Williamson have recently examined the prices of cinnamon, cloves and ginger in the different cities of Europe, which reveal that a major integration for these goods took place in the sixteenth century, suggesting that the new spice route opened up after the travels of Vasco da Gama brought a force of integration early on in the early modern period.[16] In the case of cloves, they find a convergence between Europe and Asia, but this is followed by a soaring price gap in the seventeenth and eighteenth centuries; only from the nineteenth century is convergence sustained.[17] Özmucur and Pamuk have considered the prices of sugar, which was central to the trade between Europe and the Americas. They find a convergence in prices within Europe, which also occurs in the sixteenth century, with no further convergence in the seventeenth or eighteenth centuries.[18]

Whether one looks at wheat or other goods, there is relatively little evidence of a significant improvement in goods markets in the course of the early modern period; the most significant improvements came in the medieval period, or, at the latest, in the sixteenth century, and then once again in the nineteenth century. In fact, there is evidence of a deterioration at some point in the middle of the early modern period.

European Factor Markets

Throughout this book our main focus has been on the development of markets for goods. However, markets for factors of production (land, labour and capital) are also potentially important for understanding economic growth. In the case of Europe, and as we saw in Chapter 1, Jan Luiten van Zanden and Tine de Moor have recently argued that the development of a labour market in north west Europe in medieval times provided foundations for the successful advance of the region, including by encouraging savings and an expansion of literacy.[19] The development of capital markets – which often in turn rely upon land markets given that land is a key source of collateral – could also be argued to have encouraged economic growth by facilitating greater investment, including the substitution of machinery for labour.[20] More generally, if firms are not able to acquire the land, the investment funds or the labour required for production, it is unlikely that they will be able to successfully produce goods and services. If land, labour and savings cannot make their way into the hands of those who can use them most productively, the productivity and so level of income in the economy will suffer.

The development of factor markets in Europe was far from independent of the development of goods markets; the development of goods markets affected factor markets, and vice-versa. In the Introduction we saw how, according to Adam Smith, factor markets advanced in response to goods markets, which drew labour out of subsistence farming, generated pressure for institutional changes on the land, and by encouraging the circulation of money, stimulated the development of a market for capital.[21] More recently, Allen, has argued that the development of commerce and trading centres provided incentives for change in the countryside and drew workers into urban labour markets.[22] According to economic theory, the exchange of goods between regions induces changes in factor prices which lead to a convergence of wages and rental rates, integrating factor markets. Not only did factor markets receive a boost from the development of goods markets, but the development of factor markets also helped to advance goods markets. As we saw in Chapter 2, Holland was free of the feudal system that existed elsewhere in Europe, on the basis of which labour, land and capital markets developed early on. According to Bavel, Dijkman, Kuijpers and Zuijderduijn (2011), these helped to bring about the commercialization and growing trade of the economy. Elsewhere it has been argued that the development of land markets (including through the enclosure of common land) led to the emergence of larger ('capitalist') farms which brought higher output, higher rents and an army of landless workers. In turn this provided a supply of labour for mills and factories and funds which could be either reinvested in the land or industry, helping to advance labour and capital markets.[23] By providing a source of collateral and higher streams of returns (in the form of rents), private ownership of land also supported the development of capital markets. Zuijderduijn, de Moor and van Zanden, for example, have demonstrated the wide scale use of property as collateral for loans in the fifteenth- and sixteenth-century Edam region of the Netherlands.[24] Campbell argues similarly for the period following the legal reforms of twelfth-century England.[25] Marx argued that through such channels, developments on the land and then in turn labour and capital markets ultimately explain the birth of the capitalist economy.[26]

Given the relevance of factor markets for economic growth, the measurement of factor market integration is receiving an increasing amount of attention in the literature. In this section we will survey the literature to establish where and when factor markets developed in Europe, taking land, labour and capital markets in turn. As we will see, the development of factor markets in general lagged that of goods markets, but the two periods which saw most improvement (the period before the seventeenth century and in the course of the nineteenth century) correspond neatly to the picture of goods market development that we have arrived at so far.

(i) Land

Of all of the factors of production, land was arguably the most important in the pre-modern European economy, which was dominated by the agrarian sector. For land to be put to its most productive use, property rights are commonly thought to be required. With clear and well defined rights of ownership people are able to buy, sell and rent out or lease land, with the result being that each piece of land enters into the ownership of the individual who will use it most productively (as they will be willing to pay the highest price). However, in history, feudalism and land that was held 'in common' by lords and villagers acted to limit the development of a market for land. Under such systems, rights to the land were held by multiple people, making buying and selling difficult to arrange.[27] Over time, the decline of feudalism and of communal village practices together with the development of a legal system with written title enabled more absolute and exclusive property rights in land and with it the development of a land market. According to Bavel, Italy was the first place in which land markets developed, around the time of the eleventh century.[28] North-western Europe soon followed between the twelfth and thirteenth centuries.[29] Increasingly, land was being traded on the market and being leased-out to tenants; evidence suggests that around fifty per cent of land in the Low Countries was leased out on a short-term basis, and that annual turnover of land in England and the Low Countries in the sixteenth century was comparable to that today (around 2–3 per cent).[30] Out of all these economies, England may have lagged slightly behind.[31] However, in parts of Germany, the north of France, eastern Europe and the Ottoman region, the situation was much less favourable. Here, the privatization of land and the development of a land market appears to have come much later, in the nineteenth century.[32]

(ii) Labour

In addition to land, labour provided a vital input for production in the pre-modern economy. As we know, the more productive is labour, the more the economy is able to produce. However, the productivity of labour in history was limited by slavery in Classical times and then by the feudal system and forced labour in medieval times. In each case, labour was not 'free' and so not able to choose where to work or what to produce. Since the fruits of labour did not accrue to the labourer himself, incentives to work hard and to acquire skills were blunted. With the decline of feudalism in western Europe came the potential for a labour market to develop. However, as feudalism declined, regulations on the employment and pay of labour often increased. In post-Black Death England, for example, regulations such as the Statute of Labourers and Statute of Artificers forced workers to undertake particular types of work or imposed wage restraint, and throughout Europe, guilds controlled entry into the professions (through the apprenticeship system).[33] Sticky wages, hefty skill premia and under- and unemployment point to the fact that the labour market was not free enough to reach an equilibrium at which demand equalled supply.[34]

According to de Moor and van Zanden, and as discussed in Chapter 1, labour markets in the north-west witnessed their most significant development in the century or so that followed the Black Death in the middle of the fourteenth century. They argue that the prior existence of markets in this part of Europe combined with the labour shortages created by the Black Death to increase wages and thereby drew an increasing number of people into the labour market, including, most notably, young women. Evidence suggests that by the sixteenth century, the proportion of the population in the north-west working for wages was as high as 50—60 per cent.[35] It was particularly common for young women to leave home and find work as servants on farms or in urban homes.[36] This situation resulted in a high proportion of women who were able to support themselves, which in turn gave them the freedom of choice concerning who and when to marry, leading to a higher age of marriage as each couple saved in order to set up their own independent household. The less close-knit ties with parents and grandparents that came as a result arguably led to the development of an early form of welfare state in the north-west, in which the elderly, infirm and those unable to work were provided with support from the authorities. This situation in the north-west contrasted markedly with that in the Mediterranean, where women got married at a young age, were discouraged from working (particularly as servants), and lived at home until they were married (after which it was not uncommon for them to be co-habiting with parents-in-law).[37] This would seem to suggest less involvement in the labour market in southern compared with north-western Europe. In eastern Europe (including parts of Germany) labour markets were significantly less developed than anywhere else in Europe, as they were still burdened with feudal restrictions, many of which were becoming tighter (as was discussed in Chapter 1 and as we saw in Chapter 2 in the case of Poland). In Russia, for example, feudalism was not abolished until the end of the nineteenth century.

As a means to more formally measure the development of labour markets over time, Van Zanden has made use of skill premia, which are the gaps between skilled and unskilled wages. If craftsmen are limited in their ability to monopolize labour markets and labour is freely mobile, or, in other words, if labour markets are 'integrated', then the premium that a skilled worker can command over an unskilled worker should not in the long term be significantly above that expected on the basis of differences in productivity.[38] Comparing the wages of skilled and unskilled construction workers in early modern Europe, Van Zanden finds that the skill premium was relatively high in the first half of the fourteenth century – 128 per cent in western Europe, 115 per cent in Florence and 219 per cent in

Spain. Within a century, these premia had fallen to 64 per cent, 42 per cent and 67 per cent, which, given that this is difficult to explain in terms of relative changes in productivity, could be indicative of labour markets becoming increasingly developed during this time. From 1450 to 1799, the skill premium in western Europe fell by only a small degree, to 53 per cent, indicating that the labour market had made its most significant stride in the earlier period. By contrast, in parts of eastern Europe, the skill premium was on the rise, consistent with the hypothesis that labour markets were becoming less 'free' in this part of Europe.[39]

The skill premia also allow us to compare the level of labour market development in the north-west and the Mediterranean. In Milan and Madrid, the skill premia ranged from 84–100 per cent in the years 1550–1799, which was above the levels seen in the north-west, where they ranged from 29–76 per cent over the same time period. However, there were some parts of the Mediterranean in which the skill premia were not significantly different to those of the north-west, indicating that at least parts of the Mediterranean had labour markets that, at least by this measure, were as advanced as those of the Low Countries and England. For example, the skill premia in Valencia never rose above 55 per cent in the period from 1350–1799, and the skill premia in Naples fell from 95 per cent in 1500–49 to 58 per cent in 1550–99, after which it also remained at a similar level.

In order to judge how well integrated the labour markets were between – as opposed to within – the different parts of Europe, we can look to see whether the wages received by workers were converging. We have argued that in the case of goods markets, a convergence of prices indicates that markets have become better integrated. Similarly, if labour markets are integrated, wages should converge. If the wage rate is higher in one part of Europe than another (for the same labour task), then workers should be attracted to the higher wage region, with the resultant inflow putting downward pressure on the wage, and the simultaneous outflow from the low wage region causing upward pressure on the wage, bringing the wages in the two regions into equality. However, Allen has noted that both skilled and unskilled wages in the different cities of Europe diverged rather than converged in the course of the early modern period, with wages in southern Europe falling well below those in the north-west, as we saw in Chapter 1. This suggests that labour markets were not particularly well integrated between the various parts of Europe, and particularly between the north-west and the rest of Europe.[40] In other words, labour was not able to move in sufficient quantities to prevent wages from diverging. Skilled labour certainly did migrate, and represents one of the key ways in which knowledge and techniques spread across Europe. For example, Epstein notes that in Tuscany between 1430 and 1455, 55 per cent of weavers originated from outside of the region, including from Holland, Flanders, France and Germany.[41] Frequently, skilled labour migrated in response to political turmoil (including the Huguenots from France to England, the Belgians to Holland, Germany and England following the siege of Antwerp, and from Spain to escape the Inquisition), but these flows were clearly not strong enough to bring about a convergence of the wages of skilled workers.[42] By the time we reach the nineteenth century, feudal restrictions on labour were being replaced by free labour markets in eastern Europe, and migration flows were becoming much more common both within Europe and between Europe and the 'New World'.[43] 'Many Belgians moved to France and the Netherlands, many young people from Ireland moved to England, and many Italians relocated to France and Germany.[44] Even more notably, between 1820 and the early years of the twentieth century, 50 million people left Europe for the New World, 30 million of them heading for the USA.[45] Inflows of migrants explain 32 per cent of the increase in population in the USA up to 1913. The Swedish population fell by a rather large 44 per cent as a result of such emigration (between 1871 and 1890).[46] The result was that wages started to converge between north-west and Central Europe and between all sides of the Atlantic, indicating that the labour market became significantly more integrated at this time.[47] According to O'Rourke and Williamson an explanation for this is to be found not only in the vast flows of migrants but also in the rapid integration of goods markets.[48] In other words, labour market integration came as a result of goods market integration.[49]

Altogether, the evidence with regard to the labour market indicates a significant period of development between the fourteenth and fifteenth centuries within both western and southern Europe. There is reason to believe that labour markets in the north-west were more developed than those elsewhere in Europe, although skill premia suggest that at least some parts of the Mediterranean may not have been too far behind. In eastern Europe, labour markets actually moved backwards rather than forwards between these two times. Labour markets between – as opposed to within – regions were not particularly well integrated until the nineteenth century. Hence, as is consistent with goods markets, the major periods of development occurred both well before and after the Industrial Revolution.

(iii) Capital

Capital markets serve at least three important functions in the modern day economy: the provision of a medium of exchange, credit and insurance. The development of each of these activities will be considered below.

1. The provision of a medium of exchange is vital if an economy is to evolve beyond barter, supporting the development of goods markets and specialization. Coinage is the most obvious form and, of course, the Romans are still renowned for their stable and centralized minting of coins. In medieval and early modern

Europe, the lack of a single centralized mint, due to the fragmented nature of political power, resulted in the development of the business of money-changing.

Whilst coins were useful for small local transactions, they were quite burdensome when it came to long distance (and particularly higher value) transactions. In response to the expansion of trade during the commercial boom, Italian merchants developed the 'bill of exchange', which was a written promise or, rather, obligation to pay a debtor on a future date a specified sum.[50] With this development, a merchant could, for example, buy (in pounds), issue or accept as payment a bill in London which promises to pay in Antwerp in a foreign currency six months hence, disposing of the need to transact in cash. Whilst this was a less costly means of transacting compared with carrying heavy coins, it also presented more risk in terms of potential default on the promise. This risk was minimized through the development of institutions which specialized in the settlement of bills of exchange and which were tied together across Europe through tightly knit networks. In order to maintain reputation and dealings within the network, institutions had a strong incentive to make sure that bills were settled.

The use of bills of exchange diffused throughout Europe, becoming a regular feature of the wool trade between England and the continent in the fourteenth century, and lasted through to the nineteenth century. Bills of exchange also became an accepted liquid asset. In the fourteenth century, deposit-taking banks in Italy began investing part of the deposits they received in these assets, in an effort to increase profits. This later followed in the north-west.

2. The second function of capital markets is to connect people who wish to save with people who wish to borrow. The ability for funds to flow from savers to borrowers enables firms to raise the short-term credit they need to fund the purchases of materials required for production. In medieval times, for example, credit was required to bridge the gap between sowing seeds and ultimately harvesting the crop, and at the different stages of production in the woollen cloth trade.[51] Credit was also increasingly in demand to fund longer term investments on the land, or in machinery and equipment. However, before such a system of credit could emerge, at least three significant obstacles had to be overcome. Perhaps the most basic was the lack of knowledge of the mathematical techniques required to, for example, calculate interest and present values. In 1202, Pisa's Fibonacci published a mathematical work that introduced such knowledge to Italy from the east. However, Christians were still prevented from actually paying interest, which highlights the second obstacle, usury laws. This problem was initially overcome with the help of the Jewish communities in Italy, who began lending to farmers. Whilst Christian law prohibited interest, Jewish law enabled Jews to lend to Christians, and so many of the early money lenders and merchant banks were Jewish. As Jewish communities migrated between different parts of Europe (often fleeing persecution), they took their banking practices with them,

leading to the diffusion of merchant banks across Europe. Over time, Christians found their own way around usury laws, using discounting techniques, forming what became known as 'discount houses'. Discount houses would lend by buying a bill of exchange, but at less than face value (receiving both capital and interest when the bill came due for payment). Many of these discount houses and merchant banks operated as networks, which helped to overcome a third problem, the possibility of cheating caused by 'asymmetries of information'.[52] In particular, this includes individuals who might issue bills or take on loans with no intention of repaying (which they hide from the creditor). In medieval and early modern Europe, networks developed along religious (e.g. Jewish), regional (e.g. the Lombards) or family (i.e. Medici and Rothschild) lines as a means to minimize such risks. If you belong to or are a customer of a network, there is a great reputational loss from cheating, which can affect your future income and so limits such behaviour.

With the three obstacles overcome, credit expanded in medieval Europe. As a means through which to gauge the extent to which credit markets developed at this time, a number of authors have used interest rates. In the thirteenth and early fourteenth centuries, interest rates in Europe were around 10 per cent p.a., which is similar to the level in Roman times.[53] The evidence of debt cases from the period indicates that credit 'was certainly available ... but it came at a price'.[54] Interest rates were very similar in the different parts of Europe, suggesting that capital markets were either similarly developed and/or reasonably integrated at this time. By the fifteenth century, interest rates had fallen to 5–6 per cent in Genoa, the Low Countries, England and Germany.[55] In England, the capital markets of London were now lending not only to Londoners but across the country.[56] The interest rate evidence therefore suggests that a major period of development in the capital markets occurred in medieval times, making more credit available at lower cost.[57] Chilosi and Volckart speak of an integration of European money markets in the fifteenth century.[58]

In the modern world, the everyday consumer or small business borrows from their high street bank at which they hold a deposit (or current) account, rather than from a merchant bank. This particular development came later, in the course of the early modern period. Merging deposit-taking and lending would seem natural as deposits are rarely withdrawn by all depositors at the same time, and so some of the deposits can be used to lend (at higher levels of interest) to those who want to borrow. Deposit-taking banks started to lend in the middle of the seventeenth century, with the Stockholm Bank being considered the first example of this kind. In England, the 'country banks' took on this kind of activity, expanding from a mere twelve banks in 1750 to 1100 by 1838.[59] However, few of these banks were located in areas that later went on to industrialize, which makes it difficult to argue that this development was central to the Industrial

Revolution. As Niall Ferguson points out, banks played a much less important role in Britain's industrialization than they did with those occurring later elsewhere.[60] One of the problems was that this development of 'fractional reserve banking' brought a greater risk of banking panics (involving bank runs and bankruptcies). Such banking panics became a regular feature of the economy of Europe from the seventeenth through to nineteenth centuries – including in England during the Industrial Revolution. It took some time for the state to take on the role of stabilizing the banking system, and to work out how best this could be done. Perhaps the most famous move came with the advice of Bagehot in the latter half of the nineteenth century, which was for Central Banks to take on the responsibility of acting as lender of last resort during a banking panic, lending freely, albeit at penal rates of interest. History has repeated itself in recent years when the expansion of debt and development of new (debt-packaged) financial products came with benefits at first, but then the instability and problems we are witnessing today, for which states are still working out a solution. Financial innovation will continue into the future, and with it will come a new risk from an unexpected direction, resulting in another crisis, only after which measures will be devised to prevent a recurrence. Recurrent crises followed by regulatory clampdowns are an inevitable part of the expansion of private capital markets.

Much as today, private consumers, farmers and industrialists were not the only people who were in need of credit in early modern Europe. With the emergence and development of nation states came costly wars, the funding for which was increasingly sought from the credit markets in the form of long-term bonds (state bonds which paid a fixed rate of annual interest known as a coupon). However, states were not always very good at paying the interest they owed, and some regularly declared bankruptcy (as we see in the modern world). As a result, hefty interest rates were charged. In an effort to raise funds at lower rates, the tax base was expanded, which meant that states then had a more credible commitment to servicing the coupons on the bonds, as a result of which capital markets were happy to lend at lower rates of interest. Hence, not only were interest rates falling for private individuals, as we saw earlier, but also for monarchs and governments, from 15–20 per cent in 1300 to 4–6 per cent by 1550. This reduction in interest rates suggests that a major development of state finances and capital market funding for governments took place between 1300 and 1550. The exception was England; here, the military threat was less pressing, resulting in less pressure to update fiscal and administrative systems in a way that gained the credibility necessary for the government to borrow.[61] England dramatically expanded its tax base and converged on European rates of interest for state debt between the seventeenth and eighteenth centuries. As we see in the modern day, the tax base of an economy is central to determining whether it can afford to pay its debt.

3. In addition to providing a medium of exchange and credit to both the private and public sector, capital markets also provide insurance. Insurance allows individuals to pay a specified amount on a regular basis in order to receive a pay-out should a particular incident happen (such as loss of employment, loss of life or fire), thereby allowing individuals to lower the risk to which they are exposed. Historically, marine insurance was one of the first forms of insurance to develop, as shipwrecks and piracy made shipping a risky business. Insurance allowed merchants to insure the value of their cargo onboard ships. This insurance encouraged greater participation in trade by lessening the risks. As with credit, the full-scale development of insurance required a couple of obstacles to be overcome. The first was the development of statistics, with which probabilities of events against which insurance was being sought could be calculated. The second problem facing insurers was the need for scale. If an insurance firm insures one ship, and the ship then sinks, it is likely to go bankrupt. However, if the insurance firm insures 100 ships, it is unlikely that all of them will sink, and so the premiums being received should be enough to cover any ships that do so.

The evidence suggests that the insurance industry – like the credit industry – initially developed in medieval Italy, and underwent a significant phase of development between the fourteenth and fifteenth century, when insurance premia fell from 15–20 per cent to 10 per cent.[62] In the seventeenth century, the Great Fire of London and the Navigation Acts (which stimulated English shipping) encouraged the development of an insurance industry in London, providing fire and marine insurance. The formal development of statistics together with the gathering and publication of information on life expectancy subsequently led to the development of life insurance and pensions. Scottish Widows, which initially provided insurance for the families of deceased clergymen in Scotland, was one of the first examples of its kind in Britain.[63] The development of insurance and credit positively fed back on each other: insurance provided a ready demand for liquid assets (such as bonds) in which premiums could be invested, and credit markets were happy to oblige. Since the mid-twentieth century, pension funds have also been allowed to invest their premia (or funds) in the stock market, leading to a further expansion in financial activity.

Taken together the evidence pertaining to land markets, labour markets and capital markets suggest that a major development in factor markets occurred well before the Industrial Revolution, between the fourteenth and the sixteenth century. Two fundamental historical events set the process of factor market development in motion at this time: the medieval commercial boom and the decline in feudalism, which is likely connected with the former.

With the commercial boom, trade expanded within Europe and between Europe and the east, creating a demand for new means of payment, credit and marine insurance, the result of which was a development in capital markets, as witnessed by the emergence and diffusion of bills of exchange, falling interest rates and falling insurance premia. Given the centrality of Italy in long distance trade, it is not surprising to find that Italian city-states were pioneers in the capital market; as other trading centres developed, including Antwerp, Hansa cities, Amsterdam, and later London, the finance industry spread. The last of these has managed to maintain its position as a leader in the world of finance up to the present day. Developments in capital markets did not only occur in medieval times, but continued throughout the course of the early modern period. However, such developments brought recurrent crises, which were only resolved in the nineteenth and twentieth centuries, with crises once again erupting in the present day. After developing in Europe during the medieval and early modern period, capital markets 'globalized' in the nineteenth century.

The roots of the development of land and labour markets can also be found in the medieval period, during which time feudalism declined, helping to free land and labour markets. Transactions in land markets became more frequent and an increasing proportion of the population were earning a living by working on the labour market. Evidence of a reduction in the skill premium in medieval Europe suggests that labour markets were becoming increasingly free between the fourteenth and fifteenth centuries, although an increasing premium in the east of Europe during the early modern period indicates a backward move in the east thereafter. The next major period of development in labour markets occurred in the nineteenth century, as witnessed by the convergence of wages at this time, both within Europe and in the wider Atlantic economy.

Summary

The increasing evidence of the ubiquity of markets throughout Europe's long history means that we can no longer assume that markets achieved their most significant advance in the seventeenth and eighteenth centuries, culminating in the Industrial Revolution. Given that historians tend to specialize in particular periods of history, it is difficult to bring their findings together in a way that allows us to formally track the development of markets across the long span of history. In this chapter, price data has been used in an attempt to see through the detail and pull out the path of goods market development from Antiquity to the present day. The results suggest that goods markets improved significantly between ancient times and the late medieval period, consistent with the notion of a medieval commercial boom, with a possible but smaller period of improvement – in which parts of Europe 'caught up' with the rest – between then and 1600. From that time until the nineteenth century, any improvements were relatively minor, and there are in fact signs of a disintegration followed by recovery, which may account for why some authors have found evidence of 'integration' between the seventeenth and eighteenth centuries.

The finding that markets showed little or no improvement during the seventeenth and eighteenth centuries is consistent with evidence on cross-European trade, which indicates a stabilization in the early modern Mediterranean and an initial rise followed by deterioration and recovery in the Baltic. The main element of trade that was expanding was inter-continental and not cross-European.[64] The findings are also consistent with work suggesting that total real transaction costs were no lower in the late eighteenth century than in 1600, as discussed by Bochove.[65] Indeed, on the basis of the trade and transaction costs data, it would seem a little surprising if markets had reached new heights on the run up to the Industrial Revolution.

In the nineteenth century, a second major period of market improvement occurred both in cross-European and, as shown elsewhere, inter-continental markets; in 1870, grain prices in Liverpool were 60 per cent above those in Chicago, but by 1912, the difference was less than 15 per cent.[66] Substantial integration was taking place on a global scale, driven by improvements in transport (railroads and steamships) and institutions.[67] This leaves open the possibility that markets are not only a cause but also consequence of economic growth.

The development of factor markets in Europe was closely tied to the development of goods markets. The commercial boom which saw the development of goods markets also stimulated the development of capital, labour and land markets. Increasing trade led to the emergence of bills of exchange, credit and insurance, and has also been argued to have brought about the decline of feudalism (as discussed in Chapter 1), which in turn freed labour and capital markets. The evidence suggests that a major period of development took place between the fourteenth and the sixteenth century, followed by a further period of 'integration' in the nineteenth century.

The development of both goods and factor markets in Europe therefore appears to have taken place well before the Industrial Revolution, with a further period occurring afterwards. This makes it questionable whether market improvements were enough to bring about the Industrial Revolution and initiate the sustained economic growth experienced up to the present day. After all, if they were, why didn't it occur earlier? In defence one could argue that it just took time for markets to feed through to affect growth in the economy. In the grand scheme of history, two or three hundred years might not seem like much of a time lag. In an effort to provide a final resolution, the next step is to formally juxtapose the estimates of market development with those of economic growth. This is carried out in the chapters which follow.

5 THE CAUSES OF EARLY MODERN MARKET INTEGRATION AND DISINTEGRATION

Why were English, Belgian and Dutch markets well developed early on? Why did Belgian markets subsequently disintegrate? At the same time, why did French and Italian markets improve? In an effort to answer such questions, this chapter seeks to uncover the factors affecting markets in early modern Europe. The first section considers the elements which are commonly thought to affect markets through their impact on the costs of exchange, including geography, population density and institutions. It uses the set of market estimates from the previous chapters to calculate the size and strength of the impact of each factor in turn. Using the findings, the next section goes on to explain the differences in the level of market development between the countries of early modern Europe. The chapter concludes by suggesting that market development should be thought of as a virtuous circle. Many of the factors that are commonly treated as drivers of market development are in part a result of market development, providing a positive feedback process that can help us understand how markets develop to sophisticated heights in some places but not others.

The Determinants of Market Development

When trade is costly, individuals have little incentive to use the market. They will instead obtain the means of subsistence by producing for themselves the food to feed their bellies, the shelter in which to keep safe and the clothes in which to keep warm. As a result, the benefits of specialization – and the rising income which it has the potential to bring about – fail to be realized. Hence, any factor which impacts the cost of using the market place – what economists call transaction costs – will have the potential to affect the level of market development and trade. This will principally include the costs of transport, information and insurance.

If transport costs make supplying a good to distant markets prohibitively expensive because of poorly maintained carriageways or un-navigable rivers, markets are unlikely to exist in any significant form beyond the coastal and low-lying regions. By far the cheapest way of transporting goods in history was by water. Hence, it is not surprising that we find evidence of significant trade from early on in the Mediterranean. Nevertheless, in ancient times, ships were small (holding less than one hundred metric tons) and were not capable of navigating in the 'hazardous and tempestuous' winter seas.[1] Improvements in ship design and navigational techniques took place in the medieval period, led by the Italian city-states of Genoa and Venice.[2] Further improvements were made by Dutch shipbuilders in the fifteenth and sixteenth centuries.[3] Unger and Lucassen calculate labour productivity (measured as tons/man) in ocean shipping between 1450 and 1875, and find a number of distinct stages: around 5 tons per man until towards the end of the sixteenth century, rising to 10 tons per man until the end of the eighteenth century, at which point there was a further rise to approximately 17 tons per man.[4] Von Tielhof and van Zanden argue that a major phase of increasing efficiency in shipping occurred between 1550–1620s, after which efficiency stagnated.[5] They suggest that any increase in labour productivity in shipping in the remainder of the seventeenth and eighteenth centuries was a consequence of replacing labour with capital, and so did not represent a total factor productivity improvement. As shown by Harley, further improvements in shipping took place in the nineteenth century as a direct result of applying new industrial technology (steam and metallurgy).

In comparison with using water transport, carrying goods long distances overland was prohibitively expensive unless the goods were light and valuable (such as spices). Campbell, Galloway and Murphy have calculated that the cost of transporting a quarter of grain in England *c.* 1300 was 0.24 pence per mile compared with 0.026 by river and 0.019 by sea.[6] Transport costs overland benefited from the development of the turnpike system which improved road quality and the construction of canals.[7] In Holland and England there was a dense canal network which enabled the cheap transport of goods overland. Bogart has argued that Turnpike Acts led to a lower cost road transport system in England in the eighteenth century.[8]

A reduction in transport cost will only encourage trade if information is available on market opportunities in different locations, and, in particular, on price disparities. If merchants cannot rely on reliable and fast information on the prices of goods in different regions, they will be unable to take action to ship goods from cheaper to expensive locations, meaning that markets will be unconnected. In Roman times, news took months to travel from one corner of the Mediterranean to another.[9] Markets were still able to respond, but it just took time (the speed of adjustment would not have been high). In 1319, the price of wheat in Exeter rose to 6s (above the 4s 6d per quarter elsewhere in the country) and within a few months ships arrived from eastern England and France, suggesting that information flows and arbitrage were able to take place within the space of a year in the medieval period.[10] Information costs were lowered through the publication of compendia of prices, exchange rates and insurance rates, together with the development of regular postal services. For example, from 1585, the 'prijscourant' was printed weekly in Amsterdam to provide such information.[11]

The development of marine insurance was vital for spreading the risks of trade. The Italians pioneered such insurance. In 1454, insurance cost 10 per cent for a ship travelling from Genoa to England, and 4 per cent for a ship travelling from Zeeland to London.[12] The Dutch and English economies developed their own insurance markets in the sixteenth and seventeenth centuries.[13] In early nineteenth century England, the average premium for Lloyds was around 7½ per cent.[14] Also important for lowering the risks involved in trade was the development of shared ownership ('fractional ownership'). Once again, this practice was pioneered in Italy; in thirteenth century Genoa, it was possible to purchase a 'loca' which was a share of a ship which entitled the owner to a fraction of the ship's profits. A liquid market developed for such bonds, spreading ship ownership across the population and encouraging more trading activity.[15] Such developments followed in the Dutch and English economies in the early modern era.[16] Other financial innovations which also helped to lower the costs of trade were pioneered by medieval Italians, including bills of exchange, forward contracts and the factorage system.

Altogether, the lower are the costs of uncovering information about potential consumers, of transporting goods to the customer and of insuring the goods in transit, the less costly is exchange, and so the more 'integrated' markets are likely to be. In order to explain why some economies had better developed markets, we therefore need to ask why some economies had low transport costs, improvements in transport infrastructure, and developments in insurance and communications. In other words, we need to dig beneath the 'proximate' causes of market development to identify the more fundamental or underlying determinants of transaction costs, which includes geography, population density, and institutions. In an effort to do this, the Appendix provides the results of estimating the impact of population density and various geographical and institutional variables on the level of market development using the country and city-level market estimates arrived at in the previous chapters. These will be discussed in what follows.

(i) Geography

It has become increasingly common amongst economists and economic historians to highlight the impact of geographic conditions on economic conditions, and this is nowhere more relevant than when it comes to the market.[17] Adam Smith was himself keen to point to the advantages provided by a coastal location, such as on the shores of the Mediterranean.[18] Abel (1980) and Achiles (1957) have suggested that coastal integration was achieved in Europe a century before inland integration. Using our market estimates together with data on geography, we indeed find that markets in coastal areas tended to be better developed than those inland. We find that a city located on the coast has lower price volatility and that the price gap is lower than a non-coastal city by 4 percentage-points (see Appendix Table 5.2). Elevation is a further geographical factor which is likely to have affected the costs of trade. Adam Smith recognized this when he wrote '[i]t is impossible there should be such a trade as even that of a nailer in the remote and inland parts of the Highlands of Scotland'.[19] Using modern day statistical techniques, Studer has found that lowland locations had better developed markets than highland parts of Europe.[20] Our extensive set of market estimates also suggests that higher elevation had a detrimental impact on market development. An elevation of 100 m above sea level raises the coefficient of variation of a city by around 0.01 (see Table 5.2). There is also evidence from our market estimates that the relative position of a country in Europe (east versus west and south versus north) affects the level of market development. In particular, cities located further to the east tend to have higher coefficients of variation and higher price gaps, which reflects the possibility that those countries most favoured in the early modern period (following the oceanic adventures) were located relatively closer to the Atlantic.

Our results can be used to help understand which parts of Europe had better developed markets compared with others. Perhaps the part of Europe most geographically favoured was the Netherlands. Here, the average distance to the coast was 67 km and average elevation was only 30 m. The Netherlands also benefited from proximity to the Atlantic and from an intermediate location between the Baltic and the Mediterranean. From early on, the different range of products produced in these two regions (such as wood in the north and salt in the south) made trade desirable, but sending a ship on a return journey from the Mediterranean into the Baltic (or vice-versa) took many months. It was instead more efficient for ships to meet midway and exchange goods before heading back home, or for a Dutch ship to operate in both directions. Whilst Belgium was similarly well located, average height above sea level and distance from the coast were higher than in the Netherlands. England was also well favoured by physical geography. Average distance to the cost was only 45 km. Elevation was higher than in the Netherlands, but less high (very significantly in the vast majority of cases) than many of the other countries in Europe. In comparison, Belgium and Poland had an elevation on a par with England, but were on average further from the coast (124 km and 279 km respectively). Italy benefited from its long coastline, meaning that the average distance to the coast was only 65 km, but was less favoured by its mountainous terrain (average elevation was 539 m). An intermediate location between the Middle East and western Europe was a further benefit of Italy's location, but only until the birth of the Atlantic economy. The least well favoured countries geographically are Spain and Austria.

In the former, average distance to the coast is 142 km and average elevation is 705 m, whilst in the latter it is 263 km and 899 m.

Aside from the physical geography of the land, climate is a further factor that may affect the level of market development. Over the long span of history, climate has been subject to dramatic swings. The medieval period is characterized as being a warm period (around 950–1300), after which a 'Little Ice Age' set in during 1550–1700, with a return to a warmer phase more recently.[21] Some have argued that markets may function differently in response to the poor harvests (and famines) which result from adverse climatic conditions, in part as a consequence of producers holding back their produce in anticipation of a price bubble. By contrast, others have found that markets work just as well in famines as at other times.[22] Hence, the influence of climate on the functioning of markets is open to debate. Of course, economies of the past had more pressing concerns than attempting to measure and document the state of the weather, but trees provide a natural record that scientists can tap into. By examining tree rings, we can get an idea of how favourable the weather was to the growth of plants and vegetation. Figure 5.1 shows the evolution of tree rings in Europe between 1500 and 1900.[23]

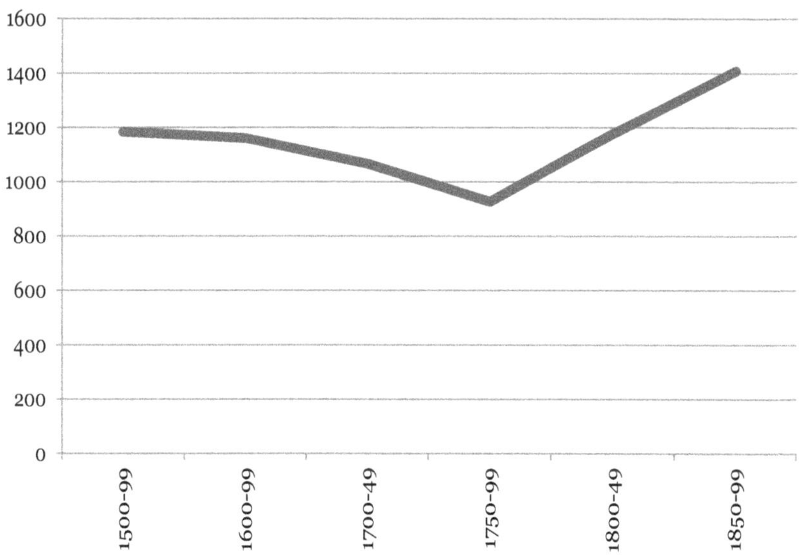

Figure 5.1: Tree ring growth in Europe, 1500–1899.

Confirming the commonly accepted picture, it is clear that the climate across most of Europe began to worsen by the sixteenth century, with tree growth reaching a low in the late eighteenth century. Thereafter, climatic conditions appear to have improved, and by the nineteenth century were better than they had been for centuries. The question is whether this had an effect on markets. To examine this, our estimates of market development are placed alongside the tree ring data from the five different tree sites for which long series of rings are available. Controlling for other factors alongside, we find that there is no relationship between the two (Table 5.1 in the Appendix). However, there are two caveats. Firstly, sufficient data is not yet available to allow us to incorporate the medieval period. This likely biases our conclusions against finding a connection between markets and climate, as we are missing out on a phase in history in which both improved alongside. Secondly, the data currently available to test the climate hypothesis cannot give us a full picture. Researchers are currently attempting to reconstruct historical climates, and this will bring more data to light in the future, on the basis of which the market-climate link can be more adequately tested.[24]

(ii) Population Density

In addition to geography, Smith argued that population density was also an important determinant of market development. Reed has developed a model in which there are economies of scale in the transactions sector, on the basis of which rising population lowers transaction costs. Insurance and information flows, for example, are both subject to significant scale economies.[25] High population also allows the fixed costs of infrastructure to be spread over more people, making it profitable to provide. Furthermore, with more potential buyers and sellers, individuals are more likely to be able to find a partner for an exchange, and as such are more likely to participate in the marketplace themselves. Their own participation then encourages others to do the same, and so the process continues, with the economy converging on an outcome in which markets are used by the majority and for the majority of activities. By contrast, if population falls, people tend to retreat from the market, which then lowers the benefits to others of remaining in the market, and the process continues until a fuller-scale retreat has taken place. Hence, for a number of reasons, population density is likely to exhibit a strong correlation with market development.

Figure 5.2 shows the evolution of population in Europe from the year 1–2000.[26] The figure reveals the collapse of population after the fall of the Roman Empire. Persson has argued that this significant fall is important for explaining the breakdown of markets after this time, resulting in convergence on a low-income equilibrium.[27] The successive recovery in population is likely to have stimulated market participation and so a recovery in markets. By AD 1300, when Europe had been experiencing a commercial boom, population was not far from triple that in AD 500. In the middle of the fourteenth century, however, population witnessed a substantial decline, only returning to the 1300 level in the latter half of the sixteenth century, after which population continued to expand to previously unseen heights.

Figure 5.2: European Population (excluding Russia, log scale), 1–2000.

When juxtaposed with evidence on population density, our market estimates confirm that markets and population density are indeed linked. We find that a rise in population density of ten people per square km lowers the coefficient of variation by around 0.02 and lowers price gaps by up to 8 percentage points (from Table 5.1 in the Appendix). We can use this estimated effect to make predictions about how market development changed over the longer run. In early modern Europe, population density was on average roughly three times that in AD 500 and not far from that in AD 1300, on the basis of which we would expect price gaps to have been around 18 percentage points lower in medieval and early modern Europe than they were in Roman times. This helps to support the view that markets reached new heights during the medieval commercial boom. We can also use our results to help explain why some parts of Europe were better integrated than others in the early modern period. Italy and Belgium had the highest population densities in the fifteenth century, and were also central to European markets. The difference in population density between Italy and France at this time is estimated to have resulted in a 10 percentage point difference in their respective between-country price gaps, which explains two thirds of the actual difference in their price gaps. Poland, which had the lowest population density, is predicted to have had a price gap that was 15 percentage points higher than Italy. Hence, in addition to geography, differences in population density between countries appear to be important when it comes to explaining differences in markets.

When interpreting the link between population density and markets a case could be made that it is better markets that lead to higher population density, rather than higher population density leading to better markets. For example, better developed markets are likely to attract more people to work in those markets, raising the level of population density. In other words, population density could be endogenous. Given this possibility, instrumental variables techniques were used to estimate the impact of population density on markets. The fact that we nevertheless found that there was still a significant link from population density to markets has an important side effect that economic development (or income) is also likely to affect markets. As economic historians know well, population density and the level of economic development were strongly linked in the past.[28] Higher levels of economic development led to higher population density as fewer people died of hunger and disease and people were able to marry sooner which (at least before the modern days of birth control) meant that more babies were born. In addition, net migration was higher where economic development was higher, as people were attracted by the associated economic opportunities. Hence, our finding that population density affected markets also tells us that economic development (or income) affected markets. In other words, that markets were better developed where the economy was better developed. This is of major importance as it tells us that any link between markets and growth cannot be straight-forwardly interpreted as markets driving growth; it opens the possibility that the sophisticated markets seen around us in the present day are a consequence as opposed to cause of growth. This is something to which we will therefore give serious attention in the next chapter.

(iii) Institutions

The final factor that we will consider as a potential driver of markets is the state of institutions. Following the seminal worth of North and Thomas, economists and economic historians have argued that the development of favourable institutions in European history led to well-developed markets and ultimately economic growth.[29] One of the most significant institutions on the rise in the period under consideration was the nation state. According to Epstein, the emergence of nation states helped to resolve the collective action problems which arose from jurisdictional fragmentation.[30] These problems included a lack of public goods provisions (such as road networks), internal tolls, uncertainty regarding the taxes and laws which were to be faced when trading outside of the local area, and multiple weights and measures (along with currencies), all of which put sand in the wheels of making transactions. Following this reasoning it can be argued that markets were well placed in Roman times, but that with the fall of the Roman Empire, and the consequent political fragmentation which took place, markets suffered. Hence, according to Epstein, it was the rise of centralized sovereign states – enforcing the rules of cooperation – that was the key driving force improving trade and markets before the nineteenth century.[31]

England had the most developed state early on and the Dutch states formed a confederation in the late sixteenth century (the Dutch Republic). Other countries like Italy and Germany were not fully developed as nation states until the nineteenth century. There is a growing literature which connects the early development of a centralized and efficient state in England to the expansion of trade. O'Brien and Duran emphasize the ways in which the Royal Navy created positive spillover effects which aided the wider trade on the English economy. The establishment of the Navy by the state led to investments in warships, which encouraged technological innovations in ship design, improvements in navigation and organizational capacity, the ability to protect commercial fleets, investments in port infrastructure and the development of specialized manpower for the manning and construction of ships.[32] Within a few years England's financial sector (including insurance) was blossoming and England's merchant marine grew from 340,000 tons of ship to 1,200,000 tons between 1686 and 1790.[33] As Rodger writes, 'British sea power benefited essentially from a breadth and depth of public support which had no equivalent in any other naval power'.[34]

For a state to be most effective in spending on the goods useful for trade (whether roads or a Navy), it needed to be able to raise funds. Dincecco argues that the centralization of the fiscal system enabled greater tax raising power, and so was an important part of this story. He provides a measure of 'fiscal fragmentation' which we can use to test the idea that the centralization of fiscal power resulted in higher levels of market development. According to this measure, England was fiscally centralized from when our data begins (in 1400), whilst many other economies were not fiscally centralized until the nineteenth century (in part a consequence of the modernization of institutions brought about under Napoleon and which continued thereafter). Using this measure, we find that a centralized state lowers price gaps by 14–19 percentage points and the coefficient of variation by 0.03 (see Table 4.2 in the Appendix).

In contrast to Epstein, North and Weingast (1989) and De Long and Schleifer (1993) have argued that the development of states had negative effects on markets and trade. They argue that states had the power to undermine property rights in the economy, and thereby discouraged markets and growth. What was therefore required was a parliament and/or constitution to limit the abuse of power. In order to test whether this was the case, we use a measure of parliamentary activity recently developed by van Zanden, Buringh and Bosker, together with the history of constitutions provided by Dincecco.[35] Using our set of market estimates alongside such measures, we indeed find evidence that parliaments and constitutions improved the level of market development. A parliament which meets regularly lowers price gaps up to by 20 percentage points (Tables

5.1 and 5.2).[36] As van Zanden et al. show, parliaments met reasonably regularly in the medieval period, but decreasingly so in the long seventeenth century. For many countries, parliaments did not again meet regularly until the nineteenth century. This could therefore help to explain the reduction in integration around the time of the seventeenth century.

Taking together the work of Epstein and others there seems little doubt that the rise of a state – if accompanied by a constitution – would have a favourable impact on the level of market development within an economy. However, the impact on integration between countries is more open to debate given that between the sixteenth and late eighteenth centuries, rising European states widely adopted a series of mercantilist policies and were often at war. Mercantilist theory placed great emphasis on a favourable balance of trade as being the route to national power. This favourable balance could be achieved through two twin engines: measures designed to encourage exports, and measures to discourage imports, both of which affect the level of cross-country market integration.[37] As far as economists of the day were concerned, trade was a zero-sum game – to get a bigger slice of the pie you needed to cut into some else's share. Mercantilist policies included those of the French minister of finance (1661–83), Jean-Baptiste Colbert, who 'increased port duties on foreign vessels entering French ports and provided bounties to French shipbuilders'.[38] The Austrian version of mercantilism, Cameralism, was practiced by Emperor Leopold I between 1676 and 1710[39], and once again by Joseph II in the latter half of the eighteenth century.[40] Across the Channel in England, the Navigation Laws of 1650 and 1651 'prohibited foreign vessels from engaging in coastal trade in England and required that all goods imported from the continent of Europe be carried on either an English vessel or a vessel registered in the country of origin of the goods'. Furthermore, '[t]he Staple Act of 1663 extended the Navigation Act by requiring that all colonial exports to Europe be landed through an English port before being re-exported to Europe'.[41] The idea was to eliminate the powerful trading middleman that was the Dutch Republic and stimulate British shipping. Given that the shipping sector is subject to economies of scale (e.g. in insurance), this can be seen in terms of an infant industry argument. Of course, not all economies were 'mercantilist'. Spanish customs were low at the beginning of our period,[42] and it was only during wartime at the very end of the sixteenth and into the seventeenth century that trade (with the enemy – England, the Dutch Republic and France) was subject to serious prohibitions and licenses.[43] However, this 'free-trade' status was far from a matter of choice. Following their wartime defeats, free trade policies were forced upon Spain by her former enemies.[44] Often thought of as key outlier in the rise of mercantilism was the Dutch Republic, which (to the exclusion of the wider Dutch Empire) followed free trade.[45] Nevertheless, in the late sixteenth century, they successfully broke the back of Belgian trade by blockading the Scheldt. Hence, where it proved useful, the Dutch Republic was not against intervention.

A further way in which the growth of the nation state may have adversely affected cross-country markets was through the battles for political supremacy, which would often spill over into the military realm, resulting in significant warfare. Hence, even if the development of nation states led to an end of the kind of local princely battles that had regularly occurred between minor political realms, they did little to reduce warfare between more distant lands. Europe experienced many such wars in the early modern era of state-building, including 'The Wars of Religion' in France (1560–98), 'The Eighty Years War' in the Low Countries (1566–1648), 'The 30 Year War' (1618–48), The Anglo-Dutch wars (1652–54, 1665–67, 1672–74 and 1780–84), 'The War of the Grand Alliance' (1688–97), 'The 7 Year War' (1756–63), various wars of succession and the Napoleonic Wars. According to Findlay and O'Rourke (2002), 'progress towards greater economic integration had been periodically impeded by war'.[46] A lagged more indirect effect of war on market integration has also been proposed by Crouzet which acts through the political economy response of industries which have prospered under wartime and thereafter favour some kind of protection.[47] According to our market estimates, war had a significant impact on markets (see Appendix Table 5.1). If a country was at war for one year in four on average, it raised the coefficient of variation by around 0.04 (the average CV being 0.23).[48] As we will see later, some economies experienced the effects of war for much longer lengths of time, which had a proportionally larger impact.

A final 'institution' which affected the level of market development was the regulation of markets. Regulations included those affecting manufactured goods (working through guilds, state sponsored monopolies and quality controls) and those affecting agricultural markets (such as limitations on exports in the case of harvest failures, limits on sales to wholesalers in an effort to avoid control of the market and maximum prices). The provisioning of grain was one of the most important concerns for rulers in early modern Europe.[49] A failed harvest risked food riots, social unrest and mass starvation, and so attempts to limit such consequences were a key political concern of the day. In addition, if population was growing in face of an insufficiently progressive agriculture, prices would increase, again posing the threat of social unrest.[50] Originally, contemporaries argued that a free grain trade would not help to ease these problems, but instead 'meant high bread prices and would cause starvation'.[51] As a result, measures that regulated the price of grain, established public granaries and banned exports in times of poor harvest were commonplace in pre-modern times.[52] Britain and the Netherlands were pioneers in the elimination of regulation (which had occurred by the start of the early modern period). Other economies liberalized much later, under the influence of economists such as Boisguillbert, Bandini, Herbert and Turgot who campaigned for the liberal cause elsewhere.[53]

All of the institutions which we have considered – the state, parliament and regulation – are typically thought of as exogenous drivers of market development. However, as with population density, we cannot assume that institutions are exogenous; they may be a product of earlier market development, and are also likely to be linked with population density. In other words, where we find a strong link between institutions and markets we should not simply interpret it as informing us that institutions drive markets. With regard to parliaments, for example, Acemoglu, Johnson and Robinson have argued that Atlantic trade led to the development of a merchant class who then pushed for institutional change in the form of greater parliamentary powers.[54] It is not difficult to imagine that where markets are better developed, there will be a class of people with both the incentive and power to push for such change. In the legal history literature there is also a vein which argues that the development of the law was in part a response to changes in the economy (rather than simply vice-versa). The legal system responded to the rise of a commercial class, as has recently been argued in the case of the development of Indian contract law.[55] In his recent work *Understanding the Processes of Economic Change,* North has himself gone some way to acknowledging the endogeneity of institutions.[56] A strong case for endogeneity can also be made when it comes to regulation. Where markets were better developed, they tended to cope with crises more easily as food could be sourced from a wider area and agricultural improvement was incentivised, leading to a greater availability of food. As a result, better developed markets (such as those in England and the Dutch Republic) were less prone to regulation. Unlike parliament and regulation, the development of the state could be viewed as exogenous to markets. It is typically argued to be a response to the need to fight and fund major wars with other powers, requiring the development of a bureaucracy and a centralized fiscal system. The 'exogenous' factor of Napoleon also had a substantial effect on the development of modern states.

By way of a summary, the chart below documents the links between markets, geography, population density (or income) and institutions. Geography and the state are shown as having a one-way effect on the level of market development. Population density and institutional developments are shown to be endogenous. The result of this seemingly small change in the way we think about market development has substantial power to help us understand why some economies in history succeeded in developing markets, whilst others were less successful. An initial spark to market development (which is likely to be geographic or as a result of state formation) has the power to create positive feed back, stimulating changes in institutions and leading to higher rates of population growth, which in turn feedback to raise market development, and so the process continues; the economy is in a virtuous circle. Economies with poor geography and political fragmentation are unlikely to have significant commercial exchange, on the basis of which institutions favourable to commerce are unlikely to arise and population is unlikely to expand.

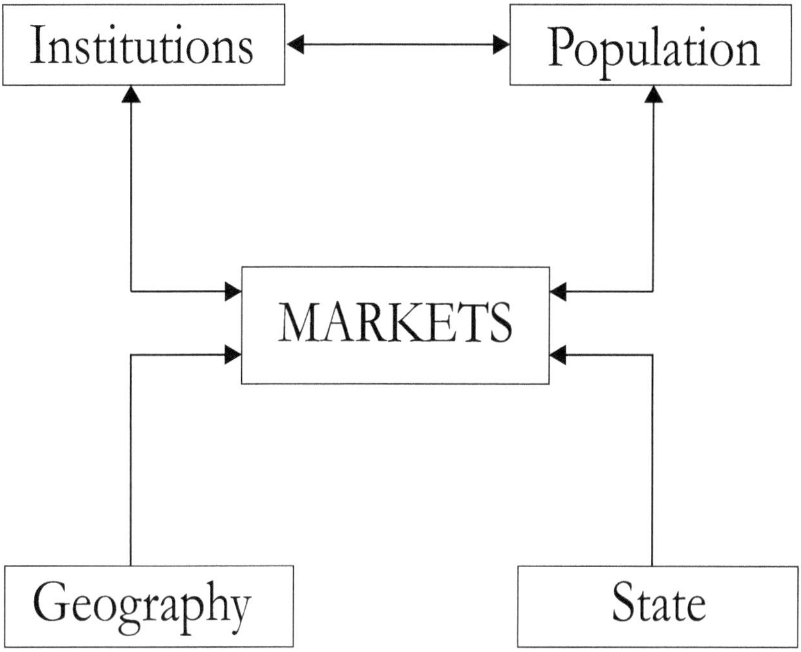

Figure 5.3: A new scheme for explaining the development of markets.

Explaining the country-level experience

Using our findings we now turn to explain some of the country-level market experience outlined in Chapter 2. We seek to explain why the north-west had a high level of market development, why Italy and France experienced market improvement over time, and why Spain had comparatively poor market experience.[57]

England

In Chapter 2 we saw how the English economy had reasonably well-developed markets internally from early on. The average domestic price gap was only 16 per cent in the fifteenth century, falling to a mere 5 per cent by the end of the eighteenth century. Over the same time period, the coefficient of variation fell from 0.25 to 0.2. England's integration with the rest of Europe also improved in the first half of the early modern period, when the between-country price gap fell from 59 per cent to a low of 39 per cent.

According to our regression results, part of the explanation for the underlying high level of market development in England compared with the rest of Europe was favourable geography: a long coastline together with reasonably low elevation compared with the mountainous parts of mainland Europe. On the basis of the latter alone, we would expect England's between country price gap to be

10 percentage points less and the coefficient of variation to be 0.03 less than for the average European economy (which was 0.23). England's island position also helped to insulate the country from the effect of wars waged on the mainland of Europe; for the average European country, wars acted to raise the CV by 0.024, which England was largely able to avoid. Another feature which created an exogenous impetus to the early development of markets was the early emergence of a centralized state. According to our estimates, this may have lowered the internal price gap by as much as 14 per cent. The commercialization that resulted from favourable geography and state development also went hand-in-hand with the existence of favourable institutions, including a high level of parliamentary activity compared with many other parts of Europe; the amount of such activity in the fifteenth century lowered England's price gap by around 7 percentage points (compared with the average early modern European economy). When the monarch acted to curtail parliamentary activity, commercial interests were on hand to re-establish the previous order, resulting in the Glorious Revolution.[58]

Rising population density over time is predicted to have further raised England's level of market development. On the basis of the change in population density, England's between-country price gap is estimated to have fallen by 17 percentage points from the fifteenth century to the early eighteenth century. However, this price gap subsequently increased in the course of the eighteenth and early nineteenth centuries. The mercantilist policy of the state together with the short-term effects of European warfare on Britain's ability to ship goods to Europe (such as during the Anglo-Dutch Wars and the Napoleonic 'Continental System') are likely responsible.

The Netherlands

Dutch markets were at a similar level of development to those of England around the time of the fifteenth century. The CV was 0.25 (or just under 0.2 if we focus on 1400–49), the domestic price gap was 20 per cent and the between-country price gap was 60 per cent. By 1600, these had fallen to 0.2, 13 per cent and 43 per cent respectively. As with England, geography supported market exchange. Few other parts of Europe were as well placed in terms of access to the sea, low elevation, an intermediate location between the Baltic and Mediterranean and a position favourable to Atlantic trade. Using our regression results (Table 5.1 of the Appendix), low elevation alone predicts that the Netherlands would have had a CV that was lower than the average European country by 0.06 (i.e. 0.17 compared with an average CV of 0.23 for Europe). This therefore goes a long way to explaining the high underlying level of market development in the Netherlands compared with other parts of Europe. Also as with England, the Netherlands had favourable institutions; regular meetings of parliament and a constitution emerged in the sixteenth century. The former can explain a 16 percentage point reduction in the price gap between the fifteenth and seventeenth centuries, which explains a large part of the reduction in the price gap during the time. Rising population density during this period is also predicted to have reduced the price gap by a similar amount. Hence, geography helps to understand the underlying high level of market development in the Netherlands, and the rise of parliament and increasing population density can explain how it further improved over time, and may very well have been in part a response to the already relatively well-developed markets.

Belgium

In Chapter 2 we saw how Belgium not only had well-developed internal markets at the start of the early modern period, but was also the centre of European exchange. The internal price gap and CV were little different to Dutch values in the first half of the fifteenth century, but the between-country price gap (at 56 per cent) was lower, indicating that Belgium was slightly ahead of England and Holland at this time. Geographically, the economy was less well placed than the Netherlands and England; the difference in elevation compared with the Netherlands added 8 per cent to Belgium's between-country price gap. However, population density was between one and a half and two times higher than elsewhere in the north-west; the difference in density compared with the Netherlands cut 15 per cent off Belgium's price gap. Netting these two effects, we can fully understand why Belgium's markets were relatively better developed in the fifteenth century.

By 1600, Belgium's between-country price gap had risen substantially (to 66 per cent), indicating that the economy became increasingly removed from European markets. According to our estimates, a large part of this can be explained by the institutional decline exogenously imposed by Spanish rule. The reduction in parliamentary activity between the sixteenth and seventeenth century is predicted to have raised the Belgian between-country price gap by 14 percentage points. Whilst population density increased, it rose by much less than in England, and the increase in wars on Belgian soil completely neutralized any positive effect on markets. Belgium's markets were pushed out of a virtuous circle and into a vicious circle.

Italy

The long coastline of Italy, together with its central location in the Mediterranean, supported the development of a number of important and vibrant trading centres from early on in history. The between-country price gap for Italy was not far from that of the north-western economies in the fifteenth century. However, internal markets appear to have been relatively less well integrated. The average internal price gap was 27 per cent in the sixteenth century and the CV for Tuscany was over 0.3. The mountainous Italian terrain – with an average height of

539 m – provides part of the explanation. The CV is predicted to have been 0.09 higher than in the Netherlands on the basis of this one geographical fact alone. Italy also lacked the kind of well-developed state that existed in England, or the cooperation between provinces that emerged in the Netherlands in the sixteenth century. Compared with England and the Netherlands, Italy also had a lower amount of parliamentary activity, and this activity only decreased between the fifteenth and seventeenth centuries. Furthermore, Italy was hard hit by war in the period 1400–1599 which added around 0.07 to the CV. Italy's relatively higher population density only partially offset these disadvantageous factors, leading to a CV of 0.33 compared with 0.25 in the fifteenth century Dutch economy.

Nevertheless, over time Italian markets witnessed improvement. By the latter half of the eighteenth century, the domestic price gap had fallen to 19 per cent and the between-country price gap had fallen to 40 per cent. However, this improvement did not come as a result of improvements in parliamentary institutions, which actually deteriorated in Italy in the course of the early modern period. Whilst on the basis of the parliamentary measure markets are predicted to have deteriorated, the reduction in jurisdictional fragmentation is likely to have improved markets. Although not captured in our measure of fiscal centralization, Epstein documents evidence of falling tolls and reduced restrictions on markets, which are likely to explain part of the market improvement.[59] A reduction in wars also cut 0.05 off the CV between the fifteenth and seventeenth centuries.

France

In terms of physical size, France was one of the largest countries of Europe. It also benefited from a coastline on the Atlantic and Mediterranean. However, vast parts of the country were both distant from the coast (with an average of 184 km) and of a high elevation (with an average of 375 m). In comparison with England, we would expect the CV to be 0.04 higher in France on account of higher elevation alone. Furthermore, parliamentary activity was not particularly high (less than a third of that in England), and only deteriorated over time. Poor geography and institutions went hand-in-hand. The result was that the domestic price gap stood firm at 24 per cent until the later eighteenth century when it fell to 18 per cent.

Despite the adverse initial conditions, French markets became more integrated over time with the rest of Europe. The between-country price gap fell from 75 per cent in the fifteenth century to 54 per cent by the sixteenth century and 40 per cent by the eighteenth century. The CV showed a similar downward trend, from 0.39 in the fifteenth century to 0.15 by the late eighteenth century. Given the lack of improvement on the institutional front, the key factors that can best explain the market improvement are the decreasing extent of military activity and the rise in population. In the fifteenth century, military activity was taking place in one out of every two years on French soil. By the next century this had fallen to just under one in three, and by the late eighteenth century to one in seven. By itself, this lowered the CV by 0.05. As with the other countries considered so far, population was also expanding, acting to further lower the CV by 0.04. Taken together these factors account for over half of the market improvement witnessed between France and Europe in the course of the early modern period.

Spain

In terms of geography, Spain and France were similarly disadvantaged, although Spain is even more mountainous. On this basis, it is unsurprising to find high internal price gaps of around 31 per cent recurring throughout the period 1400–1849. The CV for inland Madrid (which was 646 m above sea level) was 0.3, which compares with a much lower value for the coastal cities (0.14–0.15 in sixteenth century Barcelona and Valencia). Madrid's greater height above sea level can explain 0.08 of this difference, with a non-coastal location explaining another 0.02 (using the city-level regression evidence in Tables 5.1 and 5.2). Like the internal price gap, the between-country price gap (at 55 per cent) saw no sustained decrease in the period 1400–1899, reaching a temporarily higher figure of 88 per cent in 1800–49. Whilst markets benefited from a reduction in military activity between the fifteenth and eighteenth centuries, institutions deteriorated and population density increased by only a small amount compared with most other European countries. Spain appears to have been in a vicious circle in which markets were poorly developed, resulting in little pressure to maintain or improve institutions and lower rates of population growth than in the north-west.

Conclusion

This chapter has attempted to understand the causes of market development in history. Whilst falling transaction costs (including transport and insurance) are commonly held responsible, it was argued that it is necessary to uncover the fundamental factors that in turn drive these transaction costs: geography, population density and institutions. These factors were all shown to have had a significant effect on the level of market development and its evolution over time in early modern Europe. Using the results, we were able to help explain why the north-west had well-developed markets, why markets disintegrated in Belgium, why markets improved in Italy and France, and why Spain had relatively poorly developed markets.

The chapter has also suggested a new way of thinking about the evolution of markets. In the existing literature, institutions and population density are treated as exogenous to market development. Following North and Thomas, for example, it has become common to argue that the emergence of favourable institutions led to the development of markets in Europe, and that the best advice for less developed economies today is therefore to put in place 'Western' institutions.[60] Instead we have suggested that both institutions and population density should be treated as endogenous: they are likely to be affected by the level of market development and are also likely to affect each other. Not only do better institutions and higher population density lead to better developed markets, through, for example, supporting and funding improvements in transport infrastructure and enabling economies of scale in the transaction sector, but these better developed markets are in turn likely to attract more people and lead to the creation of better institutions, creating a virtuous circle. This positive feedback process can potentially help us better understand why some parts of the world have developed into sophisticated market using economies whilst others have little reliance on the market.

Geography helps us understand why some parts of Europe developed markets early on in history. It was in areas of Europe which were favoured geographically that markets received an initial boost, in turn igniting a virtuous circle of improving institutions (or protection of existing institutions), higher levels of income and greater population density, further raising market development. Well-developed markets in the Netherlands and England, and early-on in coastal areas of Belgium, Italy and Spain are easy to understand on this basis. However, with better developed states and less mountainous terrain, markets in the north-west were able to push further inland, penetrating the whole economy. Clearly, if the physical geography of a country is unfavourable, man-made transport infrastructure such as the building of canals and carriageways can act to lower transport costs, opening up the span of the market. However, it is unwise to see such improvements as falling 'like manna from the heavens'. Before the nineteenth century, they occurred in areas where markets already existed (where the expense would be justified by a ready demand), where supply-side improvements (such as the development of mines and mills) made apparent a potential and profitable need, and where supply-side improvements (such as the development of the steam engine and metallurgy) made such improvements possible technologically. Hence, it is not surprising to see that many of the transport improvements of the early modern period took place in England and the Netherlands, pushing forward the status of their markets, and not in areas in which they were geographically most needed (such as inland Spain). Countries with poor geography were stuck in a trap: where was the profit in building roads and canals if there were few merchants to use them, and where was the profit in being a merchant if there was no road and little insurance to spread risks? And, where were the merchants to instigate improvements in institutions or to protect institutions from the power of monarchs? The result was a divergence between the economies of the north-west and some other parts of Europe in the course of the early modern period. An exogenous shock was required to break into the virtuous circle experienced in the north-west, which came with the transport revolution and institutional shock of Napoleon in the nineteenth century.

Appendix

The following data has been utilized in order to explore the factors affecting market integration:

Geography:

For the country-level, average elevation, average distance to the coast, longitude and latitude came from the data work of J. L. Gallup: <www.pdx.edu/econ/jlgallup/country-geodata>. For the city-level data, longitude, latitude, elevation and a dummy for whether a city had a coastal location were taken from <www.earthtools.org>. Tree ring data was from <www.nedc.noaa.gov/paleo/treering.html>. Data was taken from five sites across Europe: Bodensee site in Baden-Wurttemberg, south Germany; Pratomagno-Bibbiena Appenine Mountains site in Italy; Siete Picos site in Spain; Fontaine Bleau site in Seine-et-Marne, France; and Ardennes Archaelogical Site in Liege, Belgium. These five sites were selected based on the time period for which tree ring records were available. For some countries sufficient length of data was not available and so it was necessary to match them to the closest site (Ardennes for England, Belgium and Netherlands and the German data for Austria and Poland).

Population Growth and Population Density:

For country-level population growth, the following were used: R. C. Allen, 'Progress and Poverty in Early Modern Europe', *Economic History Review*, 56 (2003), pp. 436–39. England's population figures were extended to 1900 using the figures in E. A. Wrigley and R. S. Schofield, *The Population History of England 1541–1871: A Reconstruction* (London: Edward Arnold, 1981). The figures for other countries were extended using C. McEvedy and R. Jones, *Atlas of World Population History* (Harmondsworth: Penguin, 1978). The size of land area for each country was used together with population to calculate population data. Land area was taken from The Economist, *Pocket World in Figures* (2009). City-level population came from P. Bairoch, J. Batou and P. Cháevre, *La Population des Villes Européennes, 800–1850: Banque de Donnâees et Analyse Sommaire des Râesultats* (Geneve: Droz, 1988).

War:

A country-level and city-level war dummy was created, taking the value of one for periods in which a city or country were subjected to military activity on their own soil. For each time period considered, the yearly dummies were then summed and divided by the total number of years in the time period. Military history came from R. E. Dupuy and T. N. Dupuy, *The Encyclopedia of Military History: From*

3500 B.C. to the Present, 2nd rev edn (London: Jane's, 1986), and M. Clodfelter, *Warfare and Armed Conflicts: A Statistical Encyclopedia of Casualty and Other Figures, 1494–2007* (Jefferson, NC: McFarland and Company, 2002).

Institutions:

For the country-level analysis, parliamentary activity data came from the data appendix of J. L. van Zanden, E. Buringh and M. Bosker, 'The Rise and Decline of European Parliaments, 1188–1789', *Economic History Review* (forthcoming) (taking an average where a country had parliaments for different regions). The data was expressed as a fraction, i.e. proportion of years in a time period that parliament met. The dates for fiscal centralization and constitutions came from M. Dincecco, 'Fiscal Centralization, Limited Government, and Public Revenues in Europe, 1650–1913', *Journal of Economic History*, 69 (2009), pp. 48–103. The variables constructed show the proportion of a time period for which a country has a constitution and fiscal centralization.

Markets:

Country-level price gaps and coefficients of variation (based on annual price data) can be found in the Appendix of Chapter 2. City-level price gaps and coefficients of variation underlay the country-level derivations, as explained in Chapter 2.

The full data files are available from the author.

Country-level Regression Results:

Table 5.1 shows the results of using a range of variables measuring population density, population growth, geography and institutions to explain the level of market development in the different countries of Europe between 1400 and 1800. As measures of market development we use the country-level average coefficient of variation (CV), which captures a combination of both within-country and between-country integration, and the between-country price gap.[61] The time periods included in the panel are 1400–99, 1500–99, 1600–99, 1700–49 and 1750–99. The panel instrumental variables estimator is used to control the potential endogeneity of population density; two instruments were chosen which affect income (and so with it population density) but which fulfil the criteria for an instrument (i.e. they do not seem to affect markets other than through their effect on population density). These were the number of academic societies relative to population in a country and factor prices interacted with a time dummy for the period from 1750 onwards. These two variables are used and described in the next chapter, and capture the Enlightenment and Factor Price views of economic growth formulated by Mokyr and Allen respectively.

Table 5.1: Country-level results, 1400–1800.

	Coefficient of Variation (annual)	Price-gap (between)
Population/land	-1658 (-1.92)*	-8163 (-3.76)**
Population growth	-2.11 (-0.56)	10.4 (1.11)
Latitude	0.019 (3.67)**	-0.0044 (-0.35)
Longitude	-0.0019 (-1.18)	0.011 (2.75)**
Elevation	0.00017 (3.19)**	-0.00052 (-3.9)**
Distance to coast	-0.00028 (-1.60)	-0.000044 (-0.10)
Tree rings	-0.000036 (-1.05)	-0.000025 (-0.29)
War	0.15 (1.98)**	-0.21 (-1.05)
Parliament	-0.026 (-0.75)	-0.20 (-2.36)**
Fiscal centralisation	-0.068 (-1.51)	0.04 (0.35)
Constitution	-0.028 (-0.81)	-0.87 (-1.00)
Constant	-0.58 (-2.73)	1.27 (2.38)**
Obs.	38	38
R-squared	0.50	0.76

T-values are provided in brackets. A single asterisk is used where a variable is significant at the 10 per cent level and a double asterisk is used where significance is 5 per cent or below.

The results show that population density and elevation significantly affect both the CV and price gap. Either latitude or longitude was also significant. The correlation between longitude and distance to the coast is 0.66, which likely explains why distance to the coast does not come out as significant in these combined regressions. In the CV regression, war was significant and fiscal centralization was not far from being significant at the 10 per cent level. The institutional variables are highly correlated (with a correlation coefficient of between 0.5 and 0.6), which may explain why they do not perform well in the regressions here. However, in the price gap regression, the parliament variable is strong enough to come out as significant, and appears to trump the effect of the other institutions on price gaps.

To envisage the size of the effect of each variable on markets (which is discussed in the text), it is helpful to have knowledge of the mean values of the variables, which are as follows: CV (0.23), latitude (49), longitude (7), elevation (365), distance to coast (155), population density (0.000033), population growth (0.0028), war (0.16), tree rings (1181), parliament (0.34), fiscal centralization (0.13), constitution (0.145).

Given the high correlations between a number of the variables, it is also useful to consider simple bivariate regressions, in which we regress markets on each explanatory factor alone.

Bivariate Regression Results:

Table 5.2 reports the bivariate regression results using panel corrected standard errors (to control for heteroskedasticity). The first three columns use country-level data to investigate whether the average market development of a country can be explained in terms of geography, institutions and population. Each regression contains between forty-two and sixty observations (depending on whether the data extend into the nineteenth century). The final two columns investigate the determinants of markets at the level of cities. Investigating markets at the level of cities has the added advantage of allowing us to increase the number of observations in each regression to around 160, introducing greater variation on the basis of which to test the significance of some of the variables. The bi-variate nature of these regressions also allows us to extend the length of time covered, as for some of the variables data is available up to the end of the nineteenth century (with the main exception being parliament).

Table 5.2: Country and city-level bivariate results.

	Country CV	Country Price-gap (between)	Country Price-gap (within)	City CV	City Price-gap
Population/land	-820	-4690	-2573	-0.000032	-0.000059
(or city pop.)	(-2.25)**	(-7.68)**	(-1.28)	(-1.15)	(-1.41)
Population growth	-3.4	-22	-4.8	0.023	-2.08
	(-1.60)	(-2.52)**	(-0.76)	(0.02)	(-0.51)
Latitude	0.0011	0.0039	-0.0013	0.0023	0.0054
	(1.08)	(1.55)	(-0.34)	(2.18)**	(1.82)*
Longitude	0.0018	0.0086	0.010	0.0014	0.0092
	(1.76)*	(3.13)**	(2.20)**	(1.17)	(5.34)**
Elevation	0.000023	-0.000044	-0.000033	0.00012	0.00013
	(1.49)	(-1.23)	(-0.46)	(3.90)**	(2.47)**
Dist. to coast	0.00013	0.0010	0.00071	-0.018	-0.036
(or coastal city)	(1.62)*	(7.36)**	(2.03)**	(-2.56)**	(-2.23)**
Tree rings	-0.000014	0.000013	-0.000062	0.000044	0.00023
	(0.53)	(0.13)	(-0.88)	(1.38)	(3.20)**
War	0.19	0.30	0.25	0.065	0.012
	(3.15)**	(2.42)**	(2.40)**	(1.24)	(0.07)
Parliament	-0.013	-0.14	-0.19		
	(-0.89)	(-2.33)**	(-4.28)**		
Fiscal centralisation	-0.021	-0.19	-0.14	0.013	-0.017
	(-1.11)	(-4.59)**	(-2.54)**	(1.15)	(-0.42)
Constitution	-0.046	-0.28	-0.14	-0.022	-0.13
	(-2.57)**	(-5.20)**	(-4.72)	(-1.71)*	(-8.28)

The geographic variables of longitude and distance to the coast (or whether a city is coastal in the case of the last two columns) appear to be most consistently linked to markets. However, elevation and latitude are also important at the level of cities. Constitution is the institutional variable that shows up most strongly across all sets of results. There is also evidence that fiscal centralization affects markets at the level of countries, as do war and population density.

6 THE CONSEQUENCES OF EARLY MODERN MARKETS: AN EXAMINATION OF THE RELATIONSHIP BETWEEN MARKETS AND ECONOMIC GROWTH

Having measured market development and understood what drives it, we are now in a position to formally test whether markets are responsible for the rich and sophisticated economy we inhabit today. Using the estimates of market development arrived at in previous chapters, including price gaps, price volatility and speeds of market adjustment, this chapter formally investigates whether economic performance at the country and city level in the period of Europe's rise between 1400 and 1900 can be explained by improving markets. Given the scarcity of historical estimates of income and growth, a range of measures of economic development are considered, including urbanization, real wages, agricultural productivity and population. The results suggest that markets were far from enough to enable sustained economic growth and that the improvements in markets taking place in the eighteenth and nineteenth century were a consequence as opposed to cause of growth. The chapter goes on to explore other factors that have been suggested by the literature, including institutions, the Enlightenment, factor prices and trade. We find that the development of the state, the Enlightenment[1] and factor prices[2] – instead of markets – were the key factors explaining the start of sustained economic growth in history.

The Relationship between Markets, Income and Growth in Europe: 1400–1850

As is strikingly shown by Maddison's historical estimates of GDP p.c., displayed in Figure 6.1, sustained economic growth is a relatively recent phenomenon.[3] Over much of history, income was relatively unchanged. With the dawn of the British Industrial Revolution, however, incomes began to rise. Initially, economic growth took time to get going. According to Feinstein, real wages rose little more than 30 per cent in total between 1781–1852,[4] whilst the work of

Harley and Crafts suggests a GDP p.c. growth rate in Britain of only 0.2 per cent p.a. 1760–1800 and 0.5 per cent p.a. 1800–30.[5] Nevertheless, significant changes were visible in economic structure and the social and political arena which indicated that a revolution was underway. Unlike any previous episodes of improvement, Malthusian constraints and vested interests failed to pull the economy backwards. Hence, as economic change diffused across the economy, economic growth increased, became sustained at a higher level and eventually spread outwards across the world – 'modern economic growth' had finally begun.

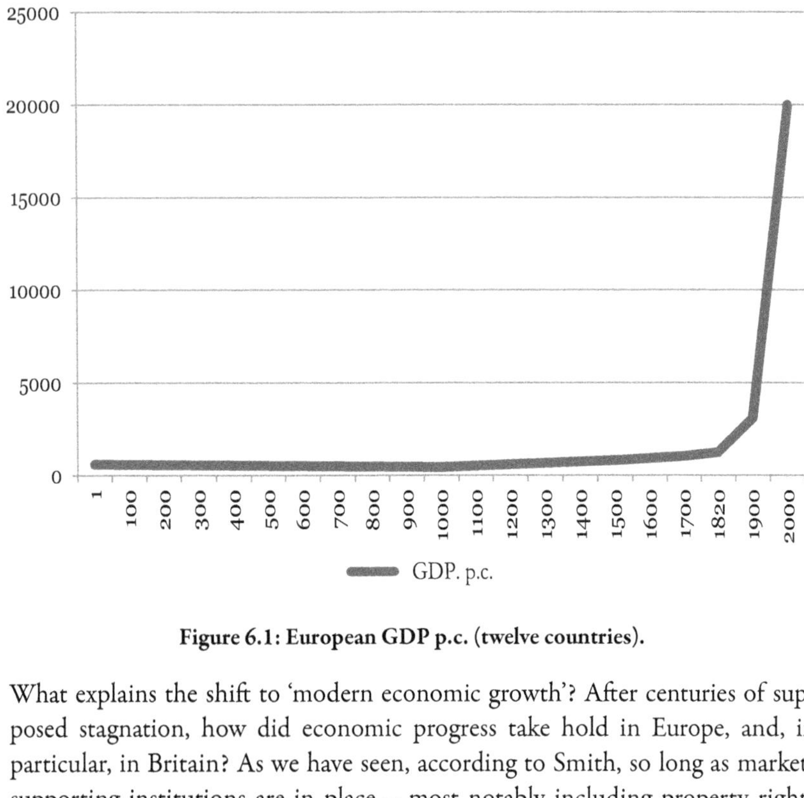

Figure 6.1: European GDP p.c. (twelve countries).

What explains the shift to 'modern economic growth'? After centuries of supposed stagnation, how did economic progress take hold in Europe, and, in particular, in Britain? As we have seen, according to Smith, so long as market-supporting institutions are in place – most notably including property rights and law and order – market exchange will naturally arise, in turn enabling economic growth. According to modern day economic theory, markets bring not only static one-off benefits in the form of a more efficient allocation of resources, factor-price convergence and a greater variety of goods, but also encourage higher rates of economic growth, allowing incomes to rise continuously year-on-year. A number of channels have been suggested: Desmet and Parente argue that larger markets raise profitability, which allows firms to invest in R&D;[6] New Growth Theory suggests that markets allow ideas to spread more easily and enable inventors to spread the fixed costs of R&D over more customers, each providing an added stimulus for invention;[7] Acemoglu, Johnson and Robinson have suggested that markets may improve institutions, which in turn stimulate investment and technological change;[8] de Vries has argued that the wider range of goods that markets make available encourage people to work harder in an effort to facilitate higher levels of consumption, and, we could suppose, invest and invent at greater rates.[9] However, as we have seen, the historical evidence raises a number of doubts. Firstly, markets have existed for much longer than sustained economic growth. Whilst economists often have in mind a transformation to market economy in the run up to the nineteenth century, we find that markets improved relatively little over this time. Many markets were as well developed at the start of the early modern period as they were at the end. If trade and markets really are enough, why didn't economic growth take off much earlier in history? Secondly, in the last chapter we found evidence to suggest that rising income has a substantial effect on markets, suggesting that the standard causality may need to be reversed. Indeed, the most significant market improvement occurred once growth was already underway, in the latter half of the nineteenth century. Thirdly, empirical work which has considered the link between economic growth and tariffs in the late nineteenth and early twentieth centuries has found relatively little support for the notion that free trade was central to growth.[10] As Chang points out, many of the now rich economies developing at this time employed tariffs and not free trade in the process of their development.[11]

In order to arrive at firmer conclusions we need to formally investigate the link between markets and growth using a quantitative approach that employs data on markets covering the long span of history. We need to place the country-level and city-level market estimates arrived at in earlier chapters alongside measures of income and economic growth in order to directly test whether there is a relationship between them. The main problem is that unlike modern day economies, economies of the past had little money and energy to put into measuring income. As a result, estimates of historical income are currently being arrived at by economic historians, but are available for only a small number of countries and are inevitably open to error. It is therefore useful to look for more concrete indicators that can be used in the process of our investigation: urbanization, real wages, population and agricultural productivity. Estimates for each of these measures have been established on the basis of more reliable data and are available for all of the countries for which we have measured markets. The correlations with the income data that is available for the early modern period are high, suggesting that this is a sensible approach to pursue: urbanization (0.5), real wage (0.68) and agricultural productivity (0.64).[12]

In addition to identifying measures of income, we also need to identify a couple of measures of economic growth. Here, the growth in each of urbanization, agricultural productivity and the real wage appear to be natural contenders. However, whilst urbanization is highly correlated with the level of income, the growth in urbanization is not highly correlated with the growth of income: the correlation is -0.11, on the basis of which this cannot be used as a measure of economic growth. The growth in agricultural productivity is a further possible indicator but has a correlation with growth of less than 0.5 and it can easily be argued that in this period, growth in incomes involved more than just rising agricultural output. In other words, such a measure would fail to capture the changes taking place in manufacturing. The growth in the real wage seems more promising as it has a reasonably high correlation with growth, at 0.55, although it does require us to assume that a more or less constant fraction of any rising incomes spilled over to workers. Real wage data is readily available to economic historians at the level of a number of European cities thanks to the work of Allen. This will prove particularly useful when placed alongside our city-level market estimates. For the country-level investigation, and given the constraints of data availability, we use one city for each country (the one for which the longest series of data is available).[13] Whilst all of the chosen cities are likely to have had wages that exceeded other towns and cities in the host country as they are large (often capital) cities, we can at least expect that their wages were correlated with the average wage in the country. In other words, that countries with a higher average wage compared with other countries will also have had higher wages (compared with other countries) in the cities for which data has been used. With this in mind, both a city- and country-level investigation of the link between markets and the real wage is pursued. In addition to using the growth in the real wage, we will also use the growth in population as a further measure of economic growth. This displays a reasonably high correlation with the growth of income at around 0.5. For economic historians, it is common to use population growth as a measure of economic growth. In history, rising incomes tended to encourage individuals to get married sooner, as they had the means to support a family unit, with the result being that more children were born. Furthermore, rising incomes lowered the mortality rate, further boosting population.

In what follows, we look at whether a relationship exists between markets and each of our measures of income and growth. We begin by looking at the level of individual countries and then move on to look at the level of individual cities.

(i) Country-level Results

Using the estimates of market development at the level of the individual countries, we find at least some initial sign of a relationship between markets and both income and growth. Table 6.1 displays the results of a battery of regressions, in which we regress each indicator of income or growth on three different market measures: the coefficient of variation (a catch-all measure); the price gap between each country and the rest of Europe (a measure of connectedness with the rest of Europe); and the price gap within each country (a measure of internal market development). The t-values are shown in brackets, as are the number of observations in each regression. If markets are the key factor at work, we would also expect to find a high R-squared, the values of which are also therefore provided in the table.[14]

Table 6.1: Country-level investigation of the link between markets and growth.

	Coefficient of variation (CV)	Between country price-gap	Within country price-gap
Measures of Income:			
Urbanisation	-57 (-3.59) R2=0.101 (N=50)	-21 (-4.89) R2=0.16 (N=53)	-18 (-2.28) R2=0.096 (N=44)
Real wage	-1.3 (-1.98) R2=0.043 (N=49)	-0.28 (-1.99) R2=0.031 (N=52)	-0.30 (-1.94) R2=0.029 (N=40)
Agricultural productivity	-0.20 (-0.34) R2=0.0017 (N=42)	-0.12 (-1.07) R2=0.0064 (N=44)	-0.07 (-0.52) R2=0.0019 (N=38)
Measures of Economic growth:			
Population growth	-0.0098 (-1.62) R2=0.034 (N=55)	-0.0044 (-2.05) R2=0.097 (N=60)	-0.00104 (-0.74) R2=0.0050 (N=44)
Real wage growth	-0.0066 (-0.63) R2=0.0103 (N=45)	-0.0055 (-1.36) R2=0.066 (N=48)	0.0043 (1.51) R2=0.069 (N=38)

Looking at the relationship between markets and the level of income, as measured through urbanization, the real wage and agricultural productivity, six out of nine cases reveal a significant relationship (shown in bold). Whilst there was no relationship between markets and agricultural productivity, we do find that countries with better markets tended to have higher wages and higher levels of urbanization. This suggests that the level of income and the level of market development were indeed likely to be related. However, following the findings of the previous chapter, we must acknowledge that any relationship between income and markets could result from the level of income affecting the level of market development, rather than the other way around. In order to control for this, or, in other words, to isolate the impact of markets on income, we can use instrumental variables techniques.[15] The results suggest that markets do not affect the real wage (or agricultural productivity), but do affect urbanization, although with an R-squared of less than 0.16 it is far from the most important factor.

Turning to the link between markets and growth (rather than income), as measured using real wage growth and population growth, we find that out of the six set of results shown in Table 6.1, only one suggests a relationship between markets and growth: countries with lower between-country price gaps tended to have higher population growth.[16] Hence, out of the six cases considered, only one suggests that growth affects markets, and even then it appears to explain very little.

(ii) City-level Results

The findings that are arrived at on the basis of the country-level evidence are also supported when we turn to the individual cities. In previous chapters, markets estimates were arrived at for over forty European cities. For all of these cities, population data is available, allowing us to test for a relationship between the size of cities, the rate of expansion of cities and the level of market development.[17] In addition to this population data, we also have data on real wages for seventeen of the cities. This greater set of data (compared with the country-level) provides us with scope for examining not only the CV and price gap measures of markets, but also the speed of market adjustment and the monthly CV, which are calculated at the city level on the basis of much more scarce data.

Table 6.2 shows the results of regressing each of the city-level indicators of income and growth on each of the measures of market development.[18]

Table 6.2: City-level investigation of the link between markets and growth.

	CV(annual)	CV(monthly)	Speed of adjustment	Price-gap
Measures of income:				
Population (42 cities)	-13	292	2505	-74
	(-0.04)	(0.75)	(2.46)	(-1.86)
	R2=0.0000	R2=0.0055	R2=0.16	R2=0.0054
	(N=168)	(N=39)	(N=35)	(N=158)
Real wage	-0.41	Insufficient obs.	Insufficient obs.	-0.04
(17 cities)	(-1.17)			(-0.56)
	R2=0.0098			R2=0.002
	(N=61)			(N=59)
Measures of economic growth:				
Population growth	0.00005	-0.026	0.027	-0.001
(42 cities)	(0.01)	(-1.81)	(1.53)	(-0.42)
	R2=0.0075	R2=0.16	R2=0.13	R2=0.01
	(N=165)	(N=37)	(N=33)	(N=156)
Real wage growth	0.016	Insufficient obs.	Insufficient obs.	-0.0007
(17 cities)	(2.66)			(-0.35)
	R2=0.077			R2=0.009
	(N=54)			(N=52)

Only two of the measures of market development display a significant relationship with a measure of income (the price-gap and speed of adjustment with population). However, the R-squareds are low and instrumental variable techniques suggest that it was city size affecting markets rather than markets affecting city size.[19] In summary, therefore, none of the set of six city-level regressions suggests that markets affected the economic performance of cities. Moving on to the question of whether markets affected growth, out of the six regressions in the bottom half of the table, two suggest that there may indeed be a link between markets and growth. One suggests that higher volatility had an adverse effect on population growth, whilst the other suggests that higher volatility may have had the opposite effect to that expected on real wage growth. However, once again, when we use instrumental variables it suggests that markets have no effect on growth.[20]

Based on the country- and city-level results, it appears difficult to argue that markets were important for explaining the variation in incomes and growth rates in Europe from 1400 to 1900, or the general increase in growth at this time. Rather than markets affecting income and growth, it was more often the case that income and growth affected markets. This is not to say that markets were not necessary for incomes to rise, but that the kinds of differences in market development exhibited in Europe between 1400 and 1900, or between for example England and France, are not capable of explaining differences in economic performance. If markets were important, they had already reached a critical point by the start of the early modern period – even in the economies with (relatively) the least developed markets. Any further improvement or difference between countries does not matter when it comes to understanding differences in economic performance. To do so, we must therefore look to other factors.

Exploring Other Factors Affecting Growth in History: Institutions, the Enlightenment, Factor Prices and Trade

Economic theory suggests that if we want to explain growth, we need to look for factors that explain technological change and investment in human and physical capital. In addition to markets, there has been no shortage of theories put forward, principally including institutions, the Enlightenment, factor prices and trade volumes. In what follows, each of these factors is briefly discussed. Alongside the set of market estimates, we investigate which best explain growth in history and, in particular, the take-off which began in England from the late eighteenth century.

'Institutions' is a word with which we are already very familiar. Good institutions are thought to include parliamentary democracy which respects the property rights of individuals and, according to some, a well-developed state system. The key way in which they are typically thought to affect growth is by lowering transaction costs and so encouraging market development. However, 'good institutions' may also encourage economic growth more directly by raising incentives for investment and technological change; or, in economist's language, by moving the private benefits of individual actions closer to social benefits.[21] Placing institutions alongside the two measures of economic growth we can examine whether countries and cities with faster growth tended to be those with better institutions. Two measures of institution are considered – whether an economy has a constitution and whether an economy has a fiscally centralized state (which may be thought of as a measure of state development). Rather than finding that constitutions were important, which is the variable traditionally emphasized, we instead find a role for fiscal centralization. Countries with a centralized fiscal system experienced population growth of 0.13 per cent p.a. higher and real wage growth of 0.15 per cent p.a. higher (on average) than ones without (see Table 6.5). Larger effects are arrived at when looking at the city-level evidence (Table 6.7).

The finding that fiscal centralization affects growth suggests that the development of centralized states aided growth in history. In the modern world, well-developed states are something which rich economies can easily take for granted. However, for many economies of the past and for many poorer economies today, power was or still is fragmented and exercised at a local level. It is easy to imagine that such a situation could be adverse to trade and markets, as fragmentation often results in different weights and measures and multiple taxation and tariff systems (not to mention frequent warfare), placing sand in the wheels of trade.[22] However, our findings suggest that poorly developed states also have a much more direct effect on the economy.[23] Given that the drivers of growth are increasing inputs (particularly through investment) and technological change, we therefore need to pin-point ways in which fragmented states may have held back investment and technology if we want to understand how states affect growth. These may include the following. Firstly, if power is held at a local level, the opportunities for corruption may be much greater than if power is held at a less familial (more anonymous) state level. Corruption gives rise to inefficiencies and diverts energies away from productive activities. Secondly, fragmentation can give rise to intermittent warfare or hostilities, meaning that resources are shifted into battle and erecting means of protection rather than into more productive use. Furthermore, the constant threat of instability is likely to disincentivize investment. Finally, fragmentation means that economies of scale in the provision of public services (such as legal systems, tax systems and bureaucracies) cannot be achieved, likely leading to a lower level of provision of such services. Furthermore, fragmentation limits the ability to raise funds to invest in such growth-generating infrastructure, as explained elsewhere by Dincecco.[24]

In Europe, England was the first economy to fiscally centralize (according to Dincecco, in 1066), and is certainly well known for having a well-developed state from early on in history. This was followed by Holland, which fiscally centralized in 1574, and formed a union with the other Dutch provinces around the same time.[25] Many other parts of Europe, such as Italy and Germany, cannot be said to have constituted well-developed states in the modern sense, and fiscal centralization did not arrive until Napoleon. If having a well-developed state created the types of advantages referred to above, then it is easy to understand why we find a strong relationship between economic growth and fiscal centralization.

In the modern world, many of the poorer parts of the world tend to be areas in which power rests at the local level with no strong state as an overseer. According to our results, this is something which limits the ability of such areas to grow.

Institutions are unlikely to be enough to fully explain the emergence of sustained growth, particularly given that England and the Dutch Republic scored well on this card from well before the Industrial Revolution. One change that did take place in Europe closer to the eve of the Industrial Revolution was the Enlightenment, which Mokyr has recently emphasized in his explanation of the Industrial Revolution.[26] According to Mokyr, the Enlightenment heralded a new – more scientific, more rational and more self-interested – way of looking at the world and it is this that explains the beginnings of growth in Europe. It is difficult to imagine that people in the past might have had a different mind-set to people today and, even if so, it is not something that economic historians have typically thought of as being crucial to understanding historical backwardness. However, Mokyr has redressed this fact, and to understand the potential power of his argument it is useful to take an example. Let us suppose that the local church roof was to collapse. Before the Enlightenment (and perhaps in some parts of the world today), the majority response to this would typically have been to think that God was unhappy with last Sunday's sermon. The reaction would therefore likely be to give a very different sermon next week and to pray for forgiveness in the meantime. After the Enlightenment, the response would instead be to question the way in which the roof had been constructed and so to try to improve engineering and construction techniques. As this example suggests, it is only when individuals hold a scientific view of the world that material progress (technological or otherwise) becomes possible. Without it, it is difficult to imagine how we could learn from our mistakes or from events around us in a way that facilitates economic improvement.

Not only did the Enlightenment make progress possible, it also made it desirable. As Mokyr discusses, before the Enlightenment, the central view of life for the majority of people was that one should accept one's position in society and behave in a way that would facilitate passage to the afterlife (which may include prayers, fasting and so on). In Mokyr's language, the aim was to be 'good' and not necessarily 'happy'. After the Enlightenment, people began to strive for improvement in the present life and in a more materialistic sense. Material fulfilment was no longer seen as completely antithetical to other goals in life. Indeed, striving to make a better life for one's children and grandchildren was something to be proud of. Hence, with the Enlightenment, progress was both possible and desirable.

In an effort to achieve the progressive goal, 'Enlightened' individuals started to work together. Nothing is more evident of this than the increasing number of societies that began to form across Europe, including geographic, meteorological, medical, scientific, agricultural and so on. Scientists shared knowledge between themselves and also began to diffuse it to the general public through the medium of publishing and public lectures. With this 'public knowledge', dots could be joined, needless repetition avoided, and connections formed between different ideas, all of which increased the knowledge base of the economy.[27] The dissemination and sharing of this knowledge helped to bring together three important parties: those with (scientific) ideas, those with the craft skills required to take an idea and build a machine which could exploit it, and entrepreneurs with a keen eye for a profit (who could see the value of using a machine). Without all three sets of people coming together through communal endeavour, even if progress is being made, it remains within the doors of the 'ivory towers' and so never has the means by which to impact the economy.

Of course, we must not forget that Adam Smith himself was an Enlightenment figure. The anti-regulation way of looking at the economy promulgated by Smith is also central to Mokyr's story. It is not enough for progress to get going; what we also need is to make sure that new technologies and new ideas that make old ones obsolete are not resisted. It was common in history that workers who were concerned about being made redundant by a new technique, or producers who felt under competition from new producers employing cheaper means of production, would lobby the authorities for policies to be enacted that would resist change. With the new Smithian laissez-faire approach to the economy, progress would no longer be held back, and so once it got going, it would continue indefinitely.

In order to test whether the Enlightenment can help explain the European growth take-off, we collect together data on the number of scientific societies that existed in each country and city in 1400, 1500, 1600, 1700, 1750, 1800 and 1850.[28] We find that growth rates are faster where more societies exist (i.e. where there is evidence of greater Enlightenment activity). A city with ten extra societies experienced higher growth rates to the tune of at least 0.3 per cent p.a (Table 6.7).[29] Now, one could of course argue that science may not only be a driver of growth, but also a consequence of growth. Higher levels of income may afford greater levels of education and R&D, resulting in scientific breakthroughs. Preliminary tests suggest that this may indeed be the case.[30] As we see in the modern world, most scientific breakthroughs occur in the rich economies, where there are sufficient funds and enough scientists to push forward the frontier of our understanding. In other words, there is a positive feedback process between science and growth, which creates a virtuous circle.

As any historian knows, the Enlightenment was something going on across Europe. It was certainly not Anglo-centric, unlike the Industrial Revolution. Indeed, many of the famous scientists or other individuals involved came from places such as France and Scotland, rather than England. Central to Mokyr's argument is therefore the view that Britain was not crucial for the Industrial

Revolution. Had Britain sunk into the Atlantic Ocean, Europe would still be where it is today in terms of its level of economic development. Mokyr argues that it was only because of a temporary advantage in terms of the number of skilled craftsmen and the very practical-focused nature of science in England (as opposed to a more abstract or academically technical nature abroad) that the Industrial Revolution got going there first.

However, according to Allen, whilst the Enlightenment was necessary, it was not sufficient.[31] Just because scientific breakthroughs occur doesn't mean that firms have an incentive to build and adopt machines which embody the new science. Scientific advances are unlikely to be put to work in the production process – generating rising output and so income – unless there is a demand for them. Where labour is cheap relative to new technologies, there will be little incentive to develop and use technologies in the real world outside of societies, institutes and universities. Hence, what mattered alongside the Enlightenment was the cost of labour relative to the cost of using technology (including the fuel required to power the technologies), known as the factor price. Allen has argued that Britain's high wage and cheap coal economy in the eighteenth century meant there was an incentive to invent and adopt labour-saving (energy-using) technologies in manufacturing, in a way that was not present in most other parts of Europe where wages were lower and where coal was less accessible. According to Allen, the high wages also acted to stimulate productivity and technical improvements in agriculture, as farmers sold their land and migrated to the cities and remaining farmers were incentivized to raise their marginal product. By the end of the nineteenth century, micro-improvements to the new technologies made them profitable at foreign factor prices, and so they diffused abroad, spreading economic growth worldwide. Allen's view is that had it not been for the peculiar factor prices in England, the technological changes of the Industrial Revolution would never have been profitable, and the Industrial Revolution would never have got off the ground. Britain was central to the Industrial Revolution.

The idea that relative factor prices may affect the incentive to *adopt* machine-based technology is difficult to dispute from a theoretical perspective. Similar conclusions were arrived at by the work of economic historians including, most notably, Habakkuk and Broadberry, and have now been extensively applied in the economic history literature.[32] To the growth theorist, this connects with the notion of 'appropriate technology' – that a technology developed in the rich economies of the west may not be suitable for use in the developing world where economic conditions are different. Hence, for poor countries catching up with rich ones it is not simply a case of copying the latter's technology, which, of course, makes development in poor economies somewhat difficult.

However, the notion that relative factor prices may affect the *rate* of technological change is altogether more challenging. According to Allen, expensive labour gives rise to the incentive for labour-saving technological change. Economies with low wages may therefore experience lower levels of technological change than economies with high wages. This contrasts with the theory that low wages enable higher levels of profit, which thereby encourage greater technological change. On balance, Mokyr's view is that factor prices are broadly neutral – he argues that so long as an economy is Enlightened, factor prices will affect the *direction* of technological change but not its rate.[33] Hence, all that matters is science. If wages are high and coal is cheap, that might place the economy on a path in which technological change tends to be machine-based in nature. However, with a different set of factor prices, technological changes would still have occurred at the same rate, they just would have taken a different (perhaps non-machine intensive) form.

If we are to form a conclusion as to whether factor prices did matter for economic growth, we need to look at whether variations in factor prices can explain the variations in economic performance for our set of European economies. Given that Allen's view is that the Enlightenment is necessary – just not sufficient – we take our measure of factor prices and multiply it by a dummy variable for the period 1750 onwards (which is when Enlightenment activity appears to have become widespread). Using our city-level data, we do not find that factor prices affected growth. However, at the level of countries, factor prices do appear to have had an effect.[34] This may be because the country-level unit of analysis is able to capture the wider spillover effects that come for the economy as a whole as a result of the incentivized technological development. Using the size of the estimated effect of factor prices on growth, we can calculate the contribution of factor prices to Britain's Industrial Revolution. On average, population growth in Britain was 1.2 per cent in the period 1800–49 compared with half that amount (0.65 per cent) in Europe on average, reflecting the fact that she was experiencing the Industrial Revolution. At the same time, the factor price in Britain was 2.2 compared with 1 on average in Europe. This suggests that Britain should have grown 0.3 percentage points faster than Europe,[35] which explains around 50 per cent of the faster growth experienced in Britain compared with the rest of Europe in the period of the Industrial Revolution between 1800–49. If we look at the general increase in Europe-wide growth from a figure close to zero (around 0.3 per cent) in the fifteenth century, to 0.65 per cent p.a. by the first half of the nineteenth century, factor prices (interacted with the Enlightenment) can also explain a large proportion of it (0.25 percentage points and so around 70 per cent of the increase in growth).

Trade, the final factor that we need to consider, is in some ways related to Allen's factor price argument. As Allen found when he constructed the real wage series, real wages in London were falling in the sixteenth century, but in the mid-seventeenth century they started to recover. He argues that the increase in trade, in part a result of mercantilist policy and the carving out of colonies, raised the demand for labour in the English port cities and so pushed up the real wage. With an increasing number of ships coming into the ports, extra labour was required to service the ships, to build and repair them, to produce clothing, ropes and anchors for onboard, and to provide insurance and retailing.

Allen is not the only author to stress the importance of trade, as we saw in Chapter 1. Others include Acemoglu, Johnson and Robinson, who stress the effect on institutions, Pomeranz who has argued that newly found access to overseas resources alleviated the Malthusian trap, and Berg, de Vries and Davis who highlight effects that worked through consumption and demand.[36] It is important to note that trade and markets are not necessarily the same thing. As O'Rourke and Williamson have pointed out, whilst market integration is to some extent correlated with trade, trade can also change as a result of supply and demand shifts that can occur for any given level of market integration.[37] Much of the increasing trade was associated with colonial and mercantilist policies, as we have seen in the case of England, which are far removed from free-trade. This means that we need to test for the impact of foreign trade separately to the impact of markets. To do so, we use Allen's measure of the trade conducted with the Americas and the East, provided at the level of our individual countries. According to the regression results, there is a strong relationship between trade and growth. However, as with markets, this could be a result of growth driving trade rather than vice-versa.[38] The results suggest that – like markets – trade is largely a consequence as opposed to cause of growth. In other words, richer economies tended to export and import more as a result.

Altogether, the literature has suggested a number of factors that may potentially help to explain the origins of modern economic growth in Europe: markets, institutions, the Enlightenment, factor prices and trade. On the basis of our empirical investigation at both the country and city levels, it can be argued that neither markets nor trade affected economic growth but were instead a consequence of such growth. The key factors driving growth were the development of the state (measured through the degree of fiscal centralization) and the scientific Enlightenment, which pushed furthest where real wages were high relative to the price of powering machines. A well-developed state and a scientific approach are both factors which we take for granted today, and so it is no wonder that it is only recently that they have been uncovered as explanations for the European growth take-off. Once fiscal centralization and the Enlightenment triggered the beginnings of growth, growth then fed back to encourage the further development of science, which then further raised incomes, placing the economy in a virtuous circle which has brought us to the present day.

Conclusion

Contrary to the view of many modern day economists, the findings of this chapter suggest that whilst markets may in some ways be necessary for growth, they are far from sufficient. The development of the state, factor prices and the Enlightenment – and not markets – gave birth to sustained economic growth. The standard causation that runs from markets to growth needs to be reconsidered; the developments in markets that occurred from 1400 onwards, including steamships, railways, finance and ICT, were in many ways a consequence rather than cause of economic expansion.

Appendix 1

The following data has been used in the course of this chapter

Income:

S. Broadberry, S. Ghosal, and E. Proto, 'Commercialisation, Factor Prices and Technological Progress in the Transition to Modern Economic Growth: History and Theory', *University of Warwick Economics Research Paper*, series number 852 (2008), Table 8.

Urbanization:

D. Acemoglu, S. Johnson and R. A. Robinson, 'The Rise of Europe: Atlantic Trade, Institutional Change and Economic Growth,' *American Economic Growth*, 95 (2005), pp. 1369–401.

Real Wages:

Building labourers welfare ratios from Allen, 'The Great Divergence in European Wages and Prices from the Middle Ages to the First World War', *Explorations in Economic History*, 38 (2001), pp. 411–47'. The cities used were as follows: London, Antwerp, Amsterdam, Paris, Madrid, Florence/Milan, Leipzig and Wurzburg (chosen to maximize the length of time which could be covered).

Agricultural Productivity:

R.C. Allen, 'Progress and Poverty in Early Modern Europe', *Economic Hisotry Review*, 56 (2003), pp. 403–43.

Population:

See Chapter 5.

Markets:

See Chapter 2.

Institutions:

See Chapter 5.

Scholarly Societies:

A record of historical societies can be found at www.scholarly-societies.org (accessed 26 July 2010 and 4 January 2012). The number of societies was found cumulatively for each country and each city involved in the investigation for 1400, 1500, 1600, 1700, 1750, 1800 and 1850.

FactorPprices:

The factor price is the nominal wage divided by the price of energy. Nominal wages were taken from Table 2 of Allen, 'The Great Divergence' and the nominal price of energy was taken from Table 4.2 of Allen, *The British Industrial Revolution*. Data was used as follows at the country level: England (London), Netherlands (Amsterdam), Belgium (Antwerp), France (Paris), Spain (Madrid), Italy (Naples), Austria (Vienna), Germany (Leipzig), Poland (Warsaw). These cities were chosen in order to obtain the longest series of data.

Trade:

Real trade figures from Allen, 'Progress and Poverty'.

Geography and War (used for instruments):

See Chapter 5.

An Empirical Investigation of the Factors which Explain Economic Growth in History:

Following the investigation conducted in the first section of this chapter, population growth and real wage growth are used as our measures of economic growth. However, in addition to considering markets, we also consider a fuller range of factors which may affect growth. These include institutions, the Enlightenment, factor prices and trade. As our measure of institutions, we use the Dincecco measures of fiscal centralization and constitution. The number of societies (per capita) in each country is used as a measure of the Enlightenment. Allen's factor price view is captured by a measure of real wages relative to energy prices. In order to incorporate his view that the Enlightenment was a necessary factor, the factor prices are multiplied by a dummy variable for the Enlightenment (which is 1 for 1750 onwards and 0 beforehand). In bivariate regressions, it has been easy to show that (with the exception of markets), each factor displays a relationship with at least one of our two measures of economic growth, the growth of population and the growth of the real wage. However, in an effort to see which factors are most powerful – which 'trump' the others – we can place them alongside each other in a growth regression model. The results of doing this at both the country and city level for the period 1500–1850 are reported below.

Country-level Results

Table 6.3 reports the results of the country-level growth regression models which include all of the key variables suggested by the literature (markets, trade, institutions, the Enlightenment and factor prices) alongside data on real wage growth and population growth. The panel corrected standard errors estimator has been used. The time periods included in the panel of countries are 1500–99, 1600–99, 1700–49, 1750–99 and 1800–49. An initial population term is included to capture any Malthusian or catch-up effects.

Table 6.3: Country-level growth regressions (P.C.S.E).

	Population growth (1400-1850)	Real wage growth (1500-1850)
Initial population density	29.5 (1.72)*	-12.44 (-0.19)
Between-country price gap	0.0045 (1.66)*	0.0033 (0.31)
Within-country price gap	-0.00090 (-0.54)	0.0057 (0.94)
Fiscal centralisation	0.00060 (0.76)	0.00058 (0.51)
Constitution	-0.00051 (-0.46)	-0.00066 (-0.33)
Society/population	0.00036 (1.88)*	0.00044 (1.54)
Enlightenment*factor prices	0.0016 (1.98)**	-0.00023 (-0.17)
Trade	0.00000013 (1.65)*	0.00000025 (1.41)
constant	-0.0011 (-0.87)	-0.0034 (-0.53)
observations	39	35
R-squared	0.60	0.23

The results suggest that the Enlightenment, factor prices, markets and trade may have a significant effect on growth. All of these factors work in the direction expected, except for the positive relationship between population growth and the between-country gap, which suggests that the better was a country's integration with the rest of Europe, the lower was their growth rate (controlling for other factors). Given that it is possible that there is a two-way relationship between growth and markets and growth and trade,[39] an instrumental variables estimator can be used to help isolate the effect of trade and markets on growth. Exogenous geographical factors are used as instruments, all of which can be shown to have a significant effect on trade and markets. This includes longitude and latitude (which pick up the proximity of an economy to the Atlantic and Mediterranean and so may be thought of as affecting trade) and average distance of a country to the coast (which can be thought of as affecting market integration in particular). A variable reflecting the extent of war is also included as this was also shown to affect markets in the previous chapter. The results are provided in Table 6.4.

Table 6.4: Country-level growth regression (I.V.).

	Population growth	Real wage growth
Initial population density	60.4 (1.37)	32.03 (0.34)
Price-gap (between)	0.012 (1.11)	0.020 (0.89)
Price-gap (domestic)	-0.0064 (-0.65)	-0.0096 (-0.45)
Fiscal centralisation	0.00083 (0.48)	0.00019 (0.05)
Constitution	0.00039 (0.26)	0.00044 (0.14)
Societies/population	0.00034 (1.05)	0.00050 (0.77)
Enlightenment*factor prices	0.0025 (1.44)	0.00079 (0.22)
Trade	-0.00000025 (-0.53)	-0.00000029 (-0.28)
constant	-0.0050 (-0.98)	-0.0099 (-0.96)
observations	39	35
R-squared	0.44	0.04

These results suggest that neither markets nor trade affect growth (both are now insignificant). On this basis, we conduct a regression which excludes these two factors, the results of which can be found in Table 6.5:[40]

Table 6.5: Country-level growth regression (P.C.S.E. excluding markets and trade).

	Population growth	Real wage growth
Initial population density	21.9 (1.12)	-0.83 (0.02)
Fiscal centralisation	0.0013 (2.04)**	0.0015 (1.93)*
Constitution	-0.0010 (-0.90)	-0.0016 (-0.93)
Societies/population	0.00019 (0.90)	0.00021 (0.60)
Enlightenment*factor prices	0.0025 (3.37)**	0.00086 (0.61)
Constant	0.0015 (2.37)	-0.00056 (-0.31)
Observations	44	37
R-squared	0.54	0.07

One finds that fiscal centralization has a significant effect on both measures of growth. A state with a centralized fiscal system experiences population growth of 0.13 per cent p.a. higher and real wage growth of 0.15 per cent p.a. higher than one with out. Allen's factor prices are found to have a significant effect on population growth when interacted with a dummy for the period 1750 onwards (for the age of Enlightenment).

City-level Results

Table 6.6 reports the results of running city-level growth regression models which include all of the key variables suggested by the literature (markets, trade, institutions, the Enlightenment and factor prices) alongside city-level data on real wage growth and population growth. Time periods included in the panel of countries are 1400–99 (for population growth only), 1500–99, 1600–99, 1700–49, 1750–99 and 1800–49. An initial population term is included to capture any Malthusian or catch-up effects. The cities involved are those for which real wage and factor price data is available: Antwerp, Amsterdam, London, Florence, Naples, Valencia, Madrid, Paris, Augsburg, Leipzig, Vienna, Gdansk, Krakow and Warsaw. Following the same procedure as at the country-level, the instrumental variables technique is employed.

Table 6.6: City-level growth regression (I.V.).

	Population growth (1400-1850)	Real wage growth (1500-1850)
Initial population	-0.0000087 (-0.89)	-0.000012 (-1.85)*
CV annual	-0.012 (-0.45)	0.021 (1.41)
Fiscal centralisation	0.0043 (1.16)	0.00044 (0.17)
Constitution	0.00048 (0.10)	0.0030 (0.82)
Societies	-0.000048 (-0.04)	0.00082 (1.13)
Enlightenment*factor prices	-0.0011 (-0.51)	-0.0019 (-1.11)
Trade	0.00000071 (0.32)	-0.00000089 (-0.62)
constant	0.0077 (1.23)	-0.0062 (-1.56)
observations	60	46
R-squared	0.1	0.25

Once again, the results suggest that neither markets nor trade affect growth (both are now insignificant). On this basis, we conduct a regression which excludes these two factors, the results of which can be found in Table 6.7.

Table 6.7: City-level growth regression (P.C.S.E. excluding markets and trade).

	Population growth	Real wage growth
Initial population	-0.000012 (-2.22)**	-0.00001 (-3.26)**
Fiscal centralisation	0.0036 (1.59)	0.0021 (2.03)**
Constitution	0.0019 (0.64)	0.00071 (0.92)
Societies	0.00033 (2.40)**	0.00036 (3.23)**
Enlightenment*factor prices	-0.00099 (-0.57)	-0.0016 (-1.5)
Constant	0.0048 (4.48)	-0.00064 (-1.04)
Observations	68	51
R-squared	0.09	0.19

Population growth and real wage growth are affected by initial population, fiscal centralization and societies. A city with ten extra societies will experience higher growth rates of around 0.3 per cent p.a., a city which is part of a fiscally centralized state will also experience faster growth of between 0.2 and 0.4 per cent p.a. (compared with a city which is not part of a fiscally integrated state). Finally, cities with higher initial populations tend to experience slower growth (assuming everything else is equal).

7 CONCLUSIONS AND IMPLICATIONS FOR ECONOMIC POLICY AND THE MODERN DAY

For much of human existence, life has involved a constant daily battle to find the means for subsistence. Not so long ago, every day consisted of constant short-term worries: Where was the next meal coming from? Would the roof withstand the winter rains? Would your children survive the latest onset of illness? By acting alone, it is difficult to mitigate the risks and achieve anything other than bare bones subsistence. Few of us have the skills or abilities required to be great hunters, builders, soldiers and doctors all in one. It is for this reason that Adam Smith argued that markets would naturally arise. Individuals will barter with each other as a means to get access to the goods and services that they find difficult to produce for themselves. Over time, money replaces payment in kind, and a full-scale market economy develops.[1]

However, markets are not the only arrangement that societies have practiced; cooperation, gift exchange and coercion have all existed in the course of European history in one form or another.[2] Acting cooperatively involves working together and dividing tasks between one another to build shelter, grow food, hunt and provide defence. In European history this includes aspects of the open-field village system and, in theory at least, the Soviet Union under communism.[3] Of course, getting people to act for the common good is not always easy, particularly if the size of the population in question makes monitoring difficult. The self-interested response is to free-ride on the efforts of others – after all, you will still be fed in the evening. But if everyone reasons the same way, the result is that nothing gets produced and everyone goes hungry. Hence, only in small groups where people can monitor each other and build up both a moral obligation and a communal spirit does such cooperation tend to be highly successful.

Another alternative to the market, and one which some anthropologists in fact argue has been the most common system (and is still practiced in parts of the Pacific Islands today) is gift exchange.[4] One person gives a gift to another and the favour is returned in the future. In effect, such economies operate with implicit reciprocity (or 'IOUs'). The result is that each person gets access to goods or resources that they are unable to produce for themselves. Barter might exist in such societies but tends to be limited to interactions between strangers and enemies who cannot be relied upon to cooperate or to 'repay' in the future.[5]

A third alternative to the market is a system of hierarchy with some form of coercion, such as slavery or feudalism.[6] This is particularly likely in situations of low population density, where labour would be expensive if paid its just reward.[7] In such circumstances, there is an incentive for those who can command power to restrict the freedom of others such that they can extract any 'surplus' that is produced above that required for subsistence, thereby supporting a luxurious and leisurely lifestyle for themselves. Such a society creates few of the conditions required for growth as the focus is instead on obtaining a bigger slice of the pie. Where markets exist in such societies, they work to supply the elites with luxury goods, playing a relatively minor role in the total consumption of an economy.

The market solution has a number of clear advantages over the cooperative, gift and coercive arrangements. Each person specializes in what they are best at doing, selling the goods or services that result and using the proceeds to buy other goods and services that it is difficult or inefficient to produce for oneself. Since we are all good at different things, or at least enjoy doing different things, the result is something that should work for everyone. Each person is incentivized to produce, as without doing so it is not possible to get access to other goods and resources; return becomes proportional to the effort you expend and your level of skill. By acting in your own self-interest, we therefore end up at an outcome that helps others by providing greater production and consumption opportunities. In Smith's words, '[i]t is not from the benevolence of the butcher, the brewer, or the baker, that we expect our dinner, but from their regard to their own interest'.[8] The market harnesses self-interest to provide for the common-good, hence side-stepping the problem of relying on cooperation, reciprocity and coercion. As a result, the economy is able to develop more successfully, reaching a higher level of sophistication and a higher level of income.

The fact that the market might enable a better solution to the problem of human existence is, however, not enough to explain why it is dominant in many parts of the world today. Just because an arrangement is 'efficient' in a long term economic sense does not mean that it will come to dominate.[9] Nevertheless, as we have discussed in this book, it certainly did so in Europe, and from surprisingly early on, helping the economy to advance. In what follows, we draw together our findings in an effort to not only explain when and why markets developed in Europe, but also why they ultimately proved insufficient for sustaining economic growth in the longer term. We will conclude with a number of important policy implications for modern day economies.

The Development of Markets in Europe: Course, Causes and Consequences

Our first task in this work has been to establish the course that markets have taken across the long-span of history, from ancient times towards the modern day. Traditionally it has been argued that economies were 'backward' before the eighteenth century. Thereafter, the economy moved from one in which government and society completely suffocated market development to one in which commercial exchange was the order of the day, leading to the Industrial Revolution and the beginning of economic growth. The picture of markets in history that we have painted in the course of Chapters 1–4 is, however, strikingly different.

As we saw in the first chapter, archaeological evidence increasingly suggests that markets existed throughout antiquity. Whilst it cannot be denied that a coercive system of slavery was a common feature of such economies, markets were used much more widely than has traditionally been thought. However, after the fall of the Roman Empire, the weight shifted away from markets and towards communal, gift and coercive systems, such as feudalism. The economy entered the Dark Ages. Our evidence, together with that of a growing body of economic historians, suggests that after this time the situation significantly improved: markets were recovering and reached new heights by the beginning of the early modern period. The level of development achieved at this time was two or three times that in ancient Babylonia, and not far from that which existed on the eve of the Industrial Revolution.[10] Alongside goods markets, the recent literature that we surveyed also suggests that factor markets developed early on, with the greatest phase of development taking place in the fourteenth, fifteenth and sixteenth centuries. From then until the Industrial Revolution, markets achieved only a relatively small advance, with some evidence of a temporary setback in the seventeenth century. The next major transformation occurred after, and not before, the Industrial Revolution, in the nineteenth century.

Chapter 5 identified geography, institutions, and population growth as being the causes of market advance. The geography of Europe has always facilitated long distance contact between strangers. As Adam Smith pointed out, unlike many other continents, the seas which surround Europe infiltrate the land, which made it relatively easy for people living before the modern age to travel outside of their local regions, compared with those living in the vast interior regions of China, India, Africa and Russia.[11] The natural landscape and climate also varied greatly across the continent, from plains suited to crops to rugged hillsides and mountains suited to vines or sheep. This provided a further motive for people to travel in search of goods and resources that could not be found in the immediate vicinity, including wine, salt and wool in western Europe and metals, cereals, furs and wax in eastern Europe.[12] Given that interactions between strangers are more likely to take the form of barter, as irregular and distant contact make cooperation and reciprocity more difficult to sustain, Europe was naturally oriented to a market as opposed to a gift or cooperative system.

Geography may have given Europe a natural bias to trade, but, as Smith himself pointed out, trade will not thrive unless it is supported by good institutions.[13] From an economists' point of view, the most vital institution for supporting markets is property rights, which in turn requires a legal system for enforcement:[14] factors of production can only be bought and sold – making their way into the hands of those who can best make use of them – if there are clear ownership rights; producers will only produce for the market if their goods cannot be confiscated and if their contracts will be upheld; lenders will only want to lend if they have legal recourse should a borrower default. Hence, the development of markets required well-defined property rights. The Roman state helped markets to flourish by providing a legal system to uphold these property rights, together with public goods (such as transport infrastructure) and a monetary system. When the Roman state collapsed, along with its market-supporting institutions, markets also collapsed. Political rule became fragmented, which led to multiple currencies, internal tariffs, cities establishing monopolies over the countryside, and a lack of provision and coordination of transport and other infrastructure. Epstein argues that the reemergence of larger states in Europe helped markets to recover by overcoming such problems.[15] Where states were lacking, alternative institutional forms developed to substitute for the functions that would otherwise have been performed by the state, including feudalism, city-states, merchant guilds, craft guilds and Christendom. Whilst these state-substitutes aided recovery, they may also have imposed a ceiling on the extent to which markets could improve.[16]

A recovery of population also helped markets to advance, and in some cases lifted the ceiling, through at least four different channels. Firstly, rising population lowered the benefits of coercion. By lowering the wage that workers could command on the market, it made it possible for the elite to generate a surplus by employing 'free' as opposed to slave or feudal labour.[17] Hence, coercion (including feudalism) waned as populations increased, raising the ceiling on the extent to which markets could improve. Secondly, a larger population meant more contact between strangers, reducing the benefits of communal and gift exchange systems relative to the market. Thirdly, more people meant more conflict, bringing incursions from foreigners in search of new land or resources. In an effort to provide wider defense systems, power was passed to a central body who was given the responsibility of coordinating and organizing defense. To fund this defense, the central body often implemented taxation, which forced individuals to start selling more of their goods on the market to enable them to pay taxes. Some have argued that Viking threats created such a transition to a market-using economy in England (and with it the early development of the state), using the name 'emergency conversion'.[18] Finally, not only did rising population reduce the benefits of communal, gift and coercive ways of living, it also helped to raise the benefits of using the market: more people enabled a finer division of labour and greater specialization, and made it more likely that participants in the market could find buyers and sellers (encouraging reliance on the market).

As markets and trade expanded in response to the establishment of institutions and rising population, positive feedback mechanisms helped to create a virtuous circle: trade encouraged population growth, feeding back to fuel further market expansion; trade also stimulated improvements in technology,[19] including bills of exchange, marine insurance and bigger and better ships, which themselves served to encourage further trade; institutions responded to trade, adapting in ways that merchants found beneficial for trade. Hence, by medieval times, parts of Europe (including the coasts of Italy, settlements along main rivers of Central Europe, and along the North Sea coast) were in a virtuous circle, experiencing rising population, improvements in institutions and technology, and expanding markets.[20] Where markets and institutions had become established in this way, the shock of the Black Death structurally transformed the economy in a way that created further scope for markets to improve; it put a final end to the remnants of feudalism, freeing labour and land markets, and, through putting upward pressure on wages, drew an increasing number of people into the labour market. The Renaissance and the oceanic adventures of the fifteenth century, which opened up the globe for the first time in history, are symbols of what had been achieved in the European economy.

The development of markets may have helped to create a more sophisticated and prosperous economy than the alternatives of a communal, gift or coercive system. They might indeed have been necessary to lay the foundations for later economic growth, but they were not enough for continued growth, as we demonstrated in Chapter 6. If they had been, then the Industrial Revolution would have taken place in the sixteenth century – and the world now would be around two centuries ahead of where it is today.

Since scientific advance and continuous technological change are the central driver of sustained economic growth,[21] the problem must have been that markets were not enough to encourage the systematic accumulation and application of knowledge to the process of production, even when accompanied with a market for invention in the form of a patent system (which was introduced in Holland in the sixteenth century and in Britain in the early seventeenth century).[22] Whilst scientific and technological advances had certainly been taking place in Europe, they were not occurring at a rapid rate or through any systematic scientific process.[23] Most intellectual activity took place in a private setting – in the parlours of gentlemen entertaining their friends – and was withheld from the public sphere.[24]

As argued by Mokyr, the engine for scientific advance was provided by the Enlightenment, which began in the seventeenth century and gathered pace in the late eighteenth century.[25] As Allen suggests, the unique factor prices which existed in Britain at this time (high wages combined with cheap fuel) meant that the engine was put to work creating new technologies that mechanized production, raising the growth of output in the economy.[26]

The Enlightenment brought the very opposite of a market system to science – a more cooperative and communal scientific research spirit, in which ideas were openly and freely distributed and scientists worked not for financial reward but for recognition and to push forward the frontier of knowledge for the common good of society.[27] The emergence of this communal and gift based system brought a number of significant advantages: it allowed ideas to spread and so be used and developed; it brought minds together in a way that was more likely to lead to results, and it allowed avenues to be explored which might – in the market's judgement – initially have seemed unprofitable but which led to unexpected advances which later brought great reward. Chapter 6 showed that countries experienced faster growth in the eighteenth and nineteenth centuries when they had a greater amount of cooperative scientific activity taking place. States harnessed the associated benefits by putting in place a publicly-funded research system.[28] In other words, the non-market systems brought to science by the Enlightenment proved useful for pushing forward the frontiers of science and for opening up new unexpected avenues at a greater rate than ever before. Only once such avenues were being continually opened would a market-based (patent) system be able to have its maximum effect, working alongside this non-market system.

As argued by Allen, Britain's high-wage economy and cheap and abundant coal created an incentive to take scientific advance and embody it in machines that could then be used in mills and factories, raising the growth of output in the economy. If wages are low, there may be little incentive to use scientific advance in a way that mechanizes production – scientific advance remains in the 'Ivory Towers', with little effect on the ground where firms are producing. In Britain, wages were high relative to the fuel (and other) cost of using machines, which stimulated the development of labour-saving machinery and provided firms with an incentive to invest in such machinery in an effort to lower costs. As Allen shows, the types of machines developed and used in Britain during the Industrial Revolution were barely profitable in other parts of Europe.[29] However, over time, Britain's engineers refined their machines, making them more efficient and so less costly to use, as a result of which the Industrial Revolution spread abroad. In the United States, wages were even higher than in Britain, which led to an even more machine intensive labour-saving growth path: mass production, which provides at least part of the explanation for why the US achieved higher labour productivity than Britain in the nineteenth and twentieth centuries.[30]

As a result of the technological advances that occurred during the Industrial Revolution, the economy entered a second phase of market development. Steamships, railroads and the telegraph dramatically cut the costs of transport and increased flows of information, bringing about a process of globalization that took Europe – and with it the world – to levels of market development not far from those seen today. Whilst globalization is thought by many to be a key driver of economic growth, nineteenth-century globalization was very much a consequence of growth.

Lessons for Economies Developing in the Modern World

The development advice given to less developed countries today often involves recommendations to copy western-style institutions, limit state intervention, liberalize markets and pursue free trade. This policy package has been highly influenced by the view that markets – underpinned by good institutions – created economic growth in the now rich economies. By suggesting a revision to our understanding of the past, our findings also therefore suggest revisions to current development policy advice, including the following.

1) Focus more on developing markets within the economy (as opposed to between economies)

As we saw in Chapter 2, the parts of Europe that witnessed most success in the early modern period were those in which domestic, as opposed to between-country, markets were well-developed. These markets were often the product of a virtuous circle, in which geography and the emergence of states sparked trade, and then population growth and institutions followed in response, fuelling more trade in turn. This suggests that the two main obstacles that prevent economies from breaking into such a virtuous circle are unfavourable geography and political fragmentation.

The regions of Europe that first advanced were those in which geography was favourable to trade, including the coasts of the Mediterranean and the North Sea. Fortunately, in the modern world, the technology of transport enables geographic disadvantages to be overcome, whilst global capital markets provide a route through which transport infrastructure can be funded. However, a more subtle way of overcoming unfavourable geography, such as mountainous terrain, involves focusing resources on developing sectors of the economy with limited need for large scale transport. In Europe, Switzerland is the most obvious example of an economy which has overcome geographic disadvantage by specializing in financial services (which do not require transportation to the consumer) and producing high-value small items, such as watches, for which the transport costs are small in proportion to the value of the good.

Even if geography is not a problem, or at least is one that can be overcome, the lack of a well-developed state or fragmented political power can place hurdles in the way of market development. Collier and Venables argue that the political fragmentation of parts of Africa has generated significant costs, including 'thin' markets (i.e. markets with too few participants to encourage specialization and market activity) and a lack of coordination on the provision of public goods, such as long-distance transport that cuts through political boundaries.[31] Political fragmentation also therefore needs to be overcome if markets are to develop.

2) Developing the state is crucial

As we saw in Chapter 6, and for reasons argued by Epstein, Voth and Grafe, a well developed centralized state is complementary to markets and growth, rather than (as it is traditionally seen) a potential hindrance.[32] Markets are not very good at producing exactly the things they need to be able to develop – legal systems, transport infrastructure and so on. Furthermore, growth requires more than just markets – such as publicly funded spending on R&D and education. Hence, the state can have a vital role to play in the process of economic development. To play this role, the state needs to have a capacity to spend, and this is somewhere that economic historians can offer advice. It would be near-impossible and unwise to place the full burden of expenditure on the current generation through the tax system; not only are poor economies likely to have relatively small tax receipts, but the benefits of spending will aid future and not just present generations, meaning the costs should be spread between them. To spread the cost into the future a country needs to be able to tap into the savings of people living in richer countries (i.e. borrow on world capital markets by issuing bonds). This then means that tax revenue only needs to be generated to the level required to pay an annual interest charge (rather than the full amount of the spending programme all at once). If the spending-plan proves successful in generating higher incomes, then as a proportion of income, the debt will fall, making the interest payments easily manageable. As economic historians like Epstein and Dincecco have shown, the extent to which the bond market is willing to lend to a country (at low rates of interest) depends on the size of the tax base and whether or not the fiscal system is centralized.[33] A broad tax base and a centralized tax system provides bond markets with an assurance that debt can be serviced, meaning that they are happy to lend at low rates of interest. Since well developed states – unlike those that are fragmented – have the power to put this in place, they are therefore more likely to be able to fund the expenditure required to help support and stimulate growth.

3) Markets have disadvantages as well as advantages

One of the reasons why free markets are insufficient for growth is that they create problems that partially offset the benefits they may bring to an economy. Economists already acknowledge that there are circumstances in which markets can fail, including where competition is inadequate, where externalities exist, and where there are information asymmetries. As a result, they are happy to recommend state intervention in a small number of cases. However, what they rarely acknowledge, even when faced with proof of the fact, is that markets can sometimes be inherently unstable, potentially destabilizing economic growth.[34]

According to mainstream economic theory, instability is created by governments (the state) rather than markets. It is for this reason that they recommend limiting state intervention and relying on the free market. However, this view has formed on the basis of economic models which rule out, by assumption, all of the possible sources of instability that markets can create in the real world. Two such influential models are the New Classical Model, which contains no recognizable financial sector (and so does not envisage the possibility of financial crises), and the main 'model' that economists use to think about financial markets, known as the Efficient Markets Hypothesis (EMH). According to EMH, financial prices are driven by 'economic fundamentals', which means that the stock market is efficient: people are able to form a judgement over the 'true' (fundamental) value of a stock, and as soon as the price of that stock starts to rise above its true value, well-informed financiers will have an incentive to sell, bringing the price back to its 'correct' value. Hence, stock market booms and busts should never occur if the market is left to its own devices. The model also predicts that movements in stock prices will follow a normal distribution (a bell curve), on the basis of which quantitative finance has developed (including the mean-variance approach, CAPM and Black-Scholes), despite the evidence of 'fat tails' (i.e. a tendency for big moves in the market) which renders much of this work – and with it the associated practices of the financial sector – erroneous.[35]

Followers of Keynes fundamentally disagree with the Efficient Market Hypothesis, and it is for this reason that they argue that financial markets – and with it the broader economy – will be inherently unstable. As Keynes argued, the root of this instability is the volatility of investment.[36] He points out that much investment in the modern world is either funded or dictated by moves in the stock market, and argues that whilst stock markets have been very helpful in terms of encouraging people to invest, by making assets liquid and so easy to sell should it become necessary, they have also made investment much more unstable and much less tied to 'fundamentals'. Unlike current mainstream economics, Keynes argued that the future is highly unpredictable, which means that it is near-impossible to predict the 'fundamental' value of a stock, on the basis of which there is no anchor to stock prices; they will therefore 'blow with the wind' as investors move between exuberance and panic, aided by the ease with which buying and selling of stocks enables them to jump on and off a bandwagon. The result is that the stock market goes through regular booms and busts and, therefore, so does investment and with it economic growth. To make matters worse, Keynes argued, the resulting volatility pushes investors to focus on the short term: if you believe that a stock is overpriced but that it will go up for the foreseeable future, you are happy to buy it; if you believe that the stock of a particular company or sector is under priced due to market sentiment, you are unlikely to buy it if you believe that it will stay low, and even fall, in the indeterminate near term. This short-termism makes it unlikely that investment will be dictated by fundamentals.

Fisher and Minsky brought debt into Keynes's story.[37] Minsky argued that as the economy booms, in an effort to make profits and compete with their peers, banks increasingly lend to riskier prospects and develop riskier investment products (recently including sub-prime mortgages and related securitized debt products). The amount of leverage, debt and risk in an economy therefore expands as an economy booms; in the USA, debt as a proportion of GDP increased from approximately 150 per cent in the late 1970s to 350 per cent in 2006.[38] As the boom turns into a bust, the unwinding of the debt creates losses that lead to a 'debt deflation', as described by Fisher. As stock and house prices fall, financial institutions are forced to fire sell such assets in an effort to maintain liquidity, but this only further deepens the asset price falls and associated losses, requiring further sales, and so the process continues. The economy gets caught in a worsening spiral. As Minsky argued, it is therefore in the period of stability, when the economy seems to be successfully expanding, in which can be found the seeds of later destruction.

The recent financial crisis has started to increase interest in the work of Keynes and his followers in intellectual circles, but many economists are still clinging to their old models. In order to resolve any problem in life, the first thing we need to do is admit it. As for alcoholics and gamblers, it is for economists. If the economic community does not face up to the realities of markets, and, as a result, economies do not take action to alleviate instability, markets will lose political support, and the result could be that we end up disposing with markets altogether (throwing the baby out with the bathwater), and then we will truly be on the 'Road to Serfdom', as Hayek called it, but for the opposite reason to that he imagined.[39]

4) Institutions do not have to be 'perfect'

It is common to argue that poor countries are poor because they lack the types of institutions which exist in developed countries, such as democracy, intellectual property rights, Central Banks, bankruptcy law and so forth. On this basis, economists advise less developed countries to copy the institutions of the west if they want to develop. As argued by Chang, economics 'almost exclusively assumes that the causality runs from institutions to economic development'.[40] However, very few now-rich economies were born with good institutions, which makes it difficult to argue that good institutions are what explains how they became rich. Whilst some minimal institutions might be a pre-requisite, other institutions could be seen as endogenous to the process of growth – in part a consequence rather than cause of growth.[41]

As economies start to develop, this development itself generates natural forces which can help to bring about institutional change, increasing the demand and funding for better quality institutions.[42] One such example is the development of political institutions in Britain: whilst some have argued that the Glorious Revolution in seventeenth-century Britain led to a transformation of markets and the start of economic growth, we have seen that markets had already developed. This suggests that rather than seeing such institutional change as a cause of market transformation and growth, it may indeed be better to view it as a consequence of what was an already developing economy.[43] Another example is the development of the role of Central Banks in assuming responsibilities for the banking system, which did not come until the late nineteenth and twentieth centuries, after the beginning of economic growth.[44] All of this means that whilst 'good' institutions may be beneficial for an economy, the economy can begin to advance without them, and this advance will likely generate the internal forces necessary for their improvement (without them needing to be imposed from outside). Rather than putting in place 'perfect' institutions from the start, what is most important for economic development is that institutions and policy are able to respond to the demands and challenges this development brings. It would be difficult to argue that the economic growth experienced in China over the last twenty years has been the product of the type of parliamentary revolution occurring in seventeenth-century Britain; instead, as people are becoming richer, it is creating pressure for political change.

5) Free trade is not guaranteed to be good for growth

Economists regularly recommend that if poor countries want to grow, they should integrate their economies into the world market, shedding protectionist barriers in pursuit of a free-trade approach. However, as we have seen in the course of this book, Britain did not grow as a result of pursuing such a free-trade policy. In fact, Britain pursued a protectionist policy from the middle of the seventeenth century to the close of the Industrial Revolution; many other economies at the time were much better integrated into the European marketplace and did not experience an Industrial Revolution. In fact, a wide body of research has shown that the economies experiencing the fastest growth in the nineteenth and early twentieth centuries (i.e. at the time at which the now rich economies became rich) were those using tariffs.[45]

There are in fact a number of ways in which involvement in international trade can be detrimental to growth, of which economies developing today need to be aware. The first works through institutions. As we saw in Chapters 1 and 2, whilst expanding trade in the course of European history resulted in improvements in institutions in a large number of cases, this was not without exception. Increasing opportunities for exports from eastern to western Europe resulted in an adverse shift in institutions – the increasing feudalization of labour. Then, as Europeans expanded their trading arena to the wider world in the course of the early modern period, whilst they were happy to take their market system and institutions with them to areas they could reasonably safely settle and inhabit, such as the United States, in less hospitable places, such as South America, the Caribbean and parts of Africa, they instead imposed a coercive system of slavery.[46] The result was that for these economies, integration into the global economy produced high levels of inequality and hindered rather than helped the development of institutions and markets in the longer run; many of them are still relatively poor today.[47]

The second channel through which free trade may cause harm is de-industrialization.[48] For countries well endowed with land, participation in the global marketplace naturally leads to specialization in exporting agricultural goods and importing manufactured goods and services in return. If the productivity growth potential of the land is lower than that of industry, this could have an adverse effect on the economy's growth rate.[49] Furthermore, as shown by Krugman, if economies of scale (or 'increasing returns') exist, meaning that costs of production fall as output expands, free international markets will not always lead to the best possible outcome for a country or indeed for the global economy.[50] Economies of scale are a feature of many industries: the longer an industry has existed, the more experience it has, and as an industry expands, it is able to benefit from agglomeration (or 'cluster') effects. This makes it difficult for a newly developing economy to 'break into' the market, even when it could potentially produce at a lower cost in the longer run; markets 'lock in' those who start to develop first and 'lock out' later developers. In such circumstances, a case can be made for 'infant industry' protection in an effort to enable economies starting from behind to develop potentially globally leading sectors, benefiting not only themselves but the wider world, as Chang argues happened successfully in South Korea in the twentieth century.[51] However, Yueh points out that there are a large number of cases in which protectionist policy has been 'a disaster'.[52] For infant industry protection to work, the state has to be competent and knowledgeable enough to manage it, the domestic market has to be sufficiently large (to enable the benefits of economies of scale to be reaped), and there has to be a good reason why the industry can in the long run push costs below the incumbent producers (such as access to sunshine in the case of film-making or highly skilled workers in the case of 'hi-tech' goods). Otherwise, the protected sector may become a 'lame-duck' rather than a successful exporter, which then hinders the development of the rest of the economy.[53] If the conditions can be met, then it may be worth risking sacrificing the gains from trade that come from specializing in agriculture in an effort to develop a higher productivity sector in the longer run. In Britain, protectionist policy was used alongside a well-developed state and well-developed internal markets, which may therefore give a guide as to the types of situations in which it could prove helpful in economies developing today.

A third situation in which free trade has been known to create problems is in economies rich in natural resources (such as oil), a situation known as the 'resource curse'. There are a number of reasons why an abundance of natural resources can create problems. The first is that 'predatory governments and interest groups are geared more to squandering rents than to creating and spreading wealth sustainably'.[54] The benefits of natural resources are rarely spread equally across the population and so can result in high levels of income inequality which have been shown to be detrimental to development. If a state can earn income through a natural resource, it may be less inclined to take measures which encourage growth in the broader economy (including putting in place good institutions and a system of education). Such a state is also more prone to 'capture' by the owners of natural resources, meaning that the types of policies it pursues are likely to be skewed in the direction of benefiting the resource owners, rather than the general population. Secondly, inflows of payments from natural resources can increase the real exchange rate, resulting in other potential export sectors (which may have higher productivity growth potential) being crowded out. This is the phenomenon known as 'Dutch Disease'. Thirdly, primary commodities tend to experience greater price volatility than other types of goods, which can be destabilizing for the economies that produce them.[55] Of course, not all resource rich and land abundant economies have suffered, as is evident in the cases of the USA, Canada and Australia. This suggests that where political institutions are strong enough to avoid capture by vested interests, and where the state creates conditions favourable to the development of the wider economy, the adverse effects of an abundance of natural resources can be avoided.

6) Copying western technologies will not necessarily bring benefits

In the medieval period, when the east led the world technologically, Europe benefited greatly from trade contact with the east, with which came the diffusion of technologies, the skills required for developing banking, and access to new goods. However, the vast differences in the costs of labour and other inputs between the rich and poor countries today mean that the types of techniques of production used in the former may not be profitable in the latter. As a result, developing countries need to pursue their own path, developing processes of production that are most appropriate to their factor endowments and factor prices. This requires researchers, engineers and entrepreneurs to work together – as they did in the British Industrial Revolution – to develop techniques that are 'appropriate' to their home countries. One thing that the government of any developing country can do to encourage productivity growth is to encourage such cooperation, possibly in combination with an 'infant industry' policy, as discussed earlier. If development was as easy as copying the technology of 'rich' economies, there would be far fewer poor countries in the world today.

7) There is nothing to fear from rising wages

Many economies today successfully compete on the basis of their low labour costs and it is common to find economic models in which low cost labour enables an economy to develop by helping firms to reap high profits, which can then be invested.[56] However, as Allen has demonstrated, and as supported by Chapter 6, Britain's Industrial Revolution came out of a high-wage and not low-wage economy. In fact, many other parts of Europe at the time had wages that were half those of Britain (see Chapter 1) and yet did not have an Industrial Revolution.

The increasing wages that result from the natural process of economic growth can have two advantages. Firstly, as argued by Allen, they can encourage the mechanization of production, raising productivity. Secondly, as argued by de Moor and van Zanden, they give young people the means by which to gain independence from their families, leading to the emergence of a new family structure in which people have more control over who they marry, and marry later in life (saving until they can set up their own independent household). The result is that people have fewer children, start to save more for their future (including once they are married in anticipation of the fact that their children won't always be around to look after them), are encouraged (and able) to invest in education and start to have more control of their spending patterns (away from the disapproving gaze of parents). The consequence is that savings, investment and education increase, and people start to work harder in an effort to be able to consume more goods. For these reasons, rising wages should not be seen as adverse to growth.

Policy Lessons for Rich Economies

The arguments of this book provide lessons not only for economies developing today but also for the more developed economies, as follows.

1) Political fragmentation is bad for markets

The problem of political fragmentation is not only evident in poorer countries but also in richer countries, including in Europe, where there has been a tendency for states to fracture into smaller political entities and where there is presently a risk of further 'breaking-up' – such as in the British Isles and the European Union. Whilst there may be very good reasons for such fragmentation, what history suggests is that should fracture occur, it will be crucial to maintain coordination between fractured units in order to ensure that markets do not suffer in response.

2) Markets cannot be taken for granted

Whilst markets are not new – they have existed for centuries – they have been subject to waves of integration and disintegration over time, as occurred with the collapse of the Roman Empire in western Europe. The recognition of this fact teaches us that markets are fragile. This creates a big risk as we are all mutually dependent on each other through the marketplace – for the food we eat at dinner, the healthcare we receive, and the clothes we wear. This works well so long as everyone keeps participating as buyers and sellers. However, the high level of specialization which has resulted means that few of us these days would know how to do even the basics required for independent subsistence (grow food, knit a jumper, repair a roof, tend to minor injuries). Hence, the ability for markets to unravel has potentially grave consequences that we need to recognize and take action to avoid.

The reason why markets can disintegrate is that if just a few people are discouraged from participating, others may do likewise, as the benefits of using the market fall when there are fewer buyers and sellers. If we want to prevent markets unraveling, we need to make sure that the state is ready to step in as a buyer or seller, should it prove necessary. By doing so, it will keep markets functioning by quelling the outflow of participants. Of course, this is effectively what the state found itself doing in response to the banking crisis, providing liquidity and acting as a ready buyer of bonds. Without it, capital markets may very well have collapsed. The lesson is that the state needs to have the knowledge, power and resources to intervene should it become necessary. In fact, if this is the case, markets are much less likely to unravel in the first place, as people will generally be happy to participate and in the case of shocks are less likely to turn-away. This is just one of many reasons why the state and the market should not be seen as substitutes, which brings us to our next point.

3) The state has a vital role to play

It is common to view the state and the market as substitutes. Hayek argued that state intervention risked putting the economy on a slippery slope in which markets were completely disposed of altogether.[57] However, as we have argued, state intervention to support markets (through providing public goods and helping to avoid unraveling), to encourage technological change (through a state-funded scientific research system), and also to correct market deficiencies (including the instabilities discussed earlier) is vital for economic growth. For these reasons, if markets are not accompanied by the state, they are unlikely to sustain economic growth. When markets are most likely to come under fire in the political arena is when they are left to their own devices; state intervention actually nurtures markets by allowing us to maintain the benefits they provide but eliminate some of the costs.

4) Markets continually create challenges that will need to be addressed

As markets develop (in part in response to economic growth), they will continually create new challenges for policy makers, which require policy and institutions to be able to adapt in response. For example, whilst developments in capital markets in the sixteenth and seventeenth centuries led to the fractional reserve banking system, bringing long-run benefits, they also made banking panics much more frequent. It was in response that the modern day system of Central Banking developed. More recent innovations in capital markets (such as the development of sub-prime mortgages and securitized products) have also created a period of instability in the form of the recent boom and bust, revealing a need to revise the duties of the institution that is the Central Bank. What history therefore teaches us is that as markets develop, they will create problems that need to be addressed, and institutions appropriate for doing this in one period may become insufficient in the next.

* * *

When it comes to the development and expansion of markets, history teaches us that the road ahead will inevitably be rocky and may even at times bring the risk of a full-scale unraveling; whether markets – and with it our current means for subsistence – will survive the storm will therefore depend on the response of the state and the advice it is given by economists. We need to begin to acknowledge that whilst markets have their advantages, they are far from sufficient for economic growth and bring with them continuous risks and challenges.

NOTES

Introduction

1. This refers to T. Hobbes, *Leviathan* (1651), pt 1, ch. 3, para. 9, where he comments that life was 'solitary, poor, nasty, brutish, and short'.
2. R. E. Lucas, 'On the Mechanics of Economic Development', *Journal of Monetary Economics*, 22 (1988), pp. 3–42, on p. 5.
3. A. Smith, *An Inquiry into the Nature and Causes of the Wealth of Nations* (1776; Oxford: Oxford University Press, 'Oxford World's Classic', 2008).
4. By contrast, D. Graeber, *Debt: The First 5000 Years* (New York: Melville House, 2012) argues that debt existed before goods markets in the system of gift exchange.
5. Building on these Smithian insights are the following: K. Desmet and S. L. Parente, 'The Evolution of Markets and the Revolution of Industry: A Quantitative Model of England's Development', *CEPR Discussion Paper* (May 2009); L. A. Rivera-Batiz and P. M. Romer, 'Economic Integration and Endogenous Growth', *Quarterly Journal of Economics*, 106 (1991), pp. 531–55; C. Jones and P. Romer, 'The New Kaldor Facts: Ideas, Institutions, Population and Human Capital', *NBER*, working paper 15049 (2009).
6. As formalized in *The First Theorem of Welfare Economics*, albeit using some rather stringent assumptions.
7. F. A. Hayek, 'The Use of Knowledge in Society', *American Economic Review*, 35 (1945), pp. 519–30.
8. D. C. North and R. P. Thomas, *The Rise of the Western World: A New Economic History* (Cambridge: Cambridge University Press, 1973).
9. Smith, *Wealth of Nations*, p. 458.
10. Usury laws limited the payment of interest.
11. Which regulated wages and entry to skilled professions.
12. K. Polanyi, *The Great Transformation: The Political and Economic Origins of our Time* (Boston, MA: Beacon Press, 1944).
13. This consensus is summarized and critiqued in H.-J. Chang and I. Grabel, 'Reclaiming Development from the Washington Consensus', *Journal of Post Keynesian Economics*, 27 (2004), pp. 273–91.
14. The extent to which this 'equality of opportunity', as Friedman called it, has been achieved in the Western world is, of course, open to debate.
15. F. M. Bator, 'The Simple Analytics of Welfare Maximization', *American Economic Review*, 47 (1957), pp. 22–59; F. M. Bator, 'The Anatomy of Market Failure', *Quarterly Journal of Economics*, 72 (1958), pp. 351–79; G. A. Akerlof, 'The Market for "Lemons": Quality Uncertainty and the Market Mechanism', *Quarterly Journal of Economics*, 84 (1970), pp.

488–500; K. J. Arrow, 'Uncertainty and the Welfare Economics of Medical Care', *American Economic Review*, 53 (1963), pp. 941–73. An alternative route to revealing market failure is Game Theory, which reveals the possibility of individuals settling on an inferior equilibrium in cases such as the Prisoner's Dilemma and Coordination Game. Interested non-economists may find the following of interest: J. Cassidy, *How Markets Fail: The Logic of Economic Calamities* (London: Penguin, 2009).

16. See also G. Hardin, 'The Tragedy of the Commons', *Science*, 162 (1968), pp. 1243–8.
17. R. H. Coase, 'The Problem of Social Costs', *Journal of Law and Economics*, 3 (1960), pp. 1–44 (which assumes minimal transaction costs).
18. At a fundamental level, such failures of markets tend to arise from the fact that humans are interdependent in the sense that the consequences of our actions depend on others, and our own actions affect them in turn. As the Prisoner's Dilemma has famously shown, self-interested actions do not always result in the common good when actions are interdependent.
19. For example, Harberger, calculated that the total losses from monopoly were no more than 1 per cent of GDP, and Baumol argued that the threat of entry in the marketplace was enough to prevent monopoly behaviour. A. C. Harberger, 'Monopoly and Resource Allocation', *American Economic Review*, 44 (1954), pp. 77–87; W. J. Baumol, 'Contestable Markets: An Uprising in the Theory of Industrial Structure', *American Economic Review*, 72 (1982), pp. 1–15.
20. F. A. Hayek, *The Road to Serfdom* (London: Routledge & Kegan Paul, 1933); Friedman, M., *Capitalism and Freedom* (Chicago, IL: University of Chicago Press, 1962); M. Friedman and R. Friedman, *Free to Choose: A Personal Statement* (New York: Harcourt Brace Jovanovich, 1980).
21. J. M. Keynes, *The General Theory of Employment, Interest and Money* (London: Macmillan, 1936).
22. D. K. Benjamin and L. A. Kochin, 'Searching for an Explanation of Unemployment in Interwar Britain', *Journal of Political Economy*, 87 (1979), pp. 441–78, on p. 474.
23. Cassidy, *How Markets Fail*, p. 107, refers to Lucas's Presidential address at the American Economic Association 2003 meeting.
24. There is an abundance of literature that looks at the effect of 'globalization' in the late nineteenth and twentieth centuries (see C. M. Meissner, 'Growth from Globalization? A View from the Very Long-Run', in P. Aghion and S. N. Durlauf (eds), *Handbook of Economic Growth*, 2 vols (Amsterdam: Elsevier, 2012), vol. 2 for a summary), but very little that considers the longer run period from before the Industrial Revolution.
25. As we will see in Chapter 4.
26. For example, R. Britnell and B. M. S. Campbell (eds), *A Commercialising Economy: England 1086 to c. 1300* (Manchester and New York: Manchester University Press, 1995).
27. W. Keller and C. H. Shiue, 'Markets in China and Europe on the Eve of the Industrial Revolution', *American Economic Review*, 97 (2007), pp. 1189–216.

1 Markets in History: A Survey

1. C. Kelly, *The Roman Empire* (Oxford: Oxford University Press, 2006), p. 2.
2. M. I. Finley, 'Technical Innovation and Economic Progress in the Ancient World', *Economic History Review*, 18 (1965), pp. 29–45. For a summary, see A. Wilson, 'Machines, Power and the Ancient Economy', *Journal of Roman Studies*, 92 (2002), pp. 1, 15 and K.

Greene, 'Technological Innovation and Economic Progress in the Ancient World: M. I. Finley Re-Considered', *Economic History Review*, 53 (2000), pp. 29–59.

3. P. Erdkamp, *The Grain Market in the Roman Empire: A Social, Political and Economic Study* (Cambridge: Cambridge University Press, 2005); C. Wickham, *Framing the Middle Ages Europe and the Mediterranean 400–800* (Oxford: Oxford University Press, 2005), p. 708.
4. On institutions in general, see E. Lo Cascio, 'The Role of the State in the Roman Economy: Making Institutional Economics', in P. F. Bang, M. Ikeguchi and H. G. Ziche (eds), *Ancient Economies, Modern Methodologies: Archaeology, Comparative History, Models and Institutions* (Bari: Edipuglia, 2006), pp. 215–34; B. W. Frier and D. P. Kehoe, 'Law and Economic Institutions', in W. Scheidel, I. Morris and R. P. Saller (eds), *The Cambridge Economic History of the Greco-Roman World* (Cambridge: Cambridge University Press, 2007), p. 113; D. P. Kehoe, *Law and the Rural Economy in the Roman Empire* (Ann Arbor, MI: University of Michigan Press, 2007); L. de Ligt, 'Roman Law and the Roman Economy: Three Case Studies', *Latomus*, 66 (2007), pp. 10–25; M. Silver, 'Roman Economic Growth and Living Standards: Perceptions Versus Evidence', *Ancient Society*, 37 (2007), pp. 191–252. On money and coinage, see R. Duncan-Jones, *Money and Government in the Roman Empire* (Cambridge: Cambridge University Press, 1994), pp. 167–70, and W. Jongman, 'A Golden Age: Death, Money Supply and Social Succession in the Roman Empire', in E. Lo Cascio (ed.), *Credito e moneta nel mondo romano* (Bari: Edipuglia, 2003), pp. 181–96. For financial development, see J. Andreau, *Banking and Business in the Roman World*, trans. J. Lloyd (Cambridge: Cambridge University Press, 1999), P. Temin, 'Financial Intermediation in the Early Roman Empire', *Journal of Economic History*, 64 (2004), pp. 705–33, W. V. Harris, 'A Revisionist View of Roman Money', *Journal of Roman Studies*, 96 (2006), pp. 1–24 and W. V. Harris, 'The Nature of Roman Money', in W. V. Harris (ed.), *The Monetary Systems of the Greeks and Romans* (Oxford: Oxford University Press, 2008), pp. 174–207 .
5. A. Bowman and A. Wilson, *Quantifying the Roman Economy: Methods and Problems* (Oxford: Oxford University Press, 2009). For a summary of Roman trade and commerce, see P. F. Bang 'Trade and Commerce, Roman', in M. Gagarin (ed.), *The Oxford Encyclopedia of Ancient Greece and Rome* (Oxford: Oxford University Press, 2009), available at <http://www.oxfordreference.com/views/ENTRY.html?subview=Main&entry=t294.e1272> [accessed 5 April 2012].
6. Silver, 'Roman Economic Growth', pp. 192, 203, 208.
7. C. Howgego, 'Coin Circulation and the Integration of the Roman Economy', *Journal of Roman Archaeology*, 7 (1994), pp. 5–21.
8. P. Temin, 'A Market Economy in the Early Roman Empire', *Journal of Roman Studies*, 91 (2001), pp. 169–81; P. Temin, 'The Economy of the Early Roman Empire', *Journal of Economic Perspectives*, 20:1 (2006), pp. 133–51.
9. W. Scheidel, I. Morris and R. Saller, *The Cambridge Economic History of the Greco-Roman World* (Cambridge: Cambridge University Press, 2008), with earlier work including, R. W. Goldsmith, 'An Estimate of the Size and Structure of the National Product of the Early Roman Empire', *Review of Income and Wealth*, 30 (1984), pp. 263–88. Further relevant references can be found below.
10. Bowman and Wilson, *Quantifying the Roman Economy*; R. B. Hitchner, 'The Advantages of Wealth and Luxury': The Case for Economic Growth in the Roman Empire', in J. G. Manning and I. Morris (eds), *The Ancient Economy: Evidence and Models* (Stanford,

CA: Stanford University Press, 2005), pp. 207–22; W. Scheidel, 'Real Income Growth in Roman Italy', *Princeton/Stanford Working Papers in Classics* (2006), p. 15; Silver, 'Roman Economic Growth', pp. 197–8, 207.

11. Silver, 'Roman Economic Growth', p. 223.
12. J. Mokyr, *Lever of Riches: Technological Creativity and Economic Progress* (New York and Oxford: Oxford University Press, 1992), chapter 2 surveys the literature to 1992, since which time more evidence has become available. See, for example, M. J. Lewis, *Millstone and Hammer: The Origins of Water Power* (Hull: Hull University Press, 1997); Wilson, 'Machines, Power and the Ancient Economy.
13. P. Fara, *Science: A Four Thousand Year History* (Oxford: Oxford University Press, 2009), p. 52.
14. One of the first authors to argue that Europe was not in fact ahead was Joseph Needham. See J. Needham, *Science and Civilisation in China* (Cambrideg: Cambridge University Press, 1956).
15. Fara, *Science*, p. 53.
16. B. Milanovic, 'An Estimate of Average Income and Inequality in Byzantium around Year 1000', Review of Income and Wealth, 52 (2007), pp. 449–70; G. Persson, *An Economic History of Europe: Knowledge, Institutions and Growth, 800 to the Present* (Cambridge: Cambridge University Press, 2012), p. 28.
17. Fara, *Science*, p. 54.
18. P. Malanima, *Pre-Modern European Economy: One Thousand Years (10th–19th Centuries)* (Leiden and Boston, MA: Brill, 2009), p. 208–11.
19. For a recent discussion of the impact of 'barbarian attacks' see B. Ward-Perkins, *The Fall of Rome: And the End of Civilization* (Oxfrod: Oxford Unievrsity Press, 2006).
20. T. Ertman, *Birth of the Leviathan Building States and Regimes In Medieval Modern Europe* (Cambridge: Cambridge University Press, 1997), p. 38.
21. F. L. Ganshof, *Feudalism* (London: Longman Group, 1996), p. 3.
22. Coordination failures are the natural consequence of this fragmentation, leading to inadequate provision of market-supporting institutions, despite the fact that everyone would benefit from them. See S. R. Epstein, *Freedom and Growth: The Rise of States and Markets in Europe, 1300–1750* (London: Routledge/London School of Economics, 2000). Also see Persson, *An Economic History*, pp. 21–8.
23. Wickham, *Framing the Middle Ages*, p. 698.
24. Persson, *An Economic History*, p. 34.
25. Malanima, *Pre-Modern*, p. 7.
26. Persson, *An Economic History*, pp. 21–8.
27. Such market unraveling can be formally modeled using what economists call a 'market participation externality model' exhibiting multiple equilibria. In such a model, the benefits of using the market are dependent on the number of other people using the market. A relatively rapid unraveling from the high market participation equilibrium to the low market participation equilibrium can be understood in this context. See R. C. Cooper, *Coordination Games: Complementarities and Macroeconomics* (Cambridge: Cambridge University Press, 1999).
28. See, for example, M. McCormick, *Origins of the European Economy: Communications and Commerce, A.D. 300–900* (Cambridge: Cambridge University Press, 2002). G. W. Bowerstock, P. Brown and O. Grabar, *Late Antiquity: A Guide to the Post-Classical World* (Cambridge, MA: Belknap Press of Harvard University Press, 1999), p. ix, and R. Hodges, *Dark Age Economics: A New Audit* (Bristol: Bristol Classical Press, 2012). For

a more optimistic view of the era of the Vikings, see R. Hodges, *Goodbye to the Vikings? Re-Reading Early Medieval Archeology* (London: Duckworth, 2006).

29. Ward-Perkins, *The Fall of Rome*.
30. Originally published in 1937: H. Pirenne, *Mohammed and Charlemagne* (London: G. Allen & Unwin, 1954). Pirenne's work has been much debated; see, for example, R. Hodges and D. Whitehouse, *Mohammed, Charlemagne and the Origins of Europe: Archeology and the Pirenne Thesis* (Ithaca, NY: Cornell University Press, 1983), E. Scott, *Mohammed and Charlemagne Revisited: The History of a Controversy* (London: New English Review Press, 2012), P. Horden and N. Purcell, *The Corrupting Sea: A Study of Mediterranean History* (Oxford: Blackwell, 2000), pp. 32–4, A. Verhulst, *The Carolingian Economy* (Cambrside: Cambridge University Press, 2002), McCormick, *Origins*, and Hodges, *Goodbye to the Vikings*.
31. McCormick, *Origins*, p. 798.
32. Wickham, *Framing the Middle Ages*, p. 803; S. R. H. Jones, 'Transaction Costs, Institutional Change, and the Emergence of a Market Economy in Later Anglo-Saxon England', *Economic History Review*, 46 (1993), p. 667.
33. See Mokyr, *Lever of Riches*, pp. 176–8. Also see N. Rosenberg and L. E. Birdzell, *How the West Grew Rich: Economic Transformation of the Industrial World* (New York: Basic Books, 1986).
34. E. Domar, 'The Causes of Slavery or Serfdom: A Hypothesis', *Journal of Economic History*, 30 (1970), pp. 18–32.
35. G. Duby, *The Early Growth of the European Economy: Warriors and Peasants from the Seventh to the Twelfth Century*, trans. H. B. Clarke (London: Weidenfield and Nicolson, 1974).
36. Domar, 'The Causes of Slavery'.
37. For which the seminal work has recently been republished as I. M. Wallerstein, *The Modern World-System*, 3 vols (Berkley, CA: University of California Press, 2011).
38. P. Sweezy et al., *The Transition from Feudalism to Capitalism* (London: New Left Books, 1976).
39. M. Mann, *The Sources of Social Power. Vol. I: A History of Power from the Beginning to A.D. 1760* (Cambridge: Cambridge University Press, 1986); E. Fernie, 'The Origins of Europe', *Journal of the Warburg and Courtauld Institutes*, 71 (2008), p. 46.
40. J. L. van Zanden, *The Long Road to the Industrial Revolution The European Economy in a Global Perspective, 1000–1800* (Leiden: Brill, 2009), p. 353; H. J. Berman, *Law and Revolution* (Cambridge, MA: Harvard University Press, 1983); Fernie, 'The Origins', p. 46; F. Fukuyama, *The Origins of Political Order: From Prehuman Times to the French Revolution* (New York: Farrar, Straus & Giroux, 2012).
41. Persson, *An Economic History*, p. 17; van Zanden, *The Long Road*, p. 353.
42. Fara, *Science*, p. 83–4.
43. Ibid., p. 83.
44. Ibid., p. 86.
45. Persson, *An Economic History*, p. 17.
46. A. Grief, P. Milgrom and B. R. Weingast, 'Coordination, Commitment, and Enforcement: The Case of the Merchant Guild', *Journal of Political Economy*, 102 (1994), pp. 745–76; A. Grief, *Institutions and the Path to the Modern Economy: Lessons from Medieval Trade* (Cambridge: Cambridge University Press, 2006); T. de Moor, 'The Silent Revolution: A New Perspective on the Emergence of Commons, Guilds, and Other Forms of Corporate Collective Action in Western Europe', *International Review of Social*

History, 53, supplement (2008), pp. 179–212. On craft guilds see S. R. Epstein, 'Craft Guilds, Apprenticeship, and Technological Change in Preindustrial Europe', *Journal of Economic History*, 58 (1998), pp. 684–713.

47. T. Scott, *The City-State in Europe, 1000–1600* (Oxford: Oxford Unievrsity Press, 2012).
48. As explained in Grief, Milgrom and Weingast, 'Coordination, Commitment, and Enforcement', Grief, *Institutions and the Path*, and de Moor, 'The Silent Revolution'.
49. Many authors point to the negative effects of the new institutions, including S. Ogilvie, *Institutions and European Trade* (Cambridge: Cambridge University Press, 2011), S. Ogilvie, 'Were Merchant Guilds Really Beneficial? A Comment on Grief, Milgrom and Weingast', Cambridge University mimeo (1995), S. Ogilvie, '"Whatever Is, Is Right"? Economic Institutions in Pre-Industrial Europe', *Economic History Review*, 60 (2007), pp. 649–84 and Epstein, *Freedom and Growth*.
50. Many authors have pushed back the origins of the European economy to this time, but place emphasis on slightly different periods within this long window (for example, Spufford on the thirteenth century, Davies on the twelfth century, Geary on the eleventh century, Fossier on the tenth century and McCormick and Verhulst on the Carolingian age). See P. Spufford, *Money and its Uses in Medieval Europe* (Cambridge: Cambridge University Press, 1988), M. A. Kishlansky, P. J. Geary and P. O'Brien, *Civilization in the West* (New York and London: Pearson Longman, 2006), R. Fossier, 'Rural Economy and Country life', in T. Reuter (ed.), *The New Cambridge Medieval History, Vol. III: c. 900–c. 1024* (Cambridge: Cambridge University Press, 1999), pp. 27–63, Verhulst, *The Carolingian Economy*, N. Davies, *Europe: A History* (Oxford: Oxford University Press, 1996) and McCormick, *Origins of the European Economy*. Significant debate amongst these authors exist as to whether the origins of economic expansion could be found in agriculture or commerce, whether they were home-grown or rooted in contact with the East, and on the role of the Mediterranean versus the North.
51. Britnell and Campbell (eds), *A Commercialising Economy*; J. Masschaele, 'Transport Costs in Medieval England', *Economic History Review*, 46 (1993), pp. 266–79; J. Masschaele, *Peasants, Merchants and Markets: Inland Trade in Medieval England, 1150–1350* (New York: St Martin's Press, 1997); G. Clark, 'Markets and Economic Growth: Grain Markets in Medieval England', Mimeograph, Department of Economics, U. C. Davis (2002); B. van Bavel, J. Dijkman, E. Kuijpers and J. Zuijderduijn, 'The Organisation of Markets as a Key Factor in the Rise of Holland, Fourteenth-Sixteenth Centuries: A Test Case for an Institutional Approach', *Centre for Global Economic History*, Working Paper number 6 (2011); R. Unger, 'Feeding Low Countries Towns: The Grain Trade in the Fifteenth Century', *Revue Belge de Philolgie et d'Histoire*, 77: 2 (1999), pp. 329–58. Also see the earlier work of R. S. Lopez, *The Commercial Revolution of the Middle Ages, 950–1350* (Cambridge: Cambridge University Press, 1976).
52. S. R. Epstein, 'Regional Fairs, Institutional Innovation, and Economic Growth in Late Medieval Europe', *Economic History Review*, 47 (1994), pp. 459–82; Malanima, *Pre-Modern*, pp. 186, 188.
53. P. Chorley, 'The Cloth Exports of Flanders and Northern France during the Thirteenth Century: A Luxury Trade?', *Economic History Review*, 40 (1987), pp. 349–79.
54. Fara, *Science*, pp. 81–2. Jean Gimpel places emphasis on a slightly earlier period, from the ninth to eleventh century. See J. Gimpel, *The Medieval Machine*: *The Industrial Revolution of the Middle Ages* (New York: Holt, Rinehart & Winston, 1976).

55. Malanima, *Pre-Modern*, p. 185; R. Findlay and K. H. O'Rourke, *Power and Plenty: Trade, War and the World Economy in the Second Millennium* (Princeton, NJ and Oxford: Princeton University Press, 2007), p. 103.
56. Fara, *Science*.
57. Reported from various sources in Malanima, *Pre-Modern*, p. 7, and Persson, *An Economic History*, p. 30.
58. For the history of Venice, see F. C. Lane, *Venice: A Maritime Republic* (Baltimore, MD and London: Johns Hopkins University Press, 1973).
59. Later, Pisa was conquered by Florentine troops and Florence took over as a centre of trade in the region.
60. R. S. Lopez, 'Market Expansion: The Case of Genoa', *Journal of Economic History*, 24 (1964), p. 457.
61. Ibid., p. 450.
62. Ibid., p. 456. On Italian merchants in Southampton in the fourteenth century, see A. A. Ruddock, *Italian Merchants and Shipping in Southampton, 1270–1600* Southampton Records Series (Southampton: University College, 1951).
63. This refers to 'L', 's' and 'd' (pounds – librae, shillings – solidi and pence – denarii); N. Ferguson, *The Ascent of Money: A Financial History of the World* (London: Penguin, 2009), pp. 42–8.
64. Epstein, *Freedom and Growth*.
65. D. Nicholas, 'Of Poverty and Primacy: Demand, Liquidity, and the Flemish Economic Miracle, 1050–1200', *American Historical Review*, 96 (1991), pp. 17–41, on p. 17.
66. Epstein, 'Regional Fairs'; A. Verhulst, *The Rise of Cities in North-West Europe* (Cambridge and New York: Cambridge University Press; Paris: Editions de la Maison des Sciences de l'Homme, 1999).
67. Nicholas, 'Of Poverty and Primacy', pp. 34–5; J. van Houtte, 'The Rise and Decline of the Market of Bruges', *Economic History Review*, 19:1 (1996), pp. 29–47, on p. 31.
68. P. R. Milgrom, D. C. North and B. R. Weingast, 'The Rise of Institutions in the Revival of Trade: The Medieval Law Merchant, Private Judges, and the Champagne Fairs', *Economics and Politics*, 2 (1990), pp. 1–23.
69. S. Ogilvie, *Institutions and European Trade: Merchant Guilds, 1000–1800* (Cambridge: Cambridge University Press, 2011).
70. J. I. Israel, *Dutch Primacy in World Trade 1585–1740* (Oxford: Clarendon Press, 1989), p. 7.
71. P. Dollinger, *The German Hansa*, trans. and ed. D. S. Ault and S. H. Steinberg (London: Routledge, 1999), pp. 191, 203.
72. See, for example, ibid., ch. 2.
73. Ibid., p. xviii.
74. On occasions in which such privileges were not upheld, Hansa merchants would regularly employ a trade blockade to protect their 'rights'.
75. Dollinger, *The German Hansa*, pp. xii, xvii. The First Hanseatic diet took place in 1356.
76. Ibid., pp. xviii (note that pp. xliii–x contains a list of all 200 Hansa towns and p. 4 contains a map which documents the expansion of the Hanseatic realm). By the middle of the fourteenth century, overland connections had been formed with French cities (such as Paris and Bourgneuf), Polish cities (such as Thorn, Cracow and Lemberg) and (along the Rhine via Cologne) with Venice. By the end of the fifteenth century, connections had also reached as far as Lisbon (by sea) and Milan and Genoa (by land) and then from there across the Mediterranean Sea to Barcelona.

77. Ibid., p. xviii.
78. Epstein, 'Regional fairs', p. 473; Jones, 'Transaction Costs'.
79. Israel, *Dutch Primacy*, pp. 20–38.
80. Malanima, *Pre-Modern*, p. 27.
81. McNeill, W., *Plagues and Peoples* (New York: Bantam Doubleday Dell Publishing Group, 1998). ch. 4.
82. P. Freedman, 'Rural Society', in M. Jones (ed.), *New Cambridge Medieval History, Vol. VI: c. 1300–c. 1415*' (Cambridge: Cambridge University Press, 2008), pp. 82–101.
83. Malanima, *Pre-Modern*, p. 25.
84. Ibid., p. 9.
85. M. M. Postan, *Essays on Medieval Agriculture and General Problems of the Medieval Economy* (London: Cambridge University Press, 1973); J. Z. Titow, *English Rural Society 1200–1350* (London: Allen & Unwin, 1969); J. Z. Titow, 'Some Evidence of the Thirteenth-century Population Increase', *Economic History Review*, 14 (1961), pp. 218–24.
86. For the most recent neo-Malthusian view of human history, see G. Clark, *A Farewell to Alms: A Brief Economic History of the World* (Princeton, NJ: Princeton University Press, 2007). For the intense debate surrounding this work, see the symposium on Clark's book in *European Review of Economic History*, 12:2 (2008). Note that those who disagree with the Malthusian view tend to argue that rising population brings benefits – such as supporting markets and enabling specialization – which raise productivity and so enable more people to be fed from a fixed amount of land.
87. A useful amalgamation of population figures for all European countries from 1300 to 1870 can be found in Malanima, *Pre-Modern*, p. 9.
88. Freedman, 'Rural Society'.
89. R. Brenner, 'Agrarian Class Structure and Economic Development in Pre-Industrial Europe', *Past and Present*, 72 (1976), pp. 30–75.
90. Also discussed in van Zanden, *The Long Road*.
91. C. Dyer, *An Age of Transition? Economy and Society in England in the Later Middle Ages* (Oxford: Oxford University Press, 2005), pp. 218–20.
92. Epstein, *Freedom and Growth*.
93. Ibid., pp. 94, 167.
94. Ibid., pp. 54–5.
95. J. R. Strayer, *On the Medieval Origins of the Modern State*, forewords C. Tilly and W. C. Jordan (Princeton, NJ and Oxford: Princeton University Press, 2005); C. Tilly, *Coercion, Capital, and European States, AD 990–1990* (Cambridge MA; Basil Blackwell, 1990); O. Hintze, 'Military Organization and the Organization of the State', in F. Gilbert (ed.), *The Historical Essays of Otto Hintze* (New York: Oxford University Press, 1970), pp. 178–215.
96. Epstein, *Freedom and Growth*, p. 55.
97. T. de Moor and J. L. van Zanden, 'Girl Power: The European Marriage Pattern and Labour Markets in the North Sea Region in the Late Medieval and Early Modern Period', *Economic History Review*, 63 (2009), pp. 1–33.
98. Higher age at marriage is associated with the more favourable 'preventive check' of the Malthusian model.
99. Fara, *Science*, p. 109.
100. Ibid., p. 99.
101. Dollinger, *The German Hansa*; Lopez, 'Market Expansion', pp. 449–56; Ruddock, *Italian Merchants*, pp. 96–9.

102. Israel, *Dutch Primacy*, p. 18.
103. G. Campbell, 'Columbus', in G. Campbell (eds), *The Oxford Dictionary of the Renaissance* (Oxford and New York: Oxford University Press, 2003): e-reference edition distributed by Oxford University Press at: http://www.oxfordreference.com/views/ENTRY.html?subview=Main&entry=t175.e906 [accessed 7 April 2012].
104. M. Prak, *The Dutch Republic in the Seventeenth Century*, trans. D. Webb (Cambridge: Cambridge University Press, 2005), p. 95.
105. Malanima, *Pre-Modern*, p. 170.
106. K. H. O'Rourke and J. G. Williamson, 'Did Vasco da Gama Matter for European Markets? Testing Frederick Lane's Hypothesis Fifty Years On', *Economic History Review*, 62:3 (2009), pp. 655–84.
107. K. H. O'Rourke and J. G. Williamson, 'After Columbus: Explaining the Global Trade Boom 1500–1800', *NBER*, Working Paper 8186 (2001), pp. 3, 32–3 (table 1).
108. This will be discussed further in Chapters 2 and 3.
109. D. Acemoglu, S. Johnson and J. A. Robinson, 'The Rise of Europe: Atlantic Trade, Institutional Change, and Economic Growth, *American Economic Review*, 95 (2005), pp. 546–79.
110. M. Drelichman, 'The Curse of Moctezuma: American Silver and the Dutch Disease, 1501–1650', *Explorations in Economic History*, 42:3 (2005), pp. 349–80.
111. In line with Epstein's view (expressed in *Freedom and Growth*), others argue that political fragmentation was responsible for difficulties. See, for example, J. Voth, 'Debt, Default and Empire: State Capacity and Economic Development in England and Spain in the Early Modern Period', Tawney Lecture, Economic History Society Annual Conference, University of Cambridge (2011); R. Grafe, *Distant Tyranny: Markets, Power, and Backwardness in Spain, 1650–1800* (Princeton, NJ and Woodstock: Princeton University Press, 2012).
112. Epstein, *Freedom and Growth*.
113. The development of absolutist states is discussed in Ertman, *Birth of the Leviathan*. Ertman discusses how the demand for a strong monarch or leader existed in areas subject to external threats, internal religious strife and where bottom-up institutions were becoming paralysed by vested interests.
114. R. C. van Caenegem, *An Historical Introduction to Western Constitutional Law* (Cambridge: Cambridge University Press, 1995); J. L. van Zanden, E. Buringh and M. Bosker, 'The Rise and Decline of European Parliaments, 1188–1789', *Economic History Review* (forthcoming).
115. J. B. De Long and A. Schleifer, 'Princes and Merchants: European City Growth before the Industrial Revolution', *Journal of Law and Economics*, 36 (1993), pp. 671–702; D. C. North and B. Weingast, 'Constitutions and Credible Commitments: The Evolution of the Institutions of Public Choice in 17th Century England', *Journal of Economic History*, 49 (1989), pp. 803–32.
116. Caenegem, *An Historical Introduction*.
117. North and Weingast, 'Constitutions and Credible Commitments'.
118. R. C. Allen, 'Economic Structure and Agricultural Productivity in Europe, 1300–1800', *European Review of Economic History*, 4 (2000), pp. 1–25.
119. Ibid.
120. Ibid.
121. Ibid.

122. R. C. Allen, 'The Great Divergence in European Wages and Prices from the Middle Ages to the First World War', *Explorations in Economic History*, 38 (2001), pp. 427. Data can be found on p. 428, table 6.
123. The provinces are as follows: Holland, Zeeland, Utrect, Fiesland, Gelderland, Groningen, Drenthe and Overijssel. The Council of State was composed of representatives from the provinces. See M. C. t' Hart, *The Making of a Bourgeois State: War, Politics and Finance during the Dutch Revolt* (Manchester and New York: Manchester University Press, 1993).
124. Quoted in Israel, *Dutch Primacy*, pp. 12–13.
125. Ibid., pp. 12–13.
126. Which includes England, France, Spain, Portugal and Germany. Wallerstein, *The Modern World-System*, vol. 3, p. 46.
127. Prak, *The Dutch Republic*, p. 91.
128. Ibid., p. 96.
129. Israel, *Dutch Primacy* (e.g. p. 11).
130. Ibid., p. 98.
131. Ibid., pp. 13–15.
132. t'Hart, *The Making of a Bourgeois State*, p. 17.
133. J. L. Price, *The Dutch Republic in the Seventeenth Century* (Basingstoke: Macmillan, 1998), pp. 42–3.
134. Prak, *The Dutch Republic*, p. 96.
135. Ibid., p. 44.
136. Ibid., p. xi.
137. Ibid., p. 48.
138. Ibid., p. 47.
139. Ibid., p. 18; t'Hart, *The Making of a Bourgeois State*, p. 27.
140. North and Weingast, 'Constitutions and Credible Commitments'. See also North and Thomas, *The Rise of the Western World*, pp. 155–6.
141. To be discussed in Chapter 2.
142. D. Ormrod, *The Rise of Commercial Empires: England and the Netherlands in the Age of Mercantilism, 1650–1770*, Cambridge Studies in Modern Economic History (Cambridge: Cambridge University Press, 2003); P. K. O'Brien 'Mercantilism and Imperialism in the Rise and Decline of the Dutch and British Economies 1585–1815', *De Economist*, 148 (2000), pp. 469–501; P. K. O'Brien, T. Griffiths and P. Hunt, 'Political Components of the Industrial Revolution: Parliament and the English Cotton Textile Industry, 1660–1774', *Economic History Review*, new series, 44 (1982), pp. 395–423.
143. Ormrod, *The Rise of Commercial Empires*, p. 55.
144. Williams, Frank and Wallerstein were some of the original authors to point to the importance of colonial trade. E. E. Williams, *Capitalism and Slavery* (Chapel Hill, NC: University of North Carolina Press, 1944); A. G. Frank, *Dependent Accumulation and Underdevelopment* (London: Macmillan, 1978); Wallerstein, *The Modern World-System*. Evidence that the direct impact of trade was too small comes from the following: S. L. Engerman, 'The Slave Trade and British Capital Formation in the Eighteenth Century: A Comment on the Williams Thesis', *Business History Review*, 46 (1972), pp. 430–43; S. L. Engerman and P. K. O'Brien, 'Export and the Growth of the British Economy from the Glorious Revolution to the Peace of Amiens', in B. L. Solow (ed.), *Slavery and the Rise of the Atlantic System* (Cambridge: Cambridge University Press, 1991), pp. 177–209; P. K. O'Brien, 'European Economic Development: The Contribution of the Periphery',

Economic History Review, 35 (1982), pp. 1–18; P. Bairoch, *Economics and World History: Myths and Paradoxes* (Chicago, IL: University of Chicago Press, 1995).

145. R. C. Allen, *The British Industrial Revolution in Global Perspective* (Cambridge: Cambridge University Press, 2009).
146. Ibid.
147. K. Pomeranz, *The Great Divergence: China, Europe, and the Making of the Modern World Economy* (Princeton, NJ and Oxford: Princeton University Press, 2000).
148. R. Davis, 'English Foreign Trade, 1700–1774', *Economic History Review*, 15:2 (1962), pp. 285–303, on p. 290.
149. R. Davis 'English Foreign Trade, 1660–1700', *Economic History Review*, 7:2 (1954), pp. 150-66, on pp. 151–3.
150. J. Mokyr, *The Enlightened Economy: An Economic and Social History of Britain 1700–1850* (Newhaven. CT: Yale University Press, 2009).
151. E. A. Wrigley, *Energy and the English Industrial Revolution* (Cambridge: Cambridge University Press, 2010).
152. C. K. Harley, 'Ocean Freight Rates and Productivity, 1740–1913: The Primacy of Mechanical Innovation Reaffirmed', *Journal of Economic History*, 48 (1988), pp. 851–76.
153. B. Cater and B. Lew, 'The Telegraph, Coordination of Tramp Shipping, and Growth in World Trade, 1870–1910', *European Review of Economic History*, 10 (2006), pp. 147–73.
154. M. Flandreau and M. Maurel, 'Monetary Union, Trade Integration, and Business Cycles in 19th Century Europe', *Open Economics Review*, 16 (2005), pp. 135–52; K. J. Mitchener and M. Weidenmier, 'Empire, Public Goods, and the Roosevelt Corollary', *Journal of Economic History*, 65 (2005), pp. 658–92; D.. Jacks, 'What Drove Nineteenth Century Commodity Market Integration?' *Explorations in Economic History*, 43 (2006), pp. 383–412; A. Estevadeordal, A. M. Taylor and B. Frantz, 'The Rise and Fall of World Trade, 1870–1939', *Quarterly Journal of Economics*, 118 (2003), pp. 359–407; J. E. Lopez-Cordova and C. M. Meissner, 'Exchange Rate Regimes and International Trade: Evidence from the Classical Gold Standard Era, 1870–1913', *American Economic Review*, 93 (2003), pp. 344–53.
155. Findlay and O'Rourke, *Power and Plenty*, ch. 7.
156. K. H. O'Rourke and J. G. Williamson, 'Late 19th Century Anglo-American Factor Price Convergence: Were Heckscher and Ohlin Right?', *Journal of Economic History*, 54 (1994), pp. 1–25; K. H. O'Rourke and J. G. Williamson (1997), 'Around the European Periphery 1870–1913: Globalisation, Schooling and Growth', *European Review of Economic History*, 1:2, pp. 153–90; K. H. O'Rourke and J. G. Williamson, *Globalisation and History: The Evolution of a Nineteenth Century Atlantic Economy* (Cambridge, MA and London: MIT, 1999); K. H. O'Rourke and J. G. Williamson, 'When Did Globalization Begin?', *European Review of Economic History*, 6:1 (2002), pp. 23–50; M. Obstfeld and A. M. Taylor, *Global Capital Markets: Integration, Crisis and Growth* (Cambridge: Cambridge University Press, 2004) .
157. T. J. Hatton and J. G. Williamson (eds), *Migration and the International Labour Market 1850–1939* (London: Routledge, 1994), p. 4.
158. M. Edelstein, *Overseas Investment in the Age of High Imperialism: The United Kingdom, 1850–1914* (London: Methuen, 1982), p. 3.
159. H.-J. Chang, *Kicking Away the Ladder: Development Strategy in Historical Perspective* (London: Anthem Press, 2002).
160. Also see D. A. Irwin, 'Trade Restrictiveness and Deadweight Losses from US Tariffs', *American Economic Journal: Economic Policy*, 2:3 (2010), pp. 111–33, who measures

the welfare loss from this policy. For evidence of any 'infant' industry learning by doing effects that in theory might outweigh these static welfare losses in the case of the USA, see, for example, P. David, 'Learning by Doing and Tariff Protection: A Reconsideration of the Case of the Ante-Bellum United States Cotton Textile Industry', *Journal of Economic History*, 30 (1970), pp. 521–601, and K. Head, 'Infant Industry Protection in the Steel Rail Industry', *Journal of International Economics*, 37 (1994), pp. 141–65. Irwin is doubtful for the case of tinplate: D. A. Irwin, 'Did Late-Nineteenth Century U.S. Tariffs Promote Infant Industries? Evidence from the Tinplate Industry', *Journal of Economic History*, 60:2 (2000), pp. 335–60.

161. Of course, this is not to say that tariffs were at the root of such growth. As argued by S. Broadberry in *The Productivity Race: British Manufacturing in International Perspective, 1850–1990* (Cambridge: Cambridge University Press, 1997), resource endowments in the US also appear to be an important part of the story. There is a big debate on the relationship between tariffs and growth in the late nineteenth century. For a summary, see C. M. Meissner, 'Growth from Globalization?'.
162. Obstfeld and Taylor, *Global Capital Markets*; Findlay and O'Rourke, *Power and Plenty*, ch. 8.
163. O'Rourke and Williamson, *Globalisation and History*, p. 30.
164. P. Mauro, N. Sussman and Y. Yafah, *Emerging Markets and Financial Globalization: Sovereign Bond Spreads in 1870–1913* (Oxford: Oxford University Press, 2006); M. Schularick, 'A Tale of Two 'Globalizations': Capital Flows from Rich to Poor in Two Eras of Global Finance', *International Journal of Finance and Economics*, 11 (2006), pp. 339–54.
165. Extending the work in V. N. Bateman, 'The Evolution of Markets in Early Modern Europe, 1350–1800: A Study of Wheat Prices', *Economic History Review*, 64 (2011), pp. 447–71.

2 The Course of Early Modern Market Integration: Country Level Results

1. In the Ricardian view, countries differ in terms of technology. In the Heckscher-Ohlin view, they differ in terms of resource endowments. Either way, trade creates benefits.
2. Using the Heckscher-Ohlin model, economists note that there will be a redistribution of income within each economy, as the abundant factor of production will gain but the scarce factor will lose, but the gains will outweigh the losses.
3. O'Rourke and Williamson have provided a compelling justification for the use of price data as opposed to volume of trade data in the study of market integration. As they point out, trade can increase as a result of factors independent of increasing integration, and so is not an ideal indicator of market development. See K. H. O'Rourke and J. G. Williamson, 'After Columbus', pp. 10–12. Whilst grain markets were subject to regulation, such regulation rarely took the form of maximum prices. See G. Persson, *Grain Markets in Europe, 1500–1900: Integration and Deregulation* (Cambridge: Cambridge University Press, 1999), p. 77. As such, the use of price data is not open to serious concern.
4. Or, in strict terms, greater consumption opportunities relative to the economy's production capacity, increasing the average welfare of its citizens.

5. Integration will be price-stabilizing if the 'world' output varies less than 'local' output of the good, as is generally the case for agricultural products.
6. An alternative approach taken by economic historians to measure market integration is to work with the gravity equation and through this to indirectly estimate (unobservable) trade costs. See, for example, D. Jacks, C. M. Meissner and D. Novy, 'Trade Costs in the First Wave of Globalization', *Explorations in Economic History*, 47 (2011), pp. 127–41. Whilst this method works well when applied to the nineteenth century onwards, a lack of data on volumes of trade makes it almost impossible to apply to the period before then.
7. Lord W. H. Beveridge, *Prices and Wages in England from the Twelfth to the Nineteenth Century* (London: Cass, 1965), pp. xlix–li; A. Cole and R. Crandall, 'The International Scientific Committee on Price History', *Journal of Economic History*, 24 (1964), pp. 381–8.
8. Malanima, *Pre-Modern*, pp. 106, 302.
9. Ibid., p. 304.
10. Such as from the Home Counties to London and from Ile de France to Paris. See D. Hay, *Europe in the Fourteenth and Fifteenth Centuries* (London and New York: Longman, 1989), p. 398; N. J. G. Pounds, *An Historical Geography of Europe 1500–1840* (Cambridge: Cambridge University Press, 1979), p. 61.
11. Pounds, *An Historical Geography*, p. 61; Nicholas, 'Economic Reorientation', p. 11; Nicholas, 'Of Poverty and Primacy', pp. 27–8, 34.
12. Nicholas, 'Of Poverty and Primacy', p. 34.
13. Pounds, *An Historical Geography*, pp. 278–80. As a rough estimate, the cost of carrying a cargo of corn from Danzig to Bruges was about 48 per cent of the value of the cargo in the early fifteenth century (Hay, *Europe*, p. 390).
14. Pounds, *An Historical Geography*, pp. 61–3, 276; Hay, *Europe*, pp. 395–8.
15. Hay, *Europe*, p. 398; R. Cameron and L. Neal, *A Concise Economic History of the World from Paleolithic Times to the Present* (New York and Oxford: Oxford Unievrsity Press, 2003), p. 58.
16. Hay, *Europe*, p. 396, p. 398.
17. For example, see the case of Dutch agriculture discussed in D. Jacks, 'Market Integration in the North and Baltic Seas, 1500–1800', *Journal of European Economic History*, 33:3 (2004), pp. 285–329.
18. Persson, *Grain Markets*.
19. Bateman, 'A Study of Wheat Prices'.
20. See, for example, Persson, *Grain Markets*.
21. E. J. Hobsbawm 'The General Crisis of the European Economy in the 17th Century', *Past and Present*, 5 (1954), pp. 33–53.
22. O'Rourke and Williamson, 'After Columbus', pp. 32–4, table 1.
23. W. G. Heeres, L. M. J. B. Hesp, L. Noordegraaf and R. C. W. van der Voort, *From Dunkirk to Danzig: Shipping and Trade in the North Sea and the Baltic, 1350–1850* (Hilversum: Verloren Publishers, 1988), esp. pp. 420-2, 38–40; A. Attman *The Russian and Polish Markets in International Trade, 1500–1650* (Göteborg: Institute of Economic History of Gothenburg University, 1973), p. 65.
24. The current website address is as follows: www.history.ubc.ca/faculty/Unger/ECPdb/Submit.html.
25. The current website address is as follows: www.iisg.nl/hpw/data.php.

26. E. J. Hamilton, *American Treasure and the Price Revolution in Spain, 1501–1650* (Cambridge, MA: Harvard University Press, 1934).
27. These percentage price-gaps can be approximated to the following: Gapi,j,t = ln(Pi,t/Pj,t). Not all pairs of cities traded directly – some were instead connected through a third market.
28. See Appendix 2.
29. See Appendix 2 for a note on the panel data method employed to arrive at the country averages.
30. Once again, these country averages are arrived at by applying a fixed effects regression with time dummies to the city-level results for each country. This avoids any biases caused by missing data.
31. The theory behind this approach can be found in S. Johansen (1988), 'Statistical Analysis of Cointegrating Vectors', *Journal of Economic Dynamics and Control*, 12 (1998), pp. 231–54. The natural logarithm of the price data is used in the VECMs calculated in this chapter. Other studies using this approach include Persson, *Grain Markets*, which also discusses the method in greater detail. For an earlier technique, see M. Ravallion, 'Testing Market Integration', *American Journal of Agricultural Economics*, 68 (1986), pp. 102–9.
32. Kindly available online at www.nuffield.ox.ac.uk/General/Members/allen.aspx.
33. S. Özmucur and Ş. Pamuk, 'Did European Commodity Prices Converge during 1500–1800?', in T. J. Hatton, K. O'Rourke and A. M. Taylor, *New Comparative Economic History: Essays in Honour of Jeffrey G. Williamson* (Cambridge, MA and London: MIT Press, 2007), pp. 59–86; O'Rourke and Williamson, 'Did Vasco da Gama Matter'. Also see, V. N. Bateman, 'Market Integration in the Mediterranean', *Economic History Society Conference Paper* (2011).
34. For soap, the cities are London, Antwerp, Amsterdam, Vienna, Naples and Madrid. For candles, the cities were London, Antwerp, Augsburg, Vienna, Madrid, Strabourg and Amsterdam. For linen, the cities were London, Antwerp, Augsburg, Munich, Leipzig, Strasbourg and an amalgamation of Florence and Milan prices. Given the annual nature of the data, volatility and speed of adjustment are not attempted.
35. For a brief summary of the development of Italy's connections with the East and of the rise of Venice, see H. Van der Wee, 'Structural Changes in European Long-Distance Trade, and Particularly in the Re-export Trade from South to North, 1350–1750', in J. D. Tracy, *The Rise of Merchant Empires: Long Distance Trade in the Early Modern World, 1350–1750* (Cambridge: Cambridge University Press, 1993), pp. 14–33.
36. A number of authors have argued that Italian success was the product of merchant capitalism (see Epstein, *Freedom and Growth*, p. 71).
37. Van der Wee, 'Structural Changes, pp. 21, 23, 27; Ashtor, 'E., The Volume of Levantine Trade in the Later Middle Ages 1370–1498', *Journal of European Economic History*, 4 (1975), pp. 573–612, on p. 609.
38. See Epstein, *Freedom and Growth*, ch. 5.
39. R. H. Britnell, 'England and Northern Italy in the Early Fourteenth Century: The Economic Contrasts', *Transactions of the Royal Historical Society*, series 5, 39 (1989), pp. 168–70; Ferguson, *The Ascent of Money* p. 42.
40. See Appendix 2.
41. Scott, *The City-State in Europe*, p. 55 contains a useful map of the city-state divisions.
42. Epstein, *Freedom and Growth*, p. 71.

43. The 'Western European average', which will be used as a comparison tool throughout the country-level markets histories, includes all countries except Poland and the Ottoman Empire.
44. Epstein (*Freedom and Growth*, pp. 162–4) has previously identified an increasing integration of Italian markets at this time.
45. Ibid., pp. 94, 167.
46. However, improvements were not without exception. Where the vested interests of cities were too strong relative to the state, they acted to prevent improvements in integration that risked introducing more competition and weakening the monopoly position of the city. See Epstein, *Freedom and Growth*, and Epstein, 'Regional Fairs', p. 472–3.
47. In particular, see R. T. Rapp, *Industry and Economic Decline in Seventeenth-Century Venice* (Cambridge, MA and London: Harvard University Press, 1976).
48. This non-wheat price data is from IISH www.iisg.nl/hpw/data.php and Allen www.nuffield.ox.ac.uk/General/Members/allen.aspx.
49. P. Sénac, 'Spain, Muslim', in A. Vauchez, B. Dobson and M. Lapidge (eds), *Encyclopedia of the Middle Ages* (Cambridge: James Clarke, 2001): e-reference edition distributed by Oxford University Press at http://www.oxfordreference.com/views/ENTRY.html?subview=Main&entry=t179.e2683-s1__[accessed 7 April 2012]; A. Rucquoi, 'Castile', in A. Vauchez, B. Dobson and M. Lapidge (eds), *Encyclopedia of the Middle Ages* (Cambridge: James Clarke, 2001): e-reference edition distributed by Oxford University Press at: http://www.oxfordreference.com/views/ENTRY.html?subview=Main&entry=t179.e494 [accessed 7 April 2012].
50. Dollinger, *The German Hansa*; R. Grafe, 'Northern Spain between the Iberian and Atlantic Worlds: Trade and Regional Specialisation, 1550–1650', Economic History Association (US) Gerschenkron prize dissertation summary, *Journal of Economic History*, 62 (2002), pp. 533–7; M. Aurell, 'Barcelona', in A. Vauchez, B. Dobson and M. Lapidge (eds), *Encyclopedia of the Middle Ages* Cambridge: James Clarke, 2001): e-reference edition distributed by Oxford University Press at: http://www.oxfordreference.com/views/ENTRY.html?subview=Main&entry=t179.e303>[accessed 7 April 2012].
51. R. E. Dupuy and T. N. Dupuy, *The Encyclopedia of Military History: From 3500 B.C. to the Present*, 2nd rev. edn (London: Jane's, 1986), pp. 430–1; G. Campbell, 'Aragon', in G. Campbell, *The Oxford Dictionary of the Renaissance* (Oxford: Oxford University Press, 2003): e-reference edition distributed by Oxford University Press at: http://www.oxfordreference.com/views/ENTRY.html?subview=Main&entry=t175.e186 [accessed 7 April 2012].
52. W. D. Phillips Jr, 'Columbus, Christopher', in D. Buisseret (eds), *The Oxford Companion to World Exploration* (Oxford: Oxford University Press, 2007): e-reference edition distributed by Oxford University Press at: www.oxfordreference.com/views/ENTRY.html?subview=Main&entry=t230.e0166 [accessed 7 April 2012].
53. J. K. J. Thomson, *A Distinctive Industrialization: Cotton in Barcelona 1728–1832* (New York: Cambridge University Press, 1992), p. 26.
54. Thomson, *A Distinctive Industrialization*, p. 27, 31; E. Ashtor, 'Catalan Cloth on the Late Medieval Mediterranean Markets', *Journal of European Economic History*, 17 (1988), pp. 233–57.
55. Thomson, *A Distinctive Industrialization*, pp. 27, 31.
56. Ibid., p. 34.
57. Ibid., p. 46.
58. Drelichman, 'The Curse of Moctezuma'.

59. Voth, 'Debt, Default and Empire'.
60. J. Simpson, *Spanish Agriculture: The Long Siesta, 1765–1965*, Cambridge Studies in Modern Economic History, 2 (Cambridge: Cambridge University Press, 1995); J. Vicens Vives, J. Nadal and F. M. Lâopez-Morillas, *An Economic History of Spain* (Princeton, NJ: Princeton University Press, 1969).
61. Simpson, *Spanish Agriculture*.
62. M. S. Anderson, *Europe in the Eighteenth Century, 1713–1783*, 3rd edn (London: Longman, 1987), p. 76.
63. Grafe, *Distant Tyranny*; Voth, 'Debt, Default and Empire'.
64. D. R. Ringrose *Madrid and the Spanish Economy, 1560–1850* (Berkeley, CA and London: University of California Press, 1983), p. 7.
65. See Grafe, *Distant Tyranny*, for a recent study on market integration in seventeenth- and eighteenth-century Spain.
66. This explains the low average volatility for Spain overall (which is an average of Barcelona, Valencia and Madrid).
67. Hamilton, *American Treasure*, p. 198.
68. G. Anes Alvarez, *Las crises agrarias en la espana moderna* (Madrid, 1970), p. 495, which is discussed in Ringrose, *Madrid*, p. 5.
69. The soap data is from IISH http://www.iisg.nl/hpw/data.php and Allen http://www.nuffield.ox.ac.uk/General/Members/allen.aspx.
70. The linen data is from IISH http://www.iisg.nl/hpw/data.php and Allen http://www.nuffield.ox.ac.uk/General/Members/allen.aspx.
71. The nail data is from IISH http://www.iisg.nl/hpw/data.php.
72. The olive oil data is from IISH http://www.iisg.nl/hpw/data.php and (for Madrid) Allen http://www.nuffield.ox.ac.uk/General/Members/allen.aspx.
73. J. R. Roses and B. Sanchez-Alonso, 'Regional Wage Convergence in Spain 1850–1930', *Explorations in Economic History*, 41:4 (October, 2004), pp. 404–25; R. Barquín, 'Transport y precio del trigo en el siglo XIX', *Revista de Historia Económica*, año XV, 1 (1997), pp. 17–48; T. Martínez Vara, 'Fluctuaciones estacionales e integración de mercados en Santander y Castilla durante la primera mitad del siglo XIX', *Studia Histórica. Historia Contemporánea*, 17 (1999), pp. 185–289; D. Jacks, 'Intra- and International Commodity Market Integration in the Atlantic Economy, 1800–1913', *Explorations in Economic History*, 42: 3 (2005), pp. 381–413.
74. Over time, silver mines were depleted and other states began to compete in the colonial domain.
75. Ringrose, *Madrid*, p. 10, 16, 312–4; Voth, 'Debt, Default and Empire'.
76. Dupuy and Dupuy, *Encyclopedia*, p. 488.
77. H. Pirenne, *Medieval Cities: Their Origins and the Revival of Trade* (Princeton, NJ: Princeton University Press, 1925); H. Pirenne, *Economic and Social History of Medieval Europe* (New York: Harcourt, Brace & Company, 1937).
78. J. M. Murray, 'Wool, Cloth and Gold', in J. M. Murray, *Bruges: Cradle of Capitalism, 1280–1390* (Cambridge: Cambridge University Press, 2005), pp. 259–99.
79. Allen, 'The Great Divergence' and Allen, 'Economic Structure'. On urbanization, also see J. de Vries, *European Urbanization 1500–1800* (London: Methuen, 1984).
80. J. Dijkman, *Shaping Medieval Markets: The Organisation of Commodity Markets in Holland, c. 1200–c. 1450* (Leiden and Boston, MA: Brill, 2011); Unger, 'Feeding Low Countries Towns', p. 334–8; H. van der, Wee *The Growth of the Antwerp Market and*

the European Economy: Fourteenth–Sixteenth Centuries, 3 vols (The Hague: Martinus Nijhoff, 1963), vol. 1, p. 22–4.
81. Nicholas, 'Economic Reorientation', pp. 10, 13.
82. J. D. Tracy, *The Rise of Merchant Empires: Long Distance Trade in the Early Modern World, 1350–1750* (Cambridge: Cambridge University Press, 1993). p. 16.
83. Murray, 'Wool, Cloth and Gold', pp. 281, 288.
84. Ibid., p. 288.
85. J. M. Murray, *Bruges: Cradle Of Capitalism, 1280–1390* (Cambridge: Cambridge University Press, 2005), p. 122.
86. This was not resolved until the opening of the Bruges-Ostend Canal in 1663.
87. F. Braudel, *La dynamique du capitalism* (Paris: Flammarion, 1985), pp. 97, 143.
88. Prak, *The Dutch Republic*, p. 95.
89. C. Lesger, *The Rise of the Amsterdam Market and Information Exhange: Merchants, Commercial Expansion and Change in the Spatial Economy of the Low Countries c. 1550–1630* (Aldershot: Ashgate, 2006), p. 187.
90. Israel, *Dutch Primacy*, p. 5.
91. J. C. H. Blom and E. Lamberts, *History of the Low Countries* (New York and Oxford: Berghahn Books, 1999), p. 230.
92. Dupuy and Dupuy, *Encyclopedia*.
93. J. van Houtte, *An Economic History of the Low Countries, 800–1800* (London: Weidenfeld & Nicolson, 1977), p. 204.
94. K. Veraghtert, 'The Antwerp Port, 1790–1814', in J. Winter (ed.), *The Interactions of Amsterdam and Antwerp with the Baltic Region 1400–1800. Papers Presented at the Third International Conference of the 'Association Internationale d'Histoire des Mers Nordiques de l'Europe', Utrecht, 30th August–3rd September 1982* (Leiden: Brill, 1983), pp. 193–9.
95. This finding is also in agreement with Unger's work on the Low Countries: R. Unger, 'Integration of Baltic and Low Countries Grain Markets, 1400–1800', in J. M. van Winter (ed.), *The Interactions of Amsterdam and Antwerp with the Baltic Region, 1400–1800* (Leiden: Brill, 1983), pp. 1–10.
96. Malanima, *Pre-Modern*, p. 222.
97. G. Dejongh, B. van Campenhout and M. Ceusters 'In de greep van de markt De integratie van de regionale landbouwmarkten in Belgie, 1700–1850', *Revue Belgie d_histoire contemporaine*, 30 (2000), pp. 5–47
98. E. Buyst, S. Dercon and B. van Campenhout, 'Road Expansion and Market Integration in the Austrian Low Countries during the Second Half of the 18th Century', *Center for Economic Studies, University of Leuven* (2000).
99. B. J. P. van Bavel, 'The Organization and Rise of Land and Lease Markets in Northwestern Europe and Italy, *c.* 1000–1800', *Continuity and Change*, 23 (2008), pp. 20–1; van Bavel, Dijkman, Kuijpers and Zuijderduijn, 'The Organisation of Markets', pp 5, 24.
100. van Bavel, 'The Organization', pp. 13–53.
101. J. De Vries and A. M. van der Woude, *The First Modern Economy: Success, Failure, and Perseverance of the Dutch Economy, 1500–1815* (Cambridge: Cambridge University Press, 1997), p. 160.
102. Bavel, Dijkman, Kuijpers and Zuijderduijn, 'The Organisation of Markets', p. 26.
103. Dijkman, *Shaping Medieval Markets*.
104. This union took place in 1579. Dupuy and Dupuy, *Encyclopedia*, p. 485.
105. Israel, *Dutch Primacy*, p. 12.
106. Prak, *The Dutch Republic*, p. 110.

107. Prak, *The Dutch Republic*, p. 89.
108. The literature on the ascent of Holland is extensive, but includes: J. L. van Zanden, *The Rise and Decline of Holland's Economy: Merchant Capitalism and the Labour Market* (Manchester: Manchester University Press, 1993); J. L. van Zanden, 'The "Revolt of the Early Modernists" and the "First Modern Economy": An Assessment', *Economic History Review*, 55 (2002), pp. 619–41; F. Braudel, *La Mediterranee* (Paris: Colin, 1949), pp. 572–5; F. Braudel, *Civilisation Materialle*, 3 vols (Paris: Colin, 1979), vol. 3, p. 174; Israel, *Dutch Primacy*; Blom and Lamberts, *History of the Low Countries*, esp. pp. 143–8; de Vries and van der Woude, *The First Modern Economy*; P. K. O'Brien, 'Mercantilism and Imperialism'; Veraghtert, 'The Antwerp Port', pp. 193–9; van Houtte, *An Economic History*, pp. 187–2010; Van der Wee, *The Growth of the Antwerp Market*.
109. de Vries and van der Woude, *The First Modern Economy*; van Zanden, 'The "Revolt"'.
110. van Zanden, 'The "Revolt"'.
111. de Vries, *European Urbanization*, p. 39.
112. J. L. van Zanden, 'Estimating Early Modern Economic Growth', *International Institute of Social History, University of Utrecht*, Working Paper (2004).
113. Israel, *Dutch Primacy*, p. 6.
114. Unger, 'Feeding Low Countries Towns'; Bavel, Dijkman, Kuijpers and Zuijderduijn, 'The Organisation of Markets' .
115. O'Brien, 'Mercantilism and Imperialism'.
116. t' Hart, *The Making of a Bourgeois State*, p. 27; J. Aalbers, 'Holland's Financial Problems (1713–1733) and the Wars Against Louis XIV', in A. C. Duke and C. A. Tamje (eds), *Britain and the Netherlands: Papers Delivered to the Sixth Anglo-Dutch Conference* (The Hague: Martinus Nijhoff, 1977), pp. 79–93; C. Wilson, 'Taxation and the Decline of Empires'.
117. Ormrod, *The Rise of Commercial Empires*, p. 307.
118. Israel, *Dutch Primacy*, pp. 292–358; O'Brien, 'Mercantilism and Imeprialism'; Ormrod, *The Rise of Commercial Empires*.
119. t'Hart, *The Making of a Bourgeois State*, p. 17.
120. Ormrod, *The Rise of Commercial Empires*, p. 55.
121. O'Brien, 'Mercantilism and Imperialism', p. 473.
122. Ormrod, *The Rise of Commercial Empires*.
123. See, for example, Bavel, Dijkman, Kuijpers and Zuijderduijn, 'The Organisation of Markets', p. 27–8.
124. E. A. Wrigley, *Energy and the English Industrial Revolution*.
125. de Vries, *European Urbanization*; van Zanden, 'Estimating Early Modern Economic Growth'.
126. A. Maddison, *The World Economy: A Millenial Perspective* (Paris: Development Centre of the Organisation for Economic Co-operation and Development, 2001), Appendix B.
127. D. C. North and B. Weingast, 'Constitutions and Credible Commitments' For a summary critique, see Allen, *The British Industrial Revolution*, p. 5.
128. Ormrod, *The Rise of Commercial Empires*; O'Brien, 'Mercantilism and Imperialism'; Chang, *Kicking Away the Ladder*.
129. In modern day economics language, the Dutch economy was a 'cluster', like the modern day City of London. Such clusters benefit from external economies of scale and increasing returns to scale, making it difficult for other areas to 'break into' the market. In such instances, a case can be made for infant industry protection. See P. Krugman, and M. Obstfeld, *International Economics* (Reading, MA and London: Addison-Wesley, 2006).
130. Acemoglu, Johnson and Robinson, 'The Rise of Europe'.

131. Jones, 'Transaction Costs'.
132. Ibid., pp. 669–70.
133. A. Bell, 'The Organization of Public Work in Society and by the State in Early Medieval England *c.* 800-*c.* 1300' (DPhil thesis, University of Oxford, 2006).
134. This quote is taken from Jones, 'Transaction Costs', p. 675.
135. R. H. Britnell, *Commercialisation of English Society, 1000–1500* (Cambridge: Cambridge University Press, 1993); C. Dyer, 'The Consumer and the Market in the Later Middle Ages', *Economic History Review*, 42 (1989), pp. 305–27; G. Clark, 'Markets and Economic Growth'; J. Masschaele, 'Transport Costs in Medieval England', *Economic History Review*, 46 (1993), pp. 266–79; J. A. Galloway (ed.), *Trade, Urban Hinterlands and Market Integration c. 1300–1600*, Working Papers, series 3 (London: Centre for Metropolitan History, Institute of Historical Research, 2000); Masschaele, *Peasants, Merchants and Markets*; J. Langdon and J. Claridge, 'Transport in Medieval England', *History Compass*, 9 (2011), pp. 864–75; R. H. Britnell, 'The Proliferation of Markets in England, 1200–1349', *Economic History Review*, 34:2 (1981), pp. 209–21; Britnell, *Commercialisation of English Society*; R. Britnell and B. M. S. Campbell (eds), *A Commercialising Economy;* B. M. S. Campbell *English Seigniorial Agriculture 1250–1450* (Cambridge: Cambridge University Press, 2000); M. Kowaleski, *Local Markets and Regional Trade in Medieval Exeter* (Cambridge: Cambridge University Press, 1995).
136. Masschaele, 'Transport Costs in Medieval England'.
137. Dyer, 'The Consumer', p. 305.
138. Britnell, *Commercialisation of English Society*, pp. 90–3.
139. Epstein, 'Regional Fairs', p. 473.
140. Using price volatility measures, Galloway in *Trade, Urban Hinterlands and Market Integration* also identifies a deterioration in market integration between Exeter and London at this time, which he argues to be a result of currency debasements, epidemic disease in 1550s and a possible destabilization of coastal markets due to the rapid growth of London.
141. V. N. Bateman, 'Market Integration and Growth in Europe: The Early Modern era' (DPhil Economics Thesis, University of Oxford, 2006), chs 1, 3.
142. Ruddock, *Italian Merchants*, p. 97.
143. Ibid., pp. 115–6.
144. Ibid., pp. 99, 106.
145. Dollinger, *The German Hansa*, p.xi.
146. According to J. L. Abu-Lughod, *Before European Hegemony: The World System A.D. 1250–1350* (New Yorka dn Oxford: Oxford Unievrsity Press, 1989).
147. B. M. S. Campbell, 'Factor Markets in England before the Black Death', *Continuity and Change*, 24 (2009), pp. 79–106, on p. 80.
148. Holland was slightly ahead, as argued by Bavel, Dijkman, Kuijpers and Zuijderduijn, in 'The Organisation of Markets', pp. 21–2.
149. R. Davis, 'The Rise of Protection in England, 1689–1786', *Economic History Review*, 19 (1966), pp. 306–17.
150. Dupuy and Dupuy, *Encyclopedia*, pp. 424–5.
151. van Zanden, 'Estimating Early Modern Economic Growth'.
152. de Vries, *European Urbanization*, p. 39; Allen, 'Economic Structure'.
153. E. Le Roy Ladurie, *Les paysans de Languedoc* (Paris: S. E. V. P. E. N, 1966); J. Meuvret, *Le problème des subsistances à l'époque de Louis XIV*, 3 vols (Paris, 1977–88). See C. O'Gráda and J-M. Chevet, 'Market Segmentation and Famine in ancien régime France', Journal of Economic History, 42 (2002), pp. 706–33, for further references and discussion.

154. P. T. Hoffman, *Growth in a Traditional Society: The French Countryside, 1450–1815* (Princeton, NJ: Princeton University Press, 1996). See J. Miller, *Mastering the Market: The State and the Grain Trade in Northern France, 1700–1860* (Cambridge: Cambridge University Press, 1998), pp. 27–8, 42, for the hazards and threat of sabotage associated with the grain trade.
155. Meuvret, *Le problem.*
156. Brenner, 'Agrarian Class Structure'.
157. Meuvret, *Le problem*, vol. 3, p. 173.
158. Ibid.; P. T. Hoffman, 'Land Rents and Agricultural Productivity: The Paris Basin, 1450–1789', *Journal of Economic History*, 51:4 (December, 1991), pp. 771–805; E. Le Roy Ladurie, *The Ancien Regime: A History of France, 1610–1774* (Oxford and Cambridge, MA: Blackwell, 1996).
159. Based on the estimation of the coefficient of variation across the set of prices. A. P. Usher, *The History of the Grain Trade in France 1400–1700* (Cambridge, MA: Harvard University Press, 1913), provides a map which details grain movements within France. Grain movements are also extensively discussed in Meuvret, *Le Problem.*
160. For evidence on declining transport costs in France originating from other sources (such as the establishment of middlemen), see J. Letaconnoux, 'Les transports en France au 18e siecle', *Revue d'histoire moderne et contemporaine*, 11 (1908/9), pp. 97–114, 269–92.
161. Reed G. Geiger, *Planning the French Canals: Bureaucracy, Politics, and Enterprise under the Restoration* (Newark, DE and London: University of Delaware Press, Associated University Presses, 1994).
162. Persson, *Grain Markets*, p. 4–6; Miller, *Mastering the Market.*
163. Such measures are discussed in detail in Miller, *Mastering the Market.*
164. Person, *Grain Markets*, p. 143; J. Miller, 'The Pragmatic Economy: Liberal Reforms and the Grain Trade in Upper Normandy, 1750–1789' (Dissertation, Duke University, NC, 1987).
165. See van Zanden, 'Estimating Early Modern Economic Growth'.
166. Israel, *Dutch Primacy*, p. 9.
167. Ibid., p. 26–34.
168. Ibid., p. 5; also Lesger, *The Rise of the Amsterdam* Market, p. 210.
169. Israel, *Dutch Primacy*, p. 20.
170. R. W. Unger (ed.), *Shipping and Economic Growth 1350–1850* (Ledien: Brill, 2011).
171. Israel, *Dutch Primacy*, p. 20; Christensen makes a similar point in A. E. Christensen, *Dutch Trade to the Baltic about 1600: Studies in the Sound Toll Register and Dutch Shipping Records* (Copenhagen and The Hague: Einar Munksgaard; Martinus Nijhoff, 1941).
172. See Israel, *Dutch Primacy*, for more discussion of how the Dutch overtook Germany.
173. M. Clodfelter, *Warfare and Armed Conflicts: A Statistical Encyclopedia of Casualty and Other Figures, 1494–2007* (Jefferson, NC: McFarland, 2002). p. 34.
174. Dupuy and Dupuy, *Encyclopedia*, p. 533, who write how '[m]uch of the area was plundered and replundered by undisciplined and motley armies whose major source of supply was the land over which they fought'.
175. P. H. Wilson, *From Reich to Revolution: German History 1558–1806* European History in Perspective (Basingstoke: Macmillan, 2004), pp. 87–8.
176. F. W. Carter, *Trade and Urban Development in Poland: An Economic Geography of Cracow, from its Origins to 1795* (Cambridge: Cambridge University Press, 2006), p. 340.
177. Ibid., p. 4.

178. On Danzig's role in the Baltic (including grain exports to Holland) on the eve of the early modern period, see Attman, *The Russian and Polish Markets*, pp. 56–66; S. Faroqhi, B. McGowan, D. Quuataert and S. Pamuk, *An Economic and Social History of the Ottoman Empire*, 2 vols (Cambridge: Cambridge University Press, 1997), vol. 2, p. xl note a connection to the Ottoman realm.
179. Carter, *Trade and Urban Development*, p. 343.
180. R. C. Allen and R. Unger, 'The Depth and Breadth of the Market for Polish Grain 1500–1800', in J. P. S. Lemmink and J. S. A. M. van Koningsbrugge (eds), *Baltic Affairs Relations between the Netherlands and North-Eastern Europe 1500–1800* (Nijmegen: Institute of Northern and Eastern European Studies, 1990), pp. 2–4.
181. A. H. Lyber, 'The Ottoman Turks and the Routes of Oriental Trade', *English Historical Review*, 30 (1915), pp. 577–88, on p. 583.
182. Israel, *Dutch Primacy*, pp. 213–4.
183. Ibid.; Attman, *The Russian and Polish Markets*, p. 66; Heeres, Hesp, Noordegraaf and van der Voort, *From Dunkirk to Danzig*.
184. Clodfelter, *Warfare and Armed Conflict*, p. 100.
185. Brenner, 'Agrarian Class Structure'; W. Kula, *An Economic Theory of the Feudal System: Towards a Model of the British Economy, 1500–1800* (London: New Left Review Editions, 1976).
186. Malanima, *Pre-Modern*, p. 127.
187. See ibid., pp. 128–9 for a brief outline.
188. P. Kriedte, *Peasants, Landlords and Merchant Capitalists: Europe and the World Economy* (Cambridge: Cambridge University Press, 1984), discussed in Kula, *An Economic Theory*.
189. Israel, *Dutch Primacy*, pp. 213–4.
190. Ibid., pp. 213–5.
191. Ibid.; Heeres, Hesp, Noordegraaf and van der Voort, *From Dunkirk to Danzig*, pp. 38–40.
192. Kula, *An Economic Theory*, p. 163 speculates that integration in Poland may have been above that of France, but without any formal comparison.
193. Faroqhi, McGowan, Quataert and Pamuk, *An Economic and Social History*, p. 474.
194. Greene in D. Abulafia (ed.), *The Mediterranean in History* (London: Thames & Hudson, 2003), pp. 219–20, 227–8, 248–9.
195. S. Pamuk 'Changes in Factor Markets in the Ottoman Empire, 1500–1800', *Continuity and Change*, 24 (2009), pp.107–36, on p. 114.
196. L. Berov, *Dvizhenieto na tsenite na Balkanite prez XVI–XIX v. i evropeiskata revoliutsiia na tsenite* (Sofia: BAN, 1976), pp. 170–3.
197. Ibid.; Faroqhi, McGowan, Quataert and Pamuk, *An Economic and Social History*, p. 758.
198. Berov, *Dvizhenieto*, p. 174.
199. T. S. Willan, 'Some Aspects of English Trade with the Levant in the Sixteenth Century', *English Historical Review*, 70 (1955), p. 405; Berov, *Dvizhenieto*, p. 174.
200. Pamuk, 'Changes in Factor Markets', p. 113.
201. Faroqhi, McGowan, Quataert and Pamuk, *An Economic and Social History*, p. 959.
202. In practice, this is known as Dutch Disease, where prices send signals to discourage exports of these other goods.
203. Berov, *Dvizhenieto*, p. 175.
204. Carter, *Trade and Urban Development*.
205. Berov, *Dvizhenieto*, pp. 170–1 which gives details of the transport costs.

206. Ibid., p. 178 makes reference to transport cost reductions at this time.
207. Data can be found in S. Pamuk, *500 Years of Prices and Wages in Istanbul and Other Cities* (Ankara: State Institute of Statistics, 2001).
208. J. G. Williamson, *Trade and Poverty: When the Third World Fell Behind* (Cambridge, MA: MIT Press, 2011).
209. Ibid.
210. Pamuk, 'Changes in Factor Markets', pp. 107–36, pp. 113–4.
211. Ibid., p. 115.
212. Greene in Abulafia (ed.), *The Mediterranean*, pp. 219–20, 227–8, 248–9.
213. Pamuk, 'Changes in Factor Markets', p. 115; Berov, *Dvizhenieto*, pp.168–9 (footnotes).
214. Pamuk, 'Changes in Factor Markets', pp. 118–120.
215. Ibid., p. 111.
216. Faroqhi, McGowan, Quataert and Pamuk, *An Economic and Social History*, p. 476.
217. Pamuk, 'Changes in Factor Markets', pp. 115–18.
218. Faroqhi, McGowan, Quataert and Pamuk, *An Economic and Social History*, pp. 474, 489–90.
219. Berov, *Dvizhenieto*. See Appendix 1 of current chapter.
220. S. Pamuk, *500 Years of Prices and Wages in Istanbul and Other Cities* (Ankara: State Institute of Statistics, 2001).
221. Faroqhi, McGowan, Quataert and Pamuk, *An Economic and Social Hisotry*, p. 496.
222. Berov, *Dvizhenieto*, p. 169.
223. Based on a Dickey-Fuller test for the co-integration of Istanbul and Balkan prices.
224. Pamuk, 'Changes in Factor Markets', p. 120.
225. Pamuk, *500 Years*.
226. In the sense of being co-integrated, with a visually stable price-gap across the period 1617–1863.
227. See Appendix 4. There is a lack of overlapping data to examine the integration of Jerusalem and Istanbul. The area around Jerusalem was a great producer of olive oil, but did not export this product to Istanbul, as much of it was used in local soap production.
228. See Appendix 5.
229. C. Verlinden (ed.), *Dokumenten voor de geschiedenis van prijzen en loonen in Vlaanderen en Brabant, gepubliceerd onder leiding van C. Verlinden, en de redaktie van J. Craeybeckx* (Brugge: De Tempel, 1959), pp. 58, 95, 481.
230. One data point was removed from the Madrid series (1654), which was exceptionally high and dwarfed all other results.
231. File titled '*Prices and Wages in Cataluña*'.
232. Pamuk, *500 Years*.
233. Much of this data is patchy – available for occasional years only.
234. Wheat and wheat flour prices have been used for Istanbul as wheat prices are patchy.
235. The regression gave the following results: gapi,j = 0.24 + 0.00026 (distancei,j). Hence the adjusted price-gap for a pair of cities is equal to: raw price-gap – (0.00026*distance).
236. The Ottoman data is very patchy and is therefore discussed separately in the text.
237. Note that the CV was not calculated where the number of observations was less than four.
238. A version of this model was applied in P. Földvári, and B. van Leeuwen 'What Can Price Volatility Tell Us about Market related Institutions? Conditional heteroskedasticity in historical commodity price series', Paper Presented at the World Economic History Con-

gress (2009), available at: http://www.basvanleeuwen.net/bestanden/2conditionalHteroscedasticity.pdf [accessed 1 August 2011].

239. The model was developed by R. Engle, 'Autoregressive Conditional Heteroskedasticity with Estimates of the Variance of United Kingdom Inflation', *Econometrica*, 50 (1982), pp. 987–1007, and T. Bollerslev, 'Generalized Autoregressive Conditional Heteroskedasticity', *Journal of Econometrics*, 31 (1986), pp. 307–27. Engle provides a more recent discussion and application to volatility in R. Engle, 'GARCH 101: The use of ARCH/GARCH in applied econometrics', *Journal of Economic Perspectives*, 15 (2001), pp. 157–68, and R. Engle, 'Risk and Volatility: Econometric Models and Financial Practice', *American Economic Review*, 94 (2004), pp. 405–20. This type of approach provides a more sophisticated approach compared with using coefficients of variation, the standard deviation of residuals from a random walk model or the AR model.
240. For an alternative version, see the previous work of the author (Bateman, 'The Evolution of Markets').
241. The 10 per cent significance level was employed in the VECM models, although when significance was found, it tended to be at a 5 per cent level.
242. A regression of the raw speeds on distance between cities (calculated as the bird flies) gives the following: speedi,j = 0.15 – 0.0001distancei,j. Hence, the adjusted speeds were calculated as follows: adjusted speedi,j=raw speed + 0.0001(distancei,j).
243. In order to gauge how well integrated each city is with the rest of Europe (as opposed to other cities in the same country), pairs of cities within the same country were excluded (e.g. Pisa-Siena). These are discussed in the text.
244. Mid-nineteenth century half lives from Persson, *Grain Markets*.
245. Antwerp soap prices are in litres, and following C. van Bochove, *The Economic Consequences of the Dutch* (Amsterdam: Amsterdam University Press, 2008) it was assumed that the density of soap is one kg per litre (p. 243).
246. 'Candles II' in Allen's CPI spreadsheet.
247. For soap, the average European price was calculated using London, Antwerp, Amsterdam and Naples prices due to gap sin the other series. For candles, the average European price was calculated using all cities except Amsterdam (for which data was only available up to 1676) and Naples (for which data was only available up to 1645). For linen, all cities were used in the calculation of the average price except for Madrid (for which there was a significant gap in the data).

3 The Course of Early Modern Market Integration: The Mediterranean and the North-West Region

1. Smith, *Wealth of Nations*, p. 28.
2. Hobsbawm, 'The General Crisis', p. 34.
3. R. C. Allen, 'Progress and Poverty in Early Modern Europe', *Economic History Review*, 56 (2003), figure 2, table 1; Allen, 'The Great Divergence', figures 7 and 8.
4. Allen and Unger, 'The Depth and Breadth'; C. van Bochove, 'Market Integration and the North Sea System (1600–1800)', in H. Brand and L. Muller (eds), *The Dynamics of Economic Culture in the North Sea and Baltic Region in the Late Middle Ages and Early Modern Period* (Hilversum: Verloren, 2007); Jacks 'Market Integration'; Jacks 'Intra- and International'.

5. D. Abulafia, *The Great Sea: A Human History of the Mediterranean* (London: Allen Lane, 2011).
6. For a map of medieval trade routes across the Mediterranean, with the principal cities involved, see F. Tabak, *The Waning of the Mediterranean, 1550–1870: A Geohistorical Approach* (Baltimore, MD: Johns Hopkins University Press, 2008), p. 32.
7. E. Hutton, *Venice and Venetia* (London: Hollis & Carter, 1954), p. 1.
8. J. H. Parry, 'Transport and Trade Routes', in E. E. Rich and C. H. Wilson, *Cambridge Economic History of Europe*, 8 vols (Cambridge: Cambridge University Press, 1967), vol. 4, p. 163.
9. Tabak, *The Waning*, p. 34.
10. Braudel, F., *La Mediterranee*; Tabak, *The Waning*, p. 5; Parry, 'Transport and Trade Routes', pp. 156–9. This picture of a northern 'invasion' has a number of followers, but has been critiqued by M. Greene, 'Beyond Northern Invasions: The Mediterranean in the Seventeenth Century', *Past and Present*, 174 (2002), pp. 40, 46–7.
11. Parry, 'Transport and Trade Routes', p. 187.
12. Ibid., p. 188.
13. Ibid., pp. 186–7.
14. Ibid., p. 189.
15. Tabak, *The Waning*.
16. Ibid., pp. 8–9.
17. Ibid., p. 9.
18. The following sections draw heavily on Tabak, *The Waning*, integrating his qualitative observations with economic theory and price-gap evidence.
19. Braudel, *La Mediterranee*, pp. 572–3.
20. Tabak, *The Waning*, p. 17; Abulafia, *The Great Sea*.
21. Tabak, *The Waning*, p. 123 (also see p. 90 and pp. 63–4).
22. Braudel, *La Mediterranee*, pp. 572–3.
23. Prak, *The Dutch Republic*, p. 10.
24. M. Ratekin, 'The Early Sugar Industry in Española', *Hispanic American Historical Review*, 34 (1954), pp. 1–19.
25. Tabak, *The Waning*, p. 16.
26. This is calculated using the set of between country market estimates discussed in Chapter 2, but using only the city-pairs which involved a Mediterranean and north-western city (which includes those in England, Belgium and the Netherlands). A fixed effects regression is applied to arrive at the 'average' trend between the two regions.
27. Tabak, *The Waning*, pp. 13–14.
28. Ibid., p. 17.
29. Ibid., pp. 7, 68.
30. R. T. Rapp, 'The Unmaking of the Mediterranean Trade Hegemony: International Trade Rivalry and the Commercial Revolution', *Journal of Economic History*, 35:3 (1975), pp. 499–525. Rapp also notes how emigration of skilled workers from Venice helped to transfer the skills and techniques to competing nations (pp. 505–6). On the advantages and disadvantages of the established versus new suppliers, see pp. 515–6.
31. K. Glamann, 'The Changing Patterns of Trade', in E. E. Rich and C. H. Wilson, *The Cambridge Economic History of Europe. Vol. 5: The Economic Organization of Early Modern Europe* (Cambridge: Cambridge University Press, 1977), p. 222; Rapp, 'The Unmaking', p. 511.
32. Davis, 'The Rise of Protection'.

33. Tabak, *The Waning*, p. 155.
34. Rapp, 'The Unmaking', table 4, p. 513.
35. For further data on the decline of industry in Venice, see D. Sella, 'Crisis and Transformation in Venetian Trade', in B. Pullan (ed.), *Crisis and Change in the Venetian Economy* (London: Methuen, 1968), p. 92, and F. C. Lane, 'Venetian Shipping during the Commercial Revolution', *American Historical Review*, 38 (1933), pp. 219–39.
36. Rapp, 'The Unmaking', p. 523, fn. 59.
37. Ibid., pp. 523–4.
38. Tabak, *The Waning*, pp.12, 13, 158.
39. Ibid., p. 13.
40. Rapp, 'The Unmaking', pp. 508, 517. For a wider discussion, see Rapp, *Industry and Economic Decline.*
41. These candle price comparisons involve Milan, Naples, Madrid and London.
42. Lopez, 'Market Expansion', p. 450.
43. F. C. Lane, *Venetian Ships and Shipbuilders of the Renaissance* (Baltimore, MD: Johns Hopkins University Press, 1934).
44. Faroqhi, McGowan, Quataert and Pamuk, *An Economic and Social History*, p. 521.
45. Parry, 'Transport and Trade Routes', pp. 186–9. The most famous ship innovation of the time was the Dutch fluit.
46. Sella, 'Crisis and Transformation', p. 92.
47. Greene, 'Beyond Northern Invasions', p. 40.
48. Ibid.. Also see M. Greene, *A Shared World: Christians and Muslims in the Early Modern Mediterranean* (Princeton, NJ: Princeton University Press, 2000).
49. R. Paris, *Histoire du Commerce de Marseille* (Paris: Plon, 1957).
50. G. Leon, 'The Greek Merchant Marine, 1453–1850', in S. Papadopoulos (ed.), *The Greek Merchant Marine, 1453–1850* (Athens: National Bank of Greece, 1972), p. 18.
51. Particularly the Dutch, whose efforts focused on trade outside of the Mediterranean. Greene, 'Beyond Northern Invasions', p. 44.
52. Ibid., p. 52.
53. Ibid., pp. 47–8.
54. Ibid., pp. 48–9, 50–1.
55. Ibid.
56. Inalcik and Quataert, *An Economic and Social History of the Ottoman Empire*, p. 499.
57. F. Trivellato, *The Familiarity of Strangers: The Sephardic Diaspora, Livorno, and Cross-Cultural Trade in the Early Modern Period* (New Haven, CT: Yale University Press, 2009), p. 6. Trade data can be found in: F. Braudel and R. Romano, *Navires et Marchandises à L'entrée du port de Livourne, 1547–1611* (Paris: Armand Colin, 1951).
58. Green, 'Beyond Northern Invasions, p. 52.
59. Tabak, *The Waning*, pp. 74, 79.
60. Ibid., p. 58.
61. See Chapter 4.
62. Tabak, *The Waning*, p. 3.
63. Ibid., pp. 58–8, 79.
64. For more details on the spice routes through the Eastern Mediterranean, see A. H. Lyber, 'The Ottoman Turks and the Routes of Oriental Trade', *English Historical Review*, 30 (1915), pp. 577–88.
65. F. C. Lane, 'The Mediterranean Spice Trade: Further Evidence of its Revival in the Sixteenth Century', *American Historical Review*, 45 (1940), pp. 581–90; N. Steensgaard,

The Asian Trade Revolution of the Seventeenth Century: The East India Companies and the Decline of the Caravan Trade (Chicago, IL and London: University of Chicago Press, 1974); A. H. Lyber, 'The Ottoman Turks', p. 586–7 (p. 587 notes the higher profits and cheapness of the Cape Route relative to the traditional spice route). As surveyed and discussed in van der Wee, 'Structural Changes'.

66. O'Rourke and Williamson, 'Did Vasco da Gama Matter'.
67. P. Blancard, *Manuel du Commerce des Indes* (Paris, 1806), p. 82; P. Masson, *Histoire du Commerce francais dans le Levant au XVII siècle* (Paris, Hachette & cie, 1896), p. 82; G. A. Olivier, *Voyage dans l'Empire Othman, l'ègypte, et la Perse* (Paris: Chez Agasse, 1801), iii, p. 326 and v, p. 320; G. Berchet, *Del Commercio dei Veneti nell' Asia* (Venice, 1869), p. 15.
68. Lyber, 'The Ottoman Turks', pp. 585–6.
69. As in the previous chapter, a fixed effects panel regression incorporating a series of time dummies is applied (this time to sub-sets of Mediterranean and north-western market estimates) in order to extract an 'average' trend for each region. As before, the average trend is calculated by summing for each period the coefficient on the time dummy and the constant term. In contrast with calculating the simple average, the use of fixed effects avoids the problems which arise from missing data. The north-western cities are as follows: Amsterdam, Arnhem, Leiden, Utrecht, Antwerp, Brussels, Bruges, Lier, Louvain, Exeter, London, Edinburgh. The Mediterranean cities are as follows: Istanbul (x2 series), Bursa, Barcelona, Madrid, Valencia, Gerona, Granada, Aix, Angouleme, Arles, Beziers, Grenoble, Toulouse, Ancona, Cantania, Milan, Naples, Pesaro, Sansepolcro, Tuscany and Udine (x2 series). The data were detailed in Appendix 1 of Chapter 2.
70. Note that these are raw estimates, i.e. they are not 'distance adjusted'.
71. The non-distance adjusted (raw speeds) increase from 0.08 at the start of the period to 0.16 at the end of the period in the Mediterranean case, and rise from 0.05 to 0.27 in the north-western case.

4 Early Modern Market Integration in a Longer Run Perspective

1. V. N. Bateman, 'Price Volatility in Late Medieval and Early Modern Europe', in R. J. Spek, J. L. van der Zanden and E. S. Leeuwen, *A History of Market Performance* (London: Routledge, forthcoming).
2. P. Földvári, B. van Leeuwen and J. L. van Zanden, 'Long Run Patterns in Market Efficiency and the Genesis of the Market Economy: Markets Around the Mediterranean from Nebuchadnezzar to Napoleon (580 BC and 1800 AD)', *Centre for Economic Policy Research*, discussion paper, 8521, in R. J. van der Spek, J. L. van Zanden, and E. S. Leeuwen, *A History of Market Performance* (London: Routledge, forthcoming); Bateman, 'Price Volatility'.
3. Epstein, *Freedom and Growth*, pp. 159–63 (esp. figures 7.3 and 7.5).
4. Including the following: W. Abel, *Agrarkrisen und Agrarkonjunktur. Eine Geschichte der Land- und Ernèahrungswirtschaft Mitteleuropas seit dem hohen Mittelalter* (Berlin-Hamburg: P. Parey, 1935), pp. 106–14; W. Achilles, 'Getreidepreise und Getreidehandelsbeziehungn Europaischer Raume im 16. und 17. Jahrhundert', in *Zeitschrift fur Agrargeschichte und Agrarsoziologie* (1959), pp. 32–55; Allen and Unger, 'The Depth and Breadth', V. N. Bateman, 'The Evolution of Markets in Early Modern Europe, 1350–1800: A Study of Wheat Prices', *Economic History Review*, 64 (2011), pp. 447–71; F. P.

Braudel and F. Spooner, 'Prices in Europe from 1450 to 1750,' in E. E. Rich and C. Wilson (eds), *The Cambridge Economic History of Europe. Vol. 4: The Economy of Expanding Europe in the Sixteenth and Seventeenth Centuries*, 8 vols (Cambridge: Cambridge University Press, 1967), pp. 374–486; D. Chilosi, T. E. Murphy and R. Studer, 'Europe's Many Integrations: Geography and Grain Markets, 1620–1913', *Innocenzo Gasparini Institute for Economic Research*, working paper 412 (2011); Jacks, 'Market Integration'; Özmucur and Pamuk, 'Did European Commodity Prices Converge'; Persson, *Grain Markets*; R. Studer, 'Does Trade Explain Europe's Rise? Geography, Market Size and Economic Development', London School of Economics, Economic History Working Papers 27877 (2009).

5. Chilosi, Murphy and Studer, 'Europe's Many Integrations'.
6. Özmucur and Pamuk 'Did European Commodity Prices Converge'; Bateman, 'The Evolution of Markets'.
7. To put this into action we regress each panel of estimates on a series of time dummies together with time-invariant dummies for each city or city-pair ('fixed effects'). The time invariant dummy for each city-pair is an estimate of the underlying level of integration for the city or city-pair – the part that does not change over time, and is, for example, explained by unchanging geographical or institutional factors. The coefficients on the time dummies will then allow us to see what is happening to the average trend over time.
8. These calculations are based on simply taking an average of the volatility levels of the countries for which we have data (provided in Chapter 2, Appendix 2), to the exclusion of Istanbul (for which data is available for a shorter period of time) and Poland (for which data is lacking in the early seventeenth century). If Poland is included, the results are little changed.
9. From annual CV wheat prices baby ch plus germ aust – sheet for ch5 and 6 regs. sheet 1, column GT.
10. See previous note.
11. This is based on taking the natural logarithms of the price data; if the price-data are not logged, which allows for a more flexible transport cost function, there is no improvement. See the results in Bateman, 'The Evolution'.
12. Persson, *Grain Markets*, p. 100.
13. Malanima, *Pre-Modern*, p. 304.
14. Özmucur and Pamuk, 'Did European Commodity Prices Converge'.
15. Soap prices: London, Amtwerp, Amsterdam, Vienna, Madrid and Naples; Candles: London, Antwerp, Augsburg, Vienna, Madrid and Strasbourg; Linen prices: London, Antwerp, Augsburg, Munich, Leipzig, Strasbourg and Florence/Milan.
16. O'Rourke and Williamson, 'Did Vasco da Gama Matter'.
17. O'Rourke and Williamson, 'After Columbus', pp. 7–8.
18. Özmucur and Pamuk, 'Did European Commodity Prices Converge'.
19. de Moor and van Zanden, 'Girl Power'.
20. Epstein, *Freedom and Growth*, pp. 61–2.
21. Smith, *Wealth of Nations*, pp. 259–73
22. Allen, *The British Industrial Revolution*, ch. 3.
23. Ibid., pp. 57–8; van Bavel, 'The Organization and Rise of Land and Lease Markets', p. 15. For a model of the way in which large capitalist farms increase rents and reduce the employment of labour in agriculture relative to small peasant farms, see J. S. Cohen and M. L. Weitzamn, 'A Marxian Model of Enclosures', *Journal of Development Economics*,

1 (1975), pp. 287–336, which was applied in N. Crafts and C. K. Harley, 'Precocious British Industrialisation: A General Equilibrium Perspective', in L. P. de la Escosura (ed.), *British Exceptionalism: A Unique Path to the Industrial Revolution* (Cambridge: Cambridge University Press, 2004).

24. C. J. Zuijderduijn, T. de Moor and J. L. van Zanden, 'Small is Beautiful: On the Efficiency of Credit Markets in Late Medieval Holland', *Centre for Global Economic History*, working paper number 11 (2011).
25. Campbell, 'Factor Markets', esp. p. 92.
26. K. Marx, *Das Kaptal* (Hamburg: Verlag von Otto Meisner, 1867).
27. Bavel, 'The Organization and Rise of Land and Lease Markets', pp. 16–19.
28. Also see Britnell, 'England and Northern Italy'.
29. Campbell, 'Factor Markets', p. 89.
30. Bavel, 'The Organisation and Rise of Land and Lease Markets', pp. 13–53.
31. Britnell, 'England and Northern Italy'.
32. Bavel, 'The Organisation of Land and Lease Markets', p. 20; Pamuk, 'Changes in Factor Markets', pp. 108, 118.
33. Campbell, 'Factor Markets' p. 88.
34. Ibid., pp. 87–8; J. H. Munro, 'Nominal Wage Stickiness and the Real Wage Problem'; J. M. Keynes, Adam Smith and the Evidence', *Research in Economic History*, 21 (2003), pp. 186–297; B. M. S. Campbell, 'The Agrarian Problem in the Early Fourteenth Century', *Past and Present* (2005), 188, pp. 26–44.
35. C. Dyer, *An Age of Transition?*, pp. 218–20; C. Dyer, *Standards of Living in the later Middle Ages: Social Change in England c. 1200–1520* (Cambridge: Cambridge University Press, 1989); pp. 211–14; B. van Bavel, 'Rural Wage Labour in the Sixteenth Century Low Countries: An Assessment of the Importance and Nature of Wage Labour in the Countryside of Holland, Guelders and Flanders', *Continuity and Change*, 21:1 (2005), pp. 37–72; B. van Bavel, T. de Moor and J. L. van Zanden, 'Introduction: Factor Markets in Global Economic history', *Continuity and Change*, 24:1, pp. 9–21 (2009); Campbell, 'Factor Markets'; L. R. Poos, *A Rural Society after the Black Death: Essex, 1350–1525* (Cambridge: Cambridge University Press, 2004), pp. 183–229.
36. de Moor and van Zanden, 'Girl Power'; C. Dyer, *Making a Living in the Middle Ages: The People of Britain 850–1520* (Newhaven, CT: Yale University Press, 2009), pp. 193–6.
37. de Moor and van Zanden, 'Girl Power'.
38. van Zanden, *The Long Road*, p. 170.
39. Ibid., pp.154–6.
40. Allen, 'The Great Divergence'.
41. Epstein, *Freedom and Growth*, p. 65.
42. Ibid., pp. 65, 67.
43. Hatton and Williamson, *Migration*, pp. 3–7.
44. Ibid., p. 4; D. Baines 'European Labour Markets, Emigration and Internal Migration, 1850–191', in T. J. Hatton and J. G. Williamson (eds), *Migration and the International Labour Market* (London: Routledge, 1994), pp. 35–54.
45. Hatton and Williamson, *Migration*, p. 3.
46. Ibid., p. 17.
47. Allen, 'The Great Divergence'; O'Rourke and Williamson, 'Late 19th Century Anglo-American Factor Price Convergence'; O'Rourke and Williamson, 'Around the European Periphery'.

48. In the fashion of the Stolper-Samuelson theorem. See O'Rourke and Williamson, 'Late 19th Century' and O'Rourke and Williamson, 'Around the European Periphery'. Also discussed in Hatton and Williamson, *Migration*, p. 24. It should be noted that if labour is not mobile between countries, an initial wage divergence could be explained by the emergence of differences in technology between countries. The emergence of differences in education could also in theory potentially explain a divergence in wages. In this case, a subsequent convergence in wages could be understood in terms of the diffusion of technology and universal schooling, rather than of labour markets truly integrating. However, O'Rourke and Williamson show that labour flows and trade (caused by goods market integration) were much more important than the diffusion of technology and schooling in explaining nineteenth-century wage convergence.
49. For a critique of O'Rourke and Williamson, see C. K. Harley, 'A Review of O'Rourke and Williamson's Globalization and History: The Evolution of a Nineteenth Century Atlantic Economy', *Journal of Economic Literature*, 38:4 (2000), pp. 926–35.
50. Persson, *An Economic History*, p. 133.
51. Campbell, 'Factor Markets', p. 95.
52. Grief, *Institutions*.
53. Clark, *A Farewell to Alms*, pp. 167–70. Also see Epstein, *Freedom*, p. 62.
54. Campbell, 'Factor Markets', pp. 83, 92.
55. Clark, *A Farewell to Alms*, pp. 167–175; G. Clark, 'The Cost of Capital and Medieval Agricultural Techniques', *Explorations in Economic Hi*story, 25 (1988), pp. 265–94; Zuijderduijn, de Moor and van Zanden 'Small is Beautiful'; Epstein, *Freedom and Growth*, p. 62; C. J. Zuijderduijn, *Medieval Capital Markets: Markets for Renten, State Formation and Private Investment in Holland (1300–1550)* (Leiden and Boston, MA: Brill, 2009), pp. 5–13.
56. Campbell, 'Factor Markets', p. 96.
57. Epstein, *Freedom and Growth*, pp. 61–2.
58. D. Chilosi and O. Volckart, 'Money, States, and Empire: Financial Integration and Institutional Change in Central Europe, 1400–1520', *Journal of Economic History*, 71 (2011), pp. 762–91; D. Chilosi and O. Volckart, 'Books or Bullion? Printing, Mining and Financial Integration in Central Europe from the 1460s', London School of Economics, Economic History Working Papers, 144/10 (2010).
59. For an excellent summary of the development of Amsterdam and London as financial centres, see A. M. Carlos and L. Neal, 'Amsterdam and London as Financial Centers in the Eighteenth Century', *Financial History Review*, 18 (2011), pp. 21–46. On developments in general in the eighteenth century, see, L. Neal, *The Rise of Financial Capitalism: International Capital Markets in the Age of Reason* (Cambridge: Cambridge University Press, 1993).
60. Ferguson, *The Ascent of Money*, pp. 53–4.
61. Epsten, *Freedom and Growth*, p. 27.
62. Ferguson, *The Ascent of Money*, p. 186.
63. Ibid., p. 197.
64. Attman, *The Russian and Polish Markets*, p. 65; Heeres, Hesp, Noordegraaf and van der Voort, *From Dunkirk to Danzig*, pp. 420–2, 38–40; Pounds, *An Historical Geography*, ch. 6 (esp. p. 282). On the path of inter-continental trade, see O'Rourke and Williamson, 'After Columbus'.
65. C. van Bochove, *The Economic Consequences of the Dutch: Economic Integration around the North Sea, 1500–1800* (Amsterdam: Askant, 2008), p. 46.

66. Hatton and Williamson, *Migration*, p. 25.
67. See the references in Chapter 1.

5 The Causes of Early Modern Market Integration and Disintegration

1. Bang, 'Trade and Commerce, Roman'.
2. See, for example, F. C. Lane., *Venetian Ships*.
3. Unger, *Shipping and Economic Growth*.
4. J. Lucassen and R. Unger, 'Labour Productivity in Ocean Shipping 1500–1850', *International Journal of Maritime History*, 12 (2000), pp. 127–41 (see esp. pp. 133–4).
5. M. von Tielhif and J. L. van Zanden, 'Productivity Changes in Shipping in the Dutch Republic', in R. W. Unger (ed.), *Shipping and Economic Growth 1350–1850* (Leiden: Brill, 2011).
6. B. M. S. Campbell, J. A. Galloway and M. Murphy, *A Medieval Capital and its Grain Supply: Agrarian Production and Distribution in the London Region, c. 1300, Historical Geography Research Series*, 30 (1993), p. 196.
7. On the development of the canal system in The Netherlands, see J. de Vries, *Barges and Capitalism: Passenger Transportation in the Dutch Economy, 1632–1839* (Utrecht: Hes Publishers, 1981); G. Crompton, *Canals and Inland Navigation*, Studies in Transport History (Aldershot: Scolar, 1996).
8. D. Bogart, 'Turnpike Trusts and the Transport Revolution in Eighteenth Century England', *Explorations in Economic History*, 42:4 (2005), pp. 479–508.
9. Bang, 'Trade and Commerce, Roman'.
10. Dyer, *Making a Living*, p. 217.
11. N. W. Posthumus, *Nederlandsche Prijsgeschiedenis*, 2 vols (Leiden, 1943), vol. 1, pp. vvv–xxviii.
12. F. E. Roover, 'Early Examples of Marine Insurance', *Journal of Economic History*, 5 (1945), pp. 192–3.
13. V. Barbour, 'Marine Risks and Insurance in the 17th Century', *Journal of Economic History*, 1 (1929), pp. 561–96; A. H. John, 'The London Assurance Company and the Marine Insurance Market of the Eighteenth Century', *Economica*, 25 (1958), pp. 126–41.
14. John, 'The London Assurance Company', p. 127.
15. Colombia University, *Chapters in Western Civilisation* (Columbia, 1948), vol. 1, p. 146; Roover, 'Early Examples', p. 173; E. M. Byrne, *Genoese Shipping in the Twelfth and Thirteenth Centuries* (Cambridge, MA: Mediaeval Academy of America, 1930), pp. 12–19.
16. Barbour, 'Marine Risks'.
17. On geography and the market, studies include those of C. Engel and J. H. Rogers, 'Regional Patterns in the Law of One Price: The Roles of Geography Vs. Currencies', *NBER*, working paper, series 5395 (1995); C. Engel and J. Rogers, 'How Wide Is the Border?', *American Economic Review*, 86 (1996), pp. 1112–25; C. Engel and J. Rogers, 'Violating the Law of One Price: Should We Make a Federal Case Out of It?' *Journal of Money, Credit, and Banking*, 33:1 (2001), pp. 1–15; Fujita, Krugman and Venables, 1998; Richards, 2003.
18. Smith, *Wealth of Nations*, p. 28.
19. Ibid., p. 27.
20. R. Studer, 'Does Trade Explain Europe's Rise?'

21. H. H. Lamb, 'Climate in the Last Thousand Years: Natural Climatic Fluctuations and Change', in H. John and R. Fantechi (eds), *The Climate of Europe: Past, Present and Future* (Lancaster: D. Reidel Publishing Company, 1984), pp. 25–64.
22. C. O'Gráda and J.-M. Chevet, 'Market Segmentation'.
23. Based on an average of tree growth in five sites from across Europe: Bodensee site in Baden-Wurttemberg, South Germany, Pratomagno-Bibbiena Appenine Mountains site in Italy, Siete Picos site in Spain, Fontaine Bleau site in Seine-et-Marne, France, and Ardennes Archaeological Site in Liege, Belgium. These five sites were selected based on the time period for which tree ring records are available. The data can be downloaded at: http://www.ncdc.noaa.gov/paleo/treering.html.
24. See, for example, R. Brazdil, C. Pfister, H. Wanner, H. von Storch and J. Luterbacher, 'Historical Climatology in Europe – the State of the Art', *Climate Change*, 70 (2005), pp. 363–430. I thank L. S. Rowlatt for bringing this to my attention.
25. C. J. Reed, 'Transactions Costs and Differential Growth in Seventeenth Century Western Europe', *Journal of Economic History*, 33: 1 (March 1973), pp. 177–90.
26. J.-N. Biraben, 'Essai sur l'evolution du nombre des homes', *Population*, 34 (1969), p. 16; Malanima, *Pre-Modern*, p. 7–8.
27. Persson, *An Economic History*.
28. P. R. Galloway, 'Basic Patterns in Annual Variations in Fertility, Nuptiality, Mortality, and Prices in Pre-Industrial Europe', *Population Studies*, 42 (1988), pp. 275–302.
29. For a summary of the literature, see D. Acemoglu, S. Johnson and J. A. Robinson, 'Institutions as the Fundamental Cause of Long-run Growth', in P. Aghion and S. N. Durlauf (eds), *Handbook of Economic Growth*, 2 vols (Amsterdam: Elsevier, 2012), vol. 2, pp. 385–472.
30. Epstein, *Freedom and Growth*.
31. Ibid.
32. P. K. O'Brien, and X. Duran, 'Total Factor Productivity for the Royal Navy from Victory at Texal (1653) to Triumph at Trafalgar (1805)', in R. W. Unger (ed.), *Shipping and Economic Growth 1350–1850* (Leiden: Brill, 2011), pp. 279–308.
33. Lucassen and Unger, 'Labour Productivity'.
34. N. A. M. Rodger, 'Queen Elizabeth and the Myth of Sea Power in English History', *Transactions of the Royal Historical Society*, 14 (2004), pp. 153–74. See O'Brien and Duran, 'Total Factor Productivity' for a cross-country comparison of naval expenditure.
35. van Zanden, Buringh and Bosker, 'The Rise and Decline of European Parliaments'; M. Dincecco, 'Fiscal Centralization, Limited Government, and Public Revenues in Europe, 1650–1913, *Journal of Economic History*, 69 (2009), pp. 48–103.
36. Note that all of the institutional variables are highly correlated, which explains why one of either parliament or constitution becomes insignificant when placed in a full regression alongside other variables (Table 4.1).
37. C. Wilson, 'Mercantilism', *Historical Association Pamphlet*, 37 (London, 1966), pp. 3–27.
38. C. W. Cole, *Colbert and a Century of French Mercantilism* (New York: Columbia University Press, 1939).
39. W. Conze, 'Review of Der Reichsmerkantilismus. Studien zur Wirtschaftspolitik des Heiligen Romischen Reiches im 17. und 18. Jahrhundert by Ingomar Bog', *Economic History Review*, 12:2 (1959), pp. 323–4.
40. E. N. Williams, *The Ancien Regime in Europe: Government and Society in the Major States 1648–1789* (London: Bodley Head, 1970), p. 438.
41. L. LaHaye, http://www.econlib.org/library/Enc/Mercantilism.html.

42. J. Lynch, *Spain Under the Habsburgs*, 2nd edn, 2 vols (Oxford: Basil Blackwell, 1981), vol. 1, p. 155.
43. Ibid., vol. 2, pp. 168–70.
44. Ibid., vol. 2, p. 171.
45. Cameron and Neal, *A Concise Economic History*, pp. 153, 130.
46. R. Findlay and K. H. O'Rourke, *Commodity Market Integration, 1500–2000* (London: Centre for Economic Policy Research, 2002), p. 25.
47. F. Crouzet, 'Wars, Blockade, and Economic Change in Europe, 1792–1815', *Journal of Economic History*, 24:4 (December 1964), pp. 567–88.
48. Based on Table 5.1.
49. R. Nielsen, 'Storage and English Government Intervention in Early Modern Grain Markets', *Journal of Economic History*, 57:1 (March 1997), p. 1; A. I. Grab, 'The Politics of Subsistence: The Liberalization of Grain Commerce in Austrian Lombardy under Enlightened Despotism', *Journal of Modern History*, 57 (1985), p. 185.
50. Grab, 'The Politics of Subsistence', p. 185.
51. G. Lefebvre, *The French Revolution from 1793 to 1799*, trans. J. H. Stewart and J. Friguglietti (London: Routledge & Kegan Paul; New York: Columbia University Press, 1964), p. 26.
52. Persson, *Grain Markets*; Grab, 'The Politics of Subsistence'; Nielsen, 'Storage and English Government Intervention'.
53. Person, *Grain Markets*, pp. 3–5 and ch. 6.
54. Acemoglu, Johnson and Robinson, 'The Rise of Europe'.
55. T. Roy, 'Indigo and Law in Colonial India', *Economic History Review*, 64 (2011), pp. 60–75.
56. H.-J. Chang, 'Reply to the Comments on "Institutions and Economic Development: Theory, Policy and History"', *Journal of Institutional Economics*, 7 (2011), pp. 595–613.
57. All calculations are based on the coefficients estimated and reported in Tables 5.1 and 5.2 in the Appendix together with data on geography, population and institutions (sources for which are provided in the Appendix). To explain how a change in a particular explanatory variable (x) can explain the evolution of markets (y), we take the change in x and multiply it by the coefficient on the x variable (estimated by regression analysis). Similarly, to explain differences in markets between countries we take the difference in the x variable and multiply it by the associated coefficient.
58. As discussed in J. D. B. Mitchell, *Constitutional Law* (Edinburgh: W. Green, 1964), p. 4, this Revolution can be seen as 'the re-establishment of a pre-existing legal order which had been wrongfully disrupted'; Acemoglu, Johnson and Robinson, 'The Rise of Europe'.
59. The last of these factors is not captured in the fiscal centralization measure of state development but, according to Epstein, was nevertheless taking place.
60. North and Thomas, *The Rise of the Western World*.
61. The evidence based on the monthly data gives us too few observations on the basis of which to examine the causes of market integration compared with the annual data.

6 The Consequences of Early Modern Markets: An Examination of the Relationship between Markets and Economic Growth

1. As argued in Mokyr, *The Enlightened Economy*.
2. As argued in Allen, *The British Industrial Revolution*.
3. Maddison, *The World Economy*. Data is available at: www.ggdc.net/maddison.

4. C. H. Feinstein, 'Pessimism Perpetuated: Real Wages and the Standard of Living in Britain during and after the Industrial Revolution', *Journal of Economic History*, 58 (1998), pp. 625–58.
5. N. F. R. Crafts, *British Economic Growth during the Industrial Revolution* (Oxford: Clarendon, 1985); N. F. R. Crafts and C. K. Harley, 'Output Growth and the British Industrial Revolution: A Restatement of the Crafts-Harley View', *Economic History Review*, 45 (1992), pp. 703–30; summarized in J. Mokyr, 'Accounting for the Industrial Revolution', in R. Floud and P. Johnson, *The Cambridge Economic History of Modern Britain*, 3 vols (Cambridge: Cambridge University Press, 2004), vol. 1, p. 4.
6. Desmet and Parente, 'The Evolution of Markets'.
7. Rivera-Batiz and Romer, 'Economic Integration'; Jones and Romer, 'The New Kaldor Facts'.
8. Acemoglu, Johnson and Robinson, 'The Rise of Europe'.
9. J. D. Vries, 'The Industrial Revolution and the Industrious Revolution', *Journal of Economic History*, 54 (1994), pp. 249–70.
10. For a summary, see C. M. Meissner, 'Growth from Globalization?'
11. Chang, *Kicking Away the Ladder*.
12. See Appendix for data sources.
13. See Appendix.
14. The panel corrected standard errors estimator is employed in order to help overcome the problem of heteroskedasticity (and serial correlation where present). The pairwise option was used where necessary. For the urbanization and agricultural productivity regressions, the values of these indicators in, say 1500, were regressed on the market estimates for the previous period (1400–99), and so on. Real wages, population growth and real wage growth were averages per period, and so the values for, say 1500–99, were regressed on the market estimates for 1500–99, and so on. The real wage growth regression also contains a variable to capture the initial level of the real wage (as would be suggested by economic growth theorists in order to control for any catch-up effects). However, the results when such a term is not included are very similar.
15. The following variables are used as instruments for markets: war and distance to the coast. As we have seen in the previous chapter, each of these displays a significant correlation with markets. Furthermore, it is highly unlikely that they are themselves affected by economic development (i.e. they can be treated as exogenous). As a result, they prove to satisfy the standard instrument tests.
16. Once again, war and distance from the coast are used as instruments. One may of course argue that both between-country and within-country price gaps should appear together in the same regression as they are capturing different angles of integration (domestic and international). The results of doing this then suggest that between-country markets no longer have a significant relationship with growth.
17. P. Bairoch, J. Batou and P. Cháevre, *La population des villes europâeennes, 800–1850: banque de donnâees et analyse sommaire des râesultats* (Geneve: Droz, 1988).
18. The panel corrected standard errors estimator is employed (as at the country-level). To control for catch-up effects, in the population growth regressions, the initial level of population is also included and in the real wage growth regressions, the initial real wage is included.
19. Instruments are city-specific geographical measures and warfare: the extent of warfare in the home country, longitude, latitude, coastal location and elevation.
20. Instruments as above.

21. For an excellent summary of the literature on institutions see Acemoglu, Johnson and Robinson, 'Institutions'.
22. Epstein, *Freedom and Growth*.
23. Markets are found to have an insignificant effect on growth. Hence, if fiscal centralization does have an effect on growth, it cannot be working through markets.
24. Dincecco, 'Fiscal Centralization'.
25. Ibid., p. 62.
26. Mokyr, *The Enlightened Economy*; J. Mokyr, *The Gifts of Athena: Historical Origins of the Knowledge Economy* (Princeton, NJ and Oxford: Princeton University Press, 2002).
27. In addition to the work of Mokyr, also see van Zanden, *The Long Road*.
28. The website www.scholarly-societies is used for this purpose.
29. For a further empirical test of the Enlightenment hypothesis, see J. Dowey, 'Mind Over Matter: Empirical Evidence of the Industrial Enlightenment as the Origin of Modern Economic Growth', *London School of Economics*, working paper (forthcoming 2012).
30. To investigate we would ideally find an instrument for societies. Since this is rather difficult, we can instead turn the regression equation around and regress societies on growth, finding an instrument for growth. Using fiscal centralization as such an instrument, we find that growth has a significant effect on societies.
31. Allen, *The British Industrial Revolution*.
32. Broadberry, *The Productivity Race*; J. Habakkuk, *American and British Technology in the Nineteenth Century: The Search for Labour-Saving Inventions* (Cambridge: Cambridge University Press, 1962).
33. Mokyr, *Lever of Riches*; Mokyr, *The Enlightened Economy*.
34. See Appendix.
35. This is computed using the relevant coefficient value of 0.0028.
36. Acemoglu, Johnson and Robinson, 'The Rise of Europe'; Pomeranz, *The Great Divergence*; M. Berg, *Luxury and Pleasure in Eighteenth-Century Britain* (Oxford: Oxford University Press, 2005); M. Berg and H. Clifford, *Consumers and Luxury: Consumer Culture in Europe 1650–1850* (Manchester: Manchester University Press, 1999); Davis, 'English Foreign Trade, 1660–1700' and Davis, 'English Foreign Trade, 1700–1774'; J. de Vries, *The Industrious Revolution: Consumer Behavior and the Household Economy, 1650 to the Present* (Cambridge and New York: Cambridge University Press, 2008).
37. O'Rourke and Williamson, 'After Columbus'.
38. To control for this possibility, we need to identify a factor which affects trade and is exogenous (e.g. cannot in turn be affected by growth). For this purpose we use geographic location. Economies closer to the Atlantic (and closer to the Mediterranean) were naturally well positioned for long distance trade.
39. Indeed, the last chapter suggested that markets may be a function of the level of income in the economy.
40. Due to the presence of heteroskedasticity, a standard error adjusted panel estimator was used. A single asterisk indicates that the variable is significant at 10 per cent level and double asterisk indicates significance at the 5 per cent level.

7 Conclusions and Implications for Economic Policy and the Modern Day

1. For an anthropological perspective of markets, and a guide to the literature, see the summary in T. C. Bestor, 'Markets: Anthropological Aspects', in N. J. Smelser and P. B. Bates (eds), *International Encyclopedia of the Social and Behavioral Sciences* (Oxford: Pergamon, 2001), pp. 9227–31.
2. D. C. North, 'Markets and Other Allocation Systems in History: The Challenge of Karl Polanyi', *Journal of European Economic History*, 6 (1977), pp. 703–16.
3. See A. J. Njoh, *Tradition, Culture and Development in Africa: Historical Lessons for Modern Development Planning* (Aldershot: Ashgate, 2006), ch. 8, on communal systems in Africa.
4. D. Cheal, *The Gift Economy* (London: Routledge, 1988); R. Kranton, 'Reciprocal Exchange: A Self Sustaining System', *American Economic Review*, 86 (1996), pp. 830–51; M. Mauss, *The Gift: The Form and Reason for Exchange in Archaic Societies* (London: Cohen & West, 1954)); Graeber, *Debt*:; M. D. Sahlins, *Stone Age Economics* (London: Routledge, 2004); L. Hyde, *The Gift: Creativity and the Artist in the Modern World* (New York: Vintage Books, 2007). For an example of gift exchange in post-Roman Europe, see P. H. Sawyer, 'Kings and Merchants', in P. H. Sawyer and I. N. Wood (eds), *Early Medieval Kingship* (Leeds: The editors, under the auspices of The School of History, University of Leeds, 1977), pp. 139–58.
5. D. Graeber, *Towards an Anthropological Theory of Value: The False Coin of our Own Dreams* (New York: Palgrave, 2001), pp. 153–4.
6. van Bavel, de Moor and van Zanden, 'Introduction: Factor Markets', p. 12.
7. Domar, 'The Causes of Slavery'.
8. Smith, *Wealth of Nations*, p. 22.
9. Ogilvie, '"Whatever Is, Is Right"'.
10. When measured in terms of volatility.
11. Smith, *Wealth of Nations*, p. 30. This point has also been made by Malanima (Malanima, *Pre-Modern*, p. 160).
12. Ibid., p. 161.
13. Smith, *Wealth of Nations*.
14. North and Thomas, *The Rise of the Western World*.
15. Epstein, *Freedom and Growth*.
16. Ibid.
17. Domar, 'The Causes of Slavery'.
18. Jones, 'Transaction Costs', p. 660. Jones takes the lead from P. Bohannan and G. Dalton (eds), *Markets in Africa* (Evanston, IL: Northwestern University Press, 1962), pp. 6–7.
19. Fara, *Science*, pp. 55, 99, 109.
20. See Chapters 1 and 5.
21. The most significant theoretical contributions came from Robert Solow. R. Solow, 'A Contribution to the Theory of Economic Growth', *Quarterly Journal of Economics*, 70 (1956), pp. 65–94; R. Solow, 'Technical Change and the Aggregate Production Function', *Review of Economics and Statistics*, 39 (1957), pp. 312–20.
22. For a critique and discussion of the patent-driven view of the Industrial Revolution, see J. Mokyr, 'Intellectual Property Rights, the Industrial Revolution, and the Beginnings of Economic Growth', *American Economic Review*, 99 (2009), pp. 349–55.
23. Mokyr, *Lever of Riches*.

24. Fara, *Science*.
25. Mokyr, *The Enlightened Economy*; Mokyr, *Gifts of Athena*. Also see, N. Crafts, 'The First Industrial Revolution: Resolving the Slow Growth/Rapid Industrialization Paradox', *Journal of the European Economic Association*, 3 (2010), pp. 525–34.
26. Allen, *The British Industrial Revolution*.
27. Mokyr, *The Enlightened Economy*.
28. For early examples of state support in the US and Australia, see I. McLean, 'Australian Economic Growth in Historical Perspective', *Economic Record*, 80 (2004), pp. 330–45; A. L. Olmstead and P. W. Rhode, *Creating Abundance: Biological Innovation and American Agricultural Development* (Cambridge: Cambridge University Press, 2008).
29. Allen, *The British Industrial Revolution*.
30. Broadberry, *The Productivity Race*.
31. P. Collier and A. Venables, 'Trade and Economic Performance: Does Africa's Fragmentation Matter', *Conference paper for the Annual Bank Conference on Development Economics* (2008). Also see, P. Collier, 'Africa: Geography and Growth', *Proceedings, Federal Reserve Bank of Kansas City* (2006), pp. 235–52.
32. Epstein, *Freedom and Growth*; Voth, 'Debt, Default and Empire'; Grafe, *Distant Tyranny*.
33. Epstein, Freedom and Growth; Dincecco, 'Fiscal Centralization'; Voth, 'Debt, Default and Empire'; Grafe, *Distant Tyranny*.
34. Known as the Sonnenschein-Mantel-Debreu Theorem.
35. This was originally revealed by Mandelbrot and Hudson, who identified 'fat tails' (i.e. more of a tendency for big moves in asset prices) and the alternation between period of stable prices and unstable prices (known as volatility clustering). See B. B. Mandelbrot and R. L. Hudson, *The (Mis)Behavior of Markets: A Fractal View of Risk, Ruin, and Reward* (New York: Basic Books, 2004).
36. Keynes, *The General Theory*, ch. 12.
37. H. P. Minsky, *Can "It" Happen Again: Essays on Instability and Finance* (Armonk, NY: M.E. Sharpe, 1982); H. P. Minsky, *Stabilising an Unstable Economy* (New York: McGraw Hill, 2008); I. Fisher, 'The Debt-Deflation Theory of the Great Depression', *Econometrica* (1933), pp. 337–57.
38. Cassidy, *How Markets Fail*, p. 224.
39. Refers to the title of Hayek, but who argued that state intervention risked placing the economy on this road.
40. Chang, 'Institutions and Economic Development', pp. 475–6.
41. Acemoglu, Johnson and Robinson, 'The Rise of Europe'; A. K. Dutt, 'Institutional Change and Economic Development: Concepts, Theory and Political Economy', *Journal of Institutional Economics*, 7 (2011), pp. 529–34; D. C. North, *Understanding the Processes of Economic Change* (Princeton, NJ: Princeton University Press, 2005); Chang, 'Institutions and Economic Development'; Chang, 'Reply to the Comments'.
42. Chang, 'Institutions and Economic Development', p. 476.
43. Acemoglu, Johnson and Robinson, 'The Rise of Europe'. Also see Chang, 'Institutions and Economic Development', pp. 475–6.
44. Ferguson, *The Ascent of Money*.
45. For a summary, see Meissner, 'Growth from Globalization?'
46. D. Acemoglu, S. Johnson and J. A. Robinson, 'The Colonial Origins of Comparative Development: An Empirical Investigation', *American Economic Review*, 91 (2001), pp. 1369–401; K. L. Sokoloff and S. L. Engerman, 'Institutions, Factor Endowments, and

Paths of Development in The New World', *Journal of Economic Perspectives*, 14 (2000), pp. 217–32.

47. Williamson, *Trade and Poverty*, ch. 9; Sokoloff and Engerman, 'Institutions, Factor Endowments and Paths of Development'.
48. Williamson, *Trade and Poverty*, ch. 10.
49. S. Redding, 'Dynamic Comparative Advantage and the Welfare Effects of Trade', *Oxford Economic Papers*, 51 (1999), pp. 15–39.
50. Krugman and Obstfeld, *International Economics*.
51. Chang, *Kicking Away the Ladder*, p. 51.
52. L. Y-C. Yueh, *The Law and Economics of Globalisation: New Challenges for a World in Flux* (Cheltenham and Northampton, MA: Edward Elgar, 2009), p. 122. For a debate on the issues, see H-J. Chang, 'Should Industrial Policy in Developing Countries Conform to Comparative Advantage or Defy It? A Debate between Justin Lin and Ha-Joon Chand', *Development Policy Review*, Overseas Development Institute, 27 (2009), pp. 483–502.
53. C. Blattman, M. Clemens and J. Williamson, 'Who Protected and Why? Tariffs the World Around 1870–1938', *Harvard Institute of Economic Research*, working papers, 2010 (2003); Yueh, *The Law and Economics of Globalization*, p. 122.
54. The literature is immense, but for a recent application to the BRICS, see R. Sally, 'Globalisation and the Political Economy of Trade Liberalization in the BRICS', in *Globalisation and Emerging Economies* (Paris: Organisation for Economic Co-operation and Development, 2009).
55. Williamson, *Trade and Poverty*.
56. One such model is the Lewis (Dual-Sector) Model.
57. Hayek, *Road to Serfdom*.

WORKS CITED

Aalbers, J., 'Holland's Financial Problems (1713–1733) and the Wars Against Louis XIV', in A. C. Duke and C. A. Tamje (eds), *Britain and the Netherlands: Papers Delivered to the Sixth Anglo-Dutch Conference* (The Hague: Martinus Nijhoff, 1977), pp. 79–93.

Abel, W., *Agrarkrisen und Agrarkonjunktur. Eine Geschichte der Land- und Ernèahrungswirtschaft Mitteleuropas seit dem hohen Mittelalter* (Berlin-Hamburg: P. Parey, 1935).

Abu-Lughod, J. L., *Before European Hegemony: The World System A.D. 1250–1350* (New York and Oxford: Oxford University Press, 1989).

Abulafia, D. (ed.), *The Mediterranean in History* (London: Thames & Hudson, 2003).

—, *The Great Sea: A Human History of the Mediterranean* (London: Allen Lane, 2011).

Acemoglu, D., S. Johnson and J. A. Robinson, 'The Colonial Origins of Comparative Development: An Empirical Investigation', *American Economic Review*, 91 (2001), pp. 1369–401.

—, 'The Rise of Europe: Atlantic Trade, Institutional Change and Economic Growth', *American Economic Review*, 95 (2005), pp. 546–79.

—, 'Institutions as the Fundamental Cause of Long-Run Growth', in P. Aghion and S. N. Durlauf (eds), *Handbook of Economic Growth*, 2 vols (Amsterdam: Elsevier, 2012), vol. 2, pp. 385–472.

Achilles, W., 'Getreidepreise und Getreidehandelsbeziehungn Europaischer Raume im 16. und 17. Jahrhundert', in *Zeitschrift fur Agrargeschichte und Agrarsoziologie* (1959), pp. 32–55.

Akerlof, G. A., 'The Market for "Lemons": Quality Uncertainty and the Market Mechanism', *Quarterly Journal of Economics*, 84 (1970), pp. 488–500.

Allen, R. C., 'Economic Structure and Agricultural Productivity in Europe, 1300–1800', *European Review of Economic History*, 4 (2000), pp. 1–25.

—, 'The Great Divergence in European Wages and Prices from the Middle Ages to the First World War', *Explorations in Economic History*, 38 (2001), pp. 411–47.

—, 'Progress and Poverty in Early Modern Europe', *Economic History Review*, 56 (2003), pp. 403–43.

—, *The British Industrial Revolution in Global Perspective* (Cambridge: Cambridge University Press, 2009).

Allen, R. C., and R. Unger, 'The Depth and Breadth of the Market for Polish Grain 1500–1800', in J. P. S. Lemmink and J. S. A. M. van Koningsbrugge (eds), *Baltic Affairs Relations between the Netherlands and North-Eastern Europe 1500–1800* (Nijmegen: Institute of Northern and Eastern European Studies, 1990), pp. 1–18.

Anderson, M. S., *Europe in the Eighteenth Century, 1713–1783*, 3rd edn (London: Longman, 1987).

Andreau, J., *Banking and Business in the Roman World*, trans. J. Lloyd (Cambridge: Cambridge University Press, 1999).

Anes Álvarez, G., *Las crises agrarias en la Espanña moderna* (Madrid, 1970).

Arrow, K. J., 'Uncertainty and the Welfare Economics of Medical Care', *American Economic Review*, 53 (1963), pp. 941–73.

Ashtor, 'E., The Volume of Levantine Trade in the Later Middle Ages 1370–1498', *Journal of European Economic History*, 4 (1975), pp. 573–612.

—, 'Catalan Cloth on the Late Medieval Mediterranean Markets', *Journal of European Economic History*, 17 (1988), pp. 227–58.

Attman, A., *The Russian and Polish Markets in International Trade, 1500–1650* (Göteborg: Institute of Economic History of Gothenburg University, 1973).

Aurell, M., 'Barcelona', in A. Vauchez, B. Dobson and M. Lapidge (eds), *Encyclopedia of the Middle Ages* (Cambridge: James Clarke, 2001): e-reference edition distributed by Oxford University Press at: http://www.oxfordreference.com/views/ENTRY.html?subview=Main&entry=t179.e303 [accessed 7 April 2012].

Bachrach, B., 'Pirenne and Charlemagne', in A. C. Murray (ed.), *After Rome's Fall: Narrators and Sources of Early Medieval History* (Toronto: University of Toronto Press, 1998), pp. 214–31.

Baines, D., 'European Labour Markets, Emigration and Internal Migration, 1850–1930', in T. J. Hatton and J. G. Williamson (eds), *Migration and the International Labour Market* (London: Routledge, 1994), pp. 35–54.

Bairoch, P., *Economics and World History: Myths and Paradoxes* (Chicago, IL: University of Chicago Press, 1995).

Bairoch, P., J. Batou and P. Chevre, *La population des villes europeennes, 800–1850: banque de donnees et analyse sommaire des resultats* (Geneve: Droz, 1988).

Bang, P. F., 'Trade and Commerce, Roman', in M. Gagarin (ed.), *The Oxford Encyclopedia of Ancient Greece and Rome* (Oxford: Oxford University Press, 2009), online at: http://www.oxfordreference.com/views/ENTRY.html?subview=Main&entry=t294.e1272 [accessed 5 April 2012].

Barbour, V., 'Marine Risks and Insurance in the 17th Century', *Journal of Economic History*, 1 (1929), pp. 561–96.

Barquín, R., 'Transport y precio del trigo en el siglo XIX', *Revista de Historia Económica*, año XV, 1 (1997), pp. 17–48.

Bateman, V. N., 'Market Integration and Growth in Europe: The Early Modern Era' (DPhil Economics Thesis, University of Oxford, 2006).

—, 'The Evolution of Markets in Early Modern Europe, 1350–1800: A Study of Grain Prices', *Economics Series Working Paper*, University of Oxford (2007).

—, 'Market Integration in the Mediterranean', *Economic History Society Conference Paper* (2011).

—, 'The Evolution of Markets in Early Modern Europe, 1350–1800: A Study of Wheat Prices', *Economic History Review*, 64 (2011), pp. 447–71.

—, 'Price Volatility in Late Medieval and Early Modern Europe', in R. J. van der Spek, J. L. van Zanden and E. S. Leeuwen (eds), *A History of Market Performance* (London: Routledge, forthcoming).

Bator, F. M., 'The Simple Analytics of Welfare Maximization', *American Economic Review*, 47 (1957), pp. 22–59.

—, 'The Anatomy of Market Failure', *Quarterly Journal of Economics*, 72 (1958), pp. 351–79.

Baumol, W. J., 'Contestable Markets: An Uprising in the Theory of Industrial Structure', *American Economic Review*, 72 (1982), pp. 1–15.

Bavel, B. van., 'Rural Wage Labour in the Sixteenth Century Low Countries: An Assessment of the Importance and Nature of Wage Labour in the Countryside of Holland, Guelders and Flanders', *Continuity and Change*, 21 (2005), pp. 37–72.

—, 'The Organization and Rise of Land and Lease Markets in Northwestern Europe and Italy, *c.* 1000–1800', *Continuity and Change*, 23 (2008), pp. 13–53.

Bavel, B. van., J. Dijkman, E. Kuijpers and J. Zuijderduijn, 'The Organisation of Markets as a Key Factor in the Rise of Holland, Fourteenth-Sixteenth Centuries: A Test Case for an Institutional Approach', *Centre for Global Economic History*, Working Paper number 6 (2011).

Bavel, B. van., T. de Moor and J. L. van Zanden, 'Introduction: Factor Markets in Global Economic History', *Continuity and Change*, 24:1 (2009), pp. 9–21.

Bell, A., 'The Organization of Public Work in Society and by the State in Early Medieval England *c.* 800-*c.* 1300' (DPhil thesis, University of Oxford, 2006).

Benjamin, D. K., and L. A. Kochin, 'Searching for an Explanation of Unemployment in Interwar Britain', *Journal of Political Economy*, 87 (1979), pp. 441–78.

Berchet, G., *Del Commercio dei Veneti nell' Asia* (Venice, 1869).

Berg, M., *Luxury and Pleasure in Eighteenth-Century Britain* (Oxford: Oxford University Press, 2005).

Berg, M., and H. Clifford, *Consumers and Luxury: Consumer Culture in Europe 1650–1850* (Manchester: Manchester University Press, 1999).

Berman, H. J., *Law and Revolution* (Cambridge, MA: Harvard University Press, 1983).

Berov, L., *Dvizhenieto na tsenite na Balkanite prez XVI-XIX v. i evropeiskata revoliutsiia na tsenite* (Sofia: BAN, 1976).

Bestor, T. C., 'Markets: Anthropological Aspects', in N. J. Smelser and P. B. Bates (eds), *International Encyclopedia of the Social and Behavioral Sciences* (Oxford: Pergamon, 2001), pp. 9227–31.

Beveridge, Lord W. H., *Prices and Wages in England from the Twelfth to the Nineteenth Century* (London: Cass, 1965).

Biraben, J-N, 'Essai sur l'evolution du nombre des homes', *Population*, 34 (1969), pp. 13–25.

Blancard, P., *Manuel du Commerce des Indes* (Paris, 1806).

Blattman, C, M. Clemens and J. Williamson, 'Who Protected and Why? Tariffs the World Around 1870–1938', *Harvard Institute of Economic Research*, Working Papers number 2010 (2003).

Blom, J. C. H., and E. Lamberts, *History of the Low Countries* (New York and Oxford: Berghahn Books, 1999).

Bochove, C. van, 'Market Integration and the North Sea System (1600–1800)', in H. Brand and L. Muller (eds), *The Dynamics of Economic Culture in the North Sea and Baltic Region in the Late Middle Ages and Early Modern Period* (Hilversum: Verloren, 2007), pp. 155–69.

—, *The Economic Consequences of the Dutch: Economic Integration around the North Sea, 1500–1800* (Amsterdam: Askant, 2008).

Bogart, D., 'Turnpike Trusts and the Transport Revolution in Eighteenth Century England', *Explorations in Economic History*, 42:4 (2005), pp. 479–508.

Bohannan, P., and G. Dalton (eds), *Markets in Africa* (Evanston, IL: Northwestern University Press, 1962).

Bollerslev, T., 'Generalized Autoregressive Conditional Heteroskedasticity', *Journal of Econometrics*, 31 (1986), pp. 307–27.

Bowerstock, G. W., P. Brown and O. Grabar, *Late Antiquity: A Guide to the Post-Classical World* (Cambridge, MA: Belknap Press of Harvard University Press, 1999).

Bowman, A., and A. Wilson (eds), *Quantifying the Roman Economy: Methods and Problems* (Oxford: Oxford University Press, 2009).

Brazdil, R., C. Pfister, H. Wanner, H. von Storch and J. Luterbacher, 'Historical Climatology in Europe – the State of the Art', *Climate Change*, 70 (2005), pp. 363–430.

Braudel, F., *La Méditerranée* (Paris: Colin, 1949).

—, *Civilisation Materielle*, 3 vols (Paris: Colin, 1979) vol. 3.

—, *La dynamique du capitalism* (Paris: Flammarion, 1985).

Braudel, F., and F. Spooner, 'Prices in Europe from 1450 to 1750', in E. E. Rich and C. Wilson (eds), *The Cambridge Economic History of Europe, Vol. 4: The Economy of Expanding Europe in the Sixteenth and Seventeenth Centuries* (Cambridge: Cambridge University Press, 1967), pp. 374–486.

Braudel, F., and R. Romano, *Navires et marchandises à l'entrée du port de Livourne, 1547–1611* (Paris: Armand Colin, 1951).

Brenner, R., 'Agrarian Class Structure and Economic Development in Pre-Industrial Europe', *Past and Present*, 72 (1976), pp. 30–75.

Britnell, R. H., 'The Proliferation of Markets in England, 1200–1349', *Economic History Review*, 34:2 (1981), pp. 209–21.

—, 'England and Northern Italy in the Early Fourteenth Century: The Economic Contrasts', *Transactions of the Royal Historical Society*, series 5, 39 (1989), pp. 167–83.

—, *Commercialisation of English Society, 1000–1500* (Cambridge: Cambridge University Press, 1993).

Britnell, R. H., and B. M. S. Campbell (eds), *A Commercialising Economy: England 1086 to c. 1300* (Manchester and New York: Manchester University Press, 1995).

Broadberry, S., *The Productivity Race: British Manufacturing in International Perspective, 1850–1990* (Cambridge: Cambridge University Press, 1997).

Broadberry, S., S. Ghosal and E. Proto, 'Commercialisation, Factor Prices and Technological Progress in the Transition to Modern Economic Growth: History and Theory', *University of Warwick Economics Research Paper*, series number 852 (2008).

Buyst, E., S. Dercon and B. van Campenhout, 'Road Expansion and Market Integration in the Austrian Low Countries during the Second Half of the 18th Century', *Center for Economic Studies, University of Leuven* (2000).

E. M. Byrne, *Genoese Shipping in the Twelfth and Thirteenth Centuries* (Cambridge, MA: The Mediaeval Academy of America, 1930), pp. 12–19.

Caenegem, R. C. van, *An Historical Introduction to Western Constitutional Law* (Cambridge: Cambridge University Press, 1995).

Cameron, R., and L. Neal, *A Concise Economic History of the World, From Paleolithic Times to the Present* (New York and Oxford: Oxford University Press, 2003).

Campbell, B. M. S., *English Seigniorial Agriculture 1250–1450* (Cambridge: Cambridge University Press, 2000).

—, 'The Agrarian Problem in the Early Fourteenth Century', *Past and Present*, 188 (2005), pp. 26–44.

—, 'Factor Markets in England before the Black Death', *Continuity and Change*, 24 (2009), pp. 79–106.

Campbell, B. M. S., J. A. Galloway and M. Murphy, *A Medieval Capital and its Grain Supply: Agrarian Production and Distribution in the London Region, c. 1300, Historical Geography Research Series*, 30 (1993).

Campbell, G., 'Aragon', in G. Campbell (eds), *The Oxford Dictionary of the Renaissance* (Oxford and New York: Oxford University Press, 2003): e-reference edition distributed by Oxford University Press at: http://www.oxfordreference.com/views/ENTRY.html?subview=Main&entry=t175.e186 [accessed 7 April 2012].

—, 'Columbus', in G. Campbel (eds), *The Oxford Dictionary of the Renaissance* (Oxford; New York: Oxford University Press, 2003): e-reference edition distributed by Oxford University Press at: http://www.oxfordreference.com/views/ENTRY.html?subview=Main&entry=t175.e906 [accessed 7 April 2012].

Carlos, A. M., and L. Neal, 'Amsterdam and London as Financial Centers in the Eighteenth Century', *Financial History Review*, 18 (2011), pp. 21–46.

Carter, F. W., *Trade and Urban Development in Poland: An Economic Geography of Cracow, from its Origins to 1795* (Cambridge: Cambridge University Press, 2006).

Cassidy, J., *How Markets Fail: The Logic of Economic Calamities* (London: Penguin, 2009).

Cater, B., and B. Lew, 'The Telegraph, Coordination of Tramp Shipping, and Growth in World Trade, 1870–1910', *European Review of Economic History*, 10 (2006), pp. 147–73.

Chang, H-J., *Kicking Away the Ladder: Development Strategy in Historical Perspective* (London: Anthem Press, 2002).

—, 'Should Industrial Policy in Developing Countries Conform to Comparative Advantage or Defy it? A Debate between Justin Lin and Ha-Joon Chang', *Development Policy Review*, Overseas Development Institute, 27 (2009), pp. 483–502.

—, 'Institutions and Economic Development: Theory, Policy and History', *Journal of Institutional Economics*, 7 (2011), pp. 473–98.

—, 'Reply to the Comments on "Institutions and Economic Development: Theory, Policy and History"', *Journal of Institutional Economics*, 7 (2011), pp. 595–613.

Chang, H-J., and I. Grabel, 'Reclaiming Development from the Washington Consensus', *Journal of Post Keynesian Economics*, 27 (2004), pp. 273–91.

Cheal, D., *The Gift Economy* (London: Routledge, 1988).

Chilosi, D., T. E. Murphy and R. Studer, 'Europe's Many Integrations: Geography and Grain Markets, 1620–1913', *Innocenzo Gasparini Institute for Economic Research*, working paper 412 (2011).

Chilosi, D., and O. Volckart, 'Books or Bullion? Printing, Mining and Financial Integration in Central Europe from the 1460s', *London School of Economics, Economic History Working Papers*, 144/10 (2010).

—, 'Money, States, and Empire: Financial Integration and Institutional Change in Central Europe, 1400–1520', *Journal of Economic History*, 71 (2011), pp. 762–91.

Chorley, P., 'The Cloth Exports of Flanders and Northern France during the Thirteenth Century: A Luxury Trade?', *Economic History Review*, 40 (1987), pp. 349–79.

Christensen, A. E., *Dutch Trade to the Baltic about 1600: Studies in the Sound Toll Register and Dutch Shipping Records* (Copenhagen and The Hague: Einar Munksgaard; Martinus Nijhoff, 1941).

Clark, G., 'The Cost of Capital and Medieval Agricultural Techniques', *Explorations in Economic History*, 25 (1988), pp. 265–94.

—, 'Markets and Economic Growth: Grain Markets in Medieval England', Mimeograph, Department of Economics, U. C. Davis (2002).

—, *A Farewell to Alms: A Brief Economic History of the World* (Princeton, NJ: Princeton University Press, 2007).

Clodfelter, M., *Warfare and Armed Conflicts: A Statistical Encyclopedia of Casualty and Other Figures, 1494–2007* (Jefferson, NC: McFarland, 2002).

Coase, R. H., 'The Problem of Social Costs', *Journal of Law and Economics*, 3 (1960), pp. 1–44.

Cohen, J. S., and M. L. Weitzamn, 'A Marxian Model of Enclosures', *Journal of Development Economics*, 1 (1975), pp. 287–336.

Cole, A., and R. Crandall, 'The International Scientific Committee on Price History', *Journal of Economic History*, 24 (1964), pp. 381–8.

Cole, C. W., *Colbert and a Century of French Mercantilism* (New York: Columbia University Press, 1939).

Collier, P., 'Africa: Geography and Growth', *Proceedings, Federal Reserve Bank of Kansas City* (2006), pp. 235–52.

Collier, P., and A. Venables, 'Trade and Economic Performance: Does Africa's Fragmentation Matter', *Conference Paper for the Annual Bank Conference on Development Economics* (2008).

Conze, W., 'Review of Der Reichsmerkantilismus. Studien zur Wirtschaftspolitik des Heiligen Romischen Reiches im 17. und 18. Jahrhundert by Ingomar Bog', *Economic History Review*, 12:2 (1959), pp. 323–4.

Cooper, R. C., *Coordination Games: Complementarities and Macroeconomics* (Cambridge: Cambridge University Press, 1999).

Crafts, N. F. R, *British Economic Growth during the Industrial Revolution* (Oxford: Clarendon, 1985).

Crafts, N. F. R., and C. K. Harley, 'Output Growth and the British Industrial Revolution: A Restatement of the Crafts-Harley View', *Economic History Review*, 45 (1992), pp.703–30.

—, 'Precocious British Industrialisation: A General Equilibrium Perspective', in L. P. de la Escosura (ed.), *British Exceptionalism: A Unique Path to the Industrial Revolution* (Cambridge: Cambridge University Press, 2004), pp. 86–110.

Crafts, N., 'The First Industrial Revolution: Resolving the Slow Growth/Rapid Industrialization Paradox, *Journal of the European Economic Association*, 3 (2010), pp. 525–34.

Crompton, G., *Canals and Inland Navigation*, Studies in Transport History (Aldershot: Scolar, 1996).

Crouzet, F., 'Wars, Blockade, and Economic Change in Europe, 1792–1815', *Journal of Economic History*, 24:4 (1964), pp. 567–88.

David, P., 'Learning by Doing and Tariff Protection: A Reconsideration of the Case of the Ante-bellum United States Cotton Industry', *Journal of Economic History*, 30 (1970), pp. 521–601.

Davies, N., *Europe: A History* (Oxford: Oxford University Press, 1996).

Davis, R., 'English Foreign Trade, 1660–1700', *Economic History Review*, 7:2 (1954), pp. 150–66.

—, 'English Foreign Trade, 1700–1774', *Economic History Review*, 15:2 (1962), pp. 285–303.

—, 'The Rise of Protection in England, 1689–1786', *Economic History Review*, 19 (1966), pp. 306–17.

De Long, J. B. and A. Schleifer, 'Princes and Merchants: European City Growth before the Industrial Revolution', *Journal of Law and Economics*, 36 (1993), pp. 671–702.

Dejongh, G., B. van Campenhout and M. Ceusters, 'In de greep van de markt De integratie van de regionale landbouwmarkten in Belgie, 1700–1850', *Revue Belgie d_histoire contemporaine*, 30 (2000), pp. 5–47.

Desmet, K., and S. L. Parente, 'The Evolution of Markets and the Revolution of Industry: A Quantitative Model of England's Development', *CEPR Discussion Paper* (May 2009).

Dijkman, J., *Shaping Medieval Markets: The Organisation of Commodity Markets in Holland, c. 1200–c. 1450* (Leiden and Boston, MA: Brill, 2011).

Dincecco, M., 'Fiscal Centralization, Limited Government, and Public Revenues in Europe, 1650–1913, *Journal of Economic History*, 69 (2009), pp. 48–103.

Dollinger, P., *The German Hansa*, trans. and ed. D. S. Ault and S. H. Steinberg (London: Routledge, 1999).

Domar, E., 'The Causes of Slavery or Serfdom: A Hypothesis', *Journal of Economic History*, 30 (1970), pp. 18–32.

Dowey, J., 'Mind Over Matter: Empirical Evidence of the Industrial Enlightenment as the Origin of Modern Economic Growth', *London School of Economics*, working paper (forthcoming 2012).

Drelichman, M., 'The Curse of Moctezuma: American Silver and the Dutch Disease, 1501–1650', *Explorations in Economic History*, 42:3 (2005), pp. 349–80.

Duby, G., *The Early Growth of the European Economy: Warriors and Peasants from the Seventh to the Twelfth Century*, trans. H. B. Clarke (London: Weidenfield & Nicolson, 1974).

Duncan-Jones, R., *Money and Government in the Roman Empire* (Cambridge: Cambridge University Press, 1994).

Dupuy, R. E., and Dupuy, T. N., *The Encyclopedia of Military History: From 3500 B.C. to the Present*, 2nd rev. edn (London: Jane's, 1986).

Dutt, A. K., 'Institutional Change and Economic Development: Concepts, Theory and Political Economy', *Journal of Institutional Economics*, 7 (2011), pp. 529–34.

Dyer, C., *Standards of Living in the Later Middle Ages: Social Change in England c. 1200–1520* (Cambridge: Cambridge University Press, 1989).

—, 'The Consumer and the Market in the Later Middle Ages', *Economic History Review*, 42 (1989), pp. 305–27.

—, *An Age of Transition? Economy and Society in England in the Later Middle Ages* (Oxford: Oxford University Press, 2005).

—, *Making a Living in the Middle Ages: The People of Britain 850–1520* (Newhaven, CT: Yale University Press, 2009).

Edelstein, M., *Overseas Investment in the Age of High Imperialism: The United Kingdom, 1850–1914* (London: Methuen, 1982).

Engel, C., and J. Rogers, 'Regional Patterns in the Law of One Price: the Roles of Geography vs. Currencies', *NBER*, working paper, series 5395 (1995).

—, 'How Wide is the Border?', *American Economic Review*, 86 (1996), pp. 1112–25.

—, 'Violating the Law of One Price: Should We Make a Federal Case Out of It?' *Journal of Money, Credit, and Banking*, 33:1 (2001), pp. 1–15.

Engerman, S. L., 'The Slave Trade and British Capital Formation in the Eighteenth Century: A Comment on the Williams Thesis', *Business History Review*, 46 (1972), pp. 430–43.

Engerman, S. L., and P. K. O'Brien, 'Export and the Growth of the British Economy from the Glorious Revolution to the Peace of Amiens', in B. L. Solow (ed.), *Slavery and the Rise of the Atlantic System* (Cambridge: Cambridge University Press, 1991), pp. 177–209.

Engle, R., 'Autoregressive Conditional Heteroskedasticity with Estimates of the Variance of United Kingdom Inflation', *Econometrica*, 50 (1982), pp. 987–1007.

—, 'GARCH 101: The Use of ARCH/GARCH in Applied Econometrics', *Journal of Economic Perspectives*, 15 (2001), pp. 157–68.

—, 'Risk and Volatility: Econometric Models and Financial Practice', *American Economic Review*, 94 (2004), pp. 405–20.

Epstein, S. R., 'Regional Fairs, Institutional Innovation, and Economic Growth in Late Medieval Europe', *Economic History Review*, 47 (1994), pp. 459–82.

—, 'Craft Guilds, Apprenticeship, and Technological Change in Preindustrial Europe', *Journal of Economic History*, 58 (1998), pp. 684–713.

—, *Freedom and Growth: The Rise of States and Markets in Europe, 1300–1750* (London: Routledge/London School of Economics, 2000).

Erdkamp, P., *The Grain Market in the Roman Empire: A Social, Political and Economic Study* (Cambridge: Cambridge University Press, 2005).

Ertman, T., *Birth of the Leviathan: Building States and Regimes In Medieval Modern Europe* (Cambridge: Cambridge University Press, 1997).

Estevadeordal, A., A. M. Taylor and B. Frantz 'The Rise and Fall of World Trade, 1870–1939', *Quarterly Journal of Economics*, 118:2 (2003), pp. 359–407.

Fara, P., *Science: A Four Thousand Year History* (Oxford: Oxford University Press, 2009).

Faroqhi, S., B. McGowan, D. Quataert and Pamuk, S., *An Economic and Social History of the Ottoman Empire* (Cambridge: Cambridge University Press, 1997).

Feinstein, C. H., 'Pessimism Perpetuated: Real Wages and the Standard of Living in Britain During and After the Industrial Revolution', *Journal of Economic History*, 58 (1998), pp. 625–58.

Ferguson, N., *The Ascent of Money: A Financial History of the World* (London: Penguin, 2009).

Fernie, E. 'The Origins of Europe', *Journal of the Warburg and Courtauld Institutes*, 71 (2008), pp. 39–53.

Findlay, R., and K. H. O'Rourke, *Commodity Market Integration, 1500–2000* (London: Centre for Economic Policy Research, 2002).

—, *Power and Plenty: Trade, War and the World Economy in the Second Millennium* (Princeton, NJ and Oxford: Princeton University Press, 2007).

Finley, M. I., 'Technical Innovation and Economic Progress in the Ancient World', *Economic History Review*, 18 (1965), pp. 29–45.

Fisher, I., 'The Debt-Deflation Theory of the Great Depression', *Econometrica* (1933), pp. 337–57.

Flandreau, M., and M. Maurel 'Monetary Union, Trade Integration, and Business Cycles in 19th Century Europe', *Open Economics Review*, 16:2 (2005), pp. 135–52.

Földvári, P., and B. van Leeuwen, 'What Can Price Volatility Tell Us About Market Related Institutions? Conditional Heteroskedasticity in Historical Commodity Price Series', Paper Presented at the World Economic History Congress (2009), available at: http://www.basvanleeuwen.net/bestanden/2conditionalHteroscedasticity.pdf [accessed 1 August 2011].

Földvári, P., B. van Leeuwen and J. L. van Zanden, 'Long Run Patterns in Market Efficiency and the Genesis of the Market Economy: Markets Around the Mediterranean from Nebuchadnezzar to Napoleon (580 BC and 1800 AD)', *Centre for Economic Policy Research*, discussion paper, 8521, in R. J. van der Spek, J. L. van Zanden, and E. S. Leeuwen, *A History of Market Performance* (London: Routledge, forthcoming).

Fossier, R., 'Rural Economy and Country Life', in T. Reuter (ed.), *The New Cambridge Medieval History, Vol. III: c. 900–c. 1024* (Cambridge: Cambridge University Press, 1999), pp. 27–63.

Frank, A. G., *Dependent Accumulation and Underdevelopment* (London: Macmillan, 1978).

Freedman, P., 'Rural Society', in M. Jones (ed.), *The New Cambridge Medieval History, Vol. VI: c. 1300–c. 1415'* (Cambridge: Cambridge University Press, 2008), pp. 82–101.

Friedman, M., *Capitalism and Freedom* (Chicago, IL: University of Chicago Press, 1962).

Friedman, M., and R. Friedman, *Free to Choose: A Personal Statement* (New York: Harcourt Brace Jovanovich, 1980).

Frier, B. W., and D. P. Kehoe, 'Law and Economic Institutions', in W. Scheidel, I. Morris and R. P. Saller (eds), *The Cambridge Economic History of the Greco-Roman World* (Cambridge: Cambridge University Press, 2007), pp. 113–43.

Fukuyama, F., *The Origins of Political Order: From Prehuman Times to the French Revolution* (New York: Farrar, Straus & Giroux, 2012).

Galloway, J. A, 'One Market or Many? London and the Grain Trade of England', in J. A. Galloway (ed.), *Trade, Urban Hinterlands and Market Integration c. 1300–1600*, Working Papers Series, 3 (London: Centre for Metropolitan History, Institute of Historical Research, 2000), pp. 23–42.

—, (ed.), *Trade, Urban Hinterlands and Market Integration c. 1300–1600*, Working Papers Series, 3 (London: Centre for Metropolitan History, Institute of Historical Research, 2000).

Galloway, P. R., 'Basic Patterns in Annual Variations in Fertility, Nuptiality, Mortality, and Prices in Pre-Industrial Europe', *Population Studies*, 42 (1988), pp. 275–302.

Ganshof, F. L., *Feudalism* (London: Longman Group, 1996).

Geiger, Reed G., *Planning the French Canals: Bureaucracy, Politics, and Enterprise Under the Restoration* (Newark, DE and London: University of Delaware Press; Associated University Presses, 1994).

Gimpel, J., *The Medieval Machine: The Industrial Revolution of the Middle Ages* (New York: Holt, Rinehart & Winston, 1976).

Glamann, K., 'The Changing Patterns of Trade', in E. E. Rich and C. H. Wilson, *The Cambridge Economic History of Europe. Vol. 5: The Economic Organization of Early Modern Europe* (Cambridge: Cambridge University Press, 1967), pp. 185–289.

Goldsmith, R. W., 'An Estimate of the Size and Structure of the National Product of the Early Roman Empire', *Review of Income and Wealth*, 30 (1984), pp. 263–88.

Grab, A. I., 'The Politics of Subsistence: The Liberalization of Grain Commerce in Austrian Lombardy Under Enlightened Despotism', *Journal of Modern History*, 57 (1985), pp. 185–210.

Graeber, D., *Towards an Anthropological Theory of Value: The False Coin of our Own Dreams* (New York: Palgrave, 2001).

—, *Debt: The First 5000 Years* (New York: Melville House, 2011).

Grafe, R., 'Northern Spain between the Iberian and Atlantic Worlds: Trade and Regional Specialisation, 1550–1650', Economic History Association (US) Gerschenkron prize dissertation summary, *Journal of Economic History*, 62 (2002), pp. 533–7.

—, *Distant Tyranny: Markets, Power, and Backwardness in Spain, 1650–1800* (Princeton, NJ and Woodstock: Princeton University Press, 2012).

Greene, K., 'Technological Innovation and Economic Progress in the Ancient World: M.I. Finley Re-Considered', *Economic History Review*, 53 (2000), pp. 29–59.

Greene, M., *A Shared World: Christians and Muslims in the Early Modern Mediterranean* (Princeton, NJ: Princeton University Press, 2000).

—, 'Beyond Northern Invasions: The Mediterranean in the Seventeenth Century', *Past and Present*, 174 (2002), pp. 40–72.

Greif, A., *Institutions and the Path to the Modern Economy: Lessons from Medieval Trade* (Cambridge: Cambridge University Press, 2006).

Greif, A., P. Milgrom and B. R. Weingast, 'Coordination, Commitment, and Enforcement: The Case of the Merchant Guild', *Journal of Political Economy*, 102:4 (1994), pp. 745–96.

Habakkuk, J., *American and British Technology in the Nineteenth Century: The Search for Labour-Saving Inventions* (Cambridge: Cambridge University Press, 1962).

Hamilton, E. J., *American Treasure and the Price Revolution in Spain, 1501–1650* (Cambridge, MA: Harvard University Press, 1934).

Harberger, A. C., 'Monopoly and Resource Allocation', *American Economic Review*, 44 (1954), pp. 77–87.

Hardin, G., 'The Tragedy of the Commons', *Science*, 162 (1968), pp. 1243–8.

Harley, C. K., 'Ocean Freight Rates and Productivity, 1740–1913: The Primacy of Mechanical Innovation Reaffirmed', *Journal of Economic History*, 48 (1988), pp. 851–76.

—, 'A Review of O'Rourke and Williamson's Globalization and History: The Evolution of a Nineteenth Century Atlantic Economy', *Journal of Economic Literature*, 38:4 (2000), pp. 926–35.

Harris, W. V., 'A Revisionist View of Roman Money', *Journal of Roman Studies*, 96 (2006), pp. 1–24.

—, 'The Nature of Roman Money', in W. V. Harris (ed.), *The Monetary Systems of the Greeks and Romans* (Oxford: Oxford University Press, 2008), pp. 174–207.

Hatton, T. J., and J. G. Williamson (eds), *Migration and the International Labour Market 1850–1939* (London: Routledge, 1994).

Hay, D., *Europe in the Fourteenth and Fifteenth Centuries* (London and New York: Longman, 1989).

Hayek, F. A., *The Road to Serfdom* (London: Routledge & Kegan Paul, 1944).

—, 'The Use of Knowledge in Society', *American Economic Review*, 35 (1945), pp. 519–30.

Head, K., 'Infant Industry Protection in the Steel Rail Industry', *Journal of International Economics*, 37 (1994), pp. 141–65.

Heeres, W. G., L. M. J. B. Hesp, L. Noordegraaf and R. C. W. van der Voort, *From Dunkirk to Danzig: Shipping and Trade in the North Sea and the Baltic, 1350–1850* (Hilversum: Verloren Publishers, 1988).

Hintze, O., 'Military Organization and the Organization of the State', in F. Gilbert (ed.), *The Historical Essays of Otto Hintze* (New York: Oxford University Press, 1970), pp. 178–215.

Hitchner, R. B., '"The Advantages of Wealth and Luxury": The Case for Economic Growth in the Roman Empire', in J. G. Manning and I. Morris (eds), *The Ancient Economy: Evidence and Models* (Stanford, CA: Stanford University Press, 2005), pp. 207–22.

Hobsbawm, E. J., 'The General Crisis of the European Economy in the 17th Century', *Past and Present*, 5 (1954), pp. 33–53.

Hodges, R., *Goodbye to the Vikings? Re-Reading Early Medieval Archeology* (London: Duckworth, 2006).

—, *Dark Age Economics: A New Audit* (Bristol: Bristol Classical Press, 2012).

Hodges, R., and D. Whitehouse, *Mohammed, Charlemagne and the Origins of Europe: Archeology and the Pirenne Thesis* (Ithaca, NY: Cornell University Press, 1983).

Hoffman, P. T., 'Land Rents and Agricultural Productivity: The Paris Basin, 1450–1789', *Journal of Economic History*, 51: 4 (December 1991), pp. 771–805.

—, *Growth in a Traditional Society: The French Countryside, 1450–1815* (Princeton, NJ: Princeton University Press, 1996).

Horden, P., and N. Purcell, *The Corrupting Sea: A Study of Mediterranean History* (Oxford: Blackwell, 2000).

Houtte, J. van, 'The Rise and Decline of the Market of Bruges', *Economic History Review*, 19:1 (1966), pp. 29–47.

—, *An Economic History of the Low Countries, 800–1800* (London: Weidenfeld & Nicolson, 1977).

Howgego, C., 'Coin Circulation and the Integration of the Roman Economy', *Journal of Roman Archaeology*, 7 (1994), pp. 5–21.

Hutton, E., *Venice and Venetia* (London: Hollis & Carter, 1954).

Hyde, L., *The Gift: Creativity and the Artist in the Modern World* (New York: Vintage Books, 2007).

Inalcik, H., and Quataert, D., *An Economic and Social History of the Ottoman Empire* (Cambridge: Cambridge University Press, 1997).

Irwin, D. A., 'Did Late-Nineteenth Century U.S. Tariffs Promote Infant Industries? Evidence from the Tinplate Industry', *Journal of Economic History*, 60 (2000), pp. 335–60.

—, 'Trade Restrictiveness and Deadweight Losses from US Tariffs', *American Economic Journal: Economic Policy*, 2 (2010), pp. 111–33.

Israel, J. I., *Dutch Primacy in World Trade 1585–1740* (Oxford: Clarendon Press, 1989).

Jacks, D., 'Market Integration in the North and Baltic Seas, 1500–1800', *Journal of European Economic History*, 33:3 (2004), pp. 285–329.

—, 'Intra- and International Commodity Market Integration in the Atlantic Economy, 1800–1913', *Explorations in Economic History*, 42 (2005), pp. 381–413.

—, 'What Drove Nineteenth Century Commodity Market Integration?', *Explorations in Economic History*, 43 (2006), pp. 383–412.

Jacks, D, C. M. Meissner and D. Novy, 'Trade Costs in the First Wave of Globalization', *Explorations in Economic History*, 47 (2011), pp. 127–41.

Johansen, S., 'Statistical Analysis of Cointegrating Vectors', *Journal of Economic Dynamics and Control*, 12 (1988), pp. 231–54.

John, A. H., 'The London Assurance Company and the Marine Insurance Market of the Eighteenth Century', *Economica*, 25 (1958), pp. 126–41.

Jones, C., and P. Romer, 'The New Kaldor Facts: Ideas, Institutions, Population and Human Capital', *NBER*, working paper 15049 (2009).

Jones, S. R H., 'Transaction Costs, Institutional Change, and the Emergence of a Market Economy in Later Anglo-Saxon England', *Economic History Review*, 46 (1993), pp. 658–78.

Jongman, W., 'A Golden Age: Death, Money Supply and Social Succession in the Roman Empire', in E. Lo Cascio (ed.), *Credito e moneta nel mondo romano* (Bari: Edipuglia, 2003), pp. 181–96.

Kehoe, D. P., *Law and the Rural Economy in the Roman Empire* (Ann Arbor, MI: University of Michigan Press, 2007).

Keller, W., and C. H. Shiue, 'Markets in China and Europe on the Eve of the Industrial Revolution', *American Economic Review*, 97 (2007), pp. 1189–216.

Kelly, C., *The Roman Empire* (Oxford: Oxford University Press, 2006).

Keynes, J. M., *The General Theory of Employment, Interest and Money* (London: Macmillan, 1936).

Kishlansky, M. A., P. J. Geary and P. O'Brien, *Civilization in the West* (New York and London: Pearson Longman, 2006).

Kowaleski, M., *Local Markets and Regional Trade in Medieval Exeter* (Cambridge: Cambridge University Press, 1995).

Kranton, R., 'Reciprocal Exchange: A Self Sustaining System', *American Economic Review*, 86 (1996), pp. 830–51.

Kriedte, P., *Peasants, Landlords and Merchant Capitalists: Europe and the World Economy* (Cambridge: Cambridge University Press, 1984).

Krugman, P., and M. Obstfeld, *International Economics* (Reading, MA and London: Addison-Wesley, 2006).

Kula, W., *An Economic Theory of the Feudal System: Towards a Model of the British Economy, 1500–1800* (London: New Left Review Editions, 1976).

Ladurie, E. Le Roy, *The Ancien Regime: A History of France, 1610–1774* (Oxford and Cambridge, MA: Blackwell, 1996).

Lamb, H. H., 'Climate in the Last Thousand Years: Natural Climatic Fluctuations and Change', in H. John and R. Fantechi (eds), *The Climate of Europe: Past, Present and Future* (Lancaster: D. Reidel Publishing Company, 1984), pp. 25–64.

Lane, F. C., 'Venetian Shipping during the Commercial Revolution', *American Historical Review*, 38 (1933), pp. 219–39.

—, *Venetian Ships and Shipbuilders of the Renaissance* (Baltimore, MD: Johns Hopkins University Press: 1934).

—, 'The Mediterranean Spice Trade: Further Evidence of its Revival in the Sixteenth Century,' *American Historical Review*, 45 (1940), pp. 581–90.

—, *Venice: A Maritime Republic* (Baltimore, MD and London: Johns Hopkins University Press, 1973).

Langdon, J., and J. Claridge, 'Transport in Medieval England', *History Compass*, 9 (2011), pp. 864–75.

Le Roy Ladurie, E., *Les paysans de Languedoc* (Paris: S. E. V. P. E. N, 1966).

Lefebvre, G., *The French Revolution from 1793 to 1799*, trans. J. H. Stewart and J. Friguglietti (London: Routledge & Kegan Paul; New York: Columbia University Press, 1964).

Leon, G., 'The Greek Merchant Marine, 1453–1850', in S. A. Papadopoulos (ed.), *The Greek Merchant Marine, 1453–1850* (Athens: National Bank of Greece, 1972), pp. 13–52.

Lesger, C., *The Rise of the Amsterdam Market and Information Exchange: Merchants, Commercial Expansion and Change in the Spatial Economy of the Low Countries c. 1550–1630* (Aldershot: Ashgate, 2006).

Letaconnoux, J., 'Les transports en France au 18e siecle', *Revue d'histoire moderne et contemporaine*, 11 (1908/9), pp. 97–114, 269–92.

Lewis, M. J. T., *Millstone and Hammer: The Origins of Water Power* (Hull: Hull University Press, 1997).

Ligt, L. de, 'Roman Law and the Roman Economy: Three Case Studies', *Latomus*, 66 (2007), pp. 10–25.

Lo Cascio, E., 'The Role of the State in the Roman Economy: Making Institutional Economics', in P. F. Bang, M. Ikeguchi and H. G. Ziche (eds.), *Ancient Economies, Modern Methodologies: Archaeology, Comparative History, Models and Institutions* (Bari: Edipuglia, 2006), pp. 215–34.

Long, J. B. de, and A. Schleifer, 'Princes and Merchants: European City Growth before the Industrial Revolution', *Journal of Law and Economics*, 36 (1993), pp. 671–702.

Lopez-Cordova, J. E, and C. M. Meissner, 'Exchange Rate Regimes and International Trade: Evidence from the Classical Gold Standard Era, 1870–1913', *American Economic Review*, 93:1 (2003), pp. 344–53.

Lopez, R. S., 'Market Expansion: The Case of Genoa', *Journal of Economic History*, 24 (1964), pp. 445–64.

—, *The Commercial Revolution of the Middle Ages, 950–1350* (Cambridge: Cambridge University Press, 1976).

Lucas, R. E., 'On the Mechanics of Economic Development', *Journal of Monetary Economics*, 22 (1988), p. 3–42.

Lucassen, J., and R. Unger, 'Labour Productivity in Ocean Shipping 1500–1850', International Journal of Maritime History, 12 (2000), pp. 127–41.

Lyber, A. H., 'The Ottoman Turks and the Routes of Oriental Trade', *English Historical Review*, 30 (1915), pp. 577–88.

Lynch, J., *Spain Under the Habsburgs*, 2nd edn, 2 vols (Oxford: Basil Blackwell, 1981).

Maddison, A., *The World Economy: A Millenial Perspective* (Paris: Development Centre of the Organisation for Economic Co-operation and Development, 2001).

Malanima, P., *Pre-Modern European Economy: One Thousand Years (10th–19th Centuries)* (Leiden and Boston, MA: Brill, 2009).

Mandelbrot, B. B., and Hudson, R. L., *The (Mis)Behavior of Markets: A Fractal View of Risk, Ruin, and Reward* (New York: Basic Books, 2004).

Mann, M., *The Sources of Social Power. Vol. I: A History of Power from the Beginning to A.D. 1760* (Cambridge: Cambridge University Press, 1986).

Martínez Vara, T., 'Fluctuaciones estacionales e integración de mercados en Santander y Castilla durante la primera mitad del siglo XIX', *Studia Histórica. Historia Contemporánea*, 17 (1999), pp. 185–289.

Marx, K., *Das Kaptal* (Hamburg: Verlag von Otto Meisner, 1867).

Masschaele, J., 'Transport Costs in Medieval England', *Economic History Review*, 46 (1993), pp. 266–79.

—, *Peasants, Merchants and Markets: Inland Trade in Medieval England, 1150–1350* (New York: St Martin's Press, 1997).

Masson, P., *Histoire du Commerce francais dans le Levant au XVII siècle* (Paris: Hachette & cie, 1896).

Mauro, P., N. Sussman and Y. Yafah, *Emerging Markets and Financial Globalization: Sovereign Bond Spreads in 1870–1913* (Oxford: Oxford University Press, 2006).

Mauss, M., *The Gift: The Form and Reason for Exchange in Archaic Societies* (London: Cohen and West, 1954).

McCormick, M., *Origins of the European Economy: Communications and Commerce, A.D. 300–900* (Cambridge: Cambridge University Press, 2002).

McEvedy, C., and R. Jones, *Atlas of World Population History* (Harmondsworth: Penguin, 1978).

McLean, I., 'Australian Economic Growth in Historical Perspective', *Economic Record*, 80 (2004), pp. 330–45.

McNeil, W., *Plagues and People* (New York: Bantam Doubleday Dell Publishing Group, 1998).

Meissner, C. M., 'Growth from Globalization? A View from the Very Long-Run', in P. Aghion and S. N. Durlauf (eds), *Handbook of Economic Growth*, 2 vols (Amsterdam: Elsevier, 2012) vol. 2.

Meuvret, J., *Le problème des subsistances à l'époque de Louis XIV*, 3 vols (Paris, 1977–88).

Milanovic, B., 'An Estimate of Average Income and Inequality in Byzantium around Year 1000', *Review of Income and Wealth*, 52 (2007), pp. 449–70.

Milgrom, P. R., D. C. North and B. R. Weingast, 'The Rise of Institutions in the Revival of Trade: The Medieval Law Merchant, Private Judges, and the Champagne Fairs', *Economics and Politics*, 2 (1990), pp. 1–23.

Miller, J., 'The Pragmatic Economy: Liberal Reforms and the Grain Trade in Upper Normandy, 1750–1789' (Dissertation, Duke University, NC, 1987).

—, *Mastering the Market: The State and the Grain Trade in Northern France, 1700–1860* (Cambridge: Cambridge University Press, 1998).

Minsky, H. P., *Can 'It' Happen Again: Essays on Instability and Finance* (Armonk, NY: M.E. Sharpe, 1982).

—, *Stabilising an Unstable Economy* (New York: McGraw Hill, 2008).

Mitchell, J .D. B., *Constitutional Law* (Edinburgh: W. Green, 1964).

Mitchener, K. J., and M. Weidenmier, 'Empire, Public Goods, and the Roosevelt Corollary', *Journal of Economic History*, 65 (2005), pp. 658–92.

Mokyr, J., *Lever of Riches: Technological Creativity and Economic Progress* (New York and Oxford: Oxford University Press, 1992).

—, *The Gifts of Athena: Historical Origins of the Knowledge Economy* (Princeton, NJ and Oxford: Princeton University Press, 2002).

—, 'Accounting for the Industrial Revolution', in R. Floud and P. Johnson, *The Cambridge Economic History of Modern Britain*, 3 vols (Cambridge: Cambridge University Press, 2004), vol. 1, p. 1–27.

—, 'Intellectual Property Rights, the Industrial Revolution, and the Beginnings of Economic Growth', *American Economic Re*view, 99 (2009), pp. 349–55.

—, *The Enlightened Economy: An Economic and Social History of Britain 1700–1850* (Newhaven, CT: Yale University Press, 2009).

Moor, T. de, 'The Silent Revolution: A New Perspective on the Emergence of Commons, Guilds, and other Forms of Corporate Collective Action in Western Europe', *International Review of Social History*, 53, supplement (2008), pp. 179–212.

Moor, T. de., and J. L. van Zanden, 'Girl Power: The European Marriage Pattern and Labour Markets in the North Sea Region in the Late Medieval and Early Modern Period', *Economic History Review*, 63 (2009), pp. 1–33.

Munro, J. H., 'Nominal Wage Stickiness and the Real Wage Problem: J. M. Keynes, Adam Smith and the Evidence', *Research in Economic History*, 21 (2003), pp. 186–297.

J. M. Murray, *Bruges: Cradle of Capitalism, 1280–1390* (Cambridge: Cambridge University Press, 2005).

—, 'Wool, Cloth and Gold', in J. M. Murray, *Bruges: Cradle of Capitalism, 1280–1390* (Cambridge: Cambridge University Press, 2005), pp. 259–99.

Neal, L., *The Rise of Financial Capitalism: International Capital Markets in the Age of Reason* (Cambridge: Cambridge University Press, 1993).

Needham, J., *Science and Civilisation in China* (Cambridge: Cambridge University Press, 1956).

Nicholas, D., 'Economic Reorientation and Social Change in 14th Century Flanders', *Past and Present*, 70 (1976), pp. 3–29.

—, 'Of Poverty and Primacy: Demand, Liquidity, and the Flemish Economic Miracle, 1050–1200', *American Historical Review*, 96 (1991), pp. 17–41.

Nielsen, R., 'Storage and English Government Intervention in Early Modern Grain Markets', *Journal of Economic History*, 57 (1997), pp. 1–33.

Njoh, A. J., *Tradition, Culture and Development in Africa: Historical Lessons for Modern Development Planning* (Aldershot: Ashgate, 2006).

North, D. C., 'Markets and Other Allocation Systems in History: The Challenge of Karl Polanyi', *Journal of European Economic History*, 6 (1977), pp. 703–16.

—, *Understanding the Processes of Economic Change* (Princeton, NJ: Princeton University Press, 2005).

North, D. C., and R. P. Thomas, *The Rise of the Western World: A New Economic History* (Cambridge: Cambridge University Press, 1973).

North, D. C., and B. Weingast, 'Constitutions and Credible Commitments: The Evolution of the Institutions of Public Choice in 17th Century England', *Journal of Economic History*, 49 (1989), pp. 803–32.

O' Brien, P. K., 'Mercantilism and Imperialism in the Rise and Decline of the Dutch and British Economies 1585-1815', *De Economist*, 148 (2000), pp. 469–501.

O'Brien, P. K., and X. Duran, 'Total Factor Productivity for the Royal Navy from Victory at Texal (1653) to Triumph at Trafalgar (1805)', in R. W. Unger (ed.), *Shipping and Economic Growth 1350-1850* (Leiden: Brill, 2011), pp. 279–308.

O'Brien, P. K., T. Griffiths and P. Hunt, 'Political Components of the Industrial Revolution: Parliament and the English Cotton Textile Industry, 1660–1774', *Economic History Review*, new series, 44 (1982), pp. 395–423.

O'Gráda, C., and J-M. Chevet, 'Market Segmentation and Famine in ancien régime France', *Journal of Economic History*, 42 (2002), pp. 706–33.

O'Rourke, K. H., and J. G. Williamson, 'Late 19th Century Anglo-American Factor Price Convergence: Were Heckscher and Ohlin right?', *Journal of Economic History*, 54 (1994), pp. 1–25.

—, 'Around the European Periphery 1870–1913: Globalisation, Schooling and Growth', *European Review of Economic History*, 1:2 (1997), pp. 153–90.

—, *Globalization and History: The Evolution of a Nineteenth Century Atlantic Economy* (Cambridge, MA and London: MIT, 1999).

—, 'After Columbus: Explaining the Global Trade Boom 1500–1800', *NBER*, working paper 8186 (2001).

—, 'When Did Globalization Begin?', *European Review of Economic History*, 6:1 (2002), pp. 23–50.

—, 'Did Vasco da Gama Matter for European Markets? Testing Frederick Lane's Hypothesis Fifty Years On', *Economic History Review*, 62:3 (2009), pp. 655–84.

Obstfeld, M., and A. M. Taylor, *Global Capital Markets: Integration, Crisis and Growth* (Cambridge: Cambridge University Press, 2004).

Ogilvie, S., 'Were Merchant Guilds Really Beneficial? A Vomment on Grief, Milgrom and Weingast', Cambridge University mimeo (1995).

—, '"Whatever Is, Is Right"? Economic Institutions in Pre-Industrial Europe', *Economic History Review*, 60 (2007), pp. 649–84.

—, *Institutions and European Trade: Merchant Guilds, 1000–1800* (Cambridge: Cambridge University Press, 2011).

Olivier, G. A., *Voyage dans l'Empire Othman, l'ègypte, et la Perse* (Paris: Chez Agasse, 1801).

Olmstead, A. L., and P. W. Rhode, *Creating Abundance: Biological Innovation and American Agricultural Development* (Cambridge: Cambridge University Press, 2008).

Ormrod, D., *The Rise of Commercial Empires: England and the Netherlands in the Age of Mercantilism, 1650–1770*, Cambridge Studies in Modern Economic History (Cambridge: Cambridge University Press, 2003).

Özmucur, S., and Ş. Pamuk, 'Did European Commodity Prices Converge during 1500–1800?', in T. J. Hatton, K. O'Rourke and A. M. Taylor, *New Comparative Economic History: Essays in Honour of Jeffrey G. Williamson* (Cambridge, MA and London: MIT Press, 2007), pp. 59–86.

Pamuk, S., *500 Years of Prices and Wages in Istanbul and Other Cities* (Ankara: State Institute of Statistics, 2001).

—, 'Changes in Factor Markets in the Ottoman Empire, 1500–1800', *Continuity and Change*, 24 (2009), pp. 107–36.

Paris, R., *Histoire du commerce de Marseille* (Paris: Plon, 1957).

Parry, J. H., 'Transport and Trade Routes', in E .E. Rich and C. H. Wilson (eds), *The Cambridge Economic History of Europe*, 8 vols (Cambridge: Cambridge University Press, 1967), vol. 4, pp. 155–222.

Persson, K. G., *Grain Markets in Europe, 1500–1900: Integration and Deregulation* (Cambridge: Cambridge University Press, 1999).

Persson, G., *An Economic History of Europe: Knowledge, Institutions and Growth, 800 to the Present* (Cambridge: Cambridge University Press, 2010).

Phillips Jr, W. D., 'Columbus, Christopher', in D. Buisseret (eds), *The Oxford Companion to World Exploration* (Oxford: Oxford University Press, 2007): e-reference edition distributed by Oxford University Press at: http://www.oxfordreference.com/views/ENTRY.html?subview=Main&entry=t230.e0166 [accessed 7 April 2012].

Pirenne, H., *Medieval Cities: Their Origins and the Revival of Trade* (Princeton, NJ: Princeton University Press, 1925).

—, *Economic and Social History of Medieval Europe* (New York: Harcourt, Brace & Company, 1937).

—, *Mohammed and Charlemagne* (London: G. Allen & Unwin, 1954).

Polanyi, K., *The Great Transformation: The Political and Economic Origins of our Time* (Boston, MA: Beacon Press, 1944).

Pomeranz, K., *The Great Divergence: China, Europe, and the Making of the Modern World Economy* (Princeton, NJ and Oxford: Princeton University Press, 2000).

Poos, L. R., *A Rural Society after the Black Death: Essex, 1350–1525* (Cambridge: Cambridge University Press, 2004).

Postan, M. M., *Essays on Medieval Agriculture and General Problems of the Medieval Economy* (London: Cambridge University Press, 1973).

Posthumus, N. W., *Nederlandsche Prijsgeschiedenis*, 2 vols (Leiden, 1943), vol. 1, pp. vvv–xxviii.

Pounds, N. J. G., *An Historical Geography of Europe 1500–1840* (Cambridge: Cambridge University Press, 1979).

Prak, M., *The Dutch Republic in the Seventeenth Century*, trans. D. Webb (Cambridge: Cambridge University Press, 2005).

Price, J. L., *The Dutch Republic in the Seventeenth Century* (Basingstoke: Macmillan, 1998).

Rapp, R. T., 'The Unmaking of the Mediterranean Trade Hegemony: International Trade Rivalry and the Commercial Revolution', *Journal of Economic History*, 35:3 (1975), pp. 499–525.

—, *Industry and Economic Decline in Seventeenth-Century Venice* (Cambridge, MA and London: Harvard University Press, 1976).

Ratekin, M., 'The Early Sugar Industry in Española', *Hispanic American Historical Review*, 34 (1954), pp. 1–19.

Ravallion, M., 'Testing Market Integration', *American Journal of Agricultural Economics*, 68 (1986), pp. 102–9.

Redding, S., 'Dynamic Comparative Advantage and the Welfare Effects of Trade', *Oxford Economic Papers*, 51 (1999), pp. 15–39.

Reed, C. J., 'Transactions Costs and Differential Growth in Seventeenth Century Western Europe', *Journal of Economic History*, 33:1 (1973), pp. 177–90.

Ringrose, D. R., *Madrid and the Spanish Economy, 1560–1850* (Berkeley, CA and London: University of California Press, 1983).

Rivera-Batiz, L. A., and P. M. Romer, 'Economic Integration and Endogenous Growth', *Quarterly Journal of Economics*, 106 (1991), pp. 531–55.

Rodger, N. A. M., 'Queen Elizabeth and the Myth of Sea Power in English History', *Transactions of the Royal Historical Society*, 14 (2004), pp. 153–74.

Roover, F. E., 'Early Examples of Marine Insurance', *Journal of Economic History*, 5 (1945), pp. 192–3.

Rosenberg, N., and L. E. Birdzell, *How the West Grew Rich: Economic Transformation of the Industrial World* (New York: Basic Books, 1986).

Roses, J. R., and B. Sanchez-Alonso, 'Regional Wage Convergence in Spain 1850–1930', *Explorations in Economic History*, 41:4 (October 2004), pp. 404–25.

Roy, T., 'Indigo and Law in Colonial India', *Economic History Review*, 64 (2011), pp. 60–75.

Rucquoi, A., 'Castile', in A. Vauchez, B. Dobson and M. Lapidge (eds), *Encyclopedia of the Middle Ages* (Cambridge: James Clarke, 2001): e-reference edition distributed by Oxford University Press at: http://www.oxfordreference.com/views/ENTRY.html?subview=Main&entry=t179.e494 [accessed 7 April 2012].

Ruddock, A. A., *Italian Merchants and Shipping in Southampton, 1270–1600*, Southampton Records Series (Southampton: University College, 1951).

Sahlins, M. D., *Stone Age Economics* (London: Routledge, 2004).

Sally, R., 'Globalisation and the Political Economy of Trade Liberalization in the BRICS', in *Globalisation and Emerging Economies* (Paris: Organisation for Economic Co-operation and Development, 2009), pp. 117–85.

Sawyer, P. H., 'Kings and Merchants', in P. H. Sawyer and I. N. Wood (eds), *Early Medieval Kingship* (Leeds: The editors, under the auspices of The School of History, University of Leeds, 1977), pp. 139–58.

Scheidel, W., 'Real Income Growth in Roman Italy', *Princeton/Stanford Working Papers in Classics* (2006).

Scheidel, W., I. Morris, I and R. Saller, *The Cambridge Economic History of the Greco-Roman World* (Cambridge: Cambridge University Press, 2008).

Schularick, M., 'A Tale of Two "Globalizations": Capital Flows from Rich to Poor in Two Eras of Global Finance', *International Journal of Finance and Economics*, 11 (2006), pp. 339–54.

Scott, E., *Mohammed and Charlemagne Revisited: The History of A Controvery* (London: New English Review Press, 2012).

Scott, T., *The City-State in Europe, 1000–1600* (Oxford: Oxford University Press, 2012).

Sella, D., 'Crisis and Transformation in Venetian Trade', in B. Pullan (ed.), *Crisis and Change in the Venetian Economy in the Sixteenth and Seventeenth Centuries* (London: Methuen, 1968).

Sénac, P., 'Spain, Muslim', in A. Vauchez, B. Dobson and M. Lapidge (eds), *Encyclopedia of the Middle Ages* (Cambridge: James Clarke, 2001): e-reference edition distributed by Oxford University Press at: http://www.oxfordreference.com/views/ENTRY.html?subview=Main&entry=t179.e2683-s1 [accessed 7 April 2012].

Silver, M., 'Roman Economic Growth and Living Standards: Perceptions Versus Evidence', *Ancient Society*, 37 (2007), pp. 191–252.

Simpson, J., *Spanish Agriculture: The Long Siesta, 1765–1965*, Cambridge Studies in Modern Economic History, 2 (Cambridge: Cambridge University Press, 1995).

Smith, A., *An Inquiry into the Nature and Causes of the Wealth of Nations* (1776; Oxford: Oxford University Press, 2008).

Sokoloff, K. L., and S. L. Engerman, 'Institutions, Factor Endowments, and Paths of Development in the New World', *Journal of Economic Perspectives*, 14 (2000), pp. 217–32.

Solow, R., 'A Contribution to the Theory of Economic Growth', *Quarterly Journal of Economics*, 70 (1956), pp. 65–94.

—, 'Technical Change and the Aggregate Production Function', *Review of Economics and Statistics*, 39 (1957), pp. 312–20.

Spek, R. J. van der, J. L. van Zanden and E. S. Leeuwen, *A History of Market Performance* (London: Routledge, forthcoming).

Spufford, P., *Money and its Uses in Medieval Europe* (Cambridge: Cambridge University Press, 1988).

Steensgaard, N., *The Asian Trade Revolution of the Seventeenth Century: The East India Companies and the Decline of the Caravan Trade* (Chicago, IL and London: University of Chicago Press, 1974).

Strayer, J. R., *On the Medieval Origins of the Modern State*, forewords C. Tilly and W. C. Jordan (Princeton, NJ and Oxford: Princeton University Press, 2005).

Studer, R., 'Does Trade Explain Europe's Rise? Geography, Market Size and Economic Development', London School of Economics, Economic History Working Papers 27877 (2009).

Sweezy, P. et al., *The Transition from Feudalism to Capitalism* (London: New Left Books, 1976).

t' Hart, M. C., *The Making of a Bourgeois State: War, Politics and Finance during the Dutch Revolt* (Manchester and New York: Manchester University Press, 1993).

Tabak, F., *The Waning of the Mediterranean, 1550–1870: A Geohistorical Approach* (Baltimore, MD: Johns Hopkins University Press, 2008).

Temin, P., 'A Market Economy in the Early Roman Empire', *Journal of Roman Studies,* 91 (2001), pp. 169–81;

—, 'Financial Intermediation in the Early Roman Empire', *Journal of Economic History,* 64 (2004), pp. 705–33.

—, 'The Economy of the Early Roman Empire', *Journal of Economic Perspectives*, 20:1 (2006), pp. 133–51.

The Economist, *Pocket World in Figures* (2009 edition).

Thomson, J. K. J., *A Distinctive Industrialization: Cotton in Barcelona 1728-1832* (New York: Cambridge University Press, 1992).

Tielhif, M. von, and J. L. van Zanden, 'Productivity Changes in Shipping in the Dutch Republic', in R. W. Unger (ed.), *Shipping and Economic Growth 1350–1850* (Leiden: Brill, 2011).

Tilly, C., *Coercion, Capital, and European States, AD 990–1990* (Cambridge, MA; Basil Blackwell, 1990).

Titow, J. Z., 'Some Evidence of the Thirteenth-Century Population Increase', *Economic History Review,* 14 (1961), pp. 218–24.

—, *English Rural Society 1200–1350* (London: Allen & Unwin, 1969).

Tracy, J. D., *The Rise of Merchant Empires: Long Distance Trade in the Early Modern World, 1350–1750* (Cambridge: Cambridge University Press, 1993).

Trivellato, F., *The Familiarity of Strangers: The Sephardic Diaspora, Livorno, and Cross-Cultural Trade in the Early Modern Period* (New Haven, CT: Yale University Press, 2009).

Unger, R., 'Integration of Baltic and Low Countries Grain Markets, 1400–1800', in J. M. Winter (ed.), *The Interactions of Amsterdam and Antwerp with the Baltic Region 1400–1800. Papers Presented at the Third International Conference of the 'Association Internationale d'Histoire des Mers Nordiques de l'Europe', Utrecht, 30th August–3rd September 1982* (Leiden: Brill, 1983), pp. 1–10.

—, 'Feeding Low Countries Towns: The Grain Trade in the Fifteenth Century', *Revue Belge de Philolgie et d'Histoire*, 77:2 (1999), pp. 329–58.

Unger, R. W. (ed.), *Shipping and Economic Growth 1350–1850* (Leiden: Brill, 2011).

Usher, A. P., *The History of the Grain Trade in France 1400–1700* (Cambridge, MA: Harvard University Press, 1913).

Van der Wee, H., *The Growth of the Antwerp Market and the European Economy: (Fourteenth-Sixteenth Centuries)*, 3 vols (The Hague: Martinus Nijhoff, 1963).

—, 'Structural Changes in European Long-Distance Trade, and Particularly in the Re-export Trade from South to North, 1350–1750', in J. D. Tracy (ed.), *The Rise of Merchant Empires: Long Distance Trade in the Early Modern World, 1350–1750* (Cambridge: Cambridge University Press, 1993), pp. 14–33.

Veraghtert, K., 'The Antwerp Port, 1790–1814', in J. M. Winter (ed.), *The Interactions of Amsterdam and Antwerp with the Baltic Region 1400–1800. Papers Presented at the Third International Conference of the 'Association Internationale d'Histoire des Mers Nordiques de l'Europe', Utrecht, 30th August–3rd September 1982* (Leiden: Brill, 1983), pp. 193–9.

Verhulst, A., *The Rise of Cities in North-West Europe* (Cambridge and New York: Cambridge University Press; Paris: Editions de la Maison des Sciences de l'Homme, 1999).

—, *The Carolingian Economy* (Cambridge: Cambridge University Press, 2002).

Verlinden, C., *Dokumenten voor de geschiedenis van prijzen en loonen in Vlaanderen en Brabant, gepubliceerd onder leiding van C. Verlinden, en de redaktie van J. Craeybeckx* (Brugge: De Tempel, 1959).

Vicens Vives, J., J. Nadal and F. M. Lâopez-Morillas, *An Economic History of Spain* (Princeton, NJ: Princeton University Press, 1969).

Voth, J., 'Debt, Default and Empire: State Capacity and Economic Development in England and Spain in the Early Modern Period', Tawney Lecture, Economic History Society Annual Conference, University of Cambridge (2011).

Vries, J. de., *Barges and Capitalism: Passenger Transportation in the Dutch Economy, 1632–1839* (Utrecht: Hes Publishers, 1981).

—, *European Urbanization 1500–1800* (London: Methuen, 1984).

—, 'The Industrial Revolution and the Industrious Revolution', *Journal of Economic History*, 54 (1994), pp. 249–70.

—, *The Industrious Revolution: Consumer Behavior and the Household Economy, 1650 to the Present* (Cambridge and New York: Cambridge University Press, 2008).

Vries, J. de., and A. M. van der Woude, *The First Modern Economy: Success, Failure, and Perseverance of the Dutch Economy, 1500–1815* (Cambridge: Cambridge University Press, 1997).

Wallerstein, I. M., *The Modern World-System*, 3 vols (Berkley, CA: University of California Press, 2011).

Ward-Perkins, B., *The Fall of Rome: And the End of Civilization* (Oxford: Oxford University Press, 2006).

Wickham, C., *Framing the Middle Ages: Europe and the Mediterranean 400–800* (Oxford: Oxford University Press, 2005).

Williams, E. E., Capitalism and Slavery (Chapel Hill, NC: University of North Carolina Press, 1944).

Williams, E. N., *The Ancien Regime in Europe: Government and Society in the Major States 1648–1789* (London: Bodley Head, 1970).

Williamson, J. G., *Trade and Poverty: When the Third World Fell Behind* (Cambridge, MA: MIT Press, 2011).

Willan, T. S., 'Some Aspects of English Trade with the Levant in the Sixteenth Century', *English Historical Review*, 70 (1955), pp. 399–410.

Wilson, A., 'Machines, Power and the Ancient Economy', *Journal of Roman Studies*, 92 (2002), pp. 1–32.

Wilson, C., 'Taxation and the Decline of Empires', *Bijdragen en Mededelingen van het Historisch Genootschap*, 77 (1963), pp. 10–23.

—, 'Mercantilism', *Historical Association Pamphlet*, 37 (London, 1966), pp. 3–27.

Wilson, P. H., *From Reich to Revolution: German history 1558–1806,* European History in Perspective (Basingstoke: Palgrave Macmillan, 2004).

Wrigley, E. A., *Energy and the English Industrial Revolution* (Cambridge: Cambridge University Press, 2010).

Wrigley, E. A., and R. S. Schofield, *The Population History of England 1541–1871: A Reconstruction* (London: Edward Arnold, 1981).

Yueh, L. Y-C., *The Law and Economics of Globalisation: New Challenges for a World in Flux* (Cheltenham and Northampton, MA: Edward Elgar, 2009).

Zanden, J. L. van, *The Rise and Decline of Holland's Economy: Merchant Capitalism and the Labour Market* (Manchester: Manchester University Press, 1993).

—, 'The "Revolt of the Early Modernists" and the "First Modern Economy": An Assessment', *Economic History Review*, 55 (2002), pp. 619–41.

—, 'Estimating Early Modern Economic Growth', *International Institute of Social History, University of Utrecht*, working paper (2004).

—, *The Long Road to the Industrial Revolution: The European Economy in a Global Perspective, 1000–1800* (Leiden: Brill, 2009).

Zanden, J. L. van, E. Buringh and M. Bosker, 'The Rise and Decline of European Parliaments, 1188–1789', *Economic History Review* (forthcoming).

Zuijderduijn, C. J., *Medieval Capital Markets: Markets for Renten, State Formation and Private Investment in Holland (1300–1550)* (Leiden and Boston, MA: Brill, 2009).

Zuijderduijn, C. J., T. de Moor and J. L. van Zanden, 'Small is Beautiful: On the Efficiency of Credit Markets in Late Medieval Holland', *Centre for Global Economic History*, working paper, 11 (2011).

INDEX

For Product Safety Concerns and Information please contact our EU representative GPSR@taylorandfrancis.com
Taylor & Francis Verlag GmbH, Kaufingerstraße 24, 80331 München, Germany

www.ingramcontent.com/pod-product-compliance
Ingram Content Group UK Ltd.
Pitfield, Milton Keynes, MK11 3LW, UK
UKHW020011200926
475702UK00014B/1830
* 9 7 8 1 1 3 8 6 6 1 7 6 9 *